W9-AZP-284

Creative Living

Butterick Publishing wishes to thank the following members of the 1977-78 Advisory Board for their input and advice during development of this text.

Bertha King, Chairperson
Educational Program Specialist for
    Vocational Home Economics
    Education Programs
B.O.A.E., United States Office
    of Education
Washington, DC

Camille Bell
Professor and Chairperson, Dept. of
    Home Economics Education
Texas Tech University
Lubbock, Texas

Marge Harouff
Program Administrator for
    Vocational Education
Division of Vocational Education
Lincoln, Nebraska

Bettie Herring
Program Director for Vocational
    Education
Fort Worth Independent School District
Fort Worth, Texas

Anne McElrath
Acting Assistant Supervising Director,
    Vocational Home Economics Programs
District of Columbia, Board of Education
Washington, DC

Donna Miller
Career, Adult, Vocational Coordinator
S.W. Georgia Cooperative Education
    Service Agency
Leary, Georgia

Joanna Smith
Consumer and Homemaking Teacher
Rochester High School
Rochester, Indiana

Aina Summerfelt
Specialist, Consumer and Family Studies
San Diego School-Education Center
San Diego, California

Creative Living

Basic Concepts in Home Economics

CONSULTING AUTHORS

Personal & Family Relationships

Josephine A. Foster, Ph.D.

Professor of Home Economics
Appalachian State University

Consumer & Home Management

M. Janice Hogan, Ph.D.

Associate Professor of Home Economics
University of Minnesota

Foods & Nutrition

Bettie M. Herring, Ph.D.

Program Director for Vocational Education
Fort Worth Independent School District

Clothing & Textiles

Audrey G. Gieseking-Williams, Ph.D.

Professor of Home Economics
California State University, Los Angeles

Co-developed by
BUTTERICK PUBLISHING
New York, New York
&
VISUAL EDUCATION CORPORATION
Princeton, New Jersey

Butterick Publishing

Project Editor: Melanie Jamgochian
Director of Production: Hugh MacDonald

Visual Education Corporation

Project Editor: Bob Waterhouse
Art Director and Designer: Leon Bolognese

Associate Editor: Joan Blessing
Writer Researchers: Carol Simons,
    Alfred Glossbrenner, Beth Hutton,
    Fenya Crown, Barbara Fishman
Editorial Staff: Susan Gordon,
    Kathleen McGinn, Molly Seibel
Special Thanks to: Rosemary Bogden, Nancy Eills,
    Cindy Feldner, Lynn Harding, Sharon Hubbard,
    Janet Jones, Elizabeth McGrail, Ann-Marie Murray,
    Cecilia Pineo, Barbara Uittenbogaard, Ann Ward
Production Coordinator: Pat Steiner
Director for Production: Bill West
Assistant to Art Director: Cathy Marinaccio
Picture Research: Rhoda Cohen, Dan Patricia

Special Acknowledgements: Marion McGill, M.S.,
    Hazel S. Stoeckler, M.A.

Cover Design: Craven Graphics, Inc.
    Marc Phelan, Designer

Copyright © 1979 by Butterick Publishing, A Division of American Can Company.

All rights reserved. No part of this work may be reproduced in any form or by any means without permission in writing from the publisher, except by a reviewer who may quote brief passages in a review.

Library of Congress Cataloging in Publication Data

Main entry under title:

Creative living.

   Includes index.
   SUMMARY: Discusses basic concepts of personal and family relationships, consumer education, housing, food, nutrition, clothing, and textiles and other aspects of home management and day-to-day living.
   1. Home economics—Juvenile literature.
[1. Home economics]   I. Foster, Josephine A., 1930-
TX167.C79   640   78-74167

ISBN 0-88421-779-5

Printed and bound by Von Hoffmann Press, St. Louis, Missouri

Manufactured in the U.S.A.
Published simultaneously in the U.S.A. and Canada.

10 9 8 7 6 5 4 3 2 1

Key for positions: R(right), L(left), T(top), C(center), B(bottom).

PHOTOGRAPHS

Advertising Council: 245; Atlantic Richfield Co.: 144; American Red Cross: 265; Bill Bernstein: 91, 217; Black Star: Charles Moore 4; Linda Blyer: 86, 102 (L), 349, 475; Campbell Soup Co.: 311 (R) CIMMYT: 273 (TL); Rhoda Cohen: 321 (B); Gene Daniels: 325 (T); Delaware-Raritan Girl Scout Council: 47; DuPont De Nemours & Co.: 393; EPA Documerica: Michael Philip Manheim 90, Dick Rowan 44 (BR), Fred Ward 223 (TL); *Family Circle* Magazine: 204 (R); General Motors Corp., Milford Michigan Proving Ground: 181; The Goodyear Tire and Rubber Co.: 161 (B); Junior Achievement: 130; Joel Gordon: 1(B); Kraft Foods Citrus Div.: 311 (TL); John Lei: 1(R), 44 (TR), 51; Linen Supply Assn. of America: 476 (T); Magnum: Gilles Perres 27; National Archives: 115; Neenah Paper Co.: 476 (BR); Oscar Mayer Corp.: 161 (T); Ivan Pintar: 225; Photo Trends: 386 (CB); Gary Seitz: 258 (R); Stock, Boston: Eric Anderson 63, Owen Franken 44 (TL), Rick Smolan 62 (TL); Dick Swift: 470; Suzanne Szasz: 289; Thayer Coggins Furniture: 205; UN Photo Library: 267, 271; UNICEF: 273 (BR); United Press International: 66 (L) (C) (R), 386 (T) (L) (R); University of Delaware: 226; USDA: 266, 273 (TR), 298 (TL) (TR) (BL) (BR), 313, 347 (BL) (BR); U. S. Office of Consumer Affairs: 245.

Other photos by: John Freeman, Doug Dempsey, Stuart Dworeck; David Gillis; Jim McDonald; Jack Beeler; Tom Dunham; Jae Carter; Karen Leeds; Les Armstrong; Dan Patricia; Gerard Guarino; Griffin Schrack; George Tiboni.

ILLUSTRATIONS

Butterick Archives: 386 (TL); Denise Donnell: 53, 56, 60, 69, 93, 103, 119, 140, 197, 215, 376, 391, 459; Michael Garland: 1, 123, 125, 129, 146, 162, 235, 242, 279, 357; Steve Hofheimer: 179, 186, 227; Cathy Marinaccio: 25, 73, 343, 407; Meredith Nemirov: 361, 364, 372, 382, 383, 389, 391, 438, 455, 468, 473; Ann Pomeroy: 136, 143, 192, 199, 200, 206, 207, 209, 239, 283, 285, 348; Trudi Smith: 7, 49, 75, 80, 117, 133, 165, 195, 261, 296, 315, 323, 327, 330, 331, 359, 424, 428, 433; Maggie Zander: 15, 18, 20, 32, 35, 84, 111, 151, 246, 269, 292, 300, 302, 304, 307, 336, 337, 338, 451, 462.

To The Reader

Cre·a·tive: having the quality or power of creating; resulting from originality of thought or expression.

Expression . . . that's what CREATIVE LIVING is all about . . . self-expression. Because whether you know it or not, you're expressing yourself all the time. Every decision you make says something about you: the way you decorate your room, the shirt you put on in the morning, the foods you eat, even what you choose to do after school.

CREATIVE LIVING can't make these decisions for you, but it can help you to set your own goals and priorities so that you'll be able to finish that book report for Friday and still have time to go to the basketball game Thursday night. We'll also give you some pointers on how to make decisions and follow through with them, while still handling your day-to-day responsibilities. To put it simply, CREATIVE LIVING will show you how to be your own manager.

As a manager, you'll be making decisions about your food, clothing, shelter, your family, friends and most importantly, yourself. This is what Home Economics is all about—managing the basics of your life.

Part of being a good manager is looking ahead. The sections in this book on careers and the future won't make predictions, but they will start you thinking. What kind of work will you be doing? Where will you live? How will clothing be different? And what will shopping centers be like? (Turn to page 179 for our view of this!)

Thinking . . . that too is what CREATIVE LIVING is all about. Whether it involves the past, the present or the future, we want you to think and to learn and most of all to be creative. Be yourself, because there's no one exactly like *you*.

We want to hear from you. Write and let us know what you think about CREATIVE LIVING. Each response we receive will be carefully read and will help us with future editions of this book. Send your comments in care of. CREATIVE LIVING FEEDBACK, Butterick Publishing, 708 Third Avenue, New York, New York, 10017.

Welcome to CREATIVE LIVING!

The Editors

P.S. When you see a word in gray it's defined in the glossary beginning on page 494 . . . Hope to be hearing from you soon!

Contents

Foods & Nutrition

Clothing & Textiles

Personal & Family Relationships

CHAPTER 1

You As an Individual

CHAPTER CONTENTS

SECTION 1 · What Is an Individual?

WANTED: Personal Replacement

"WANTED: Personal replacement. Must be 5'4" tall, have short, dark, curly hair and a nose that itches in the presence of cats. Must be able to play exactly half of 'Home on the Range' on the piano, know how to make cheeseburgers the way my dad taught me, and know how many it takes to fill up my brother Bucky. Must know where I hide my locker key and whose name to mention to drive my sister up the wall. Must be able to put up with Marty, my buddy, when he tells about his trip to Indiana for the twelfth time. If qualified, write a letter in my handwriting signed with my full name—listing the rest of your qualifications."

Could you write a want ad for someone to take *your* place? Can you list everything that makes you you?

Each of us is unique, one of a kind. We have inherited certain physical features and mental traits from our parents. We have also learned habits, customs, and beliefs from our families and communities. But each person's combination of learned and inherited traits is unique. How we look, what we think, and what we have experienced all help make us different from those around us.

Your Body—Inside and Out

People are light, dark, broad, narrow, tall, short . . . and in between. Some have freckles, some have gray eyes. Some have straight hair, others have curls. These kinds of physical traits make each person look different. Your unique appearance adds to the interesting variety of people in the world.

Each cell in your body contains genes—materials that help control how you will grow, how you will look, and how you will feel. These genes come from your parents, who got them from *their* parents. So a large part of how you look and who you are depends on who your ancestors were. Bone structure, complexion, hair, and other features connect you with your parents and other family members. You wear bits of your family history all over your body. It's because of genes that people say things like, "You have your great-grandmother's nose."

Genes are also partly responsible for

Look at any group of friends and you will find a wide range of appearances. Every person is unique.

your voice and the way you move. You may have noticed similarities among certain members of families you know. "You walk just like your father," or "You sound just like your mother," are comments you are bound to hear. Some of your temperament—the way you think, feel, and react—comes from genes as well.

Your Experiences

The traits you inherited from your parents are only a part of what makes you special. The people you have known, the things you have learned—all your experiences—have

helped make you unique. Did you have a fifth-grade teacher who encouraged you in math? This changed the way you saw yourself and the world. Have you taken violin lessons since the age of four? You have grown up differently from people who have never played a musical instrument.

You have also been loved, hurt, amused, and bored. Everything that's happened to you, from being scolded for not finishing your dinner to taking your first trip around the block by yourself, has made a difference in who you are. These experiences, and your reactions to them, have helped make the person who is you.

You and Others

You have learned a lot from the people close to you. In many ways, you have even become like them. You have come to agree with some opinions you have heard, and you have been annoyed by others.

You have also come to *mean* a lot to others. In your own way, you touch the lives of many people. You share your life with members of your family, friends, classmates, and neighbors. You may help a friend with problems, or always have a few pleasant words for a neighbor. These people care about and depend on you. No one else can be the person you are to them. Other people's feelings about you are part of what makes you unique.

Your Own Ideas

Your ideas about yourself are also an important part of you. If you accept and enjoy your uniqueness, you will be better able to appreciate yourself as a person. Don't always compare yourself to other people. Concentrate on being the person *you* want to be.

Knowing that you are unique will help you as you grow and change and make choices for your future. Recognize your own special interests and abilities, and develop them to the fullest. Pay attention to your wants and needs and make decisions that take those wants and needs into account.

Will you go out for baseball or devote your afternoons to the school paper? Will you sign up for a craft class or spend the time reading alone? Will you select a music course or the art course that your friend is taking?

Choose activities on the basis of what you know or would like to find out about yourself. The more you understand your own personality, the better you will be able to shape the future you want for yourself.

We all gain from the knowledge and experience of others. Some skills, such as needlework, may be passed from one generation to the next.

QUESTIONS

1. What are genes? What are some of the characteristics that are influenced by genes? What other factors influence the kind of person someone becomes?
2. How does each individual affect the lives of others?

3. How can recognizing your uniqueness help you shape your life?
4. Which experiences do you think have influenced you the most? How?
5. What three things would you like other people to remember about you? Why?

ACTIVITIES

1. Write a want ad for someone to take your place. Follow the model at the beginning of this section. Include the qualities that make you unique. Keep writing until you are sure that no one could qualify for the "job."
2. Find out all you can about identical twins.

Are they really identical? If not, in what ways do they differ? Research the topic in the library, and then prepare a presentation for your class.
3. List ten differences between you and a friend. Include differences in appearance, tastes, and skills, as well as other kinds of differences.

SECTION 2 · Knowing Yourself

Will the Real Bobby Please Stand Up?

Bobby worries a lot about how other people see him. At times, he has real trouble figuring out who he is and how he should act. He's really good at making people laugh, and he knows his friends enjoy his crazy stunts. But some of his classmates think he's a show-off. Bobby gets uneasy around grownups, too. He likes his parents. Though sometimes he's embarrassed when they fuss over him, he's happy that they approve of him. Bobby likes his teacher, too, but it bothers him when he's told he's immature and fools around too much for his own good.

Like Bobby, we all sometimes feel a little confused about who we are. We are all affected by what other people think of us.

The opinions of your family and friends have much to do with how you view yourself. But your mental picture of yourself—your self-concept—is made up of more than the opinions of others. It includes all the different ideas that you have been gathering about yourself since the early months of your life. Many of these ideas come from other people. Some of them come from discoveries you have made about yourself.

Your self-concept began with your awareness of yourself as an individual separate from other people and from the world around you. It includes what you expect of yourself and how you judge yourself. For example, you may expect to do well in your school's art contest. Or you may have decided that you are too tall for your age. Both of these ideas affect your feelings about yourself.

As you change and form new ideas about yourself, your self-concept changes, too. As a six-year-old, you thought of yourself as a "first-grader." At thirteen, you see yourself as a "teenager." The way you see yourself tomorrow may be very different from the way you see yourself today.

Your Own Input

Think about your own experiences. Since early childhood, you have made discoveries about yourself. You learned what you were good at, what you enjoyed, what you wanted to avoid.

If you could outrun every child in your neighborhood, you probably started to think of yourself in terms of this ability. You considered yourself a "fast runner." Experience taught you that this was an activity you could do well. If, on the other hand, you found that you didn't like or weren't good at certain activities, that information also went into your self-concept.

You have many different ways of looking at yourself. Some are based on your strengths and weaknesses. Others are based on your likes and dislikes. Still others depend on your personality traits. All of these influence your self-concept.

What Others Think

As a child, you learned from watching others and reacting to what they said and did. Young children are deeply influenced by what others think about them. Because they are not yet able to judge the truth or fairness of an opinion, the ideas others have of them form a very important part of their self-concepts.

Often such ideas remain in our minds long past childhood. The actions of little children are often inappropriate. But even though we have changed those actions, we still retain traces of other people's judgments long ago.

Learning about Ourselves Today

Today you are probably still very much affected by what others say about you. But you are less likely to accept outside opinions blindly. You evaluate these opinions, accepting certain views and rejecting others.

Other people can't know you fully. They can't always tell what your intentions are or what you are thinking. The mind is a private place. People can be very wrong about you.

The ideas that you get about yourself from other people, however, can be very valuable. First of all, they help you to see yourself from others' points of view. Since you live in a world with other people, it is important to know what kinds of behavior they find acceptable and unacceptable.

Feeling positive about yourself is important—especially during a job interview. A positive self-concept will help you present your best image.

Without their views, your opinions about yourself might be one-sided.

What Do They Know?

Your self-concept greatly affects how you respond to other people's judgments of you. If you have a positive self-concept—that is, you accept yourself as a worthwhile human being—you can benefit from the praise, and criticism, of others. If, on the other hand, you feel negative about yourself, you will find it hard to be open to others' opinions.

Suppose that you are used to thinking of yourself as "bad." This self-concept might color everything you hear about yourself. Negative remarks might be the only ones you will believe. If someone seems to think well of you, you might secretly feel that you are "fooling" that person. You might tell yourself that she or he doesn't know how "worthless" you really are.

Sometimes a negative self-concept works the opposite way. Fighting the idea that you are "no good," you might *reject* all criticism and accept only the pleasing things that are said about you. You might dismiss critical remarks by saying, "He's just an idiot, anyway," or "Who is she to tell me that?"

Either way, a negative self-concept makes you unable to learn from other people's views of you. If you assume that all praise is mistaken, you cut yourself off from the support of others. You also use criticism to put yourself down, rather than to help you change. If you deny all criticism, you limit your opportunities to grow and change as a person.

Box 1

Building a Positive Self-Concept

What can you do to develop the positive side of your self-concept? Here are a few guidelines to help you accept the person you are and become the person you want to be:

- Remember, no one is perfect. You have talents and abilities, but you have limitations too.
- Focus on your strengths and learn to do one thing well. Knowing you can succeed at one activity will give you confidence in other areas as well.
- Set goals for yourself, but be sure they are realistic. Give yourself the chance to succeed.
- Try congratulating yourself for your successes, instead of blaming yourself for failures.
- Don't moan over your mistakes. Learn from them.
- Spend some of your time helping others. Knowing you have made someone else happy can be a real boost to your self-esteem.

Dealing with Criticism

Criticism can be hard to face. Many people find it difficult to accept that they are less than perfect. But criticism does not mean that you are a bad person. It just means that someone did not approve of something you did or said.

Is it possible to learn from criticism without being upset by it? Think about Bobby. When some of Bobby's classmates called him a show-off and his teacher called him immature, these criticisms were hard to accept. Still, many of his classmates loved his sense of humor. Perhaps Bobby could learn something from the criticism.

This doesn't mean that he should give up clowning around—it sounds as if this is a part of him that people enjoy. But he could learn to choose a place other than the classroom for his playful behavior.

Of course, some criticism may be way out of line. Perhaps the classmate who said Bobby was a bore was jealous. Consider critical remarks carefully. Don't accept or reject them without thinking.

Criticism can help you learn about yourself. It can give you a truer picture of yourself than you are used to seeing. When you can see both your strengths and your weaknesses, you will find it easier to deal with other people.

QUESTIONS

1. What does the term "self-concept" mean? What are two main influences on people's self-concepts?
2. How can self-concepts affect the way people interpret praise and blame?
3. What are some practical steps toward building a positive self-concept?
4. What are some ways parents could help children improve their self-concepts? Do you think children help their parents' self-concepts?
5. What kinds of criticism are hardest to accept? Why? What can be gained from learning to accept criticism thoughtfully?

ACTIVITIES

1. Write a dialogue based on a situation in which someone criticized you. If you are unhappy with the way you reacted, rewrite the dialogue so that it reflects what you wish you had said.
2. Make a life-size silhouette of yourself. On it draw a symbol that could stand for you. Then on the silhouette write twenty statements about yourself beginning with "I am." Add pictures from magazines to suggest your personality and interests.
3. Write a description of yourself. Give it to a classmate you trust. Ask her or him to underline the comments that seem most true.

SECTION 3 · Growing Up and Your Changing Self

GROWING PATTERNS

When you're fourteen and over five foot seven, you're heads above everyone else. I couldn't feel normal. I worried that I would spend the rest of my life looking down at my friends. Now, you know, it doesn't seem to bother me at all. Being tall really helps when you play basketball!

Being a teenager was really tough for me. I had a bad case of acne, and I felt that people were always staring at my skin. I questioned everything people said, and I felt angry most of the time. Someone said I should join the debating club, and I did. I met a girl there, and we started to date. One day when my sister said she was glad to see me smiling, I realized I wasn't so angry anymore. Things had finally started to look up.

In the seventh grade, everything started to go wrong. I wasn't interested in model airplanes anymore, and I wasn't ready to start dating. I wasn't sure where I was going. The toughest thing was not being able to concentrate on anything. The people around me got upset: my parents, my teachers, even my best friend. They were angry with me because I just didn't care about doing anything. I spent a lot of time watching TV. I felt bored.

When I was ten, my body was already changing. Not one of my friends was changing, and believe me, I felt like a freak! In a few months, though, a lot of my friends started going through the same thing. I felt better when I saw that they were changing, too.

Adolescence is the time when you move from childhood to adulthood. During these years, your body, your thoughts, and your feelings go through vital changes. These changes are actually growth: physical, mental, and emotional growth. They are so strong that they bring many problems you never knew as a child. Solving these problems is part of becoming an adult.

In your teen years, you discover new things about yourself. You also have new and different feelings about your friends. Your friendships become closer and more complex. You think and question more than you did when you were younger. Your body is developing in a new way.

Your Changing Body

The first changes you probably notice as an adolescent are physical changes. Someone in your class may seem to grow six inches almost overnight. Others may start developing adult figures. Voices change, and some people develop acne. All these things are normal. They are caused mainly by changes in body chemistry. Some changes, like acne, are temporary and will disappear as you grow older. But most changes are steps on the way to adulthood.

As you move into adolescence, the glands in your body begin to release new hormones into your system. Hormones are chemicals that cause you to grow in size and to change from a girl into a woman, or from a boy into a man.

Hormones work differently in different people. Growth may speed up, and then slow down. Some adolescents grow taller in a rush, and then stop. Others grow more steadily. The process of growth varies a great deal from person to person.

You may feel awkward because of the

Regular exercise—of any kind—can keep you fit and help you feel more comfortable with your changing self.

changes that are turning you into a man or a woman. You may also feel awkward because of the unevenness of your growth. Features of your face may grow at different rates. Your arms, neck, and legs may grow faster than the rest of you. One side of your body may even grow a little bit faster than the other side. All of this takes getting used to. For a while, you may feel clumsy and uncomfortable with your changing body.

Your Changing Mind

At the same time that you are experiencing important physical changes, you are also going through important mental changes.

Box 1

Taking Charge of Your Health

It is important to take good care of your health in order to maintain strength and reach your full potential. This means eating right and getting enough rest and exercise. It also means avoiding harmful substances such as tobacco, alcohol, and drugs not prescribed by a doctor. How well you take care of yourself affects how you feel, how you work, and how much you enjoy life.

- **A balanced diet** gives your body the nutrients it needs to grow and develop properly. You need protein-rich foods such as meat, fish, and eggs; milk and milk products; fruits and vegetables; and grains, including cereals and breads. If you eat wisely, you will have energy for your daily activities. At the same time, you will store nutrients that help your body cope with periods of illness or stress.
- **Rest** is necessary for your body to renew itself. No one can go at full speed twenty-four hours a day. You need sleep and time to relax. Enough rest also helps you to think more clearly and work better.

- **Exercise** strengthens muscles and builds stamina, or staying power. To get exercise, you don't have to join a sports team. You can simply take long walks with a friend. How you get your exercise is less important than how often you get it. Regular exercise makes your body stronger and allows you to handle daily activities more easily.
- **Watchfulness** for possible health problems is only sensible. You know yourself best, so you are the person most likely to notice changes or signs that something is wrong. When you notice symptoms such as a sore throat that does not go away, or an unusual lump or swelling, alert a parent or another responsible family member. You may have to seek help from your family doctor or clinic.

Your body works full time for you, and it's the only one you've got. Protecting your health is part of being a responsible and an independent person.

In the teen years, you learn to reason and to think more abstractly. When you were a child, you might have said, "I want some cookies because I want some." As an adolescent, you see more complex reasons for things. Your reasoning ability lets you plan, argue, and even criticize better than you could before.

As you grow in mental ability, you are better able to understand how other people think. You and your best friend may even feel sometimes that you think "exactly alike."

Your new mental abilities may also lead you to question ideas you have learned in school or from your parents. Questioning is necessary for independent thinking. However, it may lead to conflicts with your family, teachers, or friends.

Learning to think for yourself includes taking responsibility for your own actions. This is a very important part of growing up, and it is one of the most difficult tasks of adolescence.

Your Changing Emotions

Another part of you that is growing along with your body and your mind is your emotions. Emotions may be more intense in adolescence than at any time before. This is partly because they are affected by the changes in your body chemistry.

The hormones that are turning you into a woman or a man may lead you to be attracted to others. And, as your body adjusts to the rapid changes in these hormones, you may also feel some "up and down" emotions. You may feel great one day and terrible the next.

The changes in your body chemistry, combined with your mental development, make you experience emotions more intensely than before. Because you can think more abstractly now, you are better at thinking *about* what you feel. Your emotions become very important to you. This can be hard for your parents or your younger brothers and sisters to understand.

During adolescence, you will be learning how to live with new adult emotions. This means you will need to practice expressing—and controlling—these new feelings. How will you deal with intense feelings of love, jealousy, or anger? Much of your adolescent energy will be spent working on answers to this question.

Your Changing Social Self

All the changes you experience in adolescence make you more aware of yourself.

This self-awareness may make you feel self-conscious at times. As a teenager, your physical appearance is changing. Your mental development helps you imagine the thoughts of other people. And your emotions make you sensitive to their opinions.

Self-awareness, though, is part of what makes human beings human. It helps you see your individuality—the fact that you are different from everyone else in the world. It makes you recognize both your talents and your shortcomings. Self-awareness helps you decide which aspects of yourself you want to develop.

Box 2

What Are Emotions?

People all over the world know what love, anger, hate, and happiness are. Different cultures may have different names for these emotions, but all human beings experience them. We are still trying to understand the many factors that make us feel emotions.

In the Middle Ages, people thought that their emotions were caused by body fluids. We still call someone with a strong temper "hot-blooded." It is not surprising that people have made this connection. Anger often does bring a rush of blood to people's faces. But it isn't the blood that causes the emotion.

Today's scientists have discovered that our emotions are accompanied by chemical changes in our bodies. Some of these changes are caused by glands in the body. Others are caused by reactions in the brain.

Different chemical changes accompany different emotions. With some emotions—for example, fear—one of the chemicals released is called epinephrine (ep i nef' rin). Epinephrine speeds up your heartbeat, and makes the pupils of your eyes enlarge. It makes your body able to react quickly—it makes you more sensitive to the situation.

Have you ever walked down a dark path at night? If you were slightly scared, epinephrine may have made you more sensitive to the situation. You were probably ready to jump at the smallest sound.

Just as it was incorrect to think that hot blood could cause a strong temper, it's also probably wrong to think that these chemical changes "cause" emotions. But they *are* a part of the emotion—they do add to the way we feel. Understanding that emotions are more than a state of mind can help us to understand—and deal with—the power that emotions can have over us.

A Time of Exploring

In developing an idea of who you are, you will be trying out many new ways of acting and reacting. You will explore the customs, feelings, and ideas that go with having new relationships outside your family. In this exploration, you may make mistakes.

You may wear the wrong thing to a party at a friend's house. You may imagine that someone dislikes you and avoid that person, then find out that you misjudged his or her feelings. You may be nervous and blurt out something that sounds rude. Mistakes such as these are made by everyone.

The social skills you will need as an adult take practice.

You may have disagreements with people you care about—no one has ever found a way to avoid these. Sometimes you will feel very hurt or angry. Remember, the people around you are experiencing the same problems you are. Your parents and their friends all went through similar problems when they were your age.

Adolescence is a time when you discover and develop yourself. You learn that neither you nor the world is perfect. As you come to accept yourself, you will discover your own special strengths.

QUESTIONS

1. What are some of the physical changes that take place during adolescence? What causes these changes?
2. What kinds of mental development take place during adolescence? How does this development lead to self-awareness?
3. In what ways are teenagers' emotions different from those of younger people? Why? What problems might these emotional changes cause? How can teenagers learn to handle their emotions?
4. How are health habits related to development?
5. Which of the changes faced by teenagers seem to cause the most difficulties? Why?
6. What could people do about their feelings of shyness or self-consciousness? How might being shy sometimes be an advantage?

ACTIVITIES

1. What sentence in this section do you consider the most important? Justify your choice to the class.
2. Make a time line of the important physical, emotional, and mental changes you have experienced. Ask a parent for help with your earlier years. When do you think you were most prepared for changes? Why?
3. Describe a time when lack of sleep affected the way you acted.

SECTION 4 · What You Communicate about Yourself

SILENT LANGUAGE

All these people are communicating thoughts and feelings—without words. By the way their bodies are positioned, they are "speaking" a silent language—body language.

Psychologists who study body language have learned that certain positions or ways of moving the body can show certain things about a person. For example, the boy standing alone with his arms crossed may be shy. His tense, closed position may be saying that he doesn't want to be approached by anyone. In contrast, the boy sitting on the bench is relaxed and appears to be

ready to greet anyone who might come along. The girl who is talking is emphasizing her point by moving her hands. The tilt of the other girl's head shows that she is concentrating on what her friend is saying.

You can learn a lot about people by observing and interpreting their body language. What else might the people in the picture be communicating? What have you seen other people communicate through body positions? In what other ways do people communicate without words?

Have you ever asked your friend, "What's wrong?" before he's said a word? Have you come home from school and known just by looking at your sister that you had better leave her alone? How could you tell your friend was upset? How did you know your sister was angry?

People communicate in many different ways. Your friend may have looked sad and moved slowly instead of with his usual bounce. Your sister may have moved quickly and stiffly instead of in her usual relaxed manner. Appearance, facial expression, tone of voice, and gestures—as well as words and actions—communicate thoughts and feelings to others.

What Shows First

When people look at each other, they see a lot of things even in one glance. The ideas you get about people when you first see or hear them are often called first impressions.

First impressions are based on the most obvious traits or qualities of a person. These traits let you make judgments about others very quickly. You may sometimes decide whether you want to know someone better from your first impression.

Remember, however, that people's appearances vary from day to day, depending on how they feel. Try to give people the benefit of the doubt. If when you first meet Carla her hair is a mess and her clothes are wrinkled, it could mean she stayed up late studying for an exam and overslept that morning. Don't assume it means she is always careless about how she looks.

When meeting new people, give them a chance. Get to know them better before you make judgments. Time will help you see the difference between what is someone's usual personality and what is the result of an unusual circumstance.

However, many people *are* quick to make judgments based on first impressions. So it helps to keep in mind what *your* outward appearance may be saying to other people.

Posture

Your posture and the way you move make an impression on others. By the way you carry yourself, people decide whether you are shy or outgoing, nervous or relaxed, bored or content.

If you slouch and look as though you want to sink into the ground, you may give the impression that you don't think very much of yourself. If you stand straight and carry yourself with pride, people will assume you respect yourself. They will take that as a cue to respect you, too.

Manners

How you behave toward people—your manners—is another way of communicating. The world today is much less formal than it used to be. Still, politeness is important for letting people know you care how they feel.

Of course, you should say "please" when you ask for something, and "thank you" when you get it. You should say "excuse me" if you can't help interrupting someone, of if someone must move to let you walk by. "Pardon?" sounds much better than "what?" or "huh?" if you don't hear what someone says.

Friends tend to be relaxed with one another about these things. If you want to make a good impression on someone, however, pay attention to your manners. Manners are a way of letting people know you are considerate of their feelings.

Face, Body, and Voice

Your face can say things that you may not be able to say in words. Facial expressions do a lot of communicating for you. In fact, it is usually hard to keep a strong emotion from showing in your face.

Your body has its own language, too. You can see this from the picture at the beginning of this section. Different people may use "body language" differently, but friends can often tell from your stance and movements how you are feeling.

Your tone of voice or manner of speaking can say almost as much as your words. The sound of your voice can let people know what you are feeling. It can also be misleading.

Suppose you have a friend named Mike who has a habit of speaking sharply to people, as though he is always angry. The people who know him well realize that often he isn't angry at all. In fact, he is shy, and speaking harshly is his way of covering up his shyness. Usually he isn't aware that he is snapping at people, and he is surprised when they respond negatively.

When people first meet Mike, they sometimes form a bad impression of him. They think he is harsh because they don't understand his behavior. If Mike stopped to listen to himself, he might realize that he is giving people the wrong impression.

Mime artists use facial expressions to show surprise, anger, happiness, and sadness. Your face too is sending emotional messages, even though you may not be aware of it.

How People React

Because of their unique experiences and personalities, people react differently to what they see and hear. An action that is considered friendly and outgoing by one person may seem too aggressive to another. What seems shy and reserved to one person may seem unfriendly to someone else. An individual's reactions to others depends on that individual's personality. It also depends on ideas and opinions developed in childhood.

Let's look at a few examples. Steve always stands up straight and tall. This is natural for him. People who don't know Steve well often form ideas about him on the basis of his posture. Most people see it as a mark of self-confidence, but some believe that he is stiff and ill at ease.

Karen has large blue eyes and likes to accentuate them with liner and shadow.

Box 1

Cleanliness and Grooming

Neatness communicates to others that you care about yourself. It says that you are ready to take the time and effort to look attractive. It often helps you make that good first impression which causes people to want to know you better.

- The most important aspect of good grooming is cleanliness. Keeping your body and clothes clean makes you nicer to be around. It also prevents the spread of germs that can lead to disease.
- Regular bathing with soap and water keeps you comfortable and helps avoid body odor and skin problems.
- Regular shampooing keeps hair clean and shining. Clean hair also means less chance of oily hair irritating your skin.
- Washing your face at least twice a day with hot water and soap, and then rinsing it carefully, can help control acne. Acne results when oil-clogged pores trap germs and dead skin particles that irritate and inflame the skin.
- It is especially important to wash your hands before preparing or eating foods. Trimmed and scrubbed fingernails are pleasant to look at, and are an important part of overall cleanliness.
- Cleaning your teeth can keep your breath fresh and your teeth looking their best. Daily brushing and flossing removes plaque, a film of bacteria that reacts with sugars in food. (Avoiding sweets also helps control plaque.) Plaque leads to cavities and gum disease. Your teeth and gums should be checked by a dentist regularly to be sure they are free from disease and that your daily cleaning routine is effective.
- Deodorants and antiperspirants are also useful for controlling odors caused by per-

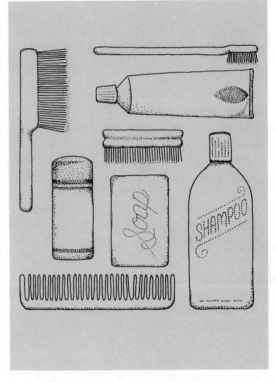

spiration. Read the labels carefully so that you can use these products properly and avoid irritating your skin.
- If you use make-up, apply it carefully. Too much make-up spoils the effect you are trying to create. While make-up can be fun to experiment with, you don't *need* it to look good.

How you dress and care for your body reflects how you feel about yourself. This doesn't mean that you have to wear expensive cologne or fancy clothes. But if you are neat and clean, it shows that you care about yourself.

Many people think that this is a sign that she always likes to look her best. Others, however, believe that she lacks self-confidence and needs to wear make-up to make herself feel attractive.

You have to expect different reactions to what you say and do. There is room for many different views. You can never hope to please everyone. But you can try to please yourself and those you care for.

Being aware of all the different ways you express yourself can help you have more control over the image you present to others.

What Do You Want to Communicate?

You are made up of much more than what shows on the surface. Your ideas, feelings, talents, and interests help make you the individual you are. But your appearance, your voice, and the way you move are important, too, because they are the first things that people notice about you. Since people are bound to form some opinions about you on the basis of these qualities, it helps to think about the picture you present to the world.

You have control over much of what you communicate. You can often choose what image you will give to others. The key to making this choice wisely is knowing clearly what your feelings and ideas are. Then see if you are communicating them well. Take a close look at some of the elements of the image you project. Then you will be more certain that what you are "saying" is what you want to say about yourself.

QUESTIONS

1. What is body language? What can facial expressions and body language communicate about a person? What else might influence the impression someone makes?
2. How do you think people usually interpret careful grooming, good posture, and thoughtful manners?
3. Why do different people sometimes interpret someone's looks and actions in different ways? What are first impressions usually based on? Should first impressions be trusted? Why or why not?
4. How can an individual control the impression he or she makes?
5. Do you think people should choose a certain image to communicate? Why or why not?
6. What could someone do if his or her appearance or manner is misinterpreted by others?

ACTIVITIES

1. Choose a snapshot or magazine photograph that shows several people. List all the ways the people are communicating, including details of posture, dress, and facial expression. After each item on your list, indicate what it communicates. (For example, being dressed up could mean that someone is ready for a special occasion.) Trade pictures with a classmate and compare your conclusions.
2. Imagine that a new student has just entered your class. Write a description of yourself based on the new student's first impression of you. Then describe yourself from the point of view of someone who knows and likes you.
3. List four of the qualities you like in yourself. Explain how you communicate each trait to other people. Then describe several practical ways you could improve your communication of these qualities. Give your plan a try-out, and keep a record of your progress.

SECTION 5 · What's Important to You?

Margie's Conflict

Margie likes to play football. Last fall, all the kids in her neighborhood played on the school field. Margie never missed a game. Since she's a fast runner for her age, she was usually picked to play tight end. She loved catching the ball and making her way through and around the other players.

All summer, Margie took any job she could get to make money for a helmet and cleats. She cut grass, picked strawberries, and washed cars. This season she wants to go out for her junior-high-school football team. At first, her parents thought she was joking. Now that they know she is serious, they are very much against the idea. Margie is really upset by their position.

Some of her friends think she is crazy for wanting to play football in the first place. Bill says that a girl could never make it in high-school football, so why bother in junior-high? But JJ and many of Margie's other friends think she should have the chance to play.

Why are her parents so against Margie's plan to try out for the team? Do you think she should be allowed to try out? Or do you think she should forget the whole idea? Should she make the team if she proves in the tryouts that she's a good player?

What you think about Margie's situation depends partly on who you are. Margie says she just wants to have fun playing. She knows all the players on the school team, and she wants a chance to be part of it.

Margie's parents are worried about her getting hurt. Some of her friends feel threatened by the fact that she is so good at football. Others take her side. They like supporting someone who has the courage to go after what she wants.

Margie's desire to play football and the advice of her parents and friends are based on different opinions of what is important for her.

Basic Needs

Human beings have certain basic needs that must be met. Satisfying these needs is necessary for health and well-being, and is important to everyone.

Some needs are physical. People need food. They need shelter and clothing for protection from the weather. They need to rest, to get exercise, and to keep themselves clean.

People have emotional needs as well. They need to know that someone cares about them. They need to feel that they are accepted. Being accepted by others helps people feel good about themselves.

These basic physical and emotional needs are shared by everyone. Other desires, however, differ from person to person. One individual may have a strong desire to be good at sports. Another would rather write well. Still another may find that organizing things is what he or she likes best. What we most enjoy and care about helps make us unique.

Our ideas about what is important are formed in many ways. Individual personal-

ity is one factor. Ideas we get from family and friends also influence our choices and goals. Our religious group, school, and community affect our sense of what is valuable in life, too.

Personal Tastes

Each of us likes some activities more than others because of our nature. We are able to handle certain situations better than others. What one person finds exciting might make another person nervous. What one person finds interesting, another might find dull.

Margie, for example, would not have her heart set on playing football if she were clumsy, tired easily, or did not like working with a team. As we grow, we find out what

Whether it's backgammon, stamp collecting, or photography, each of us has different interests and different ideas about what's important.

we are good at and what we enjoy. This knowledge helps us choose one activity over another.

What Others Think

Your family has much to do with developing your ideas. What your family expects from you now, or would like for you in the future, will certainly influence your decisions.

Parents often have strong ideas about what would make their children happy. Your close ties to your family may lead you to do some things and avoid others.

You may have a group of friends you care about and spend time with. You value their opinions and learn a lot from them. What your friends think and what they expect from you will have an effect on what is important to you.

Other Influences

Your sense of what is valuable in life is formed in other ways, too. Schools stress certain activities and goals. Religious teachings influence your ideas and behavior. Your ethnic group may follow customs and beliefs that have been passed down from parent to child over many years. All of these institutions and groups help shape what you value now and what you will want for yourself in the future.

Throughout history the written word has been important in shaping ideas. A television show may last an hour—a book can be referred to day after day.

The media—especially television—also affect what you think and how you behave. For example, a great many television programs and advertisements show women cleaning the house and men going off to work. In real life, of course, many women work and many men help clean the house. Also, older people are often shown as helpless or ridiculous. Yet the vast majority of older people are neither. Unfortunately, people unconsciously absorb false ideas about others from television.

Differing Views

Because it's natural to want to "belong," people often go along with the ideas of others in their society and in their close groups. When they disagree with those ideas, conflicts arise.

Margie is eager to use her skill. She wants the freedom to choose her own activities. Her parents, however, are concerned about her safety. They also worry that football will take up time she needs for studying. So Margie feels conflict. Not all of Margie's friends agree with her, and this makes her conflict even greater.

Not all conflicts arise over differences with others. At times, you will have to decide what you yourself value most among several different goals that are important to you.

Suppose, for example, that you were a key member of the school chorus last year. You planned to sing again this year. The director and other members of the group are counting on you.

Now you find out that a play you really want to be in has rehearsals scheduled for the same time as chorus practice. Many of your friends will be trying out for the play. Though you want very much to be in the chorus, you don't want to miss acting in the play with your friends.

Finding a Solution

Resolving conflicts can be very hard. It often helps to take a closer look at your own feelings. Margie, as we have seen, enjoys football. She is one of the best receivers in her age group and would really like to make the team.

The fact that people close to her are against the idea is very upsetting to her. She does not want to oppose their views. She also knows they have raised some very good points. Most likely, Margie herself is concerned that trying to make the team will be rough and could lead to disappointment. She may wonder if the skills she gains by playing will be of any use to her later on. These thoughts add to her conflict.

She has to decide if playing football is a goal worth going after. She has to decide if her desire to play is strong enough to overcome the problems she faces.

Sometimes you will have to change your goals in order to settle a conflict. Margie, for example, might decide to play soccer. This would satisfy some of her own needs, and answer some of her parents' concerns as well.

At other times, you will have to put off something you value or give it up altogether. You might have to miss being in the school play, for instance, unless you decide to give up singing in the chorus.

You Are the Key

Many of your ideas about what is important come from the world around you. Society as a whole, your community, your family, and your friends influence your choices and goals. But you are an individual with your own talents and abilities, your own special point of view. You add your own ideas and goals to your world. In the end, only you can decide what is important to you.

You cannot avoid conflict in your life. You can never follow all of your own and other people's ideas about what is right for you. It may be very hard to make a decision when one or more goals conflict. Sometimes you will have to accept the fact that no decision you can make will be totally satisfactory.

When you are faced with such a conflict, try to sort out your feelings about each choice. You may not be able to satisfy every need. But by weighing the choices and making a decision, you will be able to resolve the conflict to some degree. You can then apply your energy to achieving the goals that mean the most to you.

QUESTIONS

1. Give some examples of desires that differ from one person to another.
2. What is a conflict? Name two kinds of conflicts. What approaches to resolving a conflict might be helpful?
3. What are six factors that influence what people care about and consider important?

4. Which of the influences on what people care about do you think affects *you* the most?
5. Do you think that it is possible for people to be close without having any conflicts? Why or why not?
6. How do you think Margie should resolve her conflict? Why?

ACTIVITIES

1. Write a conversation in which several people who know Margie discuss her plans to try out for the football team.
2. List fifteen activities you enjoy. What does your list reveal about what you consider worthwhile? Choose five activities and explain how you got involved with them and why you enjoy them.
3. Choose three items from your billfold, handbag, or pockets that give clues to what matters to you. Explain them to your class.

SECTION 6 · Making Decisions

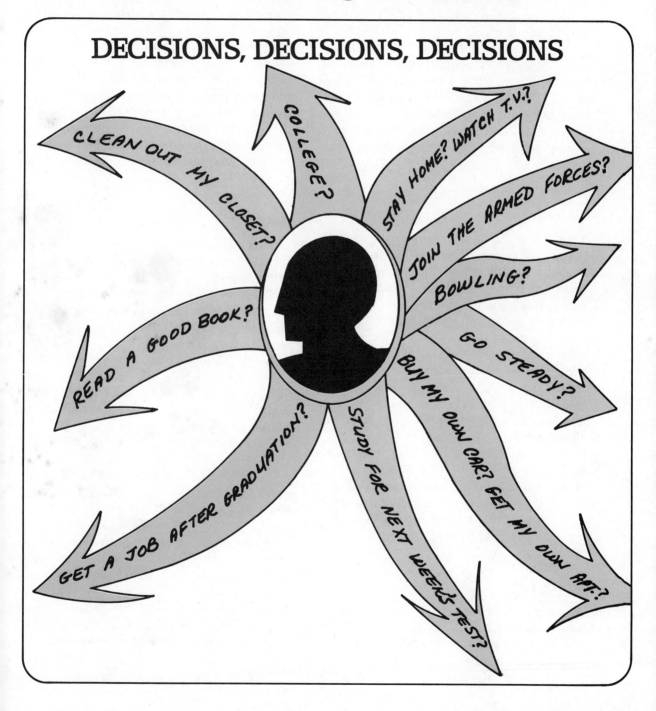

DECISIONS, DECISIONS, DECISIONS

CLEAN OUT MY CLOSET?

COLLEGE?

STAY HOME? WATCH T.V.?

JOIN THE ARMED FORCES?

BOWLING?

READ A GOOD BOOK?

GO STEADY?

BUY MY OWN CAR? GET MY OWN APT.?

GET A JOB AFTER GRADUATION?

STUDY FOR NEXT WEEKS TEST?

You are always making decisions. Some are important decisions that might affect your life for a long time. Others are less important and will affect your life only in small ways.

Decisions can be made in many different ways. Sometimes you will think long and hard before making a decision. But often you will make a decision without careful thought. Sometimes you make a decision actively. At other times, you "decide" to let events, or other people, make the decision for you.

Default

You are at home studying for a test on which you want to do well. Two friends drop by to talk about problems they are having at home. How long do you listen before telling your friends you have to study?

Many decisions are made by default. This means that people back themselves into a decision by *not* deciding. In the example just described, suppose you keep on talking with your friends until it's too late to study. You never make up your mind, and in the end you don't have any choice left.

If the decision is a small one, reaching it by default won't matter too much. But suppose the test is an important one. You need a high score to get into the school program you want. In this case, deciding by default not to study could affect you quite a bit.

Imitation

All your friends are getting their hair cut in a new hair style. It's time to have your hair cut. Do you copy your friends and get your hair cut in the new style?

You probably reach some decisions by copying another person's example. That person may be a television star, a parent, a sports hero, or a best friend. Sometimes you may imitate a group of friends. Imitation isn't always a bad idea. You may really enjoy wearing the latest hair style.

Sometimes, however, imitation doesn't work. Suppose the new hair style is short and you have ears like airplane wings. You probably won't be happy with the result. Mistakes like that can easily happen if you imitate other people blindly. Try, instead, to base your decisions on what is right for you.

Habit

You are at the store and have just received a dollar in change. Where do you put the dollar?

Perhaps you never remember where you put your money. Perhaps you decide carefully where to put it every time. But many people learn to make decisions such as this by habit. They may have once imitated someone's example. Or they may have thought carefully for themselves about the best place to put money. Then they've repeated the action over and over until it is automatic—a habit.

Habits are very useful. Without them you would have to think about every single thing you do every day. You would spend your whole day thinking about minor details!

Sometimes, though, habits get out of date. Suppose you always put change in the back pocket of your pants. Then you get some new pants without a back pocket. Or suppose you keep your change in a purse, and one day you get tired of carrying a purse. In either case, you would have to think of a new plan of action. You would need to develop a new habit.

Decisions can be as difficult as deciding on your future—or as easy as deciding how to spend a Saturday with friends.

Impulse

Your parents keep telling you that you are overweight, and you agree with them. You are with your friends, and they go out for ice-cream. Uh-oh—hot fudge sundaes, your old favorite. What do you do?

Impulse is another way people reach decisions. Impulse means doing what you feel like doing at the moment. Acting on impulse may be the ideal way to make some decisions. If there will be long-term effects, however, making a decision on impulse could be a mistake. Knowing that hot fudge sundae will add to your weight problem, should help you conquer your impulse to order it.

Coin Tossing

You are out with a friend, trying to decide what to do. Your friend wants to go bowling. You want to go to the latest movie. How do you decide where to go?

Sometimes people who can't decide

what to do flip a coin. Coin tossing may be a good way to decide between two choices. Both have an equal chance. For a small decision, a coin toss might be very satisfactory. It could even be successful for a major decision—provided the choices really *are* equal.

Suppose you have sprained your ankle and walking on it is still painful. Flipping a coin might land you at the bowling alley instead of at the movies—probably a bad decision for your ankle! In a case like this, it would be better to decide some other way.

Decision Making by Careful Thought

All of the above methods can lead to good decisions. They can also lead to decisions that are against your interests.

One way to improve your decision making is to think about decisions you have made. How did you make them? Did they turn out well? What would you do if you had another chance to decide? Thinking about decisions after the fact is a good way to improve your decision-making ability. It teaches you what methods have worked for you.

A more powerful way of using thought is to organize your thinking *before* you make a decision. This will improve your chances of making wise decisions. Organizing your thinking means knowing what questions to ask, and in what order to ask them.

Here are seven useful questions:

- What is the problem?
- What are my most important goals?
- What choices do I have?
- How well would each choice help me reach my goals?
- What results might each choice have?
- Which choice seems best?
- What is my decision?

Box 1

PROS AND CONS

A good way of seeing decisions clearly is to make a list of the points for and against each option. These are sometimes called the *pros* and *cons*. When these points are seen side by side, decisions will often look obvious.

It can also help to note how strongly you feel about each point. In the lists below, each item has a number beside it—a rating of how important the point is: (1) means it isn't too important; (5) means it's very important.

OPTIONS	PROS (for)		CONS (against)	
Going to movies	I'll enjoy it	(3)	Friend could be bored	(3)
	Give ankle a rest	(2)	More expensive	(1)
Going bowling	Less expensive	(1)	Could hurt my ankle	(4)
	Friend will enjoy it	(3)	Hurt ankle would ruin game for both of us	(5)

Add up the *pro* ratings for an option, then add up the *con* ratings. Comparing the totals will show you how attractive each option is. In the example above, which option do you think will be followed?

To see how these questions help decision making, consider the coin-tossing situation described earlier. You and your friend are trying to decide whether to go to a movie or to go bowling. Here are the questions and answers you might come up with:

What is the problem? I don't know what to do this afternoon.

What are my most important goals? To have a good time with my friend and not spend too much money.

What choices do I have? Going to a movie downtown or going bowling. (Try to think of all the other alternatives you can.)

How well would each choice help me reach my goals? Bowling is less expensive because it doesn't require a bus ride. My friend and I don't agree on which would be more fun.

What results might each choice have? If I go to the movie, my friend might be bored. If I go bowling, I might hurt my ankle again.

Which choice seems best? My friend agrees with me that it would be unfair to risk hurting my ankle. Hurting my ankle would ruin the game anyway. Decision: to go to the movie.

Following Through

Making a decision isn't the end of the process. A decision is useless unless you act on it. After you have made a decision, you may be tempted to do nothing after all. Maybe you are afraid your decision was wrong.

"Let's forget it, let's stay home and watch TV," you might say. But you owe it to yourself to act on your decision. If your decision was wrong, you will learn that only by acting on it. The experience could help you make better decisions in the future.

Take responsibility for your decisions, too. For example, if you agree to go bowling and your ankle acts up, don't blame your friend. It was your friend's idea, true, but it was your decision to go along.

Be flexible about your decisions. It may be necessary to make a change. Suppose your ankle begins to hurt in the middle of bowling. Don't continue to bowl. Tell your friend that you have to quit the game. That is certainly less painful than being laid up for another week.

When you make a decision, you are the one who must act on it. You are the one who must take responsibility for it. And you are the one who may have to change it. Keep these points in mind.

If you think carefully about your decisions, they will usually turn out well. You will gain confidence in your ability to make decisions, and you will improve your decision-making skills.

QUESTIONS

1. List and explain six ways by which people reach decisions. What are the advantages and disadvantages of each approach?
2. What steps could someone follow when thinking through a decision? What are the advantages of using this approach?
3. What steps should be taken after a decision has been made? Why?
4. How could you apply the seven-step method of decision making to one of the situations described in this section (talking to friends or studying, getting a haircut, finding a place to keep money, and having a hot fudge sundae)?
5. Which decision-making technique do you usually use? What decisions have you made during the past month by each of the methods described in this section? Do you think you could improve on any of these decisions by following the seven-step method? If so, how?

ACTIVITIES

1. Write the first few paragraphs of a story about someone who makes decisions without thinking them through. Read the opening section to the class, and ask for guesses about what might happen next.
2. Make a list of actions you usually perform by habit. Do you think you could improve on any of them? How?
3. Describe a group decision you and your friends or family recently made. How might that decision have changed if you had made a list of pros and cons?

SECTION 7 · Managing Day to Day

A Busy Evening

Dear Andy,

Dad and I have gone to pick up Grandma and we won't be home until around 8:00 p.m. Could you please make up the spare bed in Suzie's room for Grandma? Don't forget to feed and walk Sparky. I took some tomato sauce from the freezer. You can heat it and boil some spaghetti for your dinner. Don't forget your homework.

Love,
Mom

"Just what I need," thought Andy. He already had things planned for the rest of the day. Now he had these chores, too. Some days he came home from school and had nothing to do. Then, on a day like today, he seemed to have more than he could handle.

The weather was beautiful and Andy had been looking forward all day to playing basketball after school. He had also promised to rake leaves for his neighbor today or tomorrow. And there was a band rehearsal at school at 7:00 P.M. Homework, dinner, and a shower had to be worked in before that.

Andy was about to call his friends and say he couldn't make it to basketball. But then he decided to sit down and make a list of all he had to do. Perhaps there was some way to work in everything. Could he do the things that were expected of him and find time for his own activities, too?

Making plans and organizing your time are part of managing yourself. How well you manage your time can make a big difference in what you can accomplish. It can also affect how pleased you are with your efforts.

Management helps you make the best use of your time. It lets you get a lot done in a limited amount of time. A realistic schedule—or time plan—lets you avoid last-minute rushing. It helps you keep in mind all that you have to do. It allows time to do your work, and time for leisure, too.

Making a Plan

Suppose you have a lot to do in a short period of time. It makes sense to concentrate on what you *have* to do and what you most *want* to do. Making a list of those things will help you develop a good plan of action.

For example, Andy had a number of activities planned for his afternoon. He also had family responsibilities. He had a limited number of hours between getting home from school and bedtime. Andy's list to help him plan his time looked like this:

yard work	1 hr
basketball	2 hr
make bed	5 min
feed dog	5 min
walk dog	15 min
dinner	30 min
band rehearsal	2 hr
homework	2 hr
shower and dress	15 min

It was 3:00 P.M. when Andy made his list. There was no way he could do everything on it and still get to bed at a reasonable time. He studied the list for a few minutes to decide which things he would do.

What Comes First?

Looking over his list, Andy saw that certain items were "musts." Any plan he made would have to allow for these. Making the bed for Grandma, taking care of the dog, and eating dinner were absolutely necessary.

Doing his homework and going to the band rehearsal that night were also things he felt he had to do. On the other hand, the yard work *could* wait until tomorrow.

Playing basketball wasn't absolutely necessary, but it was very important to Andy. He and his friends planned to go out for the team, and they wanted this extra practice before tryouts. So Andy wanted to fit basketball into his schedule.

Making a Schedule

Once you have decided which items are most important, you have to figure out a way to do them in the time you have. In making a schedule, remember to be flexible. You must make compromises. You have to work around the schedules of other people. You have to be willing to make changes in your plans, if necessary.

By making compromises, Andy was able to find some extra time for himself. He decided to limit his basketball practice to an hour. And he saved fifteen minutes by eating a sandwich instead of the spaghetti dinner his mother had suggested.

Andy had to consider some other people's plans as he made his schedule. Grandma's bed had to be made before she got there. She might be tired from her trip and want to go right to sleep. Also, if he wanted to play basketball with his friends, he had to get to the court while the group was still there.

He would have liked to finish all his homework before band practice that evening. He had two hours of homework, however, and he was afraid he might miss meeting his friends for basketball. So Andy decided to spend an hour on homework before meeting his friends, and do the rest after band rehearsal.

A Schedule That Works

A good schedule is a realistic one. It fits you and the way you live and work. A big part of managing yourself is understanding your own pace, your habits, and how you work best.

Andy, for example, decided to spend an hour on homework in the afternoon and an hour in the evening. You might feel you need to do all your homework at one time. If so, Andy's solution would not suit you.

Making reasonable plans means taking into account your abilities and limitations. Your teacher's "half-hour" reading assign-

**The first step in managing is seeing your goals.
Then you must decide which are most
important, and how best to achieve them.**

ment may take you an hour. But then, you
may whiz through your math homework in
no time at all.

There are only so many things a person
can do in a day. There is a limit to how
much you can include in your schedule
while still enjoying what you are doing. A
tight schedule may look fine on paper. But
it won't work if someone calls you on the
phone or drops by for a visit.

It's a good idea to allow some extra time
in your schedule. Things won't always go
exactly as you planned. You will need bits
of extra time throughout the day. Use them
to relax and to deal with the unexpected.

Planning Your Free Time

Managing your time involves handling days
when there is nothing you really have to do.
You need a day of loafing and lounging once
in a while. But too many such days can be
empty and boring.

Planning a free day may call for more
thought than planning a busy one. Consider
all the activities you might pursue. Could
you help someone who is very busy that
day? Would you like to plan a joint outing
with a friend? Getting out of the house and
seeing people often helps you to think about
what you would like to be doing.

Try, Try Again

As you get older, you will be expected to manage more and more of your own time. Sometimes you will be tempted to put off chores that ought to be done right away. At other times, you will be impatient to do something that should be put off until later. In both cases, a thoughtful plan will help you to act wisely. Whatever you have to do, or want to do, planning gives you more control over your life.

The plans you make will not always go smoothly. If a schedule does not work, try to figure out what went wrong. Did you forget to list some important job? Did you allow too little time for an activity? Did you take on more than you could handle?

Whatever the reason, don't get discouraged. Use the experience to make a better plan next time. Learning to manage well takes time, practice, and patience. If you learn from experience, you will be on your way to becoming a good manager.

QUESTIONS

1. What are the advantages of good self-management?
2. What should be considered first when planning a time schedule? Why? What other factors should people take into account when scheduling their time?
3. What problems with schedules do people sometimes have? Why? What can people learn from their scheduling mistakes?
4. The schedule Andy prepared allowed no time between activities, and no extra time in case of problems. If you had to omit one activity from Andy's list, which would it be? Why?
5. What are some things about yourself that you should take into account when planning your homework time?
6. Describe a plan you once made that didn't work out as expected. How could you have better prepared yourself for what happened?

ACTIVITIES

1. Keep a day book in which you record the ways you spend your time for a week. Use categories such as *homework*, *chores*, and *time with friends*. Make a circle graph to illustrate your findings. Does the way you spend your time reflect which activities are really most important to you? If not, draw a circle graph to illustrate a more ideal way of using your time.
2. Interview several people to find out how they organize their time. Do they ever use lists, schedules, or calendars? How do they decide what to do next? Report your findings to the class.

SECTION 8 · Being Ready for the Future

THINKING AHEAD

Mandy's special interests are hiking and gardening. She also enjoys her part-time job selling shoes in a large department store. She is friendly and tries to be helpful to the customers. Her boss thinks that she could do well in retail sales. Mandy and her boss have also talked about her chances of becoming a buyer or department manager someday.

Mandy is thinking seriously about these opportunities. But she often daydreams about other careers. Sometimes she imagines herself as a forester, hiking through a wildlife preserve. Sometimes she is a landscape architect, planning yards and public parks. Mandy has decided to learn more about these jobs before making any choices for the future.

Nathan's parents own a hardware store. Nathan has been working there weekends and during the summer. For now, he enjoys being part of his family's business. But he is not sure he wants to go into it full time when he finishes school. Nathan's parents are pleased that he's learning the hardware business. They look forward to a day when their son will take over more and more responsibility for running their store.

Still, Nathan thinks some other field might suit him better. He likes working with his hands and is considering becoming a tool-and-die maker in a nearby auto plant.

Rick works in an ice-cream shop. He has become friends with Jody, the manager of the store. From watching and talking to her, he has learned a lot about her job. He thinks he would like to manage a small store or restaurant when he finishes high school.

His parents say he should go to college. But Rick thinks experience is the best teacher for the work he wants to do.

Finding a job that you can do well and that fulfills your needs is one of life's greatest challenges. In order to make a realistic choice, you must consider everything you know about yourself. You must think about your abilities, your interests, your responsibilities to others, and what you value most in life.

Gaining Knowledge

From the few things you know about Mandy, Nathan, and Rick, you have some ideas about what they might someday do for a living. Knowing all that you know about yourself, you should have no trouble thinking of ideas to explore for your own future.

Selecting a career requires more than self-knowledge, however. You will also have to find out as much as you can about jobs that might suit you. What training is required? Will there be a demand for the work when you are ready to look for a job? What satisfactions can you expect from a particular job? What are its drawbacks?

A job that you hardly considered might turn out to be very interesting once you know more about it. A job that you thought you would like at first may seem less appealing if you research it carefully.

The more you know about jobs you are considering, the greater your chances of making a satisfying decision about your career.

Clues to Your Future

Learning as much as you can about your interests will help you plan for your future.

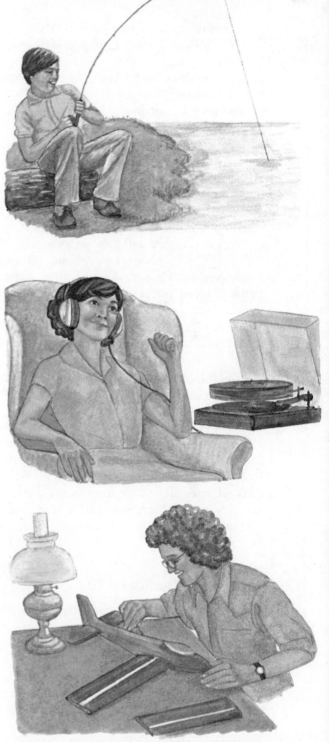

The hobbies we pursue help us to develop as individuals. They also give us clues to what we might enjoy as a career in the future.

Knowing what you like to do will enable you to choose a career that you will enjoy. Your knowledge about yourself will also suggest hobbies and leisure activities you might pursue.

In order to set realistic goals for yourself, you have to recognize your abilities and your weaknesses. You shouldn't hope to be a song-and-dance star, for example, if you can't carry a tune and have no sense of rhythm. A person who doesn't like to work with people and can't handle responsibility would not make a good manager.

Personal tastes will give you some direction as you explore future occupations. Some people like working with their hands. Others prefer working with ideas. Some people like variety in their work. Others like a regular routine. Some people like to travel, and others would rather stay put.

If you like being physically active, you might feel very confined in a small office. If you enjoy working with people, you might not like a solitary research job.

Your responsibilities to others may also affect your career decisions. One person may not consider jobs more than fifty miles from home, because the distance would make it difficult to care for a dependent relative. Someone else, who didn't have such a responsibility, might look into jobs halfway across the country.

Accepting Changes

Making decisions about your future is often difficult. You grow and change. You find out more about yourself every day. What mattered most to you last year may not seem quite so important now. You continue to discover new activities, ideas, and interests. Your plans for the future may change to fit these new discoveries.

Nathan already has some experience on which to base a career decision. He has worked in his parents' store. And he has talked many times with a neighbor about working as a tool-and-die maker. Nathan thinks he would like that trade because he likes working with tools.

He may discover other jobs, however, in which working with his hands is important. He might try carpentry, for instance, and discover that he likes working with wood a lot more than working with metal. He may decide to develop some other ability. Or perhaps he will learn more about running his parents' store and decide that the hardware business is the field for him after all.

Job Research

Try to find out as much as you can about a job that interests you. Talk to people who work in the field. See what they do every day. Ask them what they like most about the job, and what they like least. Find out if what *you* think about the job fits what others have to say.

Suppose that Mandy is looking into landscape architecture as a career. She discovers, after talking to people in that field, that it does not include as much outdoor work as she had thought. Landscape architects spend a lot of time indoors, drafting plans for yards and gardens. These activities do not particularly interest Mandy. Since she wants to be outdoors working with plants and shrubbery, she may find that nursery work would suit her better.

Mastering Skills

Once you have a clear picture of the job you want, think about preparing yourself for it. What kind of training will you need? How can you get that training? How long will it take to master the skills you will need?

College is a good place to further your education and develop your interests—but it may not be for everyone.

There may be more than one way to reach your goals. Through his job at the ice-cream store, Rick has discovered that on-the-job training could give him the practical experience he would need as a manager.

An occupational training program could be extremely valuable, too. Formal training often lets you see opportunities that you might not discover on the job. A management course at a vocational school or college would give Rick information that might take a long time to get on the job. He would benefit from the experiences of a lot of other people. He would have a broader knowledge of his field than just one job could give him.

Rick's parents want him to go to college. They feel that college will give him four more years to mature before he commits himself to a full-time job. For Rick, college could be more than a way of getting training in the field that interests him. It could give him the opportunity to develop as a person—and meet his parents' expectations for him as well.

Assistance from Others

Sometimes other people can help you find out what would suit you. Your parents, teachers, and friends may be able to help you pinpoint your interests and strengths.

An experienced counselor can help you explore the many careers open to you.

Counselors can give you tests to help determine your interests and aptitudes. They can provide you with information about jobs and how to train for them. They can help you see your potential more clearly.

No counselor can tell you exactly what to do with your life. By helping you see your career choices more clearly, though, a counselor can help you make sound decisions for your future.

QUESTIONS

1. What aspects of themselves should people consider before choosing a career? Why?
2. What kinds of questions should people ask about jobs that interest them? How can they learn the skills they will need on the job?
3. Where can people get help in setting career goals? What kinds of help are available?
4. Do you think people should stay in the same kind of work all their lives? How could people prepare themselves for job changes later in life?
5. What jobs do you think Mandy, Nathan, and Rick will eventually have? Why?

ACTIVITIES

1. Write a profile of yourself similar to the ones at the beginning of this section. Include your job goals and work experiences.
2. Take a career preference test. Write a report on the results.
3. Start a card file of job possibilities. Include work responsibilities, training and skills required, and salary ranges. Tape sample want ads on the cards.
4. Spend a day at work with someone whose job interests you. Describe the nature of the job to your class.

SECTION 9 · Some Career Choices

FAMILIAR FACES

One of the most familiar careers to you is probably that of the teacher—and a teacher's business is individual development. If you are interested in helping individuals, teaching is a career worth considering.

Your thoughts, emotions, problems and hopes are shared by many other people. What you learn about yourself as an individual can help you understand others.

Many jobs require understanding the personal concerns of other people. Hair stylists, for example, help people look the way they want to look. Teachers help people learn what they want to know. These jobs require widely different skills. But they both involve understanding people's needs and helping them to fulfill them.

Both the hair stylist and the make-up artist gain satisfaction from helping others look attractive. These careers require artistic flair and an understanding of people and their feelings.

When you plan how to earn your living, you may want to consider a job that uses your understanding of other people. What follows are brief descriptions of some jobs related to personal concerns. Different jobs require different kinds of training and different personal characteristics. Make a note of any jobs or areas of work that interest you. Try to learn more about them and how suitable they might be for you. Your teachers and counselors will be able to direct you to more information.

Helping People Look Their Best

Perhaps you have the knack of adding the right touch to your own or to your friends' dress or hair style. Many people work at jobs that involve understanding how people want to look.

Barbers and cosmetologists specialize in hair care. Barbers mainly give haircuts. They shave and trim beards and mustaches. They may also give shampoos, facial massages, and hair and scalp treatments. Barbers with advanced training provide other services, including hair styling and coloring.

Cosmetologists—who are also called beauty operators, beauticians, or hairdressers—offer a broad range of personal services. They shampoo, cut, and style hair. They curl, straighten, condition, and color hair as well. Sometimes they help their customers learn to care for their own hair. They may also give manicures, facial and scalp treatments, and advice about make-up.

Cosmetologists and barbers need stamina. They spend most of their working day on their feet. Often they are people who enjoy talking with their customers in the course of their work.

People who make and sell cosmetics are concerned with personal appearance, too. Some workers in the cosmetics industry are chemists. They develop products to help people care for their skin. Others, called demonstrators, promote and sell cosmetics. They advise customers on how to care for their skin and make the most of their appearance. Cosmetics demonstrators and salespeople may work in a store. They may also offer their products and services in the customer's home.

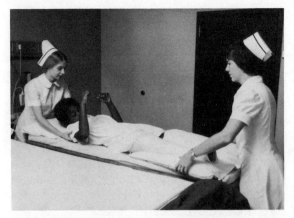

About five percent of all workers are in health related occupations. Many of them are employed as professionals in hospitals.

Helping People with Their Health

Many people work in the health-care field. Their jobs can be very satisfying, but they call for much patience and understanding. People who receive health services are often ill and uncomfortable. They may be worried or frightened. Health-care workers should be concerned for their patients' feelings as well as for their physical well-being.

Concern for the individual is important in all health-care workers, from nurses to dentists to hospital aides. Advising people on how to look after themselves is also a vital part of health care. Helping people to understand their bodies and prevent disease could save them from more serious problems.

Helping People Understand Themselves

Some jobs involve helping people understand their own capabilities, interests, and problems. People in these jobs encourage others to talk about themselves. They are skilled listeners who can pick out impor-

tant and useful information when they hear it. They take an interest in the variety of people and experiences that they hear about in the course of their day. If you enjoy the role of listener and adviser, you may want to consider a job in this field.

Psychologists are trained to help people understand what makes them act and think as they do. To become a psychologist, you must study how people grow, learn, and behave in various situations. Many psychologists devote their careers to research about human behavior and emotions. Others help people who are troubled to sort out their emotions, problems, and plans. They try to help these people learn to act independently.

Counselors show people how to evaluate their abilities, interests, and plans. Employment counselors help people figure out what jobs would best suit them. They might suggest training that would help a job seeker obtain work. They also locate jobs and help individuals adjust to new work situations. Rehabilitation counselors help the disabled and handicapped to understand their limitations and find work suited to them. School guidance counselors help people make educational and career decisions.

Helping People Learn

It can be very rewarding to teach a new idea or skill and help people achieve their goals. If you have ever helped a small child learn to tie shoelaces or spell a name, you may already have experienced the satisfaction of teaching.

Teachers must have an understanding of how people learn. They must be able to explain ideas and demonstrate skills so that students can understand them. Some teachers work in a school system or in a college. These classroom teachers must have a certificate or a degree in order to qualify for their positions.

Not all teachers work in a classroom, however. Dance and art instructors often teach in a private studio. Music teachers sometimes give lessons in the students' home. These teachers have had years of training and practice, often including college work. They must be able to demonstrate their skill and teaching ability in order to attract students.

Some people coach a sport such as tennis or soccer. Others teach practical skills like typing or driving a car. Still others teach trades like plumbing or cabinetmaking. No matter what the subject, teaching requires patience and a strong interest in both the student and the subject.

Understanding Yourself and Other People

If you enjoy working with people, you may want to try volunteer work. Many schools, hospitals, libraries, and community organizations have positions for volunteers. Volunteer work can be satisfying in itself. It can also help you decide whether or not to pursue a career in a particular field.

Maureen joined her community's volunteer rescue squad as a cadet when she was sixteen. She discovered that she enjoyed caring for people. She found she could work steadily under pressure, and remain calm in emergencies. Her experience as part of the rescue team has led her to explore different careers in health care.

The personal concerns of people will be part of your life no matter what career you choose. Understanding the needs and interests of others won't necessarily lead to a particular job. It will be important in your life and work, however. This knowledge and understanding will guide you in satisfying your own needs. And it will help you get along happily with co-workers, family, and friends.

QUESTIONS

1. Give brief descriptions of four jobs that involve helping others to look their best.
2. What qualities do psychologists and counselors need? Name three kinds of counselors and explain what they do.
3. What qualities do teachers need? Why? What different kinds of teaching jobs are there?
4. What two benefits do volunteer jobs provide?
5. Do you think people can tell when a worker in a personal service field is not truly suited to the job? How?

ACTIVITIES

1. Make a list of your personal qualities and skills. Choose five of the jobs mentioned in this section and check off the qualities and skills on your list that would help you in each of the jobs.
2. Prepare a booklet of volunteer jobs for teenagers in your community. Include job descriptions, addresses, and phone numbers, plus a list of the skills that could be learned from each job.

CHAPTER 2

You and Friends

SECTION 1 · What Are Friends?

A FRIEND IS . .

. . . someone to go places with.

. . . someone to have on your team.

. . . someone to talk to.

. . . someone to play with.

. . . someone who cares about you, understands you,
and accepts your faults.

Learning about friends begins very early in life. From the time we are born, we all need contact with others. Babies cry for attention as well as for food. They need to be picked up and cuddled. They need to hear the sound of human voices.

When infants receive love and care, they learn to trust others. Babies feel safe knowing that other family members will feed them when they are hungry, and comfort them when they are frightened. The warmth, love, and trust that children learn from these first human contacts can set the tone for later friendships. From the family, a child learns how people relate to one another.

Reaching Out

Once children are able to walk and talk, they begin to form friendships outside the family group. Preschoolers enjoy running, playing, and trying out new games and toys. Their playmates are their friends.

As children get older, they spend more time away from home. School brings new chances for friendships. Classmates become friends and form groups, often of the same sex. Or one person might single out another as a "best friend."

Friends become increasingly important as you enter your teens. Instead of going to the movies with your parents, you may go with friends. Friends provide security as you learn to handle new experiences. They help you to become more independent.

Teen and Adult Friendships

As a teenager, you probably feel a special need for someone to talk to. You may be adjusting to a changing body, and to changing emotions, as well. Friends your own age are going through the same changes, and

---

Box 1

Being Part of a Group

We are social beings. We usually like to feel that we are part of a group.

The first human societies were tribal groups with a common ancestry, language, and set of beliefs. They banded together because they needed security and support. Most of these groups have been absorbed into modern society, but human beings still need groups for security and support.

As people learn to relate to and accept others as friends, they form groups whose members have some common bond. These groups have a strong influence on their individual members.

This influence can be good or bad. A group can give us courage to do things we would not do alone. A group can lead us to sacrifice some of our own wishes for the sake of other members. But the influence of a group can be so strong that sometimes we do things that we later wish we had not done.

We become members of some groups at birth, through our parents. For example, we belong to a nationality, a neighborhood, an ethnic group. We choose to belong to other groups because of shared ideas, interests, talents, or beliefs. The friends we make throughout life usually come from the groups of which we are a part.

---

older friends have already gone through them. They are in a good position to know how you feel.

The need to share feelings and experiences goes beyond the teen years. When you start your first full-time job or move into your first apartment, it will be helpful to know others who are starting out on their own or who have done what you are doing.

The need for this kind of friendship will continue throughout your life.

Sharing Feelings

Friends share each other's joys and sorrows. They can help you celebrate your birthday and visit you when you are sick. Friends often make bad times better and good times wonderful.

When something good happens, most people are eager to tell their friends the news. When you win a contest or get the part-time job you want, your friends are glad for you. Because they share your pleasure, you feel even happier.

Just as friends can increase joy, they can make sorrows easier to bear. Everybody has unhappy times. A friend can encourage you when you are feeling down about a failure at school. A friend can help you face a death in the family. Sharing sad feelings with a friend allows you to receive comfort and support when you need them.

Sharing Problems

Friends can also help you look at your problems more clearly. They can make you see yourself from another point of view.

Suppose you are feeling bad because you didn't make the tennis team. Your friends may suggest that you go out for swimming instead—since you're a strong swimmer. They may point out that you'll have another chance to try out for the tennis team. Because you are so disappointed, you may not see these possibilities yourself. Friends can help you look at your situation in a more objective way.

When you talk over your problems with friends, you will find that others have the same worries you have. You may think you are the only one who feels shy walking into a room full of people. Then a friend says, "Hey, I know exactly what you mean. I feel the same way. I always think everyone is looking at me." It's comforting to know that someone else is shy, too, and that your problem is not at all strange or unusual. Friends make us feel that we are not alone.

Sharing Interests and Activities

At all ages, people like to share their experiences and interests with friends. A funny movie is funnier when you can laugh at it with someone else. Discussing a story with another person can help you understand it better.

Friendships are often based on common interests. Think for a moment about a friend of yours. What do the two of you have in common? Perhaps you are on the same volleyball team. Maybe you like to go shopping for clothes together. Some friends share hobbies such as painting or sewing. They like to swap ideas and compare projects.

Through shared interests and activities, you can learn a great deal from your friends. They can help you improve your skills and develop new ones. You might show your friend how to swing a tennis racket. That friend might teach you the newest dance. And when friends compete at sports, they learn how to win, how to lose, and how to work together as a team.

You may find that going places with someone else gives you a feeling of security. Walking into a party with a friend is often easier than walking in by yourself. It's fun to have someone to talk to as you walk or ride to the museum or ball park.

Whether you are exploring new places or visiting familiar ones, having a friend along can make an outing more fun.

Frequently a shared experience, such as a
wilderness camping trip, brings people together
and leads to new friendships.

Different Kinds of Friends

You probably have a different relationship
with each of your friends. This is because
each friend is an individual with a special
personality and different interests. You
may have friends who are older or younger
than you. Others may come from a different
ethnic or religious background.

You probably feel closer to some friends
than to others. The closest friends are usually the ones who are easiest to talk to
about things that are important to you. For
instance, you may have two friends who
enjoy playing tennis. One is a good player,
and improves your game. The other isn't so
good at tennis, but is easier to talk to about
other things. You enjoy spending time with
both friends, but you may feel closer to the
one with whom you talk more.

Having friends to count on makes life
easier. Friends do favors for one another. A
give-and-take attitude toward helping one
another is an important part of friendship.

When you need a favor, it's good to
know that you can depend on friends. They
like to know that they can depend on you,
too. It isn't a question of trading favors or
"keeping score." It's a question of caring
about one another.

What You Learn from Friendships

Through friendships, people learn how to
get along with others. They learn to be considerate, to share, and to work together toward common goals.

Your present friendships have value beyond the pleasure they provide now. Your friends are teaching you the art of being a friend. They are also helping you learn what qualities *you* value in a friend.

Some of the friendships you have now may last into your adult years. Even if they don't, learning to be a good friend now will help you to form other satisfying friendships later on in your life.

QUESTIONS

1. How do children first learn about getting along with others? In what ways do ideas about friendship change as children get older?
2. What do friends usually have in common? What are some of the ways in which friends help each other?
3. What are some of the ways in which friendships differ? Why do these differences occur?
4. What can people learn from having friends?
5. What kinds of groups can people belong to? How might belonging to a group influence members?
6. How have the qualities you look for in a friend changed as you've gotten older? Why do you think ideas about friendship change?
7. How many groups do you belong to? (Count informal groups, such as groups of friends, as well as formal ones, such as clubs.) How do you think these groups influence you?

ACTIVITIES

1. Interview someone older than you to find out what that person looks for in a friend. If possible, tape-record the interview.
2. Write an unrhymed poem, beginning each line with "A friend is . . . ." Find pictures to illustrate the poem, and make a display of your pictures and poem.
3. For one day, record every reference to friendship and every example of friendliness that you hear and see. Include examples from radio and television, as well as observations in your school and community.

SECTION 2 · Being a Good Friend

What's Your Problem?

Dear Nancy,

I have a problem with my friend Mark. We work on the school newspaper together and have been friends for a long time. He joined the soccer team not too long ago, and has been acting weird ever since. But last weekend was the worst.

We were supposed to go to the movies Saturday afternoon. When I stopped by Mark's house, his mother said that he had gone to a barbecue with some of the kids from the soccer team. I couldn't believe he didn't even call to let me know!

Then at school on Monday, one of the soccer crowd came up and said, "So, how's Cindy?" Cindy is my older sister's friend.

Mark is the *only* person who knew I liked Cindy, and he promised not to tell anyone else.

I found Mark after math class on Monday and asked him where he got off telling his new friends something he'd promised to keep secret. And that on top of going to the barbecue with them instead of to the movies with me!

He acted really sorry and embarrassed. It seems he was so excited about being invited to the barbecue that he forgot about going to the movies with me. He said that my secret slipped out because he was nervous about being with those other kids.

I can understand Mark wanting to be friends with this group, because they're the most popular crowd in school. But that doesn't mean that Mark should break his promise to me.

Mark and I used to have some good times together. Maybe I could forget about his skipping the movies, but I feel I can't trust him anymore. Should I stay friends with him?

A confused
Eric

Mark wants to be part of the popular crowd at school. He says he wants to remain friends with Eric, too. Mark has some things to learn about what it means to be a good friend.

Learning may sound like an odd word to use about friendship. But many of the qualities that make a good friend are learned.

The Qualities of Friendship

Sharing is one of the first aspects of friendship that people learn. Children usually start learning to share when they begin to play with others, between the ages of three and seven.

As we get older, there are other things that we need to learn to be a good friend. People want friends who are reliable, who listen well, and who are loyal. Friendship requires the ability to talk honestly and openly. It also requires being tolerant—that is, accepting people as they are.

No matter how much people's personalities and interests vary, the qualities they seek in friends are much the same.

Being Reliable

Friends want to be able to rely on each other. Suppose you are working on a project with somebody. You have divided the work, and agreed that you will each do your share before your next meeting. You have worked hard to meet the deadline. You probably won't feel too friendly if your partner calls to put the meeting off because she didn't finish the work.

The same is true of recreation plans. People who agree to meet friends, and then cancel out or arrive late, won't be popular if they do this too often. And if, like Mark, they don't even call to cancel, they will have two strikes against them. Their friends will be waiting around for them, when they could be making new plans.

Listening

Being a good listener doesn't mean simply being quiet while another person talks. Good listening means getting involved in the thoughts and emotions the other person is expressing.

To be a good friend, you must be able to get outside yourself. If you are always thinking about what *you* want to say when someone else is talking to you, you are not really *listening*. You are too involved with yourself.

If you have developed the quality of listening well, you may find that other people tell you their innermost thoughts. This is a big responsibility. It means that people trust you to keep their secrets. It demands that you respect their privacy.

Loyalty

Keeping secrets is a part of loyalty—another quality important in friendship. Loyalty can mean simply being there to talk to when things get rough. It involves actions as well.

Suppose a friend who means a lot to you is the target of unfair rumors. It can take a lot of courage to speak up for that friend, especially if you seem to be the only one who feels the rumors are unfair.

Loyalty also means not "trading in" a friendship for popularity. This is the mistake that Mark made in his relationship with Eric. Telling the soccer group about Eric's crush on Cindy made Mark the center of attention. It made him feel good for a short time, but it may have cost him his friendship with Eric.

Honest Communication

Things can go wrong in the best of friendships. That's when another quality of friendship—honest communication—can make a big difference. Many good friends find it hard to say that they are annoyed at or upset with each other.

Sometimes misunderstandings occur because friends don't talk enough about their feelings. Explaining feelings may take some effort, but keeping them inside can cause small problems to grow into large ones. If something your friend did is bothering you, tell her or him about it. Being honest about your feelings can be difficult, but it will strengthen your friendships.

Letting your friend know that the subject is hard for you to talk about is often a good way to get started. If you say something like "This is hard for me to say . . . ," it may actually be easier. Very often people do things that bother one another without even realizing it. Your friend may be very glad to learn about the problem. In fact, many people find that their friendships are better after such talks.

Tolerance

No amount of talking will bridge all the gaps that exist between people. That is where tolerance comes in. Tolerance is the ability to accept people as they are, faults and all. It is sometimes hard to accept that our friends don't behave exactly as we want. We have to make allowances.

In some ways, the future of Mark and Eric's friendship now depends on Eric. Can he forgive Mark for what he did? Will Eric be able to accept Mark's spending more time with his new friends? If Mark shows more consideration for Eric's feelings in the future, Eric will probably forgive and forget. Tolerance is a useful quality for getting along with others.

Despite all your efforts to be tolerant of others, from time to time certain people will truly bother you. Someone may be inconsiderate, rude, or bullying. The best course is to avoid such a person. There is no need to be rude about it. A firm word or two and a cool attitude will get your message across clearly.

Having a quiet talk with a close friend can sometimes help you resolve a problem.

Caring

The basic quality of friendship—the one from which all the others seem to grow—is caring. Only if people truly care about each other can they be real friends.

Caring may seem to be a natural way of responding to certain people. Expressing that feeling, however, is something that must be learned. Friendship is more than having good times with people. It means being involved in their lives during their happy moments and their sad moments.

Caring means valuing other people's feelings as much as your own. It means listening to their ideas. It means being loyal, reliable, and honest. These qualities require effort, and sometimes patience. But these are the ways to show people that you respect their friendship. These are the ways to be a good friend.

QUESTIONS

1. Define the following terms: *loyal, reliable, tolerant.* Explain why each of these qualities is valuable in a friend.
2. What does it mean to "get outside yourself" when listening to someone? What other responsibilities does a good listener have?
3. How can talking things over help a friendship? Why is it sometimes difficult to do this?
4. Which quality of a friend discussed in this section do you think is the most important?
5. What other qualities of a friend could be added to the ones in this section?

ACTIVITIES

1. Write words and phrases defining qualities of friendship on index cards. Ask several class members to arrange the cards in order of their importance. Find which quality is most popular, which least popular. Why do you think your classmates chose as they did? Post the results in the classroom.
2. Write a dialogue in which Eric and Mark discuss their disagreement. Include their definitions of friendship.
3. Organize a friendship bumper sticker, T-shirt, or banner contest. If possible, arrange to get the winning slogan or design printed.

SECTION 3 · Stereotypes and Prejudice

Filling in the Picture

Everybody makes guesses about what strangers are like. Given just a little information, we form ideas about people. Read each of the following paragraphs, look at the picture, and then answer the questions. Don't think too long before you answer. Just give your first reactions.

• You're at a party at a friend's house. Rita, a new girl at school, has just been pointed out to you across the room. She's short, blond, and rather attractive. Is she your type? Would she be a good person to borrow notes from to study for an exam?

• You've heard people talking about one of the guests—a strong swimmer named Pat—who's from a neighboring school. Suddenly, someone points to a group of people gathered at the window and says, "There's Pat." Which one do you guess is Pat? Why do you think so?

• Your friend's cousin Jess will be at the party later. You know that Jess is from a small town out of state, and that he plays football on the varsity team. Do you think you'll like him? How do you think he'll get along with your friends?

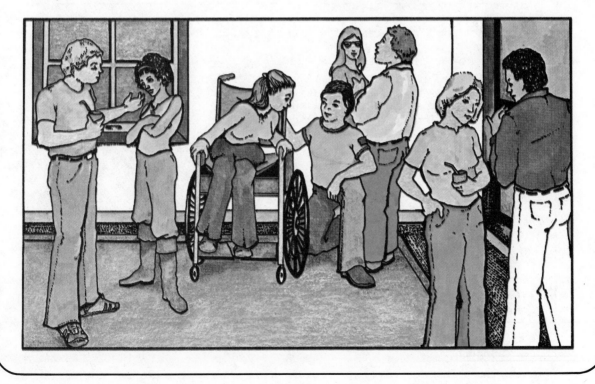

It's common to make up your mind about people before really meeting or knowing them. You hear one or two things about them, or you see them from a distance, and you begin to form some ideas about them.

Take Pat, for example. When you heard Pat was a strong swimmer, you probably started to think certain things. Did you decide that Pat was a girl or a boy? Is Pat slim or heavy? Perhaps Pat might be the person in the wheelchair. If some of these ideas surprise you, it may be because they don't match your mental picture of a strong swimmer. That "picture" made you guess that Pat would be one way, and not another.

What Is a Stereotype?

A fixed mental picture of what something or someone is like is called a stereotype. A four-year-old who says vegetables are horrible has a stereotyped view. That child sees all vegetables as being very similar. Some people think that anyone who wears glasses is studious and serious minded. They have stereotyped people with glasses as being all alike—and that isn't true.

People may be stereotyped by how they look and dress, where they come from, and what they do. Some people probably see *you* as a stereotype. If you're from California, many people would think that you spend a lot of your time surfing. They might also expect you to have blond hair. And if you do have blond hair, they might even think you have more fun!

All of us have stereotypes of what different people will be like. Stereotypes can make us approach some people and avoid others. They can make us like or dislike some people before we even meet them.

Box 1

Where Do Stereotypes Come From?

Psychologists think that stereotypes are learned in many different ways. One way is by listening to what other people say. We get ideas from our friends, our family, and other people we know. These people may have developed *their* stereotypes from the ideas of still other people.

As stereotypes get passed on, they get further and further away from real experience. For example, a person who claims that snakes are slimy (they aren't) has obviously never touched one. That person is probably just repeating what he or she heard others say.

You also encounter stereotypes whenever you turn on television, look at magazines, or go to the movies. Television commercials, for example, often show men involved only in certain activities, and women only in others. Seeing such scenes over and over can bias your thinking.

Actual experience can build up stereotypes, too. If, for example, all the lawyers you have seen are men, you may begin to think that only men are lawyers. However, there are many lawyers who are women. So, even if your stereotype fits *most* members of a group, it's unfair to assume that *every* individual in that group fits the stereotype.

Just hearing someone's voice over the telephone often gives us a mental picture of that person. And once we *do* meet people, stereotypes can affect the way we behave toward them.

Judging without the Facts

It's easy to see how stereotypes can lead to wrong guesses about people. Usually this doesn't matter, because we can quickly adjust our guess to reality.

Sometimes, however, stereotypes can lead to prejudiced thinking. A prejudice is an opinion or feeling not based on facts. Being prejudiced means judging someone before you know enough about that person to judge her or him fairly.

For example, if your sister refuses to date a football player because she thinks football players are "all brawn and no brains," she's prejudiced. She's judging the person as a stereotype, not as an individual. If you think you will like your new classmate Joan because she's attractive, you are not really judging Joan. You are prejudiced by her looks.

How Prejudice Hurts

Prejudice is harmful whether it works in favor of people or against them. The danger is that the prejudiced person is not seeing people as they really are.

Prejudice can obviously lead to all kinds of unfairness when it is directed *against* people. Suppose, for example, that you are an expert mechanic looking for work. A gas station manager refuses even to interview you because you are a woman. He has the prejudiced view that women can't fix engines. Because his view isn't based on fact, it's unfair to you.

Prejudice *in favor of* people can lead to problems, too. Suppose you become friends with someone because he's a class leader and seems to do everything well. You admire him so much that you try to be like him. You try to change yourself for his sake.

Sooner or later, you will realize that your friend is "only human." He has faults, just as you do. If you blame your friend for not living up to your ideal picture, you are being unfair. The real problem is caused not by his faults, but by your prejudice.

Prejudice—What Does It Prove?

One reason prejudices are hard to change is that they sometimes make people feel more confident about themselves. It's sad that some people can feel good only if they think they are better than another person or group. "I may have my shortcomings, but look at them—they are much worse than I am." This thought makes their own flaws seem less important.

Sometimes, too, people decide that a certain person or group is "superior." They then try to be with, or act like, the people they admire. Sometimes people try to imitate sports heroes or movie stars. In this way, they hope to be seen as superior, too.

Downgrading or upgrading other people is a very unsatisfying way of feeling good about yourself. For one thing, it can stop you from seeing yourself realistically. For another, it can prevent you from enjoying other people.

Other Problems with Prejudice

Prejudice can hurt in other ways. For example, the victims of prejudice may begin to see themselves the way others judge them. If everyone thinks the captain of your school basketball team is terrific, pretty soon he'll probably think so, too. If

Mutts
are
vulgar

Poodles
are
stuck up

Bulldogs
are
vicious

Scotties
are
snappish

Bloodhounds
are
sad-sacks

Greyhounds
are
high strung

**This is a vicious circle. Each dog has a
stereotyped view of the next. Instead of
bad-mouthing each other they could all be
playing together—still noisy, but more fun!**

he hears often enough how wonderful he is, he could easily become conceited.

If you belong to a minority group and you are continually made to feel like a second-class citizen, it can be hard to develop pride in yourself. You might become full of resentment and begin to think that everyone is against you. This can affect your relationships with others—even with those who *like* you.

Prejudice hurts everybody in society. If talented people are refused jobs or rejected for training programs because of their race or sex, the whole society suffers. We also suffer as individuals because we miss meeting people who could contribute to our lives.

Prejudice stands in the way of knowing other people. It also prevents you from knowing yourself. Unless you know yourself, you will never feel truly independent, confident, and good about yourself.

What You Can Do

Examining the ideas you learned in childhood is part of growing up. Most of us have picked up stereotypes and prejudices along the way. Whether these ideas came from others or from our own experiences, we need to think about them. It may be difficult to deal with our prejudices, but it can be done.

Are there "types" of people whom you "can't stand"? Try to avoid making snap judgments. Hold off making up your mind about someone until you have given yourself a chance to know that person better. The better we know individuals, the less likely we are to have wrong ideas about them.

Get beyond the surface differences in people. Stay open to the possibility of friendship. Overcoming prejudices can lead to a richer, fuller life.

QUESTIONS

1. What is a stereotype? What are three possible sources of stereotypes?
2. Define prejudice. Give an example of a prejudice in favor of someone, and an example of a prejudice against someone. What kinds of problems does prejudice create?
3. Why are prejudices sometimes hard to change?
4. How can prejudice harm individuals? Society as a whole?
5. What do you think an individual can do to guard against her or his own stereotypes and prejudices?
6. When do people make quick judgments about each other? What kinds of problems can these judgments cause?

ACTIVITIES

1. Evaluate ten television commercials to find out whether they encourage or discourage stereotyped thinking. How much influence do you think the commercials have on viewers?
2. Write a skit dramatizing an unfair stereotype. If you wish, base your skit on one of the situations described in the opening part of this section.
3. Describe a time you observed or experienced prejudice. What do you think caused the incident? What could be done to prevent further experiences of the same kind?
4. Interview someone you know from another country to find out what stereotypes or prejudices this person had about Americans before coming here. Did that person's views change after living in this country? How did they change, and why?

SECTION 4 · Making New Friends

ALONE OR LONESOME?

Everyone needs some time—quiet time—spent apart from other people. Listening to music, reading, or just thinking helps you get in touch with your feelings. It gives you the chance to reflect on who you are now, and who you want to be. Being alone can help you discover what you like about your life and what you would like to change. We all need time spent alone to sort out our thoughts.

Beyond a certain point, however, being alone can turn into loneliness. Too much time spent alone can heighten feelings of shyness and self-doubt. People who long for the company of others may feel there is something wrong with them because they are so often alone. Sometimes those who most want and need companionship are the people who find it most difficult to make friends. Though making new friends can be difficult, everyone can do it. But it takes some effort.

No matter how many or how few friends a person has, nearly everyone welcomes the chance to make new friends.

Different people have different needs. Some people may feel content having a few close friends to talk to and to do things with. Other people prefer having lots of friends. They like to be surrounded by people.

Making new friends is particularly important to those who feel lonely. When you break up with a close friend, you may find it difficult to get close to someone else. When you move away from old friends, you may find it hard to face having to find new ones.

Make the Effort

Making friends doesn't just "happen." It isn't only a matter of luck or chance. Making friends is a skill. Like most skills, it improves with practice.

First, you have to decide if you really want to meet new people and make new friends. Then you must be willing to take some action. If you are nervous about approaching others, remember that few people feel totally at ease when meeting new people. After all, meeting strangers means facing the unknown. It's human nature to feel a bit uncomfortable about the unknown!

Next, you must go where there are people. It will be hard to make friends if you sit home all alone.

Many schools and communities sponsor clubs for everything from chess to gymnastics. Joining a club is a good way to meet people. Talking to someone who enjoys the same activities you do is much easier than talking to someone with totally different interests. If you're doing something together—hiking, building a model railroad, or playing basketball—conversation usually flows more easily.

Even if you don't have a hobby, there is probably something you have always wanted to try. Many clubs welcome beginners. Often members go out of their way to be helpful to someone new.

Joining a club isn't the only way to make new friends. You may be passing up opportunities to make friends with people you see every day. Do you go to the library to study? Try talking to someone you see there often. If you go to a large school, you probably come into contact every day with dozens of students you don't really know. By striking up a conversation, you might end up with a new friend.

Be Honest with Yourself

One important rule for making friends is to *be yourself*. Don't join a tennis club to make friends if you hate tennis. If you're an outdoor type, don't pretend—just to get in with a new crowd—that reading and listening to music are your chief interests. It would soon become clear that you are faking it. This doesn't mean that you shouldn't try new things. It simply means that you shouldn't do things you really don't like *just* to be popular.

Make sure that you are interested in people for *themselves*. It's unfair to make friends with the class brain just so you can study for tests together.

It's also unfair to try to be friends with someone just because she or he is a school leader. You may think that being friends with a leader will make you more popular. But such friendships rarely go very far unless they are based on an honest interest in the other person.

Really knowing someone takes time and energy. If you spend that time and energy on people you truly like and relate to, you will develop lasting friendships.

Give Others a Chance

Sometimes when you meet someone new, the two of you will hit it off right away. Other times, you may feel sorry that you made the effort to begin a conversation. Don't be too hasty, however. If you judge people only on first impressions, you may misjudge them.

The person who doesn't smile and look friendly when you say hello may be shy or nervous about meeting you. Or maybe she just learned that she failed a Latin test. The person who talks a mile a minute—never giving you a chance to say any-

She thinks she's too thin—he thinks he's too fat. If these two people continue to worry about themselves, their friendship may never get started.

thing—also may be nervous. He may be worrying that the conversation will come to an embarrassing dead end if there's a silence.

At some other time, both these people might be more relaxed and much easier to talk to. Many people who started out thinking they wouldn't like each other become friends. So give the people you meet a chance. Don't rely on first impressions.

Just meeting a new person doesn't automatically mean you have made a new friend. After that first conversation, one of you will have to make a second move. When you don't hear from new acquaintances, don't assume that they aren't interested in getting to know you. They may be waiting for *you* to call. Or they may be very busy.

Make a move yourself. Follow up a pleasant first conversation with a telephone call or an invitation to do something together. Don't wait around for the other person to act.

Keep Calm

Most of us have fears about dealing with new people because of our doubts about ourselves. We worry about how we look, how we dress, and how we act. We imagine that other people are judging us—finding us too tall or too short, too fat or too thin, too this or too that.

It's important to stop worrying about yourself and to accept yourself as you are. Once you have done that, you can stop thinking about yourself and think instead of how the *other* person is feeling. Concentrate on putting the other person at ease. Then the situation becomes more comfortable for both of you. Accepting yourself can help you make new friends. And having new friends can increase your self-confidence.

Acting self-confident, even when you are not feeling that way, can sometimes help you make friends. If you enter a room full of strangers—maybe a new classroom or the cafeteria—walk tall and straight, look directly at other people, and smile. If you see someone you would like to speak to, say something. Don't wait for the other person to start a conversation.

Before you know it, you will have taken the first step toward making a new friend.

QUESTIONS

1. What is the difference between being alone and being lonely? What causes feelings of loneliness?
2. What steps could be taken by someone who wanted to make new friends? What pitfalls should be avoided?
3. Why can making new friends seem hard?
   What can be done to make it easier?
4. Do you know someone who has quite a few friends? How do you think that person met his or her friends?
5. Is it possible to decide to become a member of a certain group of friends, and then take steps to join it? Why or why not?

ACTIVITIES

1. Write a script of a telephone conversation in which a teenager asks someone older for advice on how to make new friends.
2. Look through magazines and books for teenagers to find advice on overcoming self-doubts and making friends. Choose the advice you like best and restate it in your own words.
3. Make a list of everything you like to do. Circle activities you can do alone, and check activities you can share with friends. Use the list to plan enjoyable things to do alone and with others.

SECTION 5 · Going Out Together

VARIETY

Having a date can mean anything from going to a dance or movie, to sharing a picnic or a quiet hour of studying in the library. A date may be formal or informal. It may involve a single couple, two couples, or a larger group.

Dating is a special way of exploring friendships. Through dating, people learn basic social skills. They learn to feel more sure of themselves and to be more considerate of others. They also learn to express feelings of fondness and love.

Dating Customs

In some countries, young people have little freedom to go out with friends of the opposite sex. Decisions about social life and marriage are made by parents or other family members. In North America, most young people have considerable control over their social lives. Here, socializing between sexes usually begins during the teen years.

Dating customs vary from community to community, and even from family to family. One reason for these differences is that some areas provide fewer dating opportunities than others. People may live too far from each other to arrange dates very often. There may be fewer activities available.

People's ideas, too, can make a difference in dating customs. For example, different ethnic groups may have different ideas about when teenagers should begin to date and what they should do on dates.

Most parents want to be sure their children are ready for the new freedom and responsibility that dating requires. If your parents don't want you to date yet, you may find waiting very difficult. On the other hand, you may feel pressure to start dating before you are comfortable with the idea.

Remember, there is no *right* time to begin dating. So don't worry if you're not doing what "everyone else is doing."

Going Out in a Group

Some people prefer to begin dating in groups. Group activities give people a

After a forty-foot-descent, no one worries about being self-conscious! Shared excitement can ease the tension of a first date.

chance to have fun together without the strain of one-to-one dating.

On a group date, several people might go to a movie or meet at an ice-skating rink. Or they might have a party at someone's house. They probably don't think of the occasion as a date. It's just a chance to have a good time. People find that little mistakes and awkward moments aren't nearly so noticeable in a crowd.

In some groups of young people, couples pair off. Two people may consider themselves a couple for a few weeks, and then find that they are more interested in others. Pairing off at this stage often doesn't last very long. The whole group will still go out for pizza or to a dance.

Starting to Date

When you begin dating, it's a good idea to choose an activity that doesn't require keeping up a steady conversation. Doing something together like bowling or roller-skating can be an enjoyable way to start.

Or watch a game or a movie together. It's usually best to choose casual, inexpensive activities.

On a date, you may find it hard to think of what to say—even if you are usually talkative. Unfamiliar situations make almost everyone feel tense and awkward. Be yourself. That isn't always easy when you are hoping that someone else will like you. But putting on a big act won't help. If you are nervous, don't feel you *have* to hide it. Naturalness is more appealing to most people.

You can make a date more pleasant by showing that you are having a good time. When you are feeling enthusiastic and cheerful, let your good mood show.

Let the other person know you like her or him by being considerate and asking some questions. This should help *you* relax, too. It will also give you a chance to get beyond first impressions and find out what the other person is really like.

Planning ahead can help make a date go more smoothly. Obviously, you won't plan every single thing you are going to say or do. But try to think of some activities or conversation topics ahead of time. Then, if you are feeling awkward, you can suggest something new to do or talk about. You may find you have unexpected interests in common.

Practice Makes Perfect

If a date doesn't go well, don't immediately blame yourself. Sometimes you and your date will simply find that you don't have as much in common as you thought. Or it could be that time or circumstances got in the way of things working out.

Keep your sense of humor. Remember, too, that as you date more, you will feel less awkward. After a few dates, you will probably find yourself relaxing and having a good time.

QUESTIONS

1. Give two reasons why dating customs might differ from one community to another. How do family backgrounds affect dating practices?
2. What are the two main reasons that people begin dating at different ages?
3. How can group dating help people who are just beginning to date?
4. Explain four ways to help things go more smoothly when you are on a date.
5. What can teenagers do if they differ with their parents about dating?
6. Do you think that people who go out together can also be good friends? Why or why not?

ACTIVITIES

1. Prepare a list of interesting places nearby where you and your friends could go on dates. Visit some of them, and write a report on what they are like. Perhaps you could start a column—"Dater's Guide to the Neighborhood"—for your school newspaper.
2. Write a humorous skit about a first date in which everything goes wrong. Present the skit to your class. Then discuss ways the couple could have helped the date go more smoothly.
3. Conduct a survey to determine what qualities people your age look for in others. Then take a survey of people at least two years older. How do the results compare?
4. Interview older teenagers and adults to find out how they got started dating. What do they remember about their first dates? How have dating customs changed since they were your age?

SECTION 6 · Learning to Love

LOVELORN

It loves me. It loves me not.

When is it love? People are often confused about this emotion, which can be intense and overwhelming. Sudden feelings of attraction and closeness may push everything else from a person's mind. A loved one's acceptance can make the whole world look brighter.

Love can also mean misery. It can lead to jealousy and pain. Disappointments in love sometimes hurt unbearably. They can make the world look so bleak that nothing seems to matter.

Both the joyful and the miserable feelings that love can cause affect adults as well as teenagers. As you get older, however, your ideas about love and your love relationships will change. You may first admire a friend or have a crush on someone. Later, you may experience romantic, then mature, love.

Learning to Love

Young people often have best friends whom they like and admire. Best friends may seem very interesting to each other. They may seem especially talented, or sympathetic. They may spend a great deal of time together and imitate the qualities they admire in each other. Such feelings of admiration and closeness can be a preparation for loving relationships later on in life.

Having crushes is another way to start learning how to express affectionate feelings. Teenagers may have crushes on rock stars, famous athletes, or other people who are out of reach.

Usually you don't really know the person you have a crush on. You enjoy *imagining* what it's like to care very much about this person. The feelings are real, but for the time being, it's more comfortable to keep those feelings private or to share them only with close friends. Caring for someone from afar is much easier than having to deal with the actual person.

It's quite common to be in love with someone who isn't in love with you. The person is often on your mind, and you go out of your way to be close to her or him. If the person's feelings toward you change, it can be marvelous. But that special person may not even notice you.

Often you may be too shy to say any-

Every generation has its idols—Frank Sinatra, Lena Horne, Annette Funicello, Elvis Presley are just a few. Singing stars have always been loved by millions of fans—from a distance.

thing about your love. If so, your feelings are probably a mixture of bitter and sweet. It could be a comfort to realize that these feelings won't last forever. When you find someone you *can* approach, you will certainly feel better.

Looking for Perfection

Crushes often blind people to the faults of those they love. This can lead to trouble.

Imagine someone named Leon, who likes Barbara Jean. She doesn't treat him well. Some friends think he recognizes her faults and accepts them because he also recognizes her good qualities. But Leon is not seeing Barbara Jean's faults at all.

Instead, he thinks she is perfect. He doesn't notice that she is often unkind to him. Or he may feel so imperfect compared to her that he thinks he deserves this bad treatment.

The chances that a relationship like this will be a happy one are not very good. Leon is not being fair to himself—or to Barbara Jean. It would be better for both if he were more realistic. He should try to see her the way she is, instead of as the ideal girl. She might even feel more comfortable—and treat him better.

Falling in Love

Songs and movies often portray the romantic feelings people have when they are in love. Being together is wonderful. Being separated is painful. The two people want to make each other happy. They feel that they bring out the best in each other.

This is the romantic stage of love when people can't get each other out of their minds. They may feel so excited and happy that their feet hardly seem to touch the ground. They can't concentrate on anything

Popular song titles tell their own story about romantic love.

else. Fortunately for their everyday lives, this stage of love doesn't last forever!

A couple's feelings may change. One, or both, may become interested in a new partner. Or the couple may stay together, their love gradually growing steadier and more dependable. As the newness wears off, the early thrill of love may be replaced by a strong feeling of belonging together.

When two people accept and understand each other, they can be honest about their feelings and their ideas. Both want what is best for the other, and their love allows them to keep on growing. Trust, respect, and admiration are part of such love. This is the kind of mature love that makes a good basis for marriage.

Accepting Other People as They Are

It feels terrific to know that someone you love accepts you as you are. That person may know that you have faults—and be willing to accept them because he or she cares so much about you. Take Connie and Ralph, for instance.

Connie has learned to be understanding about the way Ralph acts. When they are alone, he is always considerate. In a group, however, he sometimes interrupts her and corrects her in an annoying way.

Connie doesn't like the way Ralph acts in groups, but she accepts it because he is usually more thoughtful. She understands that Ralph acts as he does because he feels uneasy around other people. Because she cares for him, she is willing to accept him.

Trying to change people to suit yourself rarely works. Perhaps if Connie tries to help Ralph feel more comfortable in groups, he *might* change. But she shouldn't count on it.

Accepting Yourself

In order to really accept the people you love as they are, you must respect and like yourself. When you are happy with yourself, you are more capable of loving and being generous toward another person.

At the same time, love can help people accept themselves. When someone returns your love, you feel secure in each other's affection. You feel free to confide in each other. You feel free to be yourselves. This kind of trust and freedom opens the way to a truly satisfying relationship.

QUESTIONS

1. Why is love sometimes a confusing emotion?
2. What can friendships and crushes teach people about love?
3. What are the differences between romantic love and mature love? Which kind forms the best basis for marriage? Why?
4. What may happen when someone considers the person he or she loves to be perfect? How can accepting other people as they are strengthen love relationships? Why is respecting and liking yourself a good basis for loving someone else?
5. Do you think that there are people who can get along without love? Why or why not?
6. In some countries, such as India and Japan, romantic love is sometimes viewed with disapproval. It is thought to be unfriendly to other people. Why might people look at it that way?

ACTIVITIES

1. Ask members of your class what *they* think love is. Collect their thoughts, and find someone with a very different idea of love than your own. Discuss your ideas with that person, and see if you can understand each other.
2. Analyze a love story in a movie, fairy tale, or novel. What pattern does the story follow? (For example, is falling in love followed by difficulties that are resolved in a happy ending?) Write definitions of love from the points of view of several of the characters.
3. Collect a variety of popular songs about love. Post them in the classroom. After studying the lyrics, poll your class to see which ones best express their ideas about romantic love.

SECTION 7 · Expressing Emotions

Two Extremes

"You're the most inconsiderate person I've ever met!" Jack shouted. "You never think about anybody but yourself."

Nothing Sally could think of to say seemed right, so she sat in silence. She was miserable. She knew that later she would think of what she should have said, but at the moment she felt helpless.

Jack stood up abruptly. Once he lost his temper, he found it hard to stop. His emotions were getting more and more out of control. He wanted to get away before he said more things he didn't really mean.

As Jack rushed out of the door, Sally fought back tears. Why hadn't she told Jack her feelings before everything got blown out of proportion?

Jack was having second thoughts, too. Why hadn't he been a little more patient instead of losing his temper the way he always did?

Sally and Jack care about each other—even though they don't always act like it. They've gotten back together after fights before, but their constant arguments are making them both miserable. How can they avoid fighting and express themselves in less hurtful ways?

Sally wants to be able to say how she feels. Jack wishes he could keep his angry feelings under control. Both would be happier with some kind of compromise between the shouting and the silences that frustrate them now. If they learn to express their feelings directly and responsibly, their relationship could improve.

Emotions Count

Emotions matter in all human experiences, but they are especially important in relationships with other people.

Changing emotions have powerful effects on the ways people relate to each other. They are the basis for your involvement with someone else. They give value and meaning to a relationship. Without emotions, human interaction would be very mechanical.

Part of the richness of relationships is caused by differences in the ways people express emotions. Styles of expressing emotion vary from individual to individual. This is partly because of differences in background and experience.

Learning to appreciate the special ways others express and respond to emotions helps you to become close to those you care about.

Express with Care

People learn how to express their feelings from others. In early childhood, for example, we learn that hitting someone isn't the best way to express displeasure.

Experiencing a full range of emotions is part of being human. Most people know how to cope with emotions like happiness, excitement, or hope. When emotions make you feel good, you can just enjoy them. Coping with feelings of anger, fear, guilt, or sorrow is more difficult.

When you express emotions in unacceptable ways, you risk driving others away. Jack, for example, is used to shouting at people when he's angry. If he doesn't change the way he expresses his anger, he may lose his close relationship with Sally—and with others.

Keeping Quiet

It may seem that keeping quiet is the best way to deal with some emotions. If you have a bad temper, perhaps you think you should hide your anger. Keeping feelings to yourself isn't always the best solution, however. Sometimes unspoken feelings grow stronger instead of disappearing.

When feelings are strong, it's difficult to hide them. For example, if Jack is angry and decides to say nothing about it to Sally, his hidden anger might explode later. He might lose his temper over something that really doesn't matter to him. That kind of angry outburst is unfair to Sally. It's also unfair to Jack, because he's not dealing with the real reason for his anger.

Relationships can suffer, too, when people hide their feelings because of shyness or lack of self-confidence. You may not talk about your feelings because, like Sally, you aren't quite sure how to express them. By not speaking, you run the risk of being completely misunderstood.

Another reason people keep quiet about their feelings is that they are unaware of them. Because feelings such as fear or envy are difficult to face, we may deny having such feelings—even to ourselves. When we deny our feelings, we lose sight of the reasons behind some of our actions.

When You Really Care

Like the negative feelings of jealousy and anger, positive emotions—such as affection—sometimes need to be handled with care. Some people are so shy that they don't express *any* of their feelings. Others may be overbearing, and try to impose their feelings on others.

Once again, being considerate is the key. Holding back feelings of fondness isn't fair to the other person. Neither is trying to force a person to accept your affection. Think about what the other person's feelings and fears might be. Don't push another person to act in ways that are uncomfortable to him or her.

People will be flattered to know that you care for them. But you can make someone uncomfortable if you try to force a relationship. You *should* express your fondness for another person, but it is not a good idea to declare your undying love when you are just getting to know someone!

Learning to express your emotions in appropriate ways takes work. You need to be honest with yourself and with other people. With practice, you will find the right balance between openness and tact. Expressing feelings effectively and responsibly isn't easy, but it is the basis for rewarding relationships.

Even at casual gatherings, people may find it hard to communicate with others. There are times we all could use some encouragement.

Box 1

Dealing with Emotions

To handle your emotions well, you must first recognize and accept them. There is nothing wrong with having strong feelings—even the most unpleasant ones. We all feel jealousy, or fear, or even hatred at times. You must recognize and accept your feelings before you can deal with them in a positive way.

If something is bothering you, take some time to sort out your emotions. Think about what you are feeling and why you are upset. Then give some thought to how you might best handle the problem.

One constructive way to handle feelings is to express them calmly and directly. This means, for example, telling friends when you are angry at them for something they have done. It means telling your sister that her radio is annoying you—not letting your annoyance grow until you yell at her to turn it off.

When you express your feelings to others, be considerate of *their* feelings. You can express displeasure without shouting. You can tell a friend privately, rather than in front of others, that he's embarrassing you. And try to avoid being accusing. Saying to someone "I'm lonely" is better than complaining "You never spend any time with me."

Sometimes you may feel that you cannot express your emotions to someone else. Perhaps you think that more harm than good would come of telling your teacher that you're angry, or your friend that you're disappointed.

When you can't express your emotions in words, there are other things you can do to help yourself. Sometimes just waiting—and counting to ten—calms your emotions. Listening to music may help. Physical exercise can use up the physical energy emotions produce. You can rid yourself of a lot of anger, for example, by banging away at a tennis ball or by running a mile.

The best way to cope with a particular emotion depends on the situation. As you gain more experience in judging situations, you'll become better at handling your emotions.

QUESTIONS

1. Why do different people have different ways of expressing their emotions?
2. What problems can result from keeping quiet about your feelings? Give three reasons why people do not always express their feelings directly.
3. What should people consider when expressing positive feelings?
4. What hints might help people who want to express their feelings more effectively?
5. Which do you consider more important, facts or feelings? Why?
6. Do you think people are sometimes more interested in what their feelings *should* be than in what they actually are? What might result from this approach?

ACTIVITIES

1. Choose emotional scenes from plays. Practice short sequences until you can accurately communicate the feelings they contain. Tape-record your work or present it to your class.
2. Say the line, "I have dreams for my future, too," in as many different ways as you can. Emphasize different words and communicate different emotions. How does shouting the line make you feel? Whispering it?
3. Try communicating feelings nonverbally. Choose an emotion such as joy, anger, surprise, or pride. Communicate the feeling through posture, expression, and gesture, but without using any words. See how quickly the class can guess which emotion you are communicating.

SECTION 8 · Changing Relationships

BREAKING UP

Erica and Stephanie live on the same street. They have been friends since they started school together. They often spend time at each other's homes. Both are interested in art. A community college in their neighborhood offers art lessons on Saturday mornings, and the girls have been taking lessons together for three years.

Stephanie recently told Erica that she would rather spend Saturday mornings horseback riding with Jim. The news made Erica very unhappy. She is upset that they won't be going to art classes together. And she's afraid she won't see much of her friend at all, if Stephanie and Jim start spending a lot of time together.

Ben and Valerie have been going out for about a month. They were in the same math class, but didn't really know each other. Ben had a crush on Valerie for a long time before he found the courage to ask her out.

Valerie was glad Ben noticed her, because she thought he was cute. Several of the other girls in their class were attracted to him, too, and Valerie was pleased that she was "the lucky one."

After they had spent some time together, Valerie began to feel uncomfortable. They didn't have much to say to each other, beyond talking about school. The more they got to know each other, the less they had in common. Ben liked going to basketball games on their dates. Valerie thought sports were boring. She preferred going to the movies or spending time with friends.

Valerie's feelings toward Ben wore off quickly when she found out how little they had in common. But Ben was still interested in seeing her. He didn't seem to notice that they didn't have much to share. Valerie didn't know how to tell him that she felt they weren't suited for each other.

As we live our lives, we change and grow in many ways. Think back to a year ago—can you see some ways in which you have changed? Perhaps you learned to play the guitar in the last year. Through your interest in music, you may have met new people. You may have given up softball to gain time for practicing the guitar.

People change, and because they change, their relationships are bound to change, too.

Moving

Changes happen for many reasons. If your family moves to a new neighborhood, you will probably go to a new school and meet a whole new set of classmates. Separation from your old friends may seem terrible at first. You may feel as though you were uprooted and placed in a strange new world. As you make new friends and discover things that interest you, however, the new place will become your familiar world.

You may stay in touch with your old friends and see them sometimes. Your friendships with them, the feelings of caring and concern, may remain for a lifetime. But your new life will mean new interests, which your old friends may not share.

Different Needs

Relationships with people change as what you need from relationships changes. A friend you rode bikes with in childhood may not share any of your interests today. While you may have preferred having one best friend before, now you may want the variety of a group of friends.

You may also care more about the personal qualities of your friends than you did when you were younger. Do they share your sense of humor? Can they be trusted? Are they sensitive to other people's feelings?

New Groups

As your needs and interests change, so will the groups to which you belong. Some, like groups of childhood friends, may simply break up as people drift apart. Other groups may stay together, but *you* may decide to leave.

You may stay in a group, but find that the relationships within the group have changed. When you were younger, for example, perhaps you played every day with a group of friends. Now you only get together to go roller-skating some Saturdays. Skating is the one interest you all still have in common.

Dates and Change

Becoming friends is usually a slow process of learning to care for someone as you get to know her or him. You may be in the same club at school and find that you are interested in many of the same things. You enjoy spending time together. Usually you don't develop a strong emotional attachment until you get to know each other well. Then you may think of yourselves as close friends.

Dating relationships tend to start out differently. Often they are formed on the basis of physical attraction, rather than on common interests. Dating relationships often begin before either person has had time to get to know the other.

The idea of "being in love" floats in the background of most dating relationships, even if it is never openly talked about. Therefore, it is easy to form an emotional attachment.

Seeing the Real Person

People often go into dating relationships with set ideas of what they want the relationship, or the other person, to be. Valerie, for example, believed that she and Ben had many things in common. After dating him, she found out that they had almost nothing in common.

Sometimes people create an image of the other person, and love the *image* rather than the person. As they spend time together, and get to know each other better, they find the other a disappointment. Breaking up for this reason can be hard to understand. Often the people involved are unaware of what caused the problem.

Even when people seem ideally suited to each other, they may quarrel. Many couples break up eventually, often because they have lost interest in each other. They may feel that spending time together is interfering with other activities.

Growing up means going through changes, so it's not surprising that dating interests also change. That's why a relationship that works this week may not work six months from now.

Dealing with Change

Changes in a friendship affect people in different ways. Some handle them easily. They go through a short period of distress or anger. Then they set about filling up the gap in their lives. Others take a longer time to recover. Having other friends around and keeping yourself busy can help to ease the pain of separation.

When a relationship breaks up, try to remember that some combinations of people don't work forever. Neither person is to blame. It's just that these two people are no longer suited to each other.

Often a friendship changes because one person feels that a change is necessary. The other person may still be perfectly satisfied.

Few people can live up to a "perfect" image. And who wants to deal with a statue on a pedestal! Human failings usually make life more interesting.

Such changes are hard on both people. No one wants to hurt someone else, but that is often what happens.

It helps to be realistic about the situation. Weigh the awkwardness of continuing a relationship against the hurt of breaking it off. Considering the feelings of others is important, but you must do what is best for you. If you feel you must end a relationship, be gentle but honest about it. Putting off the break will only make it more difficult for you both.

Remaining Friends

Relationships can change without ending.

Some friendships change many times over, but continue for a lifetime. Some grow and deepen, while others become more casual.

If you really care about someone, but find that a close relationship doesn't work, it may be possible to remain friends. This is not always easy. It takes some effort and honest discussion. But both of you may be able to adjust and still enjoy each other's company.

Though change is sometimes hard, it is to be expected. Relationships change throughout a person's life. Knowing this can help you to accept more easily the many changes *you* will experience.

QUESTIONS

1. How might someone's expectations of a relationship change? How do changes in groups affect relationships?
2. Why do dating relationships seem to break off more often than friendships? What can happen when someone starts a relationship with fixed ideas about what the other person should be like?
3. In what ways can people make it easier to deal with changes in relationships?

4. Why do you think some relationships last much longer than others?
5. Do you think it is a good idea for a couple to remain on friendly terms after they have broken up? Why or why not?
6. What kinds of changes in groups have you seen among your friends in the past two years? Why do you think the changes happened? How can people learn to handle such changes better?

ACTIVITIES

1. Write a letter to one of the people described in the opening part of this section. Show that you sympathize, and pass along some practical advice.
2. Improvise a monologue by someone who has recently moved, lost a friend, or broken up with a boy friend or girl friend. Tape-record your monologue and play it back to see how convincing you sound.
3. Write an editorial supporting or criticizing changes in relationships. Organize your reasons to make them as persuasive as possible.

SECTION 9 · What Might the Future Hold?

The Road Ahead

What might your future hold? Later friendships will be somewhat different from those you have now. You may leave home to move in with a roommate. You may meet new people at work or through travel. What you know about getting along with others will be a great help when you begin new kinds of relationships.

Looking into the future isn't easy, but it is possible to guess at some of the situations you will face. You are likely to find a job. You will probably set up a household of your own. This may mean going away to school, moving in with a roommate, or getting married.

Friends at Work

As in all friendships, being reliable, even-tempered, and cooperative helps in a job setting. You also need to understand other points of view and to communicate clearly.

The people you work with will have varied opinions and personalities. You will have to get along with everyone, not just those you like best. Doing the job comes first. If you hold a grudge, refuse to do your share, or take advantage of other people, your work will suffer.

You will also have to learn to follow suggestions and accept criticism of your work. Criticisms and directions on the job may sound abrupt and impersonal. It takes a special effort to keep from reacting to such comments personally. Try to accept responsibility for your own work rather than blaming others if things go wrong.

The world of work can be exciting and rewarding. Part of your pleasure may come from friends you meet on the job. The job comes first, of course. But if your relationships with co-workers are pleasant, your job will be, too.

Living with a Roommate

Living with another person requires many of the same skills that living with your family does. It's much more demanding than getting along with most friends. Whether in a dormitory or an apartment, roommates must plan how decisions will be made and responsibilities shared.

Frequently roommates don't share as many activities and interests as other friends do. They need freedom to be themselves if they are to live together in peace. They must also work out their own ways to solve problems. This usually means making more compromises than you might expect.

Difficult moments occur whenever people live together. It helps to speak honestly, to listen patiently, and to be considerate. Flexibility and a sense of humor also ease the situation.

It takes some work, but sharing a room or an apartment can be both economical and fun.

The World Is Changing

As your friendships change in the years ahead, the world itself will gradually change, too. That might mean that new attitudes and customs will influence your relationships in ways that can't be predicted today.

Different expectations about what women and men should be like might affect your daily life. New trends in recreation could give friends different ways to enjoy their free time.

In the future, people may travel frequently and move often. In that case, it will be necessary to make friends quickly. On the other hand, technological advances might speed travel and make communication easier. If that happens, it will be simpler to maintain long-distance friendships.

One hope for the future is that all people will feel part of a world-wide community. As resources grow scarcer, people may gain a greater sense of shared needs and shared goals.

All of us should learn to develop friendships and a tolerant understanding of other people. This might open the way to better lives for all the people of the world.

QUESTIONS

1. What kinds of changes will probably occur in your relationships as you become an adult?
2. How are friendships at work different from other kinds of friendships? Similar to them?
3. What kinds of problems might roommates face? Why? How could they best approach these problems?
4. How might adult friendships be different from those of younger people? Why?
5. At what age do you think friendship is most important to people? Why?
6. How do you think the world of the future will be different from today's world? How might such changes influence friendships?

ACTIVITIES

1. Interview someone who lives with a roommate to find out how decisions are made and responsibilities are shared.
2. List the qualities you think people will need in the future. Rank them in order of importance.
3. Using pictures and words, make a mobile that suggests relationships in the future.

CHAPTER 3

You and Family

CHAPTER CONTENTS

SECTION 1 · Your Family and Other Families

The Typical Family?

The number of people in a particular country, divided by the number of households, gives us the size of "the average family." Your family may be larger or smaller than this average. Real families come in many forms and sizes. The number of children varies. Some families have only one parent. Many families include step-parents, stepchildren, or adopted children. Grandparents and other relatives may be part of a household, too.

The number of people in your family, and how they are related to one another, play an important part in making you the person you are. Your friends, too, are shaped by their families. Understanding how different kinds of families work can help you to understand both yourself and other people.

Families Work in Different Ways

Families differ not only in size and membership, but also in the way they work. One way to find out how a family works is to look at how decisions are made and how work is divided.

Imagine for a moment that the Kleins live next door to the Vastas. In each family, there are two children, a mother, and a father. But the families work in very different ways.

Each of the Kleins has a say in all decisions that affect the family. Even the younger child sometimes chooses the family's dessert or decides which TV show to watch.

The Kleins share family chores, too. Mr. and Mrs. Klein do the cooking and handle the family finances together. Both children help with the cleaning and laundry. When the children need advice, they go to either parent.

Just Next Door

The Vasta family works in a different way. They may talk things over, but Mrs. Vasta usually makes certain decisions, while Mr. Vasta is responsible for others.

Mr. Vasta decides, for example, how they will spend their money, and where they will go on vacation. Mrs. Vasta decides what the family will eat, how the house will be decorated, and what chores the children

must do. When the children have a problem, they usually go to Mrs. Vasta for advice.

Different ways of making decisions and dividing work make family life quite different for the Vastas and the Kleins. Other families in their neighborhood have still other kinds of family life. In fact, no two families operate in exactly the same way.

Why the Differences?

Differences in the ways families work are something like differences between individual people. One reason for the differences is a family's cultural background. In some countries, fathers make most of the decisions in their families. In other cultures, mothers or grandmothers are the decision makers.

The ways families have operated for hundreds of years are not easily forgotten. How your grandparents or great-grandparents ran their households may still be influencing the way your own works. Family patterns change, but traditional ways of running families are still important to many people.

Another reason for family differences is the makeup of the family. The Vasta and Klein families both have two children and two adults. But when children live with just one parent, that parent has all of the responsibility. And in a family that includes one or more grandparents, responsibility may be shared by several adults.

The special strengths and skills of its members affect how a family works, too. A mother may be better at budgeting money. A father may be better at organizing the household. Perhaps a teenager is especially good at fixing meals. It makes sense to arrange responsibilities to take advantage of special talents.

Box 1

The Smaller Family

Families are smaller today than they once were. Many families in colonial North America had ten or more children. What accounts for the trend toward smaller families?

- In the past, most people lived on farms. Farmers' children helped with the farm work, saving the cost of hired hands. Today, rather than saving money, raising children costs a great deal. Fewer people can afford to have large families.
- Of every hundred children born at the beginning of this century, more than fifteen died before the age of five. In earlier centuries, the death rate for young children was even higher. As a result, people used to have large families to make sure that some children survived. But today, more than ninety-eight percent of all children born live to be five years and older.
- Some people prefer not to take on the responsibilities of child rearing. Others have fewer children so they will have more time to devote to education or a career.

- Concern about overpopulation encourages some people to have fewer children. Fewer children mean less people to use the earth's limited resources.

These are just a few of the reasons why families are smaller today. Many couples consider such factors when planning their families.

How Important Is Family Life?

Just as the practical, decision-making part of family life differs from one family to the next, so does the amount of closeness within families.

For some people, family life is more important than anything else. Brothers and sisters may be one another's closest friends, even if they disagree at times. Hobbies, sports, and vacations may all be family activities that include few outsiders. Even when children grow up and move away from home, they may return to their family to celebrate joyful events and to find support in time of trouble.

Other families are quite different. Each member may have friends and interests that the others do not share. More time may be spent with friends than with parents or brothers and sisters. Feelings and ideas may be expressed most often to people outside these families.

Similarly, families express feelings in many different ways. In some families, people often show their affection for one another. In others, people argue loudly and then forgive and forget. Still other families rarely express emotions openly.

Different kinds of family life appeal to different people. People try to find the amount of closeness that seems comfortable and right for them.

How About You?

At this time in your life, you may be asking yourself questions about who you are and what kind of family you have. You may be troubled by disagreements with your parents or sisters and brothers. Sometimes you may even think that another family is better than your own.

These thoughts are not unusual. Many people wish they were part of some other family at one time or another. But a family can look quite different to an outsider than it does to an insider.

You might like certain aspects of another family's life-style. If you lived with that family all the time, though, you would probably find things you didn't like. In the same way, others may envy *your* family. But if they lived with you, they, too, might see things differently.

Each family is different. Each has its strengths and its problems. Realizing the differences will help you appreciate what is special about your own family.

QUESTIONS

1. What are two questions to ask when analyzing how a family works? What are three reasons why families operate in different ways?
2. In what ways can emphasis on family life vary from one family to another?
3. What are four ways in which family members are influenced by how their families work?
4. How has average family size changed over the last 200 years? Why? How has this change in family size influenced the ways in which families work?
5. How does your family make decisions and divide tasks? How have you been influenced by the way your family works?

ACTIVITIES

1. Imagine that you have been brought up in a family much different from your own. Write an imaginary diary entry describing a day in that family's life.
2. Write a dialogue in which all family members contribute to a decision. Then write another dialogue in which a different kind of family comes to a decision about the same issue.
3. Collect folk tales and proverbs about families. Which ideas in them are still accepted? Which are no longer accepted? Why?
4. Prepare a magazine about the family life of the members of your class. Include interviews and surveys on how families make decisions and get things done. You might also want to cover family celebrations, sports and games, and favorite family recipes.

SECTION 2 · What Families Do for People

What Does Your Family Mean to You?

BEVERLY: "I feel sorry for people who don't have anyone to talk to. I tell my sister about funny things I've heard and she laughs. And most of the time, she listens and tries to help me when something's wrong."

KEITH: "My brother's good in math. Sometimes he helps me with my homework. And I help him work on his car. I fight with my brother pretty often, but we always get over it."

JOE: "Sometimes it's no fun. My parents were divorced when I was six, so my mom works all the time. I have to work after school, too. And my sister and I take care of my two little brothers. But I guess I'd hate it if I didn't have my family. I really care about them."

KATHY: "The best thing about my family is that they'll tell me what they really think. If I'm going out somewhere and my sister and brother say I look nice, I know they really mean it—because they also tell me when I don't."

ALICE: "I don't get around as well as I used to, but my family takes good care of me. After my husband died, I moved into a small apartment near our daughter Helen and her family. I usually have my Sunday dinner over at their house. I keep treats on hand, and I just love it when one of my grandchildren stops in for a visit after school."

JOHN: "Keeping a household running smoothly isn't easy. I have to do many things I'd rather not do. But if I had to choose over again, I'd still want a family. We have great times together. I guess the thing I would miss most is seeing my children grow older. That's one of the best parts of being a parent."

Being part of a family gives people a sense of security. Because they share many of the same activities and events, family members have a lot in common. This usually makes them feel more comfortable at home than anywhere else. Both parents and children can benefit from the understanding, trust, and affection that unite many families.

Your family gives you a place in the world and provides many of your ideas. For example, your opinions about clothes and food may have come from members of your family. More importantly, your family helps you decide how to act. From your family, you learn right and wrong and what matters most in life. Your sense of who you are is strongly influenced by your family.

Satisfying Needs

Basic physical needs—food, clothing, and shelter—are usually met through family effort. Adult members usually earn most of the money to pay for these basic needs. In some families, older children hold part-time jobs so they can help pay for clothes, school expenses, or recreation.

Even when family members don't earn money outside the home, they still contribute. They can do jobs that the family might otherwise have to pay for, such as caring for young children.

At first, parents take most of the responsibility for running the household. But as children grow older, they are often gradually introduced to the idea of sharing the work of the family.

They begin by taking on small chores, such as putting away toys or emptying wastepaper baskets. Later, they accept larger duties, such as caring for their own rooms or for family pets. Older children might handle their own laundry and pre-

pare meals for themselves and their families.

Providing Guidelines

What each family expects of its members depends on the particular family situation. What is expected of a child in one family may be quite different from what is expected of a child in another.

Abby, for example, lives in the same town as her mother's relatives. Her aunts and uncles and cousins often celebrate holidays as a group. Sometimes they go shopping together. When the adults go out, all the children usually stay at Abby's house.

When Abby was younger, her brother cared for her and her cousins when their parents were away. Now he has a weekend job in a drugstore, so Abby is expected to take care of the younger family members. Abby knows that this is one of her biggest obligations to her family.

Bill, on the other hand, has extra responsibilities at home because his parents do not read and write English well. He helps them fill out forms, and he writes checks and balances the family checkbook. Bill learned to do these things because his family needed and expected his help.

Taking responsibility for meeting everyday needs can give children a sense of independence. It also helps prepare them for the time when they will have to take care of themselves.

Showing They Care

Being part of a family means more than being able to depend on family members for practical needs. Families also provide emotional support.

Most of us want to live with people who listen to us and care about us. We want to

Everyone benefits from love and attention. No matter how old or how young—we all appreciate the affection of other family members.

be able to express our feelings and ask for advice when we need it. We also want to be able to turn to our families in times of trouble.

Family members help each other simply by offering encouragement. Just knowing that others are concerned can be a real comfort to someone who has a difficult problem.

When the company their father worked for closed down, there was nothing Joe and Nina could do about it. But they were sure that their father's skills would make it easy for him to find another job. During his search for work, they offered a lot of encouragement.

Later, when their father was settled in a new job, he told Joe and Nina that their support had helped him get the job. He felt that their confidence in him had helped him keep a positive attitude, which impressed his new employers. Although Joe and Nina couldn't solve their father's problem, their emotional support was a great help to him.

Helping to Meet Others

Families teach people how to get along with others. Young children are gradually introduced to the world around them—in stores, parks, libraries, schools, and other people's homes. Watching how family members act in these situations can teach children how to feel comfortable and accepted in the world outside their homes.

Families also teach children how to communicate. This means not only how to talk, but also when—and when not—to talk. Children soon learn which words will bring smiles and which will make people uncomfortable.

As a child, you learned how your family reacted to good news and to bad news. You noticed how they felt when people came home late, and what they did when you pleased or amused them.

When you brought people into your home, *you* enriched your family's life. You helped other members socially by introducing new friends to the household. From the give and take of family life, a family learns how to deal with other people.

All-around Support

Give and take is a good phrase to describe the workings of a family. Whether it's practical help or emotional support, every family member can contribute a great deal to the family. And the more that each member gives, the more each takes into the future.

Young children like to see where grown-ups work and how they do their jobs. Parents often give their children a first taste of the world outside their home.

QUESTIONS

1. What two kinds of needs can families fulfill for their members? Give an example of each. How does a child's share in meeting these needs change as she or he gets older?
2. What kinds of ideas about the world can you get from your family? How do families teach their members to relate to others?
3. Why might two teenagers of the same age have very different roles in their families? Describe two situations that illustrate this point.
4. What effect would it have on children to be given *no* responsibilities in the family? Why?
5. What do you think children learn from being taken care of by other family members besides parents?

ACTIVITIES

1. Ask several young children to draw pictures showing what families do for people. Tape-record their explanations of the drawings.
2. What do the songs you know imply about families? Do you agree? Try making up a song about what families do for people. Use a familiar tune but write your own words.
3. Interview several members of a family to find out how the family's chores get done. Ask how it was first decided who would do particular household tasks. What changes have been made?

SECTION 3 · Understanding Your Family

DIFFERENT DREAMS

The people in this family have many things in common. But each person also has private thoughts and hopes. When family members try to understand one another's personal feelings and desires, family life is more pleasant and rewarding.

Many different factors affect your role in your family. Your age and sex influence how you interact with other family members. Your parents' ages, the size of your family, and the age differences between children all affect how your family works.

Every position in a family is unique. Each has its own problems and privileges. Understanding the special situation of each family member helps you understand her or his point of view. Mutual understanding leads to greater family harmony.

How Many Years Apart?

The age span between siblings affects how they get along (siblings are the brothers and sisters in a family). When the age difference is greater than three years, for example, siblings may not have many common interests. They may find it hard to understand each other. Still, children far apart in age may be treated more as individuals by their parents. This may make them feel less competitive with each other.

When children are close in age, parents may be less able to give them individual attention. The children may feel a greater need to compete with each other. Closeness in age, on the other hand, often results in greater companionship. Twins, particularly, are often very close friends.

Being a Younger Child

Life sometimes seems easier for younger children. Older siblings have usually paved the way for them, so that parents are more relaxed about granting privileges. If you are an older child, you may think a younger brother or sister has fewer obligations and expectations to live up to than you.

Following an older sister or brother through childhood has its drawbacks, however. If an older child has some special talent or ability, younger children may feel that they have to measure up. Or if things haven't gone smoothly at home or at school for an older child, parents may feel more uneasy or worried about younger children.

It can also be hard for younger children when the older ones have more freedom. They may feel envious that all the new and exciting things seem to happen to the older children.

If you are an older child in your family, the younger ones probably look up to you. Try to understand their feelings. Include them in your activities occasionally. They are interested in what you do because they want to understand what will soon be happening to them in their own lives.

Being an Older Child

Most people who have older sisters or brothers see plenty of advantages to being an older child. Because parents often welcome their help, older children often seem

Box 1

THE ONLY CHILD

Being an only child has its advantages. An only child does not have to get along with brothers and sisters or share belongings with them. She or he also enjoys a great deal of the parents' attention. And an only child may be included in adult conversations and activities more than a child with a sister or brother.

Being an only child has its disadvantages, too. It can be lonely sometimes. And having your parents all to yourself is not always easy. All your parents' hopes are focused on you. As a result, pressure to please parents can feel greater to an only child.

Children often depend on their older brothers or sisters for comfort and for help in solving problems.

Being older isn't always easy, however. Older children sometimes feel that too much is expected of them. Their parents may want them to act more grown up than they are. They may have to care for younger members of the family even when it interferes with their own plans. Sometimes it seems to them that the younger children get away with things that *they* weren't allowed to do.

Those of you who are younger family members can help older brothers and sisters a lot. By acting a little more grown up yourself, you can make life easier for them. Respect their privacy—let them have their own lives. And remember that if they have more privileges, they probably have more responsibilities, too.

Competing for Affection

Children sometimes compete for the attention and affection of parents. For example, older children commonly feel upset when a new brother or sister seems to get all the parents' attention.

Sharing parents' love and attention means sharing what is most important to young children. When one child gains special attention, the others may feel jealous. Everybody who has a brother or a sister feels jealous sometimes.

When members of your family seem jealous of you, you can help. Find things to do with them that take advantage of their special talents. Encourage them to follow their own interests instead of competing with other family members or trying to be just like you.

When you feel pleased with a sister or brother, don't be afraid to say so. Your affection and admiration probably mean more to them than you realize.

more capable and confident. Because parents depend on them, older children usually seem to have more freedom.

Older children learn how to be good leaders by taking charge of younger sisters and brothers. Teaching younger children how to do things can improve older children's skills. And having a younger brother or sister look up to you and admire you can make you feel good about yourself.

Male or Female in the Family

Some families have very different expectations for daughters than for sons. Young boys may be encouraged to be independent and active. Perhaps parents tolerate rougher behavior from them. But crying and acting afraid are discouraged in boys. In contrast, girls are encouraged to be gentle, affectionate, and expressive.

Such expectations probably started because of the physical differences between females and males and the different jobs they have traditionally done. Today, physical traits such as strength don't make as much difference as they used to.

Understanding your family's expectations for men and women can help you understand your brothers and sisters. Your brother may not show his feelings when he is unhappy or worried because he thinks men are supposed to be unemotional. Your sister may give up her dream of studying engineering because she thinks women shouldn't become engineers.

These family members support each other by setting aside a common time and place for studying. How does your family help its members meet personal needs?

Be alert for this kind of thinking in your family. You may get the chance to help your sisters and brothers be a little more flexible about how they think they should act.

Before you catch yourself saying, "Girls shouldn't do that," or "Boys don't act that way," stop to think. What you say and how you act can make a big difference to your sisters and brothers. If you encourage them to try out new activities, they are more likely to discover what suits them as *individuals.*

Parents Are People

Understanding your family means thinking about your parents' role, too. To very young children, parents seem to know everything and be able to do anything. But as children grow and become more capable of thinking for themselves, they realize that their parents aren't perfect. This discovery can be upsetting.

Some children react by becoming impatient and critical of their parents. If you feel this way, it's useful to remember that parents are people, too. They have weaknesses, as well as strengths, just as you have.

Parents also have different kinds of personalities. Some show their feelings openly. Others keep their emotions to themselves. Naturally, the kinds of personalities parents have make a big difference in the way they act toward their families.

Realize that your parents have their own interests and needs. As you get older, you want people to see you as an individual, not just as your parents' child. So you should be able to understand that your parents want to be treated as individuals, too.

Being a parent is not easy. When their children are young, parents hardly have time for anything but caring for them. But people do not lose their need for time to themselves when they become parents. They still need time to work on projects they care about, and time to be with their own friends. Your parents may sometimes need your cooperation to find that time for themselves.

Letting Children Grow Up

Parents sometimes have trouble judging when their children can manage without them. For many people, being a mother or father is the most important part of their lives. Because caring for young children can be very satisfying, some parents find it very hard to stop doing everything for their children, even when the children want to become more independent.

Parents also find it hard to allow their children to learn from their own mistakes. They don't like to watch their children make decisions that they feel sure will lead to disappointment. In their own lives, they have faced many of the same decisions. Naturally, they would like to give their children the benefit of their experience.

Parents are responsible for the welfare of their children. The decisions they make affect the children's happiness, health, and satisfaction. It is not always easy for parents to know how best to guide them.

Getting Along

Trying to understand one another helps family members get along together. People in your family will have opinions and beliefs that differ from yours. Learning to accept those differences is an important part of growing up. Acceptance does not necessarily mean agreement.

The bonds between family members depend on love, not on shared beliefs. The family that recognizes and respects individual viewpoints is united by understanding and affection.

QUESTIONS

1. List five factors that affect your role in your family.
2. What are some of the difficulties of being a younger child? An older child? An only child? A parent? How can you help make life easier for each?
3. What are some things to remember that can help you better understand your siblings?

Your parents? What are the benefits of increased understanding among family members?
4. Which of the five factors you listed in the answer to question one do you think most determines your role in your family? Why?
5. Do you think it is possible for brothers and sisters never to argue with one another? Explain your answer.

ACTIVITIES

1. Write a "Parents' Bill of Rights." Write a "Bill of Rights for Children." Do the two lists clash in any way?
2. Choose a memorable event that happened in your family, such as the birth of a new baby.

Write a description of the event from the point of view of another family member.
3. Evaluate a child's book, comic book, or television program to see what it suggests males and females should be like.

SECTION 4 · Sharing Problems

CONFLICT

KAREN

"Sometimes I can't stand being around my sister. She's a great swimmer, and our living room is full of her trophies. Compared to her, I feel worthless. She gets the praise, and all I get is the criticism."

EDDIE

"I have one big problem. My parents argue all the time. Nothing I do seems to help. Sometimes I don't know where to turn. Maybe it would help if I had somebody to talk to."

DOUG

"What I like to do most is sit around and read history books or study languages. I've already started to learn French and German. I like playing chess, too. My parents, though, are always after me to do something practical. I'd like to go to college, but they want me to learn a trade."

Karen, Doug, and Eddie have problems. But their problems don't affect them alone. Usually, when something is bothering one family member, it touches the lives of the others as well. Serious problems such as poor health or lack of money can upset family life. When family members have painful, frustrating problems, relationships outside the family also suffer.

Why Problems?

Families have problems for many reasons. Sometimes the cause of a problem lies outside the family. Perhaps the parents can't find jobs. Perhaps social services that the family needs are not available.

Other problems are started by conflicts within families. One child may feel unhappy and neglected when another gets a lot of attention. Family members may disagree about responsibility for household tasks.

Some family problems can be solved quickly. Talking things over sometimes results in solutions. Other problems are more difficult to solve. Sometimes families need help from friends, relatives, or trained outsiders to solve these problems.

Individual Needs

It's not unusual for people sharing the same household to have conflicts. Their needs may differ. For example, one person may want to play a record at exactly the time another would like to have absolute quiet for doing homework. This kind of conflict is very common.

Karen faces a somewhat more serious problem. She feels she is the loser in a competition with her sister. Karen needs the attention of other people, especially of her parents. But she doesn't know how to get it.

Box 1

Discussing Problems in the Family

It sometimes helps to set aside a special time to deal with family problems. Just sitting down with your family and calmly discussing whatever is upsetting you can be an effective approach to settling difficulties. When your family gets together to solve a problem, these guidelines will help make the discussion go more smoothly.

- Find a time that is convenient for everyone. It should be a time when the issue can be discussed calmly and in a relaxed atmosphere.
- Take turns listening to one another's points of view. Be sure you understand what someone else is saying before you add your own ideas.
- Attack the problem, not one another. Express thoughts and feelings in a constructive way—without blaming or name-calling.
- Brainstorm possible solutions. Write every suggestion down. Then go over the list to decide which ones might work best.

Families should try to approach problem-solving sessions with patience and good will. Each person should be encouraged to take part in the discussion. Talking over problems with other family members gives everyone a chance to air feelings—and to look for a solution everyone can live with.

Her parents know that she is upset, but they don't know what's wrong.

In Karen's case, discussing her feelings with her parents might help. She would probably discover that they admire her own special qualities. Just because her sister is a champion swimmer doesn't mean they love her sister more.

A discussion could also help Karen see that her sister's life isn't easy, either. Her sister has to get up when it's still dark and work out before school. Swimming takes up so much of her time that she can rarely relax with friends or do something just for fun.

Talking these matters over with her parents, or thinking them through for herself, could improve Karen's family life.

Disagreements

Doug's problem may be harder to solve than Karen's because it isn't caused by a misunderstanding. Doug and his parents truly disagree about how he should spend his time and what his goals ought to be. His parents expect him to grow out of his current interests. They want him to settle down to something they consider more practical.

It might help Doug to find out why his parents feel as they do. If they are worried about his future, he can reassure them by showing them that he *is* thinking about a career.

He could explore some careers that would use his special interests and knowledge. In this way, he could satisfy some of his parents' concerns as well as his own. He could also show his willingness to consider his parents' viewpoint by taking a course in a subject they consider practical.

By defending his own goals in a mature way, and by being willing to compromise, Doug might win his parents over to his point of view.

Getting Help

Sometimes people you know and trust— relatives or friends—can help you under-

stand family problems. You will probably feel better just talking things over with them. And they may be able to help you find a solution to the problems.

Families sometimes rely on neighbors for practical help. When the mother in one family had to be hospitalized because of a car accident, a neighbor helped care for the children. When the mother came home, she still needed a lot of support looking after the household. The neighbor helped again, this time by coming over to take care of the mother and the housework.

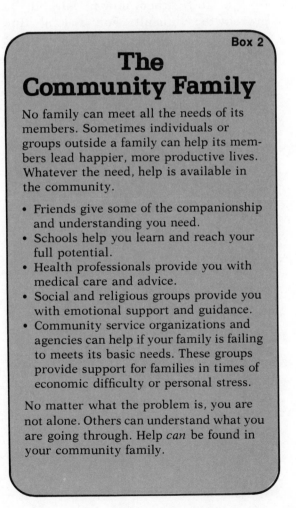

Box 2

The Community Family

No family can meet all the needs of its members. Sometimes individuals or groups outside a family can help its members lead happier, more productive lives. Whatever the need, help is available in the community.

- Friends give some of the companionship and understanding you need.
- Schools help you learn and reach your full potential.
- Health professionals provide you with medical care and advice.
- Social and religious groups provide you with emotional support and guidance.
- Community service organizations and agencies can help if your family is failing to meets its basic needs. These groups provide support for families in times of economic difficulty or personal stress.

No matter what the problem is, you are not alone. Others can understand what you are going through. Help *can* be found in your community family.

Nowhere to Turn?

Sometimes you may feel you have no one to turn to. You may feel that you can't tell family problems to friends or neighbors. Still, you do need someone to talk to.

When this happens, consider talking to people who are trained to help families work out their problems. School counselors, social workers, and religious leaders can be very helpful, and they understand that family problems are private.

Eddie was very worried and upset because his parents were fighting all the time. He tried to tell them how he felt, but this proved too difficult. For a long time, Eddie's family struggled with their problems on their own. The constant fighting bothered Eddie so much that he had trouble doing schoolwork and getting along with his friends. Finally, Eddie's mother suggested he talk to a counselor at school.

The counselor helped Eddie understand that his parents' fights weren't *his* fault.

She pointed out that solving the problem wasn't Eddie's responsibility alone. She helped Eddie to see that other families also go through difficult times. Eddie felt relieved just to talk with someone he could trust. The counselor didn't solve Eddie's problem, but she helped Eddie learn to cope with it.

Facing Problems

It helps to deal with a family problem openly. If you know there is a problem, but are not sure what it is—ask. Problems you do not understand are usually more frightening. Once you face a problem, you can begin working with your family to solve it.

Family troubles can't be wished away. Even when a family works very hard to settle differences, solutions are not always possible. But efforts to work out problems can build trust and understanding. Facing problems together can unify and strengthen your family.

QUESTIONS

1. What two different categories do most family problems fall into? Give an example of each kind.
2. List some sources of outside help for dealing with family problems.
3. Describe five things teenagers themselves can do about their family's problems. Which approaches might strengthen families?
4. What could Karen, Doug, and Eddie do about their problems?
5. One study shows that many people rate themselves as happy, yet they have personal and family problems. How can you explain this finding?

ACTIVITIES

1. Investigate the available services for troubled families in your community. Make a poster describing these services. Include how much the services cost, and who can qualify for help.
2. Choose a movie or TV show about a family with a problem. Write a description of the family's problem and an analysis of what was done about it. How might different problem-solving approaches have changed the outcome?

SECTION 5 · Changes in the Family

QUITE A CHANGE

"Things are so different now I can hardly remember what they were like before. When Mom and Dad used to come home from work, we'd make supper and then eat and talk together. On Saturdays, we all cleaned the house. After that, we could do what we wanted.

"Then, a few years ago, Mom and Dad really got fed up with their jobs. They had always dreamed of starting a restaurant together, so they decided to quit their jobs and give it a try. It was a big risk—it took a lot of courage.

"We hardly ever eat at home together anymore. Sometimes my brother and I make supper for ourselves—to save time for doing our homework. Most of the time, though, we eat here at the restaurant.

"We're all a lot busier nowadays. My brother and I do most of the work at home, because Mom and Dad usually stay at the restaurant very late. On weekends, we all work here together. We like the feeling that we're building something as a family. I think my parents are much happier. On the whole, I'd say that it's been a good experience."

Most changes come about gradually enough for people to get used to them. As your ability and independence increased, you probably made many adjustments. You took on new responsibilities a few at a time. That way, you had a chance to understand and prepare for the kinds of changes that took place in your life.

There are times, however, when change comes about suddenly. The period of adjustment to such change can be very difficult. Members of a family must learn to get along with one another in new ways. Adjusting to these changes is important because change is a necessary part of everyone's life.

Changes Because Family Members Grow

As infants develop into toddlers, and then into school-age children, the whole family changes. New routines and new ways of communicating come with the children's new activities.

Perhaps the biggest changes take place when children become teenagers. The teen years are often a time of searching for a personal identity, an individual sense of self. Teenagers want to be recognized as individuals with feelings, ideas, and tastes of their own. These changes may be difficult for the whole family.

Children are not the only family members who change and grow. The attitudes and interests of adults change, too. Grownups may try new activities and accept new challenges. Naturally, such changes in the lives of parents affect their families.

When Gail's parents started a restaurant, it changed not only who did what around the house, but also how often the family could be together at home. Gail learned to respect her parents' courage and determination. And she and her brother learned that they could take care of themselves when they had to.

When Parents Separate

Children must often learn to accept changes in their parents, even painful ones. As people change, their needs and their feelings for each other may also change. Parents who are no longer happy living together may decide to separate.

During and after a separation, parents probably need the cooperation of their children more than ever. The children may be asked to do more work at home when one parent has to manage a household alone. And because the parents may be feeling angry or sad, they may have a greater need for their children's understanding and love.

Children whose parents separate may miss family closeness. At times, they may feel lonely and unprotected. Such feelings are hard to deal with alone. If you know people who feel this way, try to make a point of listening to them and spending time with them. You may be able to help them through a difficult time.

Making a Move

Sometimes a parent's job change means that the family must move. Even when everyone knows it's necessary, moving isn't easy.

One reason moving is difficult is that people must get used to many changes at once. They may welcome the chance to meet new people, but miss their old friends very much. They may want to get away from old frustrations, yet dread leaving the things that make them feel at home. Many people look forward to living somewhere new. Still, they may feel uncomfortable with the different customs and attitudes of a new community.

Moving can bring a family closer together. Since it takes time to make friends in a new community, family members may have to rely on one another more than they usually do. They may also spend more time alone, which helps them to know themselves better.

A New Family Member

Sometimes a new member is added to the family circle. A new baby is only one example. When older sisters and brothers marry, they may bring their new husbands or wives to live in their parents' home. A grandparent or other relative may move in with a family. Or the new person may be a stepparent.

When a new member joins a household, family members' time and attention must be shared with one more person. There may also be a new division of work around the house. At first, people may be confused by new family routines. And there could be some mix-ups about who should be making family decisions.

It's very easy to resent a new family member. Getting used to another person's ways of doing things may be difficult. But think about how the newcomer feels. You are getting used to one new person. He or she must adjust to an entire family. You will make things easier all around if you make a special effort to be friendly.

Adjusting to such changes takes time. But once you do adjust, you may find that having a new family member is interesting and fun.

The family that is close can support its members through many changes—and additions!

A Death in the Family

People usually feel very sad when a family member dies. They often have a difficult time accepting the death of someone they love. It's natural to want to believe that the death never happened. It's normal to feel angry and lost.

Sometimes when a family member dies, the other people in the family feel guilty about small things that really ought to be forgotten. It's hard to get over these feelings. Learning to accept death as a natural, unavoidable part of life is painful and difficult.

Death hurts everyone in the family—adults as well as children. This means that everyone needs comfort. Lending help and support to one another can make it easier to cope with grief.

Adjusting to Change

Sometimes it just takes time to get used to a new situation at home. But at other times, a change may seem so big that you need to turn to others for help. As with many problems, talking things over with a family member or friend may help. Or you may want to talk to a school counselor. Seeking the help you need is a useful step toward accepting a difficult change in your life.

Look for positive results from a change. Don't brood on the negative effects. You will find that you are a lot stronger than you think. Remember that changes are part of life. They can help you grow.

QUESTIONS

1. What are five kinds of changes that families may go through? What kinds of emotions might each one cause?
2. How can even a welcome change put a family under a strain? How can dealing with a negative change benefit a family?
3. Explain several things people can do to help themselves handle changes.
4. What kinds of changes do you think have the biggest effect on families? Why?
5. Which technique for coping with change do you think would be most helpful? Why?

ACTIVITIES

1. Draw a time line illustrating changes in your own family or in a family you have read about. Include births, moves, and other events in the family's life.
2. Assume that your family faces an important change, such as a move to a new community. Write a diary entry telling what would happen and how you would react.
3. Form a committee to consider ways to make life easier for families moving into your community. Try to find some practical ways to help. Consider becoming a big brother or big sister to a new student. Or try forming a newcomers' club.

SECTION 6 · Ready for Parenthood?

WHAT IF . . .?

Sally's husband, Tom, had just taken their four-year-old son, Robbie, to get his hair cut. Robbie was mad at having to go, and yelled all the way out the door. Sally was thankful to have some peace and quiet at last. Just as she started clearing away the breakfast dishes, the doorbell rang.

To Sally's surprise, her old friend Laura was at the door. The two hadn't seen each other since high-school graduation five years before. Sally made some tea, and they sat down to talk.

"Laura, you look terrific," said Sally. "What are you doing now?"

"Well, right now I'm home for Christmas. But since I got my biology degree, I've been working in the city as a lab technician. The job's hard, but I love it. What about you? You sure have kept your figure. I heard you have a baby now."

"Yes, but he's not a baby anymore. He's four years old and full of energy. Being a mother is more work than I ever thought it would be. I'm working part time at the shopping center—just to help out with our bills. Between my job and Robbie and the housework, I'm always busy."

"Sounds as though you don't have much time to play the piano, the way you used to," said Laura sympathetically.

"No, I don't," said Sally. "But I'm teaching Robbie how to play a little bit. He's only four, but he can play 'Twinkle, Twinkle, Little Star' already."

"It must be sort of fun being a mother," remarked Laura.

"Oh it is," said Sally. "But sometimes I wonder what my life would be like right now if I hadn't had Robbie so soon."

Sally met Tom when she was a senior in high school. They began seeing a lot of each other, and soon felt that they were in love. Tom and Sally knew they were very young to marry, but they wanted to, anyhow.

Sally's parents asked her to wait and go to music school. Tom's parents hoped he would enroll at the community college. Despite their parents' wishes, Sally and Tom got married right after high-school graduation.

Dreams and Reality

Two months later, Sally was pregnant. Neither she nor Tom had thought much about having a baby. Sally quit her job at

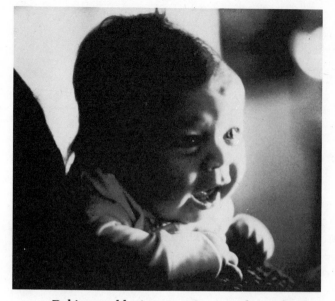

Babies need loving attention in order to develop properly. Parents must be ready to meet emotional as well as physical needs.

the local department store. Tom withdrew his college application and found a job driving a delivery truck.

Tom liked being the breadwinner for their home. Sally was very happy, too. She enjoyed taking care of their apartment and planning for the baby. She was healthy during her pregnancy and looked forward to having her own baby.

Robbie's arrival, however, totally changed Sally and Tom's lives. Parenthood was not exactly what they had expected. Instead of having a little baby just to love and play with, they found themselves bogged down with diapers, bottles, and doctor's bills. Caring for a baby was more work than they had ever dreamed.

Tom and Sally were just beginning to take charge of their own lives. This in itself was a challenge. They were beginning to make plans for their future. Then they had

to face the extra responsibility of taking care of a baby. At times, both Sally and Tom felt resentful at being so tied down and overworked.

A Big Challenge

Being a parent can be one of life's most satisfying experiences. Giving of yourself to a child can be very rewarding. But being a parent is also one of the most serious responsibilities anyone can assume. Before having a baby, you need to consider all that parenthood involves.

A couple must be physically ready to have children. If the mother is too young, the child may be harmed. In addition, a couple needs to know something about children and child care. A baby is a helpless individual who must rely on parents to meet every need.

Because parents are responsible for a child's total welfare, their own needs often come second. Being a responsible parent requires willingness to give freely to meet your child's needs.

Changing diapers is only one of many tasks that young parents need to do.

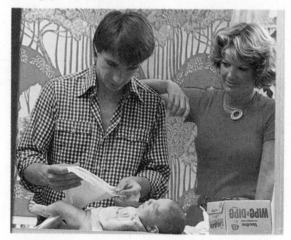

Energy, Time, and Money

Caring for children requires a great deal of energy. Babies need attention at all times—in the middle of the night, and early in the morning. And when *you* are tired, *they* can't take care of *you!*

All this giving allows parents little energy for other activities. It is very hard to further your education, or develop special skills, while giving young children the attention they need.

Being a parent is a twenty-four-hour-a-day job. Even though every minute is not spent on the child, long periods of free time are rare. Combining child care with a job or housekeeping may take up nearly all day, every day. It may be difficult to find time for personal hobbies or entertainment. Unless you can afford a sitter, or have friends who are willing to take over sometimes, going out together as a couple may be impossible.

Often young parents have no idea how costly bringing up a child can be. If you think that having a baby around would be nice, try figuring out what it would cost you *alone* to live for a year. Then think of the costs for two people. *Then* add on the cost of a child. Children mean extra medical bills and increased food and clothing costs. Having a child may also mean that you need a larger place to live.

Baby food is expensive because it is specially processed and packaged. Clothing, and equipment to help care for the baby, add to the expenses.

Emotional Readiness

In addition to energy, time, and money, parenthood requires emotional maturity. One sign that you are emotionally mature is the ability to give love freely. Many young parents become jealous of their child because they feel they aren't getting enough love themselves. But without love a child suffers. Parents should be mature enough to share in the experience of giving love. They should not make selfish demands.

Emotional maturity also means being able to manage your life independent of your parents or other adults.

A good relationship with your own parents helps you get ready for parenthood.

Watching your parents helps you decide what traits you would like to have as a parent. But if you still need to consult your parents on many decisions, or ask them to help you with everyday things, you are not ready to have a baby depending on you.

Young people need to develop faith in their ability to manage their own lives. They need to sort out their ideas and be prepared to act on their personal beliefs and views. Maturity and self-confidence are necessary for handling the challenge of being a parent. Both are qualities that take time to develop.

A loving family is largely the result of preparation and hard work by the parents.

QUESTIONS

1. What four things must parents be prepared to invest in a child?
2. What personal qualities are required of parents? Why?
3. What can people's relationships with their own parents teach them about their readiness to have children?
4. In what ways did parenthood differ from Sally and Tom's expectations? How might they have better prepared themselves for parenthood?
5. What other personal qualities do you think a person needs before he or she is ready for parenthood?

ACTIVITIES

1. Write a continuation of the conversation between Sally and Laura. Make Sally explain the qualities she feels parents need to have.
2. Interview a young parent to find out how life changed after the baby was born. What are some of the rewards of parenthood that a parent enjoys?
3. Prepare a photo essay on parenthood. Take the photographs yourself, find them in magazines, or use family snapshots. Write a caption for each photo.

SECTION 7 · Caring for Babies

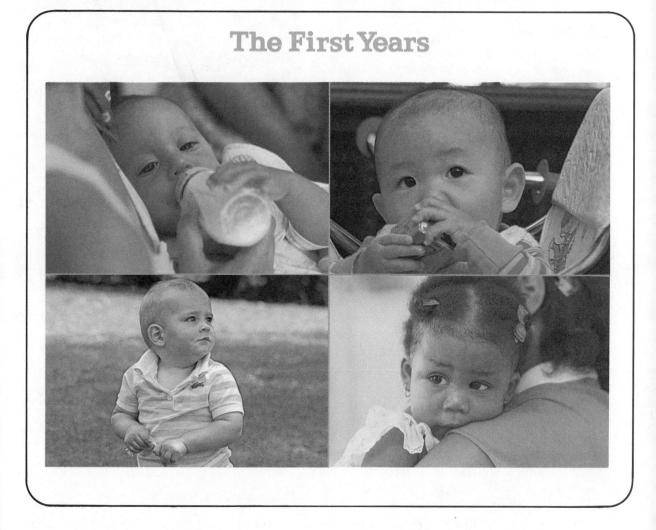

The First Years

We often divide babies into two groups: infants and toddlers. The word *infant* comes from a Latin word meaning someone who cannot speak. We generally think of infants as babies who can neither walk nor talk. When babies begin to walk a little, we call them *toddlers* because of the unsteady way in which they move.

As babies grow, they go through several stages of physical development. The age at which each occurs varies greatly from child to child. The most obvious stages are:

1. sitting up—five to seven months
2. standing—six to seven months
3. crawling—six to eight months
4. walking (toddling)—nine to fifteen months

Of course, there are many other signs of growth—for example, saying a first word or learning to eat solid foods.

Mental Development

One of the most important aspects of growth is mental development. The human brain is very complex and takes a long time to develop fully. Although babies younger than two years do not "think" in the sense that adults are able to, important steps in mental growth occur during infancy.

Babies' minds develop as they respond to the world around them. During the first eighteen months of life, babies grow to understand that things that are out of their sight have not totally disappeared. They begin to understand relationships between things. They also start to develop a sense of time. Even before the age of two, babies learn about cause and effect—that if they drop a toy, for example, it will fall to the floor. They also learn what they can do to get something they want.

Dependency

None of us can remember what it was like being a baby. Babies are totally dependent on their parents or other caregivers. When babies have their needs met and live in a secure and loving environment, they develop a positive view of the world. They learn that they can count on adults. Children who have this basic feeling of trust have an easier time later in life.

Meeting a baby's needs is not as simple as it might seem. One reason why babies are so helpless is that they can't say what they want. Imagine how it would feel to wake up one morning, unable to do anything for yourself, and unable to ask anyone for help. That's what it must be like to be a baby.

A baby has a whole new world to explore—exciting, but sometimes frightening. Parents can make the world seem more secure just by being there.

Communication

Babies have many needs. They need food, sleep, comfortable clothes, warmth, and loving attention. Yet the only way they can communicate these needs is by crying. Babies cry without really understanding what they are crying about. Their cries are general calls for help.

Babies' cries for hunger or pain or boredom do sound different, however. Caregivers often learn to recognize these different cries. This helps them give babies what they need.

Unlike infants, children of fifteen months or older can communicate with more than cries. They are learning to talk. Toddlers can usually speak only in short sentences of one, two, or three words. They might say "See truck," or "Want cookie."

Toddlers can understand longer sentences than they can say. If you ask them, "Where is the truck, is it in the closet?", they can answer "Yes" and know what they mean. But they couldn't ask a long question. They would say something like "Where truck?"

The speech of toddlers may be difficult for strangers to understand. But those who care for them—parents, or other family members, or regular sitters—usually have no trouble figuring out what toddlers are trying to say.

Babies' Diets

Babies must be fed often. They aren't born able to eat three meals a day. At first, a baby only drinks mother's milk or a special formula.

Babies nurse or take a bottle by sucking rather than drinking. The ability to suck vigorously is an in-born trait. Babies don't have to be taught to suck. Some babies have even sucked their thumbs inside the womb!

Babies soon take solid foods. By the time they are six months old, they are eating a variety of strained foods. When they reach twelve months, they eat regular foods cut up into small bite-size pieces. Babies from ten months to eighteen months enjoy "finger foods" they can pick up and eat. Toddlers learn to use a spoon and fork and to drink from a cup.

One of the more difficult tasks of this period is encouraging a baby to give up the bottle. The bottle means more than food to many babies. It also means love and security.

Babies' Schedules

After a feeding, infants usually sleep for as long as five hours at a stretch. The time they sleep after a night feeding slowly becomes longer and longer, until they sleep through the night. Most babies take morning and afternoon naps until they are between one

Young parents must try to make their work and leisure plans fit in with their baby's schedule.

6:00 a.m.	Bottle + change diaper
7:00 a.m.	Cereal + fruit
8:00 a.m.	Bath
9:00 a.m.	Nap + bottle
11:00 a.m.	Juice
12:00 p.m.	Lunch
2:00 p.m.	Nap
4:30 p.m.	Juice + play
5:30 p.m.	Dinner
6:00 p.m.	Ready for bed
6:30 p.m.	Bed

and two years of age. Then they graduate to taking only an afternoon nap. If children do not get the sleep they need, they cry a great deal and are generally fussy or cranky.

Babies appreciate regularity. They soon adopt a consistent rhythm of bedtime, naps, and meals. This is not only because regularity meets their rest and food needs. It is also because it makes babies more comfortable about the way the world works. It makes them feel secure.

Physical Comfort for the Infant

Physical comfort for an infant is largely a question of not being hungry or wet or tired. It also means being dressed comfortably and staying within a reasonable temperature range.

Unlike adults, infants don't have well-developed temperature control. Infants can quickly become too hot or too cold. Therefore, they should be warmly dressed when it's cold, and be kept free of heavy clothing in warm or hot weather. Many new parents mistakenly allow their infant to become overheated because they think a baby should *always* be well covered. Being too hot or too cool reduces a baby's resistance and may lead to illness.

Infants' digestive systems are not fully mature, so they often have gas after feeding. Sometimes this is caused by swallowing air during the feeding. Gas may be very painful for infants. They should be burped—patted gently on the back—either stomach down on a lap, or upright against the shoulder.

Nobody likes to change a baby's diaper. It's unpleasant for the caregiver *and* the baby. But it must be done. Most children can't control their bowel movements until they are two to three years old. Many can't control urination until they are even older.

Burping not only eases a baby's discomfort, it also brings parent and child close together.

Babies don't like to sit in wet and messy diapers, so they should be changed whenever their diapers are soiled.

Protecting the Baby

Caring for a growing baby requires a good deal of planning for health and safety. Babies need to be watched for signs of illness, such as being irritable or listless. They need to be checked by a doctor regularly to ensure that they are healthy and growing normally. And they need injections to protect them from diseases.

As babies grow older, their natural curiosity makes them want to taste, touch, and smell everything they see. Once babies can crawl around, they must be carefully supervised.

The house must be "child-proofed." That means that objects that can be grabbed and pulled down must be put up higher. *All* medicines and poisonous substances must be completely out of the baby's reach. Staircases must be blocked and light sockets covered. Remember, babies and young children poke into everything—whether it is safe or not.

Babies must be removed from danger. Just telling them no will not work. Until children are at least two years of age, the word *no* has little meaning. The accident rate for crawling and toddling babies is very high. They must be carefully watched and distracted from potentially dangerous situations.

Babies' Emotional Needs and Sociability

Babies thrive on loving care. They like to be held near a person's heart while they nurse or take their bottle. The heartbeat calms them, and the warmth of the caregiver's body soothes them. They also are very in-terested in the faces of the people who hold them.

At four weeks, infants can identify the face of their main caregiver. By three to six months, they can recognize people in their family and may have a fretful reaction to strange faces. They like to see faces smiling at them and hear people talking to them. They smile and often make cooing noises in return.

The development of this early social be-havior depends on the loving attention of caregivers. As babies grow, they develop the skill to show emotions to others more clearly. Toddlers who have been loved, cared for, and talked to are better able to show their emotions.

The ability to express emotions will be very important in later life. Babies who feel secure enough to show what they are feel-ing have a good chance of growing up to be happy and well-adjusted adults.

QUESTIONS

1. Describe three differences between toddlers and infants.
2. In what ways do secure, loving relationships help babies develop?
3. What can people do to make a baby comfort-able? How do babies benefit from regular schedules? What steps can caregivers take to ensure babies' safety?

4. What differences have you noticed between what toddlers can understand and what they can say?
5. What theories have you heard about sched-ules for babies? How could various ap-proaches be defended?
6. What special problems do you think babies in orphanages might have?

ACTIVITIES

1. Write an autobiography of your first two years. Describe the routines you followed, and the ways your needs were met.
2. Interview someone who has taught or taken a course for prospective parents. What infor-mation is covered in the classes? Why?
3. Make a poster with pictures of infants and toddlers at various stages of development. Find out about their needs and abilities at each stage, and add this information to the display.

SECTION 8 · Caring for Children

A CHILD CARE QUIZ

If you've ever done any baby-sitting, you know that there is very little "sitting" involved. Child care—whether for younger family members or for other children—involves a lot of activity. It also requires a certain amount of knowledge. To check what you know about caring for children, try to answer the following questions.

1. Who needs more care—older or younger children?
2. How should you behave toward children under six, children six to nine, and children ten or over?
3. Is a sitter more a playmate, a teacher, or a protector?
4. What are some things that you can teach a younger child? An older child?
5. Why might a child enjoy learning more from a sitter than from a schoolteacher?
6. As a sitter, are there times when you should be more strict than a parent?
7. What are some reasons why a child might act unreasonable?
8. What kinds of information do you need from parents who leave their children in your care?
9. Why might people say that baby-sitting is more than a job?

As babies change from infants to toddlers to pre-school-age children, they learn to do many things for themselves. They get dressed. They feed themselves. They no longer need formula or specially prepared foods. By school age, children can even make simple meals for themselves. They are independent enough to spend a great deal of time playing with children their own age.

Babies No Longer

As children get older, they go without naps, they walk, and they learn to communicate their needs. They enjoy being Mom or Dad's little helper. Perhaps you remember when you learned how to set the table, or take out the garbage, or feed the dog. You probably felt very adult doing your first chores.

As children grow, their increasing independence might lead you to think that they need less attention than when they were babies. In fact, a growing child needs just as much care and concern as a baby does from parents and other caregivers. Perhaps the actual amount of time spent caring for the older child is less than that spent on an infant. Even so, the time spent is critical. A child needs guidance, discipline, and love in order to be happy and successful.

Beyond babyhood, a child's growth can be divided into early childhood, middle childhood, and the preteen years. There are no absolute age limits, but generally early childhood includes children three through five, middle childhood is between the ages of six and nine, and the preteen years are ten to twelve. A good caregiver understands how a child's needs change as time goes by.

Early Childhood

Children in the early childhood years are constantly exploring and testing the world around them. They need encouragement for their unfolding curiosity about the world. But they also need careful supervision.

At this age, children may go to nursery school or kindergarten. They are just be-

ginning to know what it is to be social. Their behavior toward others is being shaped and formed. They begin to learn manners, and how to share toys and play organized games with other children.

They need guidance and a firm sense of rules for getting along with others.

Middle Childhood

By middle childhood, children are going to school. Besides learning basic skills such as reading and writing, they are developing socially. They are learning what it means to have best friends. They want to grow up and be like their mommy or daddy. They

Young children often are not aware of what they can realistically handle. They need guidance, and a sense of humor, from those around them!

Learning skills from a qualified instructor can improve confidence and be fun!

may like certain teachers more than others.

They enjoy learning things that make them feel special. Middle childhood is a good time to begin dancing or music lessons, to take up sports or hobbies.

A sitter may help seven- to nine-year-olds with their special projects, or show interest in whatever new skills they are learning. Children in this period may want to be like their sitters. They may have a special baby-sitter they like best.

Preteen Years

The preteen years bring a growing awareness of sex differences. Girls have girl friends. Boys have boy friends.

Children at this age may sometimes feel uncertain of themselves. They may try to hide such feelings by being loud and boastful. Or they may be moody and not get along with their parents as well as they did in the past. They often wish to test authority, making things difficult for their parents and sitters alike.

Though they sometimes feel sad to be leaving childhood behind, they want very much to be teenagers. In fact, they look up to teenagers, and sometimes imitate their behavior. They would usually prefer to be treated as teenagers than as children.

The Roles of the Baby-sitter

A baby-sitter is a substitute parent while the real parents are away from home. Like a parent, a sitter must take on different roles. At all times, a baby-sitter is a protector. To different children, and to children of different ages, a sitter may be a playmate or a teacher as well.

Playing games with the children you baby-sit for can be an enjoyable part of the job. An occasional game of hide-and-seek can be fun. And even a ten-year-old can offer challenging competition in a game of Monopoly. Playing with children is a good way to make friends with them.

One possible problem is that if you become a playmate, you may lose authority as a sitter. You must be careful to remain firm even though you have had a good play session.

Baby-sitting gives a special opportunity to share a skill or a hobby. You may know something about a subject that is very interesting to younger children. You might teach a four-year-old a song you know. A seven-year-old might love to hear about the book you read on pirates.

Children may find learning from a baby-sitter more fun than learning from teachers at school. Having a baby-sitter may be a special event for them, whereas school may seem more routine.

Protector

The main task of baby-sitters is protecting the children in their care. If anything, a baby-sitter should be more protective than a parent because a sitter doesn't know the child as well as the parent does. For example, you may not know that a child is a very good tree climber. You would have to keep the child out of trees. The parent, however, might let the child climb a tree.

The other side to being a good protector is being reassuring when a child is upset. A scratched knee or a banged elbow may not be very serious—but they can seem so to a young child. Children appreciate warmth and loving care.

Being a protector is important with children of all ages, but it is most important with younger children. They may need comforting more often. And they have not yet learned all the hazards of their home and neighborhood.

Managing Children

You must be able to manage children in order to fulfill your role as protector. Rules and limits must be clear from the start. Before the parents leave, ask them to discuss general rules of behavior with you and the children together.

Frequently, the parent or baby-sitter can head off trouble. Providing plenty of interesting activities can prevent children from becoming bored and getting into trouble.

If a child for whom you are sitting does something that isn't allowed, there may be many reasons for the misbehavior. Perhaps the child is tired, or angry that the parents are away. Understanding the reason for a child's behavior can help you deal with the situation.

Perhaps the child has not yet fully learned the rule. In that case, a reminder—"You know your parents don't want you to do that"—could help. If the child is simply tired, you could try reading a quiet story or playing a record.

Occasionally, the child may be testing you. In that case, you must know how the parents usually enforce their rules. Ask them in advance what you should do if the child becomes difficult to manage. That way you will know whether it's acceptable

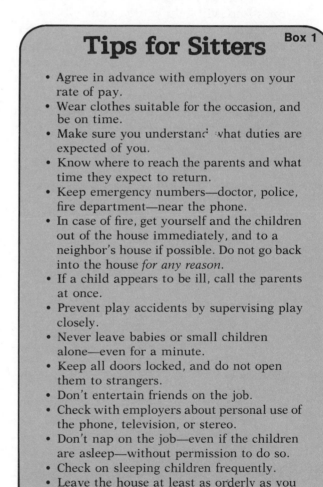

Tips for Sitters
Box 1

- Agree in advance with employers on your rate of pay.
- Wear clothes suitable for the occasion, and be on time.
- Make sure you understand what duties are expected of you.
- Know where to reach the parents and what time they expect to return.
- Keep emergency numbers—doctor, police, fire department—near the phone.
- In case of fire, get yourself and the children out of the house immediately, and to a neighbor's house if possible. Do not go back into the house *for any reason.*
- If a child appears to be ill, call the parents at once.
- Prevent play accidents by supervising play closely.
- Never leave babies or small children alone—even for a minute.
- Keep all doors locked, and do not open them to strangers.
- Don't entertain friends on the job.
- Check with employers about personal use of the phone, television, or stereo.
- Don't nap on the job—even if the children are asleep—without permission to do so.
- Check on sleeping children frequently.
- Leave the house at least as orderly as you found it.

to take away special privileges. You will know how you may discipline the child if he or she misbehaves.

Information You Will Need

As a protector, you need to have information about the children you sit for. Do they take any medicines? Are there limits to how or where they may play? What foods are they allowed to have for meals or snacks? Do they have any special allergies or fears? Knowing the answers to these kinds of questions will help you do your job.

Parents should also give you information about their doctor, the police, an ambulance, and where they are going to be while they are out. If the parents don't tell you these things, ask them. This kind of information could be critical if there is an emergency—for example, if the child has an accident or becomes ill.

It is very important to learn about any dangers in the house. If the parents have cleaning supplies, hobby materials, or dangerous tools around, you should know.

Learning by Baby-sitting

Some people view baby-sitting as merely a job. It can be much more. Caring for children presents a great challenge and teaches you many things.

As a sitter, you learn to assume responsibility and to make decisions. You become sensitive to the needs of others. You learn to adjust to new people and new situations.

Working with children now can help you plan your future. Sitting can help you decide if you would like a career working with children. Sitting can also help you gain the maturity and confidence needed for dealing with young children later in your life.

QUESTIONS

1. What are three roles that a baby-sitter takes? Which is most important? Why?
2. What are the three stages of childhood? How do a child's interests and needs differ at each stage?
3. What information does a baby-sitter need?
4. What do you think teenagers can learn from baby-sitting?
5. Do you think it is a good idea for a parent to bring in a new baby-sitter after the children have gone to sleep? Why or why not?

ACTIVITIES

1. Make a baby-sitter's check list of questions to ask parents and advice to remember. Consult parents and children for ideas about what to include. Duplicate the check list for your classmates.
2. Start a scrapbook or card file of games and stories to use when caring for children.
3. Go to a toy store and make a note of the kinds of toys made for different age groups. Do you see any general differences between toys for six-year-olds and toys for ten-year-olds? How would you explain the differences?

SECTION 9 · The Family and the Future

PAST, PRESENT AND FUTURE

These two families are quite different. In the past 100 years, families have gotten smaller. And they are much less likely today to work together on a family farm or in a family business. Today's family gets much more help from outsiders with recreation, education, health care, and other responsibilities.

Can you imagine what kinds of changes in the family will take place in the next 100 years? How do you think a photograph of a typical family of the future would look?

As the world changes—and it is changing ever more rapidly—the family changes with it. Chances are that family life will be somewhat different by the time people your age have children. Important technological and social changes may influence who makes up a family and how it works.

New Inventions Will Change Family Life

Technology has brought people pocket calculators and microwave ovens, nuclear energy and space flight. More inventions will certainly affect family life in the future. Every aspect of life a hundred years from now will be influenced by inventions that haven't yet been made. Exactly how family life will be different is hard to predict.

The homes of the future may be heated and lit by new sources of energy, such as solar and nuclear power. New ways to cook, do laundry, and clean will help family members get more done in less time.

Robots that prepare meals and take out the garbage may free family members to spend more time with one another, or to devote time to other interests.

Technological progress has made space flight a reality. In the future, groups of people may live together for years as they explore the solar system and beyond. Perhaps other people will care for and educate children while their parents are exploring the galaxy. Space flight could change family life considerably.

Space-age technology may also allow people to choose the sex of their children, or to produce exact duplicates of themselves. These possibilities raise questions that are already causing concern about the future.

Risks Families May Face

One way to imagine family life in the future is to think of the benefits of technology. More free time, less disease, and a whole new range of possibilities may make life easier and better for each family member.

On the other hand, the progress that has made it possible to live longer, safer lives than ever before has also led to new dangers. Technological advances have brought with them noise, pollution, and the threat of nuclear war. People must sort out conflicting information about additives in foods and other risks that are not yet fully understood.

Still another threat to world-wide family welfare is the limited amount of food and fuel available. Recognition that some of the world's resources are running out could change the ways families live. Facing the needs of the whole human family may help people set aside their separate claims and work together for the good of all.

New Patterns for Work

Because of improved technology, many kinds of work are done faster and better today. Over the last few generations, the number of hours people have to spend on the job has decreased.

Chances are that people will have even more free time in the future. They may spend this new leisure time with their families. And they may be able to devote more time to hobbies and education.

Another change in current work patterns is that more women are working outside the home. In some families, this means that men are sharing more day-to-day responsibilities for running a household and caring for children.

Because the world is growing more complex, certain jobs that families used to do—such as educating children—are now done outside the home. In many cases, the care of young children is largely handled by outsiders. This trend may continue. Families may get even more help in the future.

On the other hand, the world of the future may allow family members more leisure time and flexibility. Parents may be able to arrange their work schedules so that they both can devote more time to their children.

New Patterns for Families

People may feel freer to form different kinds of families in the future. Even today there are more families headed by single parents. Stepparents and families that include children from earlier marriages are also becoming more common.

There is also a chance that more people

Box 1

TV: Turn-on or Turn-off?

Television is one example of a modern invention that has had a great impact on family life. Like many other inventions, television offers important benefits, and problems, too.

Families are brought together in front of their TV set. Some people feel, however, that family time would be better spent in discussions, games, or other more active pastimes. There is also concern about the impact of television on family members too young to make sense of violent shows and repetitive commercials. In some families, television takes time away from meals together. And, too often, deciding what shows to watch leads to bickering.

Families must use television wisely in order to avoid the problems and enjoy the benefits. Television offers inexpensive entertainment families can share. It can broaden horizons by exposing people to events and entertainments they couldn't experience any other way. It also exposes viewers to different opinions and different life-styles.

Seeing how others think and live can make people more willing to accept differences in other people—including their own family members. By choosing programs thoughtfully and talking about what they see, families can use television as a group learning experience.

may decide not to marry. Such people may find that close friends can help fill some of the needs usually met by a family.

Because people are living longer, more will reach old age in the future. Perhaps more families will once again include several generations in the same household.

One hope for the families of the future is that they will provide trust and closeness in a rapidly changing world. Changes in the world will necessarily change the family. However, the people of the future will still need the human warmth and feelings of belonging that families provide. In fact, the family may be very much needed, to provide comfort and encouragement as the world becomes more complex.

What Do You Think?

As you imagine families in the future, think about the kind of family you would like to have when you grow up. What will your family be like? Where will you live? What will you do? Because of today's fast-changing world, these questions are much harder for you than they were for your parents and grandparents. But it is not too early to begin thinking seriously about the family of the future.

What you choose for your future will be influenced by how you feel about the world around you and what you think of your family and your place in it. The choices your generation makes will have an effect on the future of family life.

QUESTIONS

1. What are some of the ways in which family life has changed during the past 100 years? Why?
2. How might technological advances and limited resources change family life in the future?
3. What kinds of family patterns may become more widespread in the future? What role will the family continue to play despite any changes that may occur?
4. What do you think an average family of the future will be like? Why? In what ways might family life be better? Worse?
5. What inventions have you seen in your lifetime? What influences have they had on your family? What inventions do you think families need? Which ones are likely?
6. How does television influence *your* family?

ACTIVITIES

1. Draw a picture of an average family of the future. Include evidence of the technological and social changes you consider likely. Be ready to explain your drawing.
2. Do research to learn experts' predictions about homes and families of the future. Post the predictions in the classroom, and discuss them with your class. Add predictions made by class members.
3. Write a story about how family life would change if there were no more television.

SECTION 10 · Careers with Families and Children

What Does a Social Worker Do?

Tony Wade is a social worker in a large Midwestern city. He spends part of his time meeting with people in his office, and sometimes he goes to see people in their homes.

Q: Why did you go into social work?

A: I like working with people. And I like the feeling that I'm able to help people who really need me. For example, right now I'm working with a boy who was caught stealing and was sent away to a juvenile detention center. After his release, he couldn't get a job. I helped him get into a special program that lets him earn his high-school equivalency diploma and learn a trade. I'm hoping things work out so that he can get a job and support himself before long.

Q: How did you become a social worker?

A: When I was fifteen, I did volunteer work in a mental hospital. That really got me interested in working with people. Then I decided to go to college to study sociology, and I eventually went on to get a graduate degree in social work.

Q: What do social workers do?

A: They do different kinds of things. Some work in hospitals with families of patients. Others have jobs in schools or with city or state agencies. A few teach other social workers how to do their jobs. Others work with the elderly.

Q: What are the disadvantages of your job?

A: I wish I were responsible for fewer clients. If I had more time for each family, I could do a better job. I also get tired of filling out so many forms. There's just too much paperwork.

Q: How important would you say family life is—on the basis of what you've learned from your job?

A: I think your experiences as a child have tremendous impact on you throughout your life. Some people say the family is disintegrating, but I don't really agree. I do feel that family patterns are changing, but I wouldn't say the family is falling apart. Most people seem to want to have some kind of family, even people who come from unhappy homes.

Do you think, as Tony Wade does, that family life is very important? Would you like to help families meet the demands of daily life? Do you enjoy working with children? Then a career helping people solve their problems, handle their responsibilities, and make their family life more rewarding might be for you.

Families no longer provide for all the educational, recreational, and health-care needs of family members. Instead, they often depend on others to meet many of these needs. Such services are provided on a day-to-day basis, as well as in emergency situations.

Working with Families

Like Tony Wade, you may someday want a job helping families. This might mean working in a counseling center, a hospital, or even an employment agency. You might work as a school counselor or psychologist, helping children deal with their problems. You might work with individual people whose problems disrupt their families. Or you might work with all the members of a family together.

Family therapy is one career involving work with entire families. Family therapists help family members learn to communicate more clearly and to understand themselves and one another better. Specialists in family therapy must complete many years of formal education.

When serious family problems occur, people with jobs in the court system may step in. A judge may require a parent to provide financial support for his or her children. Lawyers and judges may also get involved when parents abuse or neglect their children. Or they may be needed when a child's behavior is uncontrollable and becomes a threat to others.

Box 1

Creating for Children

Your job may be related to the needs of children even though you don't work with children directly.

Many people design, make, and sell products for children. These products include children's clothing, furniture, games, and toys. An interest in meeting the needs of children could lead to a career designing attractive dolls or unique puzzles—or even running the local toy shop.

People interested in education, for example, may plan, write, or publish textbooks, storybooks, or educational materials. Many artists have built careers illustrating books for children.

Other jobs involve writing and producing children's movies and TV shows. Live entertainment for children also provides jobs for clowns, actors, dancers, and puppeteers.

Some jobs working with families require less training. Senior citizens, adults, and teenagers may work in agencies and child-care centers as paraprofessionals or volunteers. Such work gives them a good chance to contribute to the well-being of families. And it helps them find out what this kind of work is like. When family members work in local agencies, they find out what is being done to help people in their own community.

Providing Everyday Help

Most new parents need help learning how to care for babies and manage their households. When family members or friends are not available to give advice, a nurse or homemaker aide may go into a home to help. Homemaker aides also help people learn how to shop wisely for items such as clothes, and how to budget their money. And they teach people to cook nutritious, economical meals.

An important goal of jobs like these is preventing problems such as child abuse and delinquency. Another goal is keeping families together rather than allowing children to be placed in foster homes or institutions.

Health for the Young Family

Counselors and doctors sometimes help couples decide how many children to have and when to have them. Even before babies are born, their mothers need medical care to help the babies develop normally. Expectant mothers need to have regular medical checkups so that they get help if problems occur.

Some doctors, nurses, and other health-care workers specialize in working with children. They help children not only when they are sick, but also when they need advice on building good health habits and preventing disease. They work in clinics, hospitals, schools, and private offices.

Child Care

Many jobs involve caring for young children. Child care includes helping children learn the mental, physical, and social skills they need to know. Workers in these jobs answer the children's questions, help them plan and carry out activities, and show them how to get along together.

You may already have experience in this field. When you help with Sunday school or day camp or take care of younger sisters and brothers, you have a chance to see if you like this kind of work.

Adults may find part-time or full-time employment caring for children. In child-care centers, they may look after the children of working parents. And, of course, homemakers who have children provide this kind of care for their own families.

Special Needs

Many children have special needs that must be met by trained helpers. For example, children who are unable to speak clearly need the help of speech therapists. Audiologists help those with hearing problems. Speech therapists and audiologists work with children in hospitals and clinics, as well as in schools.

Some teachers work with children who have special learning problems. They may teach particular subjects, such as remedial reading. Or they may work with children

The right teachers and the right training can make it possible for people with special needs to become highly skilled and successful workers.

who have unusual difficulties with their school work.

Some institutions help care for children without families, the elderly, and people who are very ill or handicapped. People with severe problems may need to live in homes where their care can be closely supervised. Those who work in such homes help the residents live as comfortably and as normally as possible.

Part of helping families function well is helping people whose physical or emotional problems make them difficult to care for at home. Elderly or handicapped people sometimes need help with the details of everyday living.

Some workers provide transportation for them, or bring them hot, nutritious meals. Others provide recreational and educational activities. This can help them lead richer and more interesting lives.

A Closing Word

You may be responsible for a family of your own someday. Or you may have a job working with families. In either case, you will be helping to ensure that the family continues to thrive. Because families are so important to the development of individuals, your efforts could help fulfill the dream of a good start in life for everyone.

QUESTIONS

1. Name four areas in which workers who deal with families and children provide help or care.
2. Describe one job in each of the above areas.
3. What two basic goals are common to most of the careers that involve families and children? What might be another goal of those who work with families and children?
4. Which two jobs in the field do you think are most important? Why?
5. Do you think the number of jobs in the field is increasing or decreasing? Why?

ACTIVITIES

1. Select help-wanted ads for jobs that require people to work with families. Using them as models, write a help-wanted ad for a job with families or children which you feel is needed. What qualifications do you think are important for such a job?
2. Role-play an interview for a job as a homemaker aide, a family therapist, or a school counselor. Explain why you are interested in the job and the qualifications you have for it.
3. Observe a preschool or kindergarten class and make notes on what teachers and students are doing. What do you think are the rewards and frustrations of teaching at this grade level?

Consumer & Home Management

Consumer & Home Management

CHAPTER 4

Managing

CHAPTER CONTENTS

SECTION 1· What Is Managing?

THE MANAGERS

When you think of a manager, maybe you think of the person in charge at your favorite record shop. That person runs the store, hires and pays employees, orders records, and arranges for advertising. The manager's job is to organize the shop and the employees so that the store makes a profit.

What Is Management?

Management is a thoughtful approach to setting goals and achieving them. All managers try to make sure that certain aims or goals are reached. This involves careful planning.

You are a manager when you think about your future career and make plans to gain experience and qualifications. A basketball coach is a manager when he or she plans plays and organizes the team to win a game.

Managing a group of people—whether a sports team or a business—involves more than managing yourself does. *You* are trying to reach only your own personal goals. Someone who manages a group has the job of organizing members to work together toward shared goals.

Steps in Management

Whether decisions are made for one person or for many, following certain basic steps makes it easier to reach goals.

1. Decide what your aims are (goals).
2. Decide what you have to work with (resources).
3. Decide what procedures to use (plan).
4. Carry out your plan (action).
5. Think about how well your plan worked and why (evaluation).

These management steps are the same whatever the management task. Each step deserves careful thought and sound decision making. This is as true in your personal life as it is in a large business. And it is also true in family management.

Management and the Family

Sports teams and businesses aren't the only groups of people who need managing. Families, too, benefit from organized plans to reach goals.

Think about the single goal of feeding family members. How are meals handled in your family? Does one person cook for everybody, or does everybody cook for him or herself? Imagine half a dozen people in the kitchen at one time—all preparing different meals. Think of the confusion. Worse, think of the number of dirty pots! Organization can help in reaching family goals.

Families need management in areas besides cooking. How are the cleaning chores done in your family? Do you all go on family outings together, or do you each spend time on individual projects instead? And

Managing a family involves a lot of planning. Have you ever thought of parents as managers?

Decision Making and Management

Box 1

Management requires decision making every step of the way. You decide what your goals are and which are most important. You decide what resources to use to reach your goals. Careful thought about each of these decisions will help you make the best choices.

Thinking through a decision starts with setting aside a special time to deal with the decision. Then, by answering certain basic questions, you can improve your chances of a successful decision.

Suppose you are planning your electives program in high school. Your first step will be to decide on your goals—what you plan to do when you get out of high school.

Clearly, you must look further ahead to make this decision. What do you think you want to do later in life? Do you want to become a manager? Do you want to work with your hands? Do you want to travel? Do you want to start saving money right away? Such questions affect your decision about what to do after high school.

Next, you should look at the alternatives available. You could try to get into college. You could apply to the armed services. You could plan to get a job right away. But which job might you aim for, what armed service, what kind of college? The more alternatives you explore, the greater your chance of a satisfying decision.

A key step is comparing these alternatives with your long-term goals. If you want to gain management experience, for example, some jobs will give you a better chance to do this than others. The armed services may teach you management if you have the right qualifications. College courses, too, could give you a strong background in management techniques. Which option best fits your own personal goals?

Now you are ready to consider the effects of each alternative. If you go to college, you might study subjects that would help you in your future career. On the other hand, you might find much of the course work unsatisfying. Perhaps the armed services would give you more of what you want. Or maybe if you started working at the right kind of job after high school, you would have a valuable head start.

In considering these points, you have gone through key steps in decision making.

1. You have clearly defined the decision.
2. You have examined your goals.
3. You have checked the alternatives.
4. You have seen how well each alternative fits your goals.
5. You have thought about the effects of each alternative.

Now that you have thought clearly about your goals, you can begin to make further decisions about how to *achieve* these goals. Each decision will be improved if you go through these five basic steps. And because decision making is the heart of management, you will be on your way to becoming a good manager.

---

how is the family income spent? Do you buy the desk lamp your mother needs, or the new record player you want?

The answers to such questions vary from family to family. In most homes, parents have the most say in decisions about money. But many families give members equal votes on goals that have to do with leisure time.

Why Families Are Special

Families, like all groups, are made up of individuals with personal goals. But family members are usually bound together by a closeness rarely found in other groups. This closeness means that family members share more goals with one another than most group members do.

Families usually work to fulfill the basic needs of their members—food, clothing, and shelter. In other groups that care for basic needs, the care is usually offered for only a short time. But the family meets basic needs day in and day out.

Most groups exist for a few goals only. You may belong to a tennis club. You can hardly expect that club to pay for a backpack so that you can camp this summer. Your family, however, may help you buy a backpack even though no one else in the family will use it. Families help members with many goals—education, travel, hobbies, and companionship.

Another way in which families are different from other groups is that families are always changing. Businesses and clubs pursue much the same goals year after year.

But family needs and wants change as their members grow and change.

Good Management for All

Individuals, families, clubs, businesses—all try to achieve certain aims. How well they succeed depends on several things. Some groups are so limited in time or money that it is hard for them to do anything. Other groups are so large that it is hard for members to agree on many goals.

All groups, however—even those with little to work with—benefit from good management. Good management makes a little money go a long way. Good management lets you achieve more in a given time. Careful planning to reach goals can achieve wonders.

QUESTIONS

1. Describe the ways in which all managers are alike.
2. How is a family group like other groups? In what ways is it different?
3. What problems arise when a typical family tries to meet group goals? How might these problems be solved?
4. How does your family go about making major decisions, such as where to go on vacation?
5. How might the whole family benefit from helping one member reach an individual goal, such as taking music lessons?
6. How might membership in another group help you get along in your family group?

ACTIVITIES

1. Interview the members of your family to find out what their individual goals are. Also ask them what they think the goals of your whole family are. Do these goals conflict?
2. Write a skit in which each member of a family wants to go somewhere different on vacation. Show how the family could solve this problem.
3. Talk to someone who comes from a very large family about how that family is managed. Did you learn anything about successful family management?

SECTION 2 · Getting Your Goals Straight

Rocking the Boat

Neil, the bass player in a student rock group called the Solar Eclipse, is fifteen minutes late for rehearsal. The other players are beginning to get annoyed. The group has a performance at a picnic only a week away, and they're not ready for it yet.

"This isn't the first time Neil has been late for rehearsal," complains Jenny, the group's drummer. "Before, his playing was good enough to make up for it. But lately, he's not playing so well. I'm afraid he'll let us down next week."

"Wait a minute," says Peter, the lead guitarist. "Neil told us he was tired last Tuesday because of the soccer match. I don't think his playing is really worse. But it makes me mad that he's always busy and comes to rehearsal late. He doesn't seem to care much about us. I think we should get a new bass player."

"I don't agree with you," interrupts Althea, the lead singer. "We'd never get another bass in time for the picnic. Anyway, he's never *that* late. We'll still get in almost two hours of practice."

"Now, just a minute," says Josie, keyboard. "What are we here for, anyhow? I didn't join the group just for performances. I wanted to put in a lot of time rehearsing—that's the part I really enjoy. That's how we get to be better players."

Just then, Neil walks in, saying he's sorry he's late. He missed the bus because he was trying to finish his homework.

For an individual, setting goals is usually not hard. Most people know plenty of things they would like to do. More often the problem is setting a limit to goals. People want far more than they can manage to achieve.

For a group, setting goals is more difficult because different people want different things. In the Solar Eclipse, each member seemed to have a different idea about what the band was for.

Jenny and Althea were most concerned with playing well at performances. Josie wanted to enjoy herself at long rehearsals. Peter thought the best thing about the band was its group spirit. The question is: Can a group like this get together and agree on goals for the band? If they can't, then they probably won't be able to agree on what to do about a problem like Neil either.

Setting Group Goals

Imagine a family planning a vacation. The parents want a quiet, restful week. They would like to get away from it all—perhaps in a remote mountain cabin.

The children in the family don't mind going to the mountains, but they're not looking forward to a week of quiet. They want to get together with some other teenagers and go dancing or see some movies.

If the family members don't talk about their different goals, someone will probably be very unhappy throughout the vacation.

For group goal setting to work, the members must all say what they really want. If group members disagree strongly about goals, discussion can often lead to a compromise.

In a compromise, each person gives up part of what she or he wants, but no one gives up everything. Maybe the family will choose a fairly quiet vacation site that has entertainment nearby. The vacation will not be quite as restful as the parents want, nor quite as social as the teenagers want. But there will be something for everyone.

Priorities

Agreeing on goals isn't the end of the decision-making task. Everyone faces times when one goal or another has to come first. Deciding which goals are most important is called setting priorities.

Choices among goals are usually not clear-cut. Think about a choice involving other people. Your parents are leaving to go shopping, and they ask you to do a few chores before they return. Shortly after they leave, your grandmother calls. When you tell her your parents are not home, she sounds upset. She says she is in bed with a bad cold and was hoping your mother or father could come over and fix some soup for her.

You are now faced with three choices. You can drop everything and go help your

The conflicting goals and priorities of individuals in a group may lead to problems. Compromise may be the only solution.

grandmother. You can do the most important chore first, and then go to your grandmother's. Or you can take the message and continue to work on the jobs your parents gave you.

What do you do in this situation? Which responsibility should take priority?

Sorting Out Goals

To set goals in order of priority, it helps to divide them into groups. Two groups might be goals you *need* to reach and goals you *want* to reach.

Needs are goals you have to reach. If you don't meet your needs, you could be in real trouble. Getting food, clothing, and shelter are basic needs. Preparing yourself to earn a living is a need. Wants are goals that make life more satisfying.

Another way of looking at your goals is to decide which are *short-term* and which are *long-term*. The Solar Eclipse had the short-term goal of playing well at the picnic. It also had the long-term goal of improving each player's talents as a musician.

Getting Things in Order

Dividing your goals into groups will help you set priorities. You *must* meet certain needs—even if they aren't very exciting. You must have a place to live and food to eat.

Once these basic needs are met, however, you have many choices in setting priorities. Which of your wants is more important—tickets to the rock concert or new clothes for a party? Should you pass up going out for pizza tonight so that you'll have enough money for the movies tomorrow?

Your wants—particularly your short-term wants—may be the goals you think

Planning can be achieved by thinking about what is important to you and then making notes of these thoughts.

about most. It's easy to think only about short-term goals—they are what you want right now. But you should consider long-term goals, too—such as what you want to do with your life.

Considering long-term goals can make the difference between someday having a satisfying job and having a job that only lets you get by. Thinking about long-term goals can help make your dreams come true—a trip around the world, perhaps, or a place on the Olympic team. Before you set priorities, consider *all* your goals.

Sharing Goals

Setting priorities is as important for groups as it is for individuals. But when groups set priorities, they have to consider their shared goals as well as the personal goals of group members.

If the members of the Solar Eclipse had discussed their goals, they might have easily solved their problem with Neil. The group might have agreed with Althea that keeping the band together was the first priority. If so, they might have decided to overlook Neil's habit of being late. But the group might have agreed with Peter that the band's spirit came first, and that Neil's behavior was spoiling it. Then they might have decided to look for a more reliable bass player.

By considering all the goals involved, any group—or individuals in a group—can decide what is most important to them. Knowing the things you want, and how much you want each one of them, is a major step in successful management.

QUESTIONS

1. Why is it harder to set goals for a group than for an individual? What are the benefits of setting goals?
2. What is meant by the term "setting priorities"? Into what kinds of groups should you divide your goals when setting priorities?
3. What can happen when a group or an indi-vidual does not sort out goals?
4. What do you think the Solar Eclipse ought to do about Neil? Why?
5. How could sorting out goals and setting priorities help in your own life?
6. How do you and your friends decide upon your activities as a group? What changes, if any, would you make in the process?

ACTIVITIES

1. Make a chart that illustrates your needs and your wants. Number them in order of importance. Compare your chart with your classmates'. How can this list help you to achieve your goals?
2. Speak to one of the officers of a school or community group about what the goals of that group are. Ask how they were arrived at and how often they have changed. Describe your conversation to the class.
3. List what you think are the goals for this course. How does your list compare with your teacher's?

SECTION 3 · Resources: Time, Energy, Money, and More

GORN TALK

Things are different on the planet Algon IV. The grass is purple and the sky is red. The people have heads like parking meters and bodies like beach balls. They call themselves "gorns," and they live in an unusual way.

Every morning, as the blue sun is just beginning to appear, each gorn bounces over to its local bank to get a daily portion of resources.

Each day, he, she, or it receives a stack of disks that look like coins. The disks can be fed into two slots on the side of its head, marked "**T**" (for time) and "**E**" (for energy). They can also be put into a stomach pouch labeled "**M**" (for money—some things are the same everywhere).

It's not known whether gorns are "alive" or just very advanced machines. But one thing is clear: If a gorn doesn't keep feeding the **T** and **E** slots on the side of its head, it shuts off and no longer functions. Once gorns have used up their portion of time and energy, that's it—until the next day. Then the rising sun activates their transceiver units, and they bounce over to the bank again.

The gorns have only one enemy—the grass. It grows so fast that soon they can't jump over it, and they become "grass-tied." So gorns spend a lot of time and energy cutting their purple grass.

A power mower is one of the many popular consumer items on Algon IV because it saves a lot of energy. But every gorn must ask itself, "Should I spend my disks as money on a power mower? Or should I save them and use them for energy to mow the grass by hand?"

Gorns have other decisions to make, too. Their bodies aren't perfect, so every now and then they need tune-ups. These, too, cost disks. Gorns are always trying to decide if a tune-up is worth paying disks.

Many gorns would love to own a gorn-mobile. It's a prestige item that makes traveling faster. But gorns can bounce pretty quickly without wheels. So they must decide whether it is better to spend extra time bouncing or to spend their disks on a gornmobile.

Gorns use these trade-offs to get what they want out of life. The system works very well. In fact, it's probably fair to say that most gorns are happy most of the time.

Disks are the gorns' basic resources. In trading these resources, the gorns are similar to people here on Earth. We, too, exchange our resources to get what we want. By using resources wisely, we can get more with what we have.

What Are Resources?

Anything you can use to help with what you are doing can be called a resource. If you have a paper route, then a bicycle is a useful resource because it helps you do your work. If you baby-sit, your telephone is a resource because that is how people get in touch with you.

Objects such as bicycles and telephones are one kind of resource. **Money** is another. You can use money to buy goods and services from other people.

Other resources are less obvious than objects and money, but are very valuable just the same. **Time**, for instance, is an invisible resource, but it is necessary for reaching goals. If you use your time for homework and sports, then you may have no time for a paper route.

Information is another resource. It is useful when it helps you reach your goals. Sometimes you can gain information by doing research. For example, you can find out about careers by reading and listening to others. Other times you can learn what you need to know by experience—through a summer job, for instance.

Human Resources

Besides objects, money, time, and information, there are other resources called human resources. Human resources, too, are important in reaching goals.

Knowledge is a human resource closely related to information. When you learn some information, it becomes knowledge that you carry around with you. And, unlike some of the other resources, knowledge cannot be used up. Once you know how to cook hamburgers, for example, you don't use up that knowledge by cooking one. The next time you're hungry for a hamburger, you'll still know how to cook one!

In fact, you'll probably cook it better. With practice, you can improve your **skills,** another human resource. Skills are worth developing. They enable you to reach goals quickly and efficiently.

Imagination picks up where knowledge and skills leave off. If you need to do something but don't know how, you can use your imagination to think of a way to do it. Imagination helps you to use your skills to accomplish what you want.

Energy is one of the most valuable human resources. It is what allows you to get things done. Mental and physical energy are always needed to reach a goal. Using imagination, knowledge, money, or objects can mean using *less* energy. But if you don't have enough of the other resources, determination and physical energy can often help you reach your goal anyway.

Choosing Resources

You can use different resources to accomplish the same goal.

Suppose that washing the family car is your job. You can use your own time and energy to do the job. If you are busy or feeling lazy, you can spend money to have it done at the local car wash. Or, if you are both lazy and broke, you can use your imagination and skill to persuade your little brother that washing the car is fun. Then you could save money, time, and energy—and *still* get the job done!

If you use resources wisely, you will

reach more of your goals. When you use your time and energy to wash a car, you reserve your money for things your energy can't produce—a ticket to a concert, for example. When you use your sewing skill and time to make curtains, you have more money to spend for things you can't make.

Trading Resources

If you feel that your resources are all wrong for what you want, remember that most resources can be traded. This is as true for human beings as for gorns.

Suppose you have a tennis racket you rarely use, and you want to become a better baseball pitcher. Your friend has a wicked curve ball, and she wants to start playing tennis. Perhaps you could trade, or barter, the racket for pitching lessons from your friend. You would gain a skill, and your friend would gain some sports equipment.

Trading resources is a basic part of life. When people go to work, they are trading their time and skills for money. When you eat dinner in a restaurant, you are trading your money for both food *and* the time and energy needed to cook at home.

If you trade resources carefully, you can make them go much further toward meeting your goals.

Sharing Resources

When a group works together to achieve a goal, all the members are pooling their skills. Members' skills are an important part of a group's resources. The more resources each member is willing to share with others, the more successful the group is likely to be.

Suppose you are an expert volleyball player and your class is scheduled to play another class. By helping your classmates

At flea markets, many people get together to exchange resources, usually in the form of goods and money.

improve their skills, you will expand the volleyball-playing resources of the group. That will give your team a better chance of winning.

Families, too, benefit by sharing resources. If the person who usually does the cooking teaches someone else to cook, there will be one more person in the family who can fix dinner. When everyone devotes

In what ways do you think these family members are exchanging resources with one another?

some time and energy to keeping the house neat, housekeeping isn't a burden for any one person.

By sharing resources, you help your group reach its goals. And in helping your group, you help yourself.

QUESTIONS

1. What is a resource? List four resources that are available to us in limited quantities. List four resources that are available in unlimited quantities. What is another name for this second group of resources?
2. Briefly describe the ways in which various resources can be combined to reach a goal.
3. Explain two ways in which resources can be traded. How can you benefit from sharing resources?
4. Which two resources do you think are most important? Why?
5. How do you think your resources will change as you get older?
6. How might sharing resources be turned into a barter system?

ACTIVITIES

1. Make a poster that illustrates what you think are your unique resources.
2. Set up a table at which students trade unwanted objects with one another.
3. Evaluate the skills and talents of three of your friends. How could you share your individual resources with one another?

SECTION 4 · Making Plans

How Is a Manager Like a Juggler?

Have you ever watched a professional juggler closely? Jugglers make what they do look easy, but it is concentrated work. They have to be sure that a hand is always ready to catch the object that is falling.

A skillful juggler can keep several objects in the air at the same time. A good manager can make progress toward several goals at the same time. Just as a juggler has only two hands to keep objects in the air, a manager has only a limited amount of resources to reach goals. Both need to have careful plans.

What Makes a Good Plan?

A plan starts with knowing your goals, your priorities, and your resources. But knowing goals, priorities, and resources is not enough. You must also know how to use your resources to reach your goals.

A good plan lets you use your resources most effectively. This means you will come closest to achieving what you want. Few plans will make sure that you reach all your goals. But if you fail to reach some of them, a good plan makes sure that the ones you miss are the least important.

Suppose the circus is in town for the week and your family is planning to see it. Everyone is looking forward to the trip. You all agree that it's your top priority. Your cousin's birthday is also coming up, and you are staging a big celebration. Everyone is getting presents for the occasion. Then there's a TV special that you'd all like to watch. To top it off, your family has scheduled spring-cleaning for this week! Will your family have enough time and money for all these activities?

A good plan would guarantee that you all went to the circus—your top priority. It would no doubt put buying the presents

ahead of watching the special. And it would probably put watching the special, which is on only once, ahead of spring-cleaning, which can be done some other time. With a poorer plan, you might end up with the presents and a clean house, but miss the circus and the special.

Your best plan follows your priorities. It lets you achieve as many goals as possible, in order of their importance.

Fixed or Flexible?

An important part of making a plan is seeing which activities are fixed, or have to be done at a certain time. The time for watching a TV special or buying a birthday present is fixed. If you don't do these things now, you'll have missed the chance to do them at all. Other activities are more flexible. You can spring-clean next week. And the circus will be in town for several days.

When you are making a plan, decide which activities are flexible. Flexible activities make planning much easier because you can save them for times when nothing is fixed. However, don't be fooled into thinking that just because an activity is fixed, it's more important. Perhaps you would do better to miss the TV special altogether, and go to the circus at that time.

Deciding on Standards

Your plan is also affected by the standards you set for yourself. For example, how much do you want to spend on your cousin's present? How long are you willing to spend searching for "the right gift"? Your standards here obviously affect how much money and time you will have for your other goals.

Some people try for the most rigorous standards no matter what they are doing.

Other people always prefer the quickest and most convenient methods. A good manager, however, decides which standards are right for which goals.

A good manager also decides when it is necessary to adjust a standard slightly for the sake of the whole plan.

Suppose you want to buy a humorous T-shirt for your cousin—one that you saw someone wearing at a party. You have been to five stores, and none of them has that particular design. But you know where to buy another shirt that you like almost as much. Change your plan and buy the second T-shirt. Your cousin will probably enjoy it just as much.

By adjusting your standard, you won't waste time searching through even more stores. You might, instead, have time to finish your part of the spring-cleaning. Then you'll have free time on another day for your other plans.

Budgets

Perhaps the most important part of making a plan is working out a budget. A budget is

Family members must cooperate to make the best use of the family's resources by planning a budget that works.

a detailed account of how you will use a resource.

Once you work out a budget—either in your head or on paper—you will know whether your plan is possible. You will know if it can be achieved with the resources you have available.

You might start by budgeting your money. See how much money your plan requires. Compare this sum with the money you have available. If the trip to the circus and your cousin's present would cost more money than you have, you know right away that another plan is needed.

A schedule, or time budget, could be your next step. See how much time you have. Then see how much time your plan calls for. Perhaps you have more time than you need. If so, you could use the extra time to save money. You could *make* a present for your cousin. Then your money budget might work out and you would be able to reach both your goals after all.

You could also use your extra time to earn money. This would be another way of changing your plan to reach your goals. Budgeting your resources can show the way to making a better plan—better because it achieves what you want.

Planning Ahead

Thinking about goals, resources, standards, and budgets helps you avoid problems *before* they happen. If you do this, you can really improve your chances of success.

A good plan can help you just as it helps a juggler. A juggler who threw five objects into the air without a plan wouldn't have any act. A person who has goals but no plan usually ends up disappointed.

Managing is like juggling in another way: you improve with practice. If you work at making plans and budgeting your

Box 1
Notes and Records

Writing down the details of a management plan can help you carry it out successfully. If you have a very clear idea of how to achieve your goals, you may not need to do this. But making notes as you plan has many advantages.

At the beginning, making notes can help you sort out your goals. Notes let you see all your ideas at once, and that makes it easier to compare them.

Once you have decided on your goals, the details of achieving them will be clearer if they are collected in one place. You can list the pros and cons of each idea, and make decisions by comparing the lists.

It often helps to make notes on steps you plan to take to reach your goals, and to keep records of the steps you do take. By doing this, you will be able to compare your performance with what you planned. If you have missed an important step, you will see it immediately. Forgetting a crucial detail can mean the failure of a plan.

A written budget is useful in the same way. Write down how much of a resource you plan to use. Then, as you carry out your plan, check against your budget to see how much you are actually using. If you are overspending, you can adjust your plan before it's too late.

A record of your actions will help you evaluate your plan after you've completed it. You can compare what you planned to accomplish with what you were able to achieve. Often it's easy to see how you might have done things differently after you've completed a project. Using your records to evaluate your plans will make you a better planner in the future.

Keep your records as simple as possible so that writing them will be less of a chore. If you use a file card box or a loose-leaf notebook you will be able to add ideas or rearrange them easily. Develop your own system for keeping notes and records. It will make you a better manager.

resources, you will become a better manager. And being a good manager affects more than your everyday life. People will trust you more, because you are more reliable. You will be better prepared for job opportunities in the area of management. And when you manage your own home, whether alone or with a family, you will be able to handle your responsibilities far more easily.

QUESTIONS

1. List four things you should know before making a plan. What does a good plan allow you to do?
2. Into what two categories should you divide activities when making a plan? How do standards affect a plan?
3. What is a budget? How can it help you in making a plan? How can keeping records help you carry out a plan and evaluate it later?
4. Have you ever gotten so carried away in achieving one goal that other goals suffered? Describe what happened.
5. How do you think planning ahead could help your family achieve its goals?
6. What might happen to a plan if you do not adjust your standards?

ACTIVITIES

1. Make a list of all your activities each morning before school. Show how you budget your time each morning on a picture of the face of a clock. Number your activities in order to show which ones you skip if you oversleep. Compare your chart with your classmates'.
2. Keep a three-week record of how you spend your money. What pattern do you see in your spending? How might a budget change this pattern?

SECTION 5 · From Plan to Action to Evaluation

What Made the Difference?

Two groups were competing to raise money for their school. Both planned to hold a car wash on the same day. There were forty students in one group and only ten in the other.

The forty students felt they had it made. Each person contributed fifty cents, and the group had posters made to advertise their car wash. Once the advertising was taken care of, they relaxed. They were sure that with so many people in the group, they were bound to make a lot of money. It was a beautiful day, so all they had to do was wait for customers to appear.

The small group of students realized that it would be hard to compete with the large group. But they had a plan. Because they couldn't afford posters, each member of the group telephoned several people to let them know about the project. The students ar-

ranged times when different customers would show up. This schedule meant that they could plan lunch breaks for their workers.

At the end of the day, the small group had made twice as much money as the large group. At all times, there were at least eight people working at the small group's car-wash station. The large group's attendance ranged between four and seven—more than twenty students didn't show up at all. The small group had ten pails and plenty of soap and sponges. The large group had only six pails, and they had to make a trip to the store for more sponges at midday.

The large group had far more resources. They had enough money for an advertising campaign, and they had four times as much people power. But the smaller group won. What made the difference?

For a plan to work, it must be detailed enough to be useful. And it must be followed. Even the best plan is useless if it isn't followed.

Both groups of students had made plans for the car wash. Both had lined up workers and purchased supplies. And both groups had advertised—though in different ways.

The group of ten—because they felt they had to work harder—had planned in detail. They wrote a schedule assigning each person certain work times. They planned their supplies very carefully.

Because the large group was so confident, their plan was more loosely organized. They assumed that everybody would show up at the station to work. They didn't give careful thought to their supplies.

The result of such a casual plan was that it wasn't followed. Many of the group members didn't show up. So the smaller group—with careful attention to a detailed plan—won the competition.

Checking the Details

Having a written budget or schedule allows you to check your progress in carrying out a plan.

The small car-wash group had planned to wash one car about every twenty minutes. Once they started working, however, they discovered that each car took only fifteen minutes. Knowing that they were ahead of schedule allowed them to adjust their plan. They sent one of their workers to make phone calls to drum up more business. They also gave each worker a morning break.

Knowing how well you are following a plan can help you carry it out successfully.

Problems

Even the best plans are rarely carried out

without some problems. Unexpected things always happen. Good managers learn to deal with problems as they come up. They make decisions as they're needed and adjust plans when necessary.

Your family might have planned to drive to a lake this morning for a fishing trip. You might have planned to use the afternoon to clean out the basement—a job you've been putting off. But at breakfast, the phone rings. Your mother finds out she has to go in to work for the morning. She needs the car to get there.

You obviously can't stick to the plan you made for the day. You have some decisions to make. Perhaps you'll decide to reverse the order of your plan. You'll clean the basement in the morning, then go fishing in the afternoon, when your mother gets home from work.

Or maybe you will decide to cancel your fishing trip. Then you can do something else in the morning and still clean out the basement after lunch. Whatever your decision, you were able to make it because your plans were flexible.

Flexibility

Flexible plans allow for several contingencies. Contingencies are events that might affect what you plan to do, but are largely out of your control.

Rain is a contingency if you are planning an outdoor party to celebrate the end of the school year. It might affect the success of the party. Trying to move indoors at the last minute could be a disaster. Your plan should include a "rain plan."

If you stop at the grocery store to buy hot dogs and corn on the cob for dinner, what do you do if the store is out of corn? It's a good idea to have some plan—at least in the back of your mind—of what to buy in case the store is out of an item you want.

Flexible plans allow you to make new decisions as new circumstances arise. Flexibility lets you deal with contingencies.

A Little in Reserve

An important part of dealing with contingencies is making sure that all your resources are not scheduled for use. You need to reserve some time and money for the unexpected.

If you budget your money down to the last penny, you might not be able to take advantage of a bargain that you suddenly hear about. Suppose you plan to buy school clothes in September. Then you come across a special back-to-school sale in August. If all your money is committed until September, you'll end up spending more money later for the same new clothes.

Or suppose that the small group of car washers had not scheduled time off for lunch. When an extra car showed up unexpectedly, they were only able to do the job because two people were taking a lunch break. They had these two spare workers to

step in and handle the contingency. Their lunch break was rescheduled for a time when business was slower.

Evaluation

After you have carried out a plan, one important, final step remains. That is to think about how well your plan worked.

If you failed to reach some or all of your goals, evaluating your plan can help you judge why things went wrong. Even if you reached all your goals, evaluating your plan is still worthwhile. You might discover that you could have reached your goals more easily if you had changed your plan in some ways. You might see how you could have reached other goals in addition to the ones you did achieve.

Whether your plan succeeded or failed, evaluation can teach you more about planning. It will let you see the mistakes you made and the opportunities you missed. It will also let you enjoy the successes you had. Evaluation makes you a better manager.

QUESTIONS

1. What two things caused the failure of the large group's car-washing plan? Why are these things so important?
2. What is a contingency? Describe a situation in which planning for contingencies would be a good idea.
3. What specific ability is at the heart of good

management? How does this ability relate to flexibility?
4. Do you think "the more the merrier" is always a good idea when recruiting people for a group activity? Explain your answer.
5. How do you usually react when a problem affects a plan you have made? Does your reaction help you solve the problem?

ACTIVITIES

1. Write a skit in which a group of teenagers tries to carry out an activity from a plan that leaves out an important detail.
2. In a group, brainstorm all the problems that might arise in carrying out a plan for a class fair. How many of these problems can you

solve? How would you solve them?
3. Read several chapters of the book *Robinson Crusoe* to see how a man marooned on an island uses creative decision making to solve the problems of daily survival. Describe the chapters to your class.

SECTION 6 · Responsibility to Others

How Is Janet Like a Chemical Plant?

Janet was baby-sitting with her two-year-old brother Mike while her parents were out shopping. Her friend Donna came to the door and said she'd just bought a new bike. Mike was playing happily on the living room floor with his toys. So Janet stepped outside for a couple of minutes to look at the bike. When she came back indoors, her heart leapt to her throat. Mike was standing on the kitchen counter, reaching for his bottle. She realized that anything could have happened to him while she was outside.

The BTU Chemical Company was built near a river about thirty years ago. The location seemed ideal. The river would wash away the chemical wastes. But over the years, much of the life in the river has been poisoned by the chemicals. The company's planners never suspected that something like that would happen. It didn't occur to them to think beyond the needs of their company.

If you lived alone in the wilderness, growing your own food and making everything you needed yourself, your actions would hardly matter to others. If you forgot to chop wood or to water the corn, or if you weren't too careful about disposing of your garbage, only you would be affected.

Few people live that kind of life. Most of us depend on others to help meet our needs, and other people depend on us. We live and work together in a large community that includes everyone on earth. So we have to consider other people as well as ourselves.

Both Janet and the BTU Chemical Company failed to consider others. Both are guilty of the same thing—a lack of responsibility to other people.

This public service ad urges people to use energy resources wisely. Even large corporations which make money selling energy recognize the importance of energy conservation.

Understanding Your Responsibilities

A responsibility is any task or area of your life that you take charge of. Your homework is your responsibility. It's up to you to get it done. Your health is your responsibility. You can begin to take charge of seeing that you eat the right foods and get enough rest and exercise.

Sometimes a task you take charge of obviously involves other people. If you promise to make sandwiches for a class picnic, you have a clear responsibility to the class members. If you promise to feed your neighbors' cats while they are out of town, you know exactly what you have to do.

With some actions, however, it's harder to see how other people are involved. Both Janet and the BTU Chemical Company failed to see that their actions might affect others. Both failed to meet their responsibilities to other people.

Last night after dinner I told my family the bad news. I had this class assignment to monitor our use of energy at home for a week. Our family got an F.

Tuesday night my brother watched the same two hour movie on his TV set that we were watching in the living room. Not too smart. Thursday Mom ran an entire dishwashing cycle for three cups, two plates, a knife and three little spoons. That's a lot of electricity and hot water down the drain.

Dad drives twenty-eight miles back and forth to work. Alone. When two men he works with live right nearby. They could carpool and save about a thousand gallons of gas a year. And me. I'm guilty too. I went out and left the radio blaring in my room all Saturday morning. Dummy.

So last night at the dinner table we all agreed to do everything we could to conserve energy. Faster showers. Lower thermostats. Fuller cars. It's a fact that this country's using up energy faster than we produce it. I read where we may run out of oil—forever—in thirty years. Pretty scary. Unless every person in every house on every block does his part, the future looks pretty dim.

I'm getting more and more concerned about the future. Because that's where I'm going to be.

ARCO

As a manager, you should always think about how your plan might affect others. Could what you are doing, or not doing, be a problem for someone else? Small things that seem unimportant now can develop into trouble for others later.

The Law and Responsibility

Some responsibilities are clearly stated in the law. The law forbids certain actions that have been proven harmful to other people. For example, it is against the law to drive at night with only one headlight. And today there are laws to control the pollution of streams and rivers.

A good manager, however, tries to think about effects that are not covered by the law. When the BTU Chemical Company started polluting the river, there was no law against it. Yet the effect of pollution on life in the river was the same then as it is now. Responsibility to other people means more than obeying the law. It means considering other people's interests as well as your own.

Responsible Planning

At every step of planning—from goal setting to evaluation—you need to think of how your plans might affect other people. Good management means planning to reach your goals in ways that don't hurt or inconvenience others.

Suppose you and your family plan to celebrate your birthday with an outdoor party. To plan responsibly, you need to consider the effects your party might have on the neighbors. A game of Frisbee might mean a lot of people running across their yard. Playing a stereo might disturb their evening.

If you think of the possible effects of your plan, you can probably arrange to do the things you want without being unfair to others. You might plan to hold the party in a park near your home. Or maybe you could begin the party with quiet activities outdoors, and then move inside for music and dancing. By making responsible decisions when you plan, you can avoid many problems.

As a responsible manager, you should consider all possible outcomes of a plan. You should realize that a good plan is considerate of others. That makes you a better member of the community of Earth.

QUESTIONS

1. Besides Mike, who else could have been affected by Janet's actions?
2. Explain the saying, "No man is an island." Give an example of a responsibility that would involve only yourself, one that would involve a few people, and one that would involve many other people.
3. How are responsibility and thoughtfulness involved in the decisions of a good manager?

ACTIVITIES

1. Make a collage of newspaper articles that describe community problems that concerned citizens are trying to solve. You might also try to interview one of the citizens about the

Why should your responsibilities to others go beyond those demanded by the law?
4. How can being responsible to others benefit you as well?
5. Do you think it is possible, or desirable, to pass laws to control all kinds of irresponsible behavior? Give examples to explain your answer.
6. Why do you think so many people have the attitude, "I don't want to get involved"?

reasons for his or her involvement.
2. Make a list of laws that you would pass to protect people from the irresponsibility of others.

SECTION 7 · Careers in Management

HELPING OTHERS MANAGE

Anita Martin is a college graduate with a degree in home economics. She works in a large city for the Community Action Program, an agency that assists families on public aid.

Anita's job requires good management skills. One of her main responsibilities is teaching families how to budget their resources. She teaches adult classes on nutrition, clothing care, and family relationships. In her classes on nutrition, her students learn to stretch their budgets while still eating well.

"The people in our classes have very little money," she says. "When they meet, they learn not only from us, but also from each other. And what they learn really helps them to manage. You should have seen Mrs. Peters's face when she had finished repairing her daughter's overalls. Replacing a zipper instead of buying a new pair meant money for something else the family needed."

Besides teaching, Anita helps individual families work out their home management problems. She provides information on nutrition, child care, and income budgeting. And she's involved in other projects, too. She supervises a day-care center and sometimes serves as a consultant to other government agencies.

With so much to do, Anita must budget her own time and energy wisely. "The job is exciting. I come home tired sometimes, but never bored."

Anita Martin is only one person who uses management skills professionally. Just as individuals and groups need some form of management to function well, every organization and business needs trained managers to help it run smoothly.

In managing personal and family life, you have certain goals for which you budget time, energy, money, and other resources. Professional managers also sort out goals. They, too, budget their resources, including their employees' time, energy, and talents.

If you enjoy planning and you like responsibility, a career in management might be right for you.

Management and Home Economics

Many careers combine management and home economics. People with such training often become management advisers. Federal, state, and local government agencies provide many such jobs. For example, nearly every county in the United States employs a home economics agent or home adviser. These home economists organize 4-H and other clubs and help develop programs that meet the members' needs.

Public utility companies hire home economists to staff home service departments. These employees advise families how to manage their energy resources. They sometimes demonstrate the efficient use of appliances. They may also write pamphlets telling customers how to use and care for appliances.

Home economists also work in restaurant management and nutrition. Hospitals and other institutions provide many jobs in this field. Job responsibilities include planning menus for large numbers of people.

Banks and other financial institutions hire people to teach management skills to their customers. These managers advise consumers on budgeting, spending, and saving money.

There are many other management jobs in which training in home economics is useful. Hotel management, home products development, textile manufacture—in all these fields home economics skills and the ability to manage are important.

Business Management

Of course, the need for managers extends beyond the home economics fields. Industrial expansion and a growing population have created an increased demand for skilled managers. New shopping centers, apartment buildings, parks, and recreation centers all need managers. It has been estimated that by the early 1980s, there will be nearly eleven million people employed in management.

In large corporations, there are many levels of management. There are supervisors who oversee production work. There are middle managers who are responsible for particular projects or functions—finance, sales, and maintenance, for example. And there are top managers who set overall goals and see that everyone in the corporation works towards these goals.

Some firms hire industrial engineers, who study the way work is done and suggest how it can be done more efficiently. They may study how people work in a factory, or they may study how managers work together. Then they recommend more efficient work techniques, or more efficient management systems.

What Managers Do

Although the details vary with each management job, there are certain responsibilities that most managers have in common.

To help reach the company's goals, a good manager often meets with employees to discuss schedules and solve problems.

Good management involves planning for the future. By gathering and evaluating information, a manager can anticipate people's future wants and needs and plan for them effectively.

Managers are responsible for organizing people and resources to achieve certain goals. They decide how money will be spent and how employees will be placed in jobs. Seeing that a company's resources work together smoothly is one of a manager's most important responsibilities.

Managers often choose those who will work for them. Even the most carefully worked out plans will fail if the wrong people try to carry them out. A manager must try to find the best qualified person for each job.

A manager may also have to set up record-keeping systems. Records help a manager judge how well things are going and how closely a plan is being followed.

Communication is another skill essential to good management. Directing other people is often a major part of a manager's job. If a manager can't write well and speak effectively, he or she will have a hard time explaining to others what they are supposed to do.

Too Much Like Hard Work?

Anita Martin says that her job is challenging and tiring, but that she feels good about it. Managers sometimes take their responsibilities and their work home with them.

Long hours, frustration, and pressure are sometimes part of a manager's job. However, although managers are rarely paid for overtime work, they usually earn a good salary.

For many managers, there is the extra benefit of working with people. If you enjoy working with others, management may appeal to you. Managing other people is a big responsibility, but it can be a very rewarding career.

QUESTIONS

1. List and explain four skills necessary for success as a manager.
2. What kinds of businesses and organizations need managers? Why?
3. Describe the tasks involved in two different careers in the field of management.
4. If you were interested in a career in management, how could you start preparing for it now?
5. What do you think is the most difficult part of a manager's job? Why?

ACTIVITIES

1. The principal of your school is a manager. Invite your principal to speak to the class about the responsibilities of the job.
2. Check the job listings for managers in the classified section of your local newspaper. What kinds of qualifications are called for?
3. At your local library, obtain one of the pamphlets printed by the federal, state, or local government listing currently available civil service jobs. Report to your class on the different management jobs listed.

CHAPTER 5

You the Consumer

YOU, YOU AND YOU

People are consumers for most of their lives. From the time that toddlers begin to ask for toys and candies in the store, they help to make consumer decisions. Years ago, when a badly made toy you saw on TV fell apart the first day you had it, you made your first consumer discovery.

Important at Any Age

Now, of course, you are a much wiser consumer. But you probably also have more wants than you did back then. That record you just bought, that stereo you're saving for, those tennis lessons you're taking—these are all wants you didn't have a few years ago. Being a wise consumer is much more important now. And it will become still more important.

Up to now, most of what you ate, wore, and used was bought for you by others. But now, you may receive an allowance or have a part-time job. You may pay for some of your clothes, school supplies, and recreation. And as time goes on, you will be responsible for purchasing more and more of the things you want or need. Eventually, as an adult, you will be buying nearly *everything* for yourself and, possibly, for a family as well.

Careful consumer decisions today will develop your consumer skills for the future.

No matter who pays right now, though, you affect decisions about what to buy. You may help decide which restaurant your family chooses for dinner. You might ask for a certain kind of tennis racket for your birthday. Already, you take part in many consumer decisions.

As your life goes on, you will face many more—what, where, when, and how to buy, and why to buy at all. These are all very personal decisions.

The Consumer as an Individual

The qualities of a product or service are not the only things to consider when making a decision about buying. Clearly, your own feelings are important, too. What you buy should suit your own tastes. It should also suit your future goals and your resources.

Like most people, you probably have more than one goal, so you want a number of things. Again like most people, you probably have a limited amount of money to spend. That means you must make choices. These choices should be made on the basis of what is most important to you as an individual.

Two people on the same budget may make very different decisions when faced with the same choices. You and a friend, while out shopping, may be attracted to a display of calculators on sale. You like math and would enjoy owning a calculator. But you're saving for a backpack for your next camping trip. The backpack is more important to you than the calculator, so you pass up the chance to get one on sale.

Your friend, on the other hand, loves to do woodwork and plans to be a carpenter. The calculator will be useful for his hobby now, and maybe for his career later, so he buys one. Each of you has made a decision by setting priorities, or deciding what comes first.

Exercise your rights as a consumer by returning faulty goods.

The Consumer as a Citizen

Your consumer decisions about priorities can involve many people besides yourself. In a world where natural resources are running short, good consumer habits are important. As a good consumer, you can discourage faulty or wasteful products. You can refuse to buy them or tell the manufacturer about their shortcomings. In some areas, for example, consumers had laws passed to make soft drinks available only in returnable bottles. This saves many tons of aluminum a year. It also reduces litter.

A concerned citizen can bring a product's faults to the manufacturer's attention. Suppose your new tennis racket cracks after just a few weeks of use. If you write to the manufacturer, your letter may have several good effects besides a new racket for yourself. The manufacturer may be able to improve the product. That would bring satisfaction to the thousands of consumers who purchase the improved racket. Then the manufacturer's sales might increase.

And that would bring satisfaction to the manufacturer!

Improved products benefit not only consumers, but the environment as well. Good-quality products mean less waste of natural resources and human effort because they last a long time. If all buyers took the time and effort to be good consumers, the savings in energy and resources could mean a better world.

Consumers in a Changing World

Consumer skills are more important every year. Products and services are becoming harder to judge. Many are so complicated that only an expert can say how well made they are or how well they do the job they're supposed to do. And often there are so many varieties that making the best choice may seem impossible. Even the purchase of a simple loaf of bread can turn out to be difficult if you are faced with twenty different kinds of bread.

"Basic" items such as clothing and food are not so basic anymore. Today clothes are made from coal and oil as well as from cotton, wool, and silk. The new materials may look like the old ones, but they have very different qualities. More and more food is bought precooked and ready to serve. Sometimes people don't know exactly what they're buying.

In order to make sound consumer decisions, you need to know how to decide what to buy and where to look for information. You must learn to evaluate advertising, to compare prices, and to make your complaints heard. Consumer education can teach you these skills. And once you learn them, these skills will serve you for the rest of your life.

QUESTIONS

1. How do even very young children affect the consumer decisions of their families?
2. How will your role as a consumer change with time?
3. Explain the relationship between natural resources, the environment, and consumer decisions. Give an example of how consumers can affect the production of wasteful or harmful products.
4. What kinds of consumer decisions face you now that you didn't make five years ago?
5. Consumer decisions are a very personal matter. Think back to a recent purchase. What were your reasons for buying it? Which of those reasons are special to you as an individual, in that they matter very much to you as a person?
6. Can you think of any products that waste natural resources or harm the environment? What would be an alternative to each of these products?

ACTIVITIES

1. Ask five friends to list, in order of preference, the first ten things they would buy or do if they were suddenly given a large amount of money to spend. What does this show you about their goals and priorities? How do they compare with yours?
2. Go to your local supermarket and count the different kinds of bread displayed on the shelves. How would you choose from among them?
3. Make a collage that shows all the different kinds of consumer decisions you take part in, ranging from the snacks you eat to the clothes you wear.

SECTION 2· Plenty to Choose From

CHOICES, CHOICES, CHOICES

Whatever you want to buy, you usually have an enormous number of choices. There is a wide variety of brands from which to choose. Each brand probably has several different styles and sizes. And there is a large supply in each size. If you are buying services, too—having your hair cut, or getting your shoes fixed—there are many places to go. A wise consumer takes advantage of the choices, and isn't overwhelmed by them.

From socks to shoe polish, from ten-speed bikes to tennis rackets—no matter what you buy today, you face many choices. Which brand will you buy? There are usually many to choose from. Where will you buy? Drugstore or department store, supermarket or convenience store, or even through the mail—all these choices are open to you. How will you pay? You can pay cash for your purchase, charge it, or pay it off on the installment plan.

Consumers today have to make more decisions than ever before. Thousands of advertisers are trying to help us make up our minds about which product, which store, and which method of payment to choose. That is why it is especially important to become a wise consumer and learn as much about the marketplace as possible.

Marketplace Economy

Some countries have a free or **marketplace** economy. A marketplace economy means that people can sell anything, if they can find buyers.

Of course, this isn't strictly true. In the United States, for example, it's illegal to sell dangerous toys, or harmful cosmetics, or unsafe cars. There are laws about buying and selling to protect people's basic rights. But most decisions about what will be sold and bought are left to producers and consumers.

In other countries, the economy is **controlled** by the government. For example, a central committee in the Soviet Union decides what will be sold in that country. That makes a big difference in how the economy works. Since the people have very little say about what will be produced, they are often unable to satisfy their needs and wants. Manufacturers may be told to produce millions of pairs of brown boots in a

year when most people want other colors. That means one of two things: millions of pairs of unsold brown boots, or millions of people wearing boots they don't like.

Competition

In a marketplace economy, each manufacturer tries to produce what *consumers* need and want. If one manufacturer's product doesn't please you, you can buy another's. You have a great deal of choice, since manufacturers compete with one another for money.

Because of this competition, sellers are always looking for ways to attract customers to their own products and services. Advertising is one technique they use. They may also make their prices as low as possible.

To offer low prices, manufacturers must produce the product or service as efficiently as possible. In most cases, this means mass production.

Mass Production

Mass production is based on the idea that work goes faster when many people do just one task on each item being made. For example, you may be wearing a pair of blue jeans that was made by several people. One worker sewed only leg seams, another sewed only belt loops, while a third made the buttonholes.

Organizing a team of workers to make just *one* pair of jeans would be expensive. Mass production pays off only if large quantities of jeans will be made. With the help of special equipment, even a small group of workers can turn out hundreds of pairs of jeans a day.

If you compare that with the amount of time you would need to make one pair of

Some consumer goods, such as light bulbs, are needed in great quantities. Only mass production can meet the demand.

jeans at home, you can see how well mass production works. Mass production gives people both variety and quantity at prices they can afford.

Buying Markets

To sell all these mass-produced products, sellers must attract buyers. This is more difficult than it sounds, because consumers are not all interested in the same things. However, some groups of consumers have very similar needs and wants. So, to plan their sales, sellers divide consumers into different buying groups, or markets. Young parents, for example, are all interested in products for baby care. So sellers try to place diaper ads where the "young parents market" will see them.

One of the markets that sellers value highly is the teenage market. That's because the teenage market is a big one. In the United States, for example, it includes twenty-one million people aged fifteen to nineteen, and millions more aged thirteen to fifteen. That adds up to a lot of buying power!

The Teenage Market

Each year, in the United States alone, teenagers spend fifty billion dollars. It's hard even to imagine so much money! But suppose a six-dollar record album earns a gold record by selling a million copies. This means six million dollars in sales. When you think of all the other products that you and millions of others buy, you can see how quickly these sales add up.

Because of the impressive size of the

teenage market, manufacturers do everything they can to sell you their products. They design special products for you, such as medications to clear up acne. They advertise in the magazines you read and on the TV shows you watch. They pay a great deal of attention to your wants and needs. All this attention can have some unpleasant side effects.

Consumer Confusion

Since all these companies are competing for a share of the teenage market, you may be faced with a confusing selection of products. Many companies use advertising that tries to sell you products you don't really need or want.

Much of this advertising promises a lot.

How can you be sure that a toothpaste will give you whiter teeth and fresher breath? And can it really make you more popular with others? How can you know whether balsam or protein added to a shampoo really makes a difference in the way your hair looks? How can you decide whether a product *really* answers your wants or needs, or whether some company is trying to expand its market?

There is really only one way to be sure. And that is to learn as much as possible about the way our marketplace works. Only then will you be able to make satisfying decisions about what to buy. Only then will you get your money's worth. And only then will you be able to take best advantage of our plenty-to-choose-from marketplace economy.

QUESTIONS

1. Explain the basic difference between a marketplace economy and a controlled economy. Who decides what will be sold in each?
2. What are the benefits of competition to consumers? What are the problems?
3. Explain how mass production works.
4. Why are producers so interested in the teenage market? What are two techniques they use to attract this market?

ACTIVITIES

1. Write a story about two teenagers in a controlled economy who go shopping for a new _____. (Choose your own product.)
2. Look at a copy of a magazine aimed at teenagers. Make a list of all the products advertised in the magazine. How many different brands for each product are there? What general categories do these products fall into?

5. Name some products that are bought mainly by teenagers. Which ones do you think were created especially for teenagers?
6. Can you think of any examples of producers who guessed wrong about what products consumers would buy? What do you think happens to these products?
7. Do you think it would be a good idea for our economy to be more controlled? Why or why not?

Which of these categories do you think you would *not* find in a magazine aimed at adults? (Check this by looking through a popular adult magazine.)

3. Choose a product (it could be anything from cars to chewing gum) and find out how it is mass-produced. Then make a wall chart that shows the steps in its production, from raw material to finished product.

SECTION 3 · Giving You the Message

Reaching the Public

"Thank you very much, but I've always mowed my own lawn," Mr. Simpson said as he closed the door.

Lisa turned to walk away. Her shoulders were slumped and her feet were dragging. She was tired. She had tried every house on the street. Her plans to start a lawn-mowing business were not working out.

"I don't understand it," she thought. "There must be many people who need their lawns mowed. But where are they? Will I have to knock on every door in town to find them?"

Her thoughts were interrupted. A newspaper sailed by and landed on a front porch. She waved to Jimmy, and thought, "Maybe I should forget the lawn mowing and get a paper route. Everyone reads a newspaper." That's when the idea popped into her head. "A newspaper ad! That's it!"

Now Lisa was excited. She remembered how her aunt had placed an ad in the paper when she opened her art studio. Lisa, too, would use the newspaper to advertise her lawn-mowing services.

Lisa talked the idea over with her parents. Her mother offered to lend her the money for the ad. Lisa promised to pay the loan back out of the money she would earn.

Lisa's ad ran in the Sunday edition of the local newspaper:

> LAWN MOWING BY LISA. FAST SERVICE AT REASONABLE PRICE. SHADYBROOK AREA ONLY. CALL 532-9849.

Her phone started ringing on Sunday morning. By Tuesday, she had lined up nine lawns to mow. And her phone was still ringing.

Advertising worked for Lisa. It works for the large businesses which produce and sell goods. Through advertising, producers tell consumers about products and services they have to offer.

Why So Much?

Ads are everywhere. Radio programs, newspapers, and magazines are filled with them. Buses, subway cars, and taxis all carry advertising cards. As you ride along the highway, billboards urge you to buy things. As you walk through stores, special displays try to catch your eye. Even a product's package is designed to make you want to pick it up. The daily mail often brings advertising letters and catalogs. And just by watching television, an average viewer is exposed to more than 40,000 commercials a year.

Each year in North America, billions of dollars are spent on advertising. Businesses wouldn't spend that kind of money if they didn't think advertising was very important. And it is. People can't buy a product or service if they don't know it exists. So advertising is used to make people aware of a product and to persuade them to buy it.

Box 1

Mail Order and You

Mail-order companies sell their products through the mail instead of in stores. Some send out catalogs to advertise their products. Others advertise in newspapers or magazines, or on radio or television.

Mail-order companies allow you to shop at home. They may also offer products that aren't available in stores. Sometimes, too, mail-order prices are lower than those in stores. But ordering through the mail can involve problems.

The main problem is that you don't *see* the merchandise until it arrives. To order a product, you have to rely on drawings or photos and written descriptions.

Another problem is getting satisfaction if the product is damaged or disappointing, or doesn't arrive.

To avoid problems when ordering by mail, make sure that you are dealing with a reputable company. There are many honest mail-order firms. But there are also mail-order rackets. Some of these involve fake business opportunities, phony correspondence schools, and shoddy merchandise.

If you have any doubts about a company, check it out before ordering its product. Contact your local Better Business Bureau, chamber of commerce, or consumer protection office.

Who Pays?

The cost of advertising is almost always included in the price tag of the product or service. Paying an extra few cents, or even fractions of a cent, to cover the cost of advertising a product may not seem like much. But those fractions add up—fast.

In a recent year, for example, there were 56.7 million families in the United States. The total amount of money spent on all forms of advertising was at least thirty billion dollars. That works out to about 530 dollars per family, or 180 dollars a year for every man, woman, and child in the country.

Two Sides to the Coin

Is it fair to expect consumers to pay the cost of advertising? There are two sides to this issue.

One side claims that, without advertising, sellers couldn't reach as many buyers. This would mean sellers would have to charge higher prices because they would have to make a living selling fewer products. Also, advertising pays for almost all television and radio programming. When you consider this, you might think the cost of advertising is a bargain. And magazines and newspapers without ads would cost much more. Without advertising, you might spend more than 180 dollars a year on news and entertainment.

The other side argues that advertising doesn't exist to benefit consumers. Most businesses advertise because increased sales mean increased profits. Critics of advertising say that the many ads we see and hear each day convince us to buy more than we need or really want. They say that ads get us to place too much value on possessions. Also, they say, large companies have a big advantage over small companies because they can afford to advertise more. If small companies can't afford the high cost of advertising, they may go out of business. That could decrease competition and limit consumer choice.

Gentle Persuaders

Most criticism of advertising is aimed at the ways in which ads convince us to buy.

Since manufacturers want to increase sales, they often use ads to persuade people who don't really need their products to buy them anyway. They make what they are advertising appear very attractive, without telling the consumer anything very specific about it.

To make a product attractive, they suggest that it will help you in ways that have nothing to do with the product's real use. A shampoo ad, for example, may promise a lot more than clean hair. It may also suggest that using the shampoo will make you more popular. Such emotional appeals are used often by advertisers. Box 2 in this section shows how some ads appeal to your emotions instead of your mind.

In the Store

Advertisements aren't the only method stores and manufacturers use to persuade you to buy. With their colorful displays, attractive atmosphere, and appealing merchandise, many stores are pleasant places to be.

Department stores have restaurants and snack bars to keep the customer in the store and spending. Shopping malls provide play areas for children, special entertainment, and even art and antique shows. With so much going on, it's easy to forget how much money you are spending.

Companies may go to great lengths to get their names before the public. These unusual forms of advertising have become famous in their own right.

More Temptations

It's no accident that the first things you often see as you enter a clothing store are especially attractive, expensive-looking items. These are usually displayed in eye-catching ways. Scarves may be arranged in a rainbow pattern, or sweaters may be decorated with autumn leaves. The items in such a display usually earn the store a good profit. The display encourages people to buy them.

Suppose you intend to buy something in the budget department. You might stop to look at the display and buy an item then and there. So, instead of the bargain you intended to buy when you went into the store, you get an expensive item.

Box 2

AD APPEAL

MISLEADING COMPARISON

But shinier than what?

POPULARITY PLOY

Does popularity come in a toothpaste tube?

TESTIMONIAL

But is it right for you? And does the fact that John Dalton uses it make it better than a dryer he doesn't use?

IT'S THE GIFT THAT COUNTS

Do you need a ring to tell someone that you really care? And what about the ring's quality?

Color and style coordination also tempt people to buy. Jackets, pants, and sweaters that match are displayed together. Shoes are shown with matching handbags, wallets with key cases. These items look attractive together. The store hopes that the shopper will buy the whole outfit rather than just a single piece.

Lighting is another important selling tool. Sellers design their lighting to make merchandise look as good as possible. Used car dealers, for example, often use strings of bright lights to make the cars on the lot look shiny.

Even the way a product is packaged can have a big influence on buying decisions. Sellers know this and spend a great deal of time and money on package designs.

Remember when you shop that the important part of your purchase is not the package, but what's inside it. Avoid being tempted by ads and merchandise displays. Before you spend, ask yourself some questions. Do you *really* need or want the product on display? Are the ads you see true or misleading?

> ## People Pressure
> Box 3
>
> Ads and displays are not the only sales techniques. Salespeople—selling door to door or in stores—help persuade customers to spend their money. These tips can help you to avoid being pushed into unwise purchases.
>
> - Make a list before you shop. Sticking to a list helps you avoid *impulse buying*.
> - Listen carefully to the information the salesperson gives about a product. Ask questions and try to separate facts from emotional appeals.
> - Watch out if an advertised item is said to be out of stock and the salesperson tries to sell you something more expensive. You could be a victim of *bait and switch*, an illegal sales technique.
> - If you're unsure about a purchase, don't be pushed into buying it right away. Wait and think it over.
> - Don't feel that you must buy just because the salesperson has spent time with you. Salespeople are paid to help you whether you buy or not.

Keeping Advertising Honest

Most states have laws to control advertising and sales techniques. The advertising industry itself has set up standards for honest advertising. The Association of Better Business Bureaus and trade organizations also try to encourage fair ads. So do some independent consumer action groups.

The federal government keeps an eye on advertising through its Federal Trade Commission. The FTC has the power to make advertisers prove their claims. It welcomes reports from concerned citizens about advertising claims that seem to be false. If the claims can't be proved, the advertising must stop.

A few years ago, the FTC made one bread company stop advertising its product as a "diet" bread. The only reason that particular bread had fewer calories per slice than other brands was that the slices were thinner!

In some cases, the FTC requires companies to pay for advertising to correct the claims made by false ads.

You Are in the Driver's Seat

You are your own best protection against misleading ads and sales techniques. Be on your guard. Think about the product being promoted and the claims being made. Do the ads try to persuade you through the use of attractive pictures and appeals to your emotions? Do they offer any useful facts about the product?

An ad that gives you new information can be very helpful. But once you have studied the ad, try to find out more about the product itself. Ask your family and friends if they have ever used it. Check consumer magazines to see if the product has been tested.

After you have studied the product, you may then decide to buy it. And that's fine. Because you've looked into things yourself, you'll know that you're buying the product because *you* want it and not because the manufacturer or retailer wants to sell it to you.

QUESTIONS

1. List three ways advertising can help consumers. List three ways it can harm them.
2. Explain three approaches advertisers use to persuade people to buy. What can consumers do about false advertising?
3. How do stores encourage spending?
4. List four techniques you can use to avoid making unwise purchases.
5. If you had the power to control advertising, what changes would you make?
6. What kinds of emotional appeals do advertisers use to attract teenagers?
7. Have you bought anything on impulse recently? What convinced you to make the purchase?

ACTIVITIES

1. Turn Lisa's ad into a full-page magazine advertisement, using the kinds of appeals a professional advertiser might use. Illustrate the ad with drawings or photographs you cut out from newspapers and magazines.
2. Go to a local clothing store and make a chart that shows how the merchandise in one department is arranged. At the bottom of the chart, explain the reasons for this arrangement. Would you change anything? Why?
3. Pick a common classroom object and write a sales talk that would convince people to buy it.

SECTION 4 · Finding Out Before You Buy

JUDGING BY APPEARANCES

Buying was simpler a century ago. There were fewer products. People had little trouble judging how well something would work and whether it was worth the money.

Today things are different. We have products undreamed of 100 years ago. Many are so complicated that it's hard to tell how well they will work or whether they are good values. If you're buying a cassette player, just looking at it won't tell you if it's worth buying. You need sound information before you buy.

What you need to know, of course, depends on what you're buying. For some purchases—especially inexpensive ones—you may already know enough to make a wise decision. For a small purchase such as a note pad, for example, it may not be worth the time it takes to shop around.

For larger purchases, though, it makes sense to ask yourself some questions before you buy. How well does the product work? How do the different brands compare? What should I look for before buying? Is it really worth what they're charging?

Consumers who don't know how to answer these questions are spending their money carelessly. Without this kind of information, it's almost impossible to make a wise decision.

Fortunately, there are many places consumers can find the information they need. Among these are the advertisements and promotional brochures produced by many manufacturers.

Some advertisements make you aware of the features or main qualities of a particular product. They give you an idea of what the product sells for and where to buy it. Ads can give you important knowledge. But they rarely tell you all you need to know.

Ask Your Friends

Friends and relatives who have already bought a particular product are another source of information.

Suppose you want to buy a ten-speed bicycle. You've found a model with all the features you want. But you're not sure if it's a good buy. If you have a friend who has owned that model for a couple of years, you have a good source of information.

Ask your friends what they like or dislike about a product, where they bought it, and how they made their choice. You might be able to learn from their experiences. You may even be able to borrow the product itself for a while to see how you like it.

Read All About It

It isn't always possible to borrow a product or to ask someone else about it. And even when it is, you may not get the information you need.

You can sometimes get excellent, up-to-date information from consumer magazines. You can get these magazines through subscriptions, at a newsstand, and usually at your school or local library. For advice on how to find and use them, see box 1 in this section.

Consumer magazines test a wide variety of products and services and publish the results. They report on services ranging from medical care to auto repair. They also provide information on products from ice cream to suntan lotion. In particular, they often compare different manufacturers' versions of the same product.

Consumer magazines avoid any relationship with manufacturers so they can be fair. Most are published by nonprofit groups, and they refuse to accept any advertising. They send unidentified shoppers into stores to buy the products to be tested. That way they choose from the same range of quality available to everyone.

Shop Around

Collecting information before you buy is important. But once you have information about a product, there's really no substitute for seeing it yourself.

Go to a store and look at the product. If possible, try it out or try it on. Examine it closely and study the quality of work. If it's a bicycle, for example, test the comfort of the seat. Examine the brakes to see how well they are made and how smoothly they work. Check the gear shift, the strength of the frame, the paintwork.

Labels may also help you decide on the quality of the product, as well as tell you how to care for it. Compare several brands or models. Ask the salesperson any questions you may still have about the product. And check to see if there's a warranty.

Get the Best Price

Once you've decided on the best brand, the

Box 1

Using Consumer Magazines

Before you go shopping, you may wish to find out if consumer magazines rate the product you're looking for. Here's how you do it.

At your library, ask for the most recent issue of *Consumers Index*. This magazine, published four times a year, lists by topic all articles in the major consumer magazines.

Suppose you are gathering information on bicycles. Turn to the back of *Consumers Index*. The topics in the index there are listed alphabetically.

Look up the word "bicycles," and then turn to the page indicated. There you will find a list of the articles on bicycles published in the last three months. You will also find a brief summary of each article. The summary will be followed by the magazine's name, volume number, date, and the page number of the article. Make a note of the articles that interest you.

If you cannot find enough articles in *Consumers Index*, ask the librarian to help you find other consumer reference materials.

Once you know which magazines contain the information you need, you can find them in the library. Reading these articles will help you compare various brands.

The two leading consumer magazines listed in *Consumers Index* are *Consumer Reports* and *Consumers' Research*. These magazines test products, and they also include general advice to consumers.

Consumer Reports provides point-by-point factual information on how various brands compare when tested. It often selects certain brands as "best buys."

A toaster test!

Consumers' Research also rates brand-name products on the basis of their performance in tests. Products are rated with letters from A (Recommended), to C (Not Recommended).

Other magazines also focus on general consumer information, though they don't actually test products. *Consumer Digest* and *Changing Times*, for example, publish articles such as "How to Buy a Car at a Discount." Articles like this may tell you how much profit a seller is making. If you know this, you may be able to tell whether or not you're getting a bargain. The articles may also tell you what time of year certain products are sold at the lowest prices.

Even popular magazines have articles on consumer issues. Many run monthly columns offering general consumer advice. Some of them rate products, too.

The federal government is another source of consumer information. Many publications are either free or available at a small charge. *The Consumer Information Catalog* lists many of these pamphlets and booklets. You can find it at your local library.

next step is to shop for the best price. Prices may vary from store to store for the same item.

While shopping for the lowest possible price, you should consider each store's reputation. Find out whether your friends have shopped there, and how well the store has treated them. It's worth paying a bit more for some products if a store offers outstanding service or a money-back guarantee. Some stores are more willing to exchange products or refund money than others. If a store guarantees the quality of its products, you are more likely to be satisfied.

Studying a purchase thoroughly takes more effort than buying the first thing you see. But finding out all you can *before* buying will help you make a wiser decision.

You'll make fewer buying mistakes and get more for your money.

Evaluating Your Purchases

Careful shopping habits will greatly improve your chances of being happy with what you buy. Yet even wise consumers make mistakes sometimes. What's important is that you learn from your mistakes.

Suppose you've had a transistor radio for a while. Ask yourself whether you're still pleased with it. Is the sound quality as good as you had expected? Are the switches convenient, or is it too easy to leave in an *on* position? Do you still think it's worth the money you spent for it? If you wish you'd made another choice, try to figure out why.

Evaluating purchases is a smart way to improve your consumer skills.

QUESTIONS

1. List three sources of consumer information. What kinds of knowledge can you learn from each?
2. Why is it a good idea to shop around before making a final decision about a product?
3. What questions can you ask yourself to help you learn from past purchasing mistakes?

ACTIVITIES

1. Call different stores in your area to find out the price of a specific brand of a product that you are interested in buying. Also ask about each store's return policy. Discuss the results of your survey with your class.
2. Bring to class an unsuccessful purchase you recently made. Explain why you aren't

4. Why do you think some stores will not tell consumers prices over the phone?
5. What would you do if you received conflicting advice from friends about a particular product?
6. Are there any situations in which it might be wise to make a major purchase without shopping around?

pleased with it. How would you go about making a similar purchase in the future?
3. Using a consumer magazine as your guide, make up a list of all the things you would test if you were writing an article on "The Best Buy in Roller Skates." Also describe any special equipment you would design to help you make your tests.

SECTION 5 · Making Your Complaints Heard

WATCH OUT!

Mr. John Jensen
Manager
Jensen Jewelers
    The watch I bought at your store is defective. It doesn't keep the right time. Please send me a refund as soon as possible.

Yours truly,
Barbara Palateno

Ms. W. R. Miller
President
Tick Tock Watch Co.
Dear Ms. Miller:
    A week ago I bought a watch made by your company. The watch was sold by Jensen Jewelers here in town. (a copy of the sales slip is enclosed.)
    Your watches are known to be of good quality, so I am surprised that the one I bought doesn't work right. Even though I have followed the directions for setting the time, my watch loses ten minutes each day.
    I think that I should get either a refund or a new watch. I would like your help in this matter.
    Thank you for your time and attention.

Sincerely,
Alan Yamashita

Customer Service Department
Tick Tock Watches, Inc.
Dear Customer Service Department:
    I have just bought a watch made by your company near where I live. I have had it for only a week, and it is always ten minutes slow.
    I believe that there is something wrong with the watch and would like a refund..
    I am sending you a copy of my sales slip and hope to hear from you soon.

Juan Ramirez

- Put yourself in the place of the person receiving each of these letters. How would you react in each case?
- Which letter do you think will get the best results? Which the worst? Why?
- If you bought a defective watch, what would be your first step in trying to get satisfaction? If that failed, what might you do next?

There are close to 240 million people in the United States and Canada. There are hundreds of thousands of companies and stores. You might think that one lone consumer is powerless to get satisfaction when he or she has a problem.

Consumers do have power, though. If you know how to make a complaint, and are willing to spend a little time and energy doing so, you can usually get satisfaction. Manufacturers and stores usually take complaints seriously. Many respond to them quickly.

Why Sellers Listen

If no one had complained, the watchmaker at the beginning of this section might not have known about the defective watches. That would have been very bad for the company. Sooner or later, people would have stopped buying the company's watches because they didn't keep time. A customer's complaints can help a company correct a problem or produce a better product.

Stores also realize that a satisfied consumer is good for business. You probably prefer to shop at stores that will exchange things or give you a refund without an argument. By caring about consumer problems and complaints, a store builds a good reputation. And a good reputation may earn thousands of dollars in increased sales.

When Should You Complain?

Before you complain, make sure your complaint is fair. Suppose you throw a wool sweater into the washing machine when the care instructions read: "Dry clean only." If the sweater shrinks, you have no right to complain.

On the other hand, suppose the tag reads: "Machine wash in warm water, machine dry at low temperature." If you follow these instructions and the sweater shrinks, then you have every right to a refund or a new sweater.

Whenever you buy merchandise that is defective or doesn't perform the way it should, you have a fair complaint.

How to Complain

Once you decide that you have good reason to complain, you should do so promptly. The longer you've had an item, the harder it might be to get a replacement.

Find the sales receipt if you can, and also any warranty which came with the product. Write down exactly what is wrong with the product. Then you will be ready to complain. (For information on warranties, see box 1 in this section. You should always try to save both your warranty and your sales slip. To be protected under some warranties, you may have to prove that you bought the product before a certain date or that you are the original owner.)

Usually, the first step in making a complaint is to take the item back to where you bought it. If it's a big department store, go to the department where you made your purchase. A salesperson there may help you solve your problem on the spot. Or you may be directed to the store manager.

If the store manager doesn't satisfy your complaint, you can contact a consumer agency. These agencies help consumers with their problems. They can help you decide what to do next. Occasionally, they may investigate a complaint themselves, especially if it seems the law was broken.

You can find the names of consumer agencies in the phone book. Check the white pages under the name of your city, county, or state.

Your Rights as a Buyer

Box 1

IMPLIED WARRANTIES

As a consumer in the United States, you do have certain rights and protections by law. These are called implied warranties.

Implied warranties are not stated in writing. They are automatic and apply to each purchase you make. Some can be canceled only if the seller informs you that you are buying "as is." Otherwise, the seller must guarantee certain things.

For example, if you buy an umbrella, you can assume that the seller is not offering you stolen goods. The umbrella must also do what it's supposed to do—keep off the rain. And if you're buying from a sample model, the umbrella you receive must be exactly the same as the one you saw in the store. This also applies to mail-order purchases. The umbrella you receive must be exactly the same as the one pictured and described in the ad.

If the umbrella you buy isn't the same as the sample, or if it lets the rain soak through, or if it wasn't the seller's to sell—then you have a legal right to get your money back. These rules are implied warranties, backed by law.

There are other implied warranties. They generally differ from state to state.

EXPRESSED WARRANTIES

Written promises are called expressed warranties. They are also often called guarantees. In an expressed warranty, the manufacturer or retailer promises certain things about the quality, performance, and condition of the product.

LIMITED WARRANTY

Schwinn and Schwinn-Approved bicycles, parts and accessories are warranted to be free from defects in materials and workmanship...no time limit. Schwinn will replace...without charge...any Schwinn or Schwinn-Approved part or accessory that is determined by the factory to be defective under the terms of this warranty.

NOTICE: The user assumes the risk of any personal injuries, damage to or failure of the bicycle and any other losses if Schwinn bicycles are used in any competitive event, including bicycle racing, or in bicycle motocross, dirt biking or similar activities, or training for such competitive events or activities. DO NOT USE Schwinn bicycles for stunt riding, ramp jumping, acrobatics or similar activities, or with motors as power driven vehicles. This Warranty does not cover any personal injuries, damage to or failure of the bicycle or any other losses due to accident, misuse, neglect, abuse, normal wear, improper assembly or improper maintenance.

An expressed warranty often makes a product more desirable. For example, you would probably prefer to buy a bicycle that has a three-year warranty than a bicycle without one. You might even be willing to pay a little more for it, since the warranty gives you some insurance against a big repair bill later on.

Companies are not legally *required* to give expressed warranties. However, if they are offered, warranties must be expressed in ordinary language and printed in clear, readable type. And for products costing more than fifteen dollars, warranties must be displayed in the store for you to look at before you buy.

Both kinds of warranties—implied and expressed—offer you protection. Knowing what is covered, and what isn't, can help you avoid disappointment.

Writing a Letter of Complaint

A consumer agency might suggest that you write to the store president or to the company that manufactured the item.

If you write a letter, it's a good idea to find out the name of the person you want to contact. A letter addressed to "Ms. Joan Smith, President, Towne Shops," for example, will have more impact than one sent simply to "President, Towne Shops." A librarian can help you find reference books that list the names of company officers.

Box 2

THE TEENAGE CONSUMER

As a teenager, you may feel that people in stores won't listen to you. This is sometimes true, but most stores are eager to please. They know that teenagers spend over 50 billion dollars each year, and they want your business.

So when you have a complaint, don't remain silent. Politely bring your problem to the attention of the store or manufacturer.

Many people feel that it takes special courage to complain in person at a store. Here are some tips for getting the best results.

• STATE YOUR PROBLEM CLEARLY

Plan what you want to say ahead of time. If you are well prepared, you'll feel more confident. Say when you bought the item and exactly what your problem is. Be businesslike. Don't beat around the bush.

• STATE YOUR PROBLEM PLEASANTLY

There is no reason to get angry. The store has probably made an honest mistake, and you are simply calling it to the salesperson's attention. Getting angry wastes your energy. Besides, the person you get angry with might become angry with you and refuse to help solve your problem.

• LISTEN TO THE OTHER SIDE

Tell the person representing the company your side of the story. If she or he agrees that your complaint is fair, the solution is easy.

There may be times when a company representative does not agree with you. When this happens, listen to the other side of the story. You may find that your complaint is not fair after all. In this case, you should consider dropping the complaint. If you expect to be treated fairly, you, too, must have a fair attitude.

Even if you do everything right, you may find that your complaint is being ignored. If you think this is because of your age, ask your parent or some other adult to help you press your complaint. As a consumer, you have a right to get what you pay for.

Your letter should state where and when you bought the product and why you are dissatisfied. If your letter is not answered within a couple of weeks, call your local consumer agency for advice.

When All Else Fails

If contacting the store or the manufacturer, or both, does not produce results, there are other ways to get satisfaction.

Newspapers and radio and television stations are sometimes interested in doing stories on consumer problems. Perhaps you could write to a consumer reporter, or call an action line. Publicity can force an unwilling company to deal promptly with a complaint.

Finally, if no other method works, you can sue a company in court. This doesn't always cost a lot. If you aren't suing for a large sum of money, you can pay a small fee and get a hearing in a small claims court. You won't need a lawyer.

In court, you and a representative of the company explain your sides to a judge. If the judge orders the company to pay you, you will finally have satisfaction.

Sticking with It

Making a consumer complaint and getting action may take time and energy. If your complaint isn't taken care of the first time you make it, you may have to keep on complaining until it is.

Some businesses hope that if they ignore a complaint, the consumer will get tired and give up. To most companies, though, a consumer's complaint and warning of further action means there's a problem. Once it becomes clear that you have no intention of giving up, a business may solve your problem quickly.

QUESTIONS

1. How can stores benefit from taking care of consumer complaints as effectively as possible? Why are they especially interested in listening to teenagers?
2. What is the buyer's responsibility in making a complaint?
3. What two things should you do *before* you complain? What should you include in a good letter of complaint?
4. When you have a complaint, whom should you contact first? What can you do if that person does not satisfy your complaint?
5. Have you ever been dissatisfied with a purchase? What did you do about it?
6. One large department store has a policy of accepting merchandise for return that was *not* purchased there. Why do you think the store does this?
7. Why is it harder to get satisfaction for a complaint the longer you keep an item?
8. Why is it a good idea to be polite when stating a complaint?

ACTIVITIES

1. Write a letter of complaint to the manufacturer about a record that skipped the first time you played it. Give your letter to a classmate, and discuss how you could make the letter even more effective.
2. Make a survey of local consumer agencies to find out (a) how many complaints they receive a month, (b) what general categories these complaints fall into, (c) how many and what kinds of complaints they take individual action on, and (d) how often they get results from their action. (Feel free to add other questions to your survey.)
3. Attend a session of small claims court and describe the session to your class.

SECTION 6 · Consumer Power / Consumer Responsibility

WHO PAYS?

"No matter how hard I try," sighs Marianne, "things keep getting damaged. And the shoplifting is getting worse, too."

Marianne Best works as a salesperson at a clothing store called Riverdale Casuals. She tries hard to keep the clothes in good condition, but customers keep undoing her work. They knock suits and dresses off the racks, get makeup on sweaters, and tear seams by trying on clothes that are too small.

"Don't these customers care at all?" she says. "Between damages and shoplifting, we've had to raise prices. That hurts business. And it hurts our good customers, too."

"This shirt is just what I want, but I'm not paying $15.95 for it. Everytime I come in here, the prices are higher. What a ripoff!"

Paul Sutphen is annoyed and disappointed. Riverdale Casuals is his favorite place to shop. None of the other stores in town has such a good selection. But now he feels he's being taken advantage of. Many of his friends feel the same way. A group of them get together and agree not to shop at Riverdale Casuals until the store lowers its prices.

"My customers don't understand my problems at all!" complains the owner of Riverdale Casuals.

Carol Dubois is a worried woman. She has heard that a group of customers have decided not to shop at her store until prices are lowered. But she can't lower prices while her losses from customer damage and shoplifting continue to rise. In fact, she may even have to increase prices because she may have to hire a security guard. She feels very discouraged. "What in the world can I do if customers won't realize that they have a responsibility, too?"

Each of these people has a problem. How are their problems related? How might their problems be solved?

These people have related problems. Paul's problem—higher prices—is the result of Marianne and Carol's problem—losses from damage and shoplifting. If the problem isn't solved, Marianne could lose her job, Carol could lose her business, and Paul could lose his favorite place to shop. Paul does have a right to reasonable prices. But Carol also has a right to a reasonable profit.

The relationship between seller and consumer isn't always as simple as it seems. Sellers and consumers both have power. Sellers have the power to sell whatever they want. They also have the power to set prices. But consumers, too, have power. If the buyer-seller relationship is to work, both sides must use their power fairly.

Dollar Power

Consumers have dollar power. If people didn't buy their products, manufacturers and retailers couldn't exist. They wouldn't be able to pay people to work for them. They wouldn't be able to develop new products or advertise. Because you spend money, companies stay in business.

An individual decision not to shop in a certain store affects that store's business. Paul Sutphen used his dollar power when he decided not to shop at Riverdale Casuals. And when he convinced his friends to stop shopping there as well, his decision affected the store's business even more. Consumers can add to their dollar power when they convince others to stop dealing with a store. This is known as a boycott.

Consumer dollar power can also work in favor of a store. Each time you recommend a store or a product to someone, you're giving the seller a little free advertising. Your recommendation probably increases sales.

Your Opinion Counts

Stores know the impact of recommendations. When consumer magazines rate a product, the top-rated brand often quickly disappears from the shelves. Brands that receive low ratings may remain in the stores unsold.

When you follow the advice of a friend or the recommendation of a consumer magazine, you cast a vote for a product. Manufacturers know that individuals like you add up, so they pay close attention to what you buy. Knowing what you buy helps them in developing new products and improving old ones.

A boycott is using consumer power to pressure companies to improve faulty goods, poor services, or unfair policies.

Store owners, too, care about what people think. They know that a bad reputation can cost them many sales. The owner of Riverdale Casuals, for example, was very concerned about Paul Sutphen's complaint.

Being Fair to Sellers

When Paul decided to boycott Riverdale Casuals, he was using dollar power. But was he using it fairly?

If Paul and his friends had understood the reasons for the price increases, perhaps they would not have boycotted the store. After all, the price increases were really caused by consumers—the small number of customers who steal and damage clothes.

When consumers use their dollar power to complain, they have a responsibility to be fair toward sellers.

Being fair also means treating a store's merchandise with care. Until you pay for an item, it belongs to the store. It's okay to pick up a sweater, examine it, and try it on. But if you damage the sweater, the store won't be able to sell it. Losses from damage usually result in higher prices for all consumers.

Shoplifting costs you. Prices are raised to pay for TV monitors and guards.

Customers who shoplift are unfair both to stores and to other consumers. In North America, dishonest customers steal more than ten million dollars' worth of merchandise *every day!* This means that stores have to spend extra money on security equipment, store detectives, and insurance against losses.

Being fair with sellers means pointing out mistakes made in your favor—such as getting too much change. If you get more change than you should, especially on a high-priced item, you may feel good. But remember, all consumers will suffer because stores have to charge higher prices to make up for dishonest customers.

Be fair when you use credit, too. Credit plans are based on trust between the consumer and the seller. If people don't pay their bills, stores lose money.

More Than Dollar Power

Besides the power of their dollars, consumers have legal rights. Legal rights are based on consumers' power as voters.

Laws concerning consumer rights, and agencies to protect those rights, are created by elected officials. When you vote for candidates who agree with you about consumer issues, you will be voting for laws and agencies that protect your interests.

The effects of a book called *The Jungle* are an early example of how voter power works. In 1906, Upton Sinclair wrote about the unsanitary conditions in meat-packing firms. The facts in his book angered consumers. As a result of their anger, laws were passed. These laws forced the meat-packing industry to use more sanitary methods. The United States Food and Drug Administration (FDA), a government agency that tests and inspects products, was formed at that time.

Box 1

Consumer Rights

In 1962, the United States federal government officially recognized consumer rights in a speech by President John F. Kennedy. This "declaration of rights" included the following:

- The right to safety—to be protected against products that are dangerous to health or life.
- The right to be informed—to be protected against false and misleading information, and to be given the facts needed to make informed choices.
- The right to choose—to be guaranteed a selection of products and services at competitive prices, whenever possible.
- The right to be heard—to know that consumer interests will be given careful consideration by the government at all times.

Other agencies besides the FDA are now at work to protect your rights. Federal and state agencies protect you from dirty food, unsafe products, and false or misleading advertising. These agencies help protect your rights as a consumer and add to your power in the marketplace.

As a consumer, you have the legal right to complain to these agencies. You also have the power to take complaints about sellers to court. But you have a responsibility to be fair. Bringing unfair complaints to a court or an agency takes time away from those who really deserve attention.

A Balance of Power

All power isn't on the side of consumers. Industry has a voice in government, too. It's a powerful voice, made strong by careful organization and large sums of money. Industries hire people to present their views to lawmakers. These people lobby, or try to convince, government officials to pass laws favorable to industry.

Government has the responsibility of trying to balance power between consumers and sellers. It is this balance that makes the buyer-seller relationship work.

QUESTIONS

1. List three types of consumer power and three types of seller power.
2. Describe two consumer responsibilities. How do irresponsible consumers harm others?
3. What are the four basic consumer rights? Name two things you can do when you think your consumer rights have been violated.

4. What do you think would happen if buyers became much more powerful than sellers? What would happen if sellers became much more powerful than buyers?
5. What do you think Paul and his friends could do to help the situation at Riverdale Casuals?
6. What consumer rights would you add to the list in box 1 of this section?

ACTIVITIES

1. Make an illustrated poster with a slogan that reminds people to act responsibly in stores.
2. Find out how the work of the FDA has expanded over the years and write a report on your findings.
3. Interview the manager of a local store about the shoplifting problem. Ask how much merchandise the store loses each month and how that affects prices. Ask what security methods the store uses to cut down on its losses. Has the store become stricter over the years in the way it handles shoplifters? Why?

SECTION 7 · Consuming and the Future

What Will the Future Bring?

As any science fiction writer will tell you, predicting the future is difficult. But just for the fun of it, let's give it a try. Think about each of the following questions. Try to use what you know of the world today to predict the world of tomorrow.

- Space flight, color television, and instant photography didn't exist fifty years ago. But today we take them for granted. What other products and inventions can you name that didn't exist fifty years ago?
- What products do you think people might buy twenty years from now? For example, what kind of food will people eat? What kind of clothes will they wear? What will they do for fun?
- What products and services would you like to see become available in the next ten years?
- What effect do you think the products of the future will have on consumers? What problems might these products cause?

Making predictions is very difficult. There are so many unknowns. So many unexpected things can happen. It's impossible to say exactly what the future will bring.

This much, however, is certain: the future will be different. For consumers, this could mean a great number of new products, as well as new ways of buying them. It could also mean new problems.

Consumer interests may need more protection. That could mean more consumer laws and more powerful consumer organizations. It could also mean a different relationship among consumers, producers, and government.

Environment

One very important concern of the future will be the long-term effects new products will have on the environment. Pollution has increased a great deal in this century. And resources such as oil and natural gas, which once appeared limitless, seem to be running out at an alarming rate.

In the future, manufacturers, consumers, and government may have to make joint decisions. A new product may have short-term advantages—pleasure for consumers, profit for manufacturers. But will it really improve our lives if it severely damages the environment? We might be better off in the long run without such a product.

Today you would be surprised to find jetports, monorails, and moving sidewalks in your local shopping center, but in the year 2000—who knows?

New Ways to Package, New Ways to Pay

Concern for the environment might make it necessary to change our methods of packaging. Products such as food and personal care items might be sold in refillable containers. Instead of throwing empty packages away, we might take them to the stores for refills.

The future could also bring new ways to pay. It might not be necessary to carry money. Many bankers predict a cashless, checkless society. Others think cash will be used only for small purchases.

Instead of paying cash, you might use a system such as Electronic Funds Transfer. Under this plan, all stores and banks would be linked by computer. To buy something, you would hand the salesclerk a plastic card. A machine connected to the computer would read the card. Then the computer would instantly subtract the amount of the purchase from your bank account.

Many banks favor cashless buying. But some consumers have doubts about how well it will work. They think they would lose control of their money under an Electronic Funds Transfer system. They also worry about computer error and computer fraud.

New Products, New Choices

Choosing how to spend our money may be harder in the future. Products are already so complex, it's sometimes hard to choose wisely. We almost need to be electronics experts to decide which microwave oven, digital clock, or calculator to buy.

Tomorrow's products may require even harder decisions. For example, computer-run robots already exist. It's probably only a matter of time before they are mass-produced at prices most consumers can afford. How will we choose the best robot for our money?

Science may also develop more computer-controlled machines for *producing* goods. Such machines may be able to make many styles of a product as cheaply as they now turn out a single mass-produced style. Imagine if you had 5,000 styles to choose from when you bought a T-shirt! You might suffer from what one writer has called overchoice—too much to choose from.

Some Things Never Change

Some things, however, will always be the same. The rules you use to make a wise buying decision today will help you buy wisely tomorrow. There will be little difference between buying a transistor radio now and buying a home computer in the future. Comparing brands, shopping around for the lowest price, and carefully reading the guarantee will always be important.

As long as there are consumers, there will also be dishonest people who try to cheat them. So the fight for consumer protection will go on.

As a consumer, you will always be responsible for your own satisfaction. Laws will help protect you. Various organizations will supply you with information. But no amount of outside help can guarantee your personal satisfaction. Being a wise consumer will always be up to you.

QUESTIONS

1. Describe a decision-making process for new products to be produced in the future. Why might such a process be necessary? Who would be involved in the decision? What questions might have to be answered before a new product is produced?
2. What new shopping and paying techniques

might exist in the future? What concerns do consumers already have about some of these changes?

3. What consumer skills will you probably need in the future?

4. Do you think consulting consumers about what products to produce would tend to in-

crease or decrease the number of products on the market? Why?

5. How do you think overchoice will affect consumers in the future? Do you think overchoice already exists?

6. How might having a home robot change people's lives in the future?

ACTIVITIES

1. Make a list of existing products that you think would not be accepted by a "new products committee" of the future. Explain your choices.

2. Write a skit in which two teenagers of the future go to a store to buy a T-shirt, and discover that they have to choose from among 5,000 on display.

SECTION 8 · Careers in Consumerism

SMASHING FOR SAFETY

Can you imagine a job where you see this kind of crash every day? This is a safety test at an automobile proving ground. Major car manufacturers have their own proving grounds. Several other groups too test cars at such grounds for safety, endurance, and performance. Engineers, technicians, mechanics, and drivers work together in these tests. The result is a safer product and a more satisfied consumer.

Consumerism, the drive for consumer protection, is a fairly new field. Its roots go back to the early 1900s, when the public complained about the poor quality of meat.

Since that time, the field of consumerism has grown. Jobs are available in government, industry, public service, and the media—newspapers, magazines, television, and radio.

Some of these jobs are concerned with the safety of products and services. Some provide consumers with the information they need to buy wisely. There are also jobs to create and develop new products. And there are jobs to see that the wants and needs of consumers are heard by the government and by producers of goods and services.

Keeping Consumers Safe

Since the meat-packing scandal of 1906, thousands of field inspectors, special investigators, and product testers have been employed by government, industry, and consumer groups. These workers help safeguard the consumer's health and safety.

Food and drug inspectors, for example, work for the United States Food and Drug Administration (FDA). Some visit food-processing plants to see if foods are being prepared in a sanitary manner. Others spend their time in laboratories. They conduct scientific tests to see if various foods, drugs, cosmetics, and household products are safe to use.

Product testers also test products by using them as consumers will. For example, to judge a hair dryer, it's not enough to examine how safely it is built. People also want to know how well it dries hair. These testers may be home economists, engineers, or chemists.

Keeping Consumers Informed

Testing and inspecting products and places where products are produced helps consumers only if they hear about it. Many workers are employed simply to keep consumers informed.

Magazines, newspapers, radio, and television have consumer advisers and reporters. They present information on a wide variety of topics such as local consumer laws, best buys in food, and gas mileage in cars.

State and local governments also hire people to keep the public informed. Consumer education specialists, often with home economics training, give advice on community resources and services directed to the family. They also study the effect of laws on the family as a consumer unit. Consumer education specialists share their information with the public through lectures, workshops, and pamphlets on consumer affairs.

Public health inspectors check eating places to make sure they are sanitary.

Writers are needed in the field of consumerism. The United States government alone publishes almost 30,000 different pamphlets on consumer concerns. Many businesses have public relations departments that prepare pamphlets for their customers.

Workers in all these jobs keep consumers informed on everything from how to judge a sewing machine to how to find a good auto mechanic. With their help, consumers can make wiser choices in the marketplace.

Giving Consumers a Choice

Perhaps when you got home from school yesterday, a sample of a new toothpaste was hanging on your front door knob. If so, you were just given another choice in the marketplace, thanks to the work of people known as new product developers. These workers, often home economists, invent ideas for new products.

The idea itself is just the beginning, however. Developing a product requires great patience. Often many test models are thrown away before a workable one is developed. That new toothpaste, for example, may have gone through dozens of versions before it reached you.

Some workers help give consumers choices by making sure that all producers have an equal chance to sell their goods. Government agencies such as the United States Federal Trade Commission (FTC) employ lawyers, economists, and marketing specialists to guarantee competition in the marketplace. The FTC needs people who know how products are produced, advertised, and sold. It also needs consumer protection specialists to investigate business practices and deal with consumer groups.

Box 1

A Tough Test

In recent tests of bicycles, engineers decided to duplicate real-use conditions. They recruited two eleven-year-old boys to put the bikes through their paces. The engineers took careful notes on the handling ease of each bike. They noted braking distance on wet and dry roads, and how the bikes reacted to some typical hard knocks. The two boys were even asked to run the bikes into a curb so the engineers could test the strength of the frame.

When the engineers had learned all they could in the field, they took the bikes back to the lab. There they took them apart to test the safety of the construction.

It often takes months to test a product fully. The testers must be both patient and creative. Above all, they must never forget that people's lives may depend on the results of their work.

Helping Consumers Be Heard

Most companies have customer relations departments. Here workers, called adjustment clerks, handle complaints and pass on suggestions sent in by consumers. Better Business Bureaus employ representatives who deal with consumer problems and suggestions on a local level.

Local newspapers may have consumer complaint columnists. If members of the public let them know of a complaint, they may investigate and try to solve the problem.

Many communities have bureaus that handle consumer complaints. These bureaus often help people who have complaints against the government. They may also help people with complaints against a private industry. The public advocates and consumer affairs officers who work in these bureaus must know the laws about consumer rights. They must also have an interest in helping people. Many lawyers, law students, and other young people work for these services. They find solving consumer problems very satisfying.

What You Need for the Job

Consumerism attracts people with different backgrounds and skills. There are jobs that call for writing or legal skills. There are also jobs that require a strong background in science. Some jobs place more stress on the ability to deal with people.

Many high schools and colleges now offer courses in consumerism. Experts predict that jobs in consumerism will continue the growth that began in the 1960s.

If you're interested in the field of consumerism, there are already many opportunities. And as consumerism becomes a more powerful force in society, there may be even greater opportunities in the future.

QUESTIONS

1. How and when did consumerism become a career field?
2. In what four ways do different jobs in the field of consumerism protect the rights of consumers?
3. Describe the steps in the development of a new product. Who informs the public about the product? Who makes sure the product is safe to use? What kind of background is needed for each of these jobs?
4. How do you think our lives would differ if the field of consumerism did not exist?
5. Which job in the field do you find most interesting and why?

ACTIVITIES

1. Clip out a consumer information column or article from your local newspaper. What kind of research do you think the reporter had to do before writing the article?
2. Find out what kinds of courses in consumerism your local college or junior college offers. What kinds of backgrounds do the instructors of these courses have? How many courses in consumerism did the school offer five years ago? Is it planning more for the future? What kinds of people usually take these courses?

CHAPTER 6

Home Is Where You Live

SECTION 1 · Homes and Their Functions

Visitor from the Planet Lorana

Suppose for a moment that you live on a wonderful planet called Lorana. It's never too hot or too cold there. It never rains. Plants get all the water they need from the soft, rich earth.

Food is plentiful. Whenever you're hungry, you reach up and take food from the trees. When you're thirsty, you drink from a pleasant spring or stream nearby.

Lorana is a peaceful, friendly place. There is no crime and all the animals are tame. There are no houses in Lorana because there is no need for shelter or protection.

If you were to visit the planet Earth, perhaps as a cultural exchange student, many things would seem strange to you. One of the strangest would be the homes. You might wonder why there are so many different kinds, from small cottages to huge apartment complexes.

As an Earthling, you know that everyone needs a place to live. But why? And why are there so many types of homes?

People live in many different types of housing. There are single-family houses and houses built for two or three families. There are large apartment buildings and rooming houses, as well as mobile homes. Each type of housing has advantages and disadvantages. Yet, all housing fills the same human needs.

Shelter and Protection

The most basic of these needs is the need for shelter. People need protection from the weather. To survive, the human body must maintain a certain temperature.

That would be easy to do if the outside temperature were always perfect, as it is on Lorana. Earth temperatures, however, vary widely with location and season. So people need homes to protect their bodies from extreme heat or cold, as well as from the wind, rain, snow, and intense sun.

Food and water are not as easy to get on Earth as they are on Lorana. People need a place to store and prepare their food. Water rarely comes from nearby streams. It must usually be piped into each home from a central source.

The inhabitants of Lorana just lie down on the plush grass and go to sleep. They have no worries about danger. Earth, though, is not so safe. There is danger from wild animals. Unfortunately, there is also danger from people. So, whatever Earthlings are doing—sleeping, eating, working, or playing—they need a place where they can be safe. A home fills this need.

A Place Called Home

Besides physical needs for shelter and protection, human beings have psychological needs. One of these is the need to belong somewhere, to have roots.

Remember the movie *The Wizard of Oz?* Dorothy, the main character, has marvelous, though sometimes frightening, adventures in the strange land of Oz. When she awakens to find herself in the safety and security of her own bedroom, she says, "Oh, Auntie Em, there's no place like home."

Like Dorothy, most people find home a warm and comforting place. It doesn't really matter if home is small or large, simple or elegant. What's important is the feeling of belonging that it gives us.

In a changing world, we all need a place that is familiar. When people go home, they enjoy seeing their own things. Knowing what to expect when they walk through the door gives them a feeling of security and comfort.

Room to Be Yourself

Home is a place where people can express themselves. Whether they live in a very large house or in a single room, people reveal themselves in their homes. The way they furnish and care for their homes says something about their tastes and interests.

People find it easier to express their true thoughts and feelings when they are at home. In fact, "I feel at home" is another way of saying "I feel able to be myself."

Housing Choices

Besides the basic human needs for shelter and protection, people have their own special needs and tastes. A family with four children, for example, usually needs more space than a single person living alone. A young couple with jobs in the city would look for different features in a home than a retired older couple moving to a small town. It is because of these different needs that there are so many types of housing available.

The places where people live fall into two main categories. There are single-family houses and buildings that house many families. Any building designed for more than one family is called a multiple-family dwelling.

What do people look for when they choose a place to live? Whether they are looking for a house, an apartment, or a room, they first try to find a place they can afford. Then they look for features that satisfy their individual needs and tastes.

Space for Living

After deciding what housing they can afford, people must think about how much space they will need. Naturally, the more people living in a home, the more sleeping space they need. People may also want space for other reasons. A writer who works at home may need a room in which to work uninterrupted. Someone who has a home business doing clothing alterations may need a special sewing area.

Some people want extra space—for a hobby, or to use as a playroom or TV room. Others don't like extra room because it calls for more maintenance. They like having no more space than they need.

Layout and Style

People also differ in the way they like their spaces arranged. Some people like the closed-in, cozy feeling of a home where all the rooms are separated by solid doors. Others prefer an airy, open plan. In an open plan, the dining room and kitchen may be separated by only a counter. Or, instead of a separate dining room, there may be a dining area in the living room.

Land space is also an important factor in choosing housing. A family with small children might want a back yard—especially if there's no park nearby. A person who loves to garden might want a place to grow flowers or vegetables. On the other hand, taking care of a back yard might be a bother to someone who is rarely home.

In addition to thinking of layout, people usually have ideas about how a home should look. A great many styles are available in both homes and apartments.

Some people like buildings that remind them of the past. Others want a very modern home. Big windows and glass doors appeal to some individuals. Others prefer the intimate feeling that small windows can give a room.

Single-Family Homes

Many people like the privacy of a single-family house. When you are the only family living in a space, you don't have to worry as much about the noise you make. And you are less likely to be bothered by the sounds of other people. Privacy is an important reason for choosing a single-family home.

People with large families usually find that houses offer them more space than apartments. Houses are likely to have more bedrooms and yard space.

Houses come in many styles, shapes, and sizes. There are houses to suit just about every taste. Some houses are built on one level. Many people find that having all the rooms on one floor is convenient and makes cleaning easier. But single-level homes take up more land space than houses with two or more floors.

Houses that have two or more floors allow more yard space on the same amount of land. This yard space can be used for a garden, play area, or pool. It can also be used for another building such as a garage or toolshed.

The split level house on the left and the split entry house on the right are both good choices for a small piece of land. They give as much interior space as possible without adding height.

In two- and three-story homes, the bedrooms are usually on the upper floors. Many people find that having the bedrooms set apart from the rest of the house adds to their privacy.

There are other types of single-family homes. One is the split-level home, in which different sections of the house are built on different levels. Another is the split-entry home, in which the front door is on a level between the two stories.

Yet another kind of single-family house is the mobile home. A mobile home is not built on a lot. It is made and assembled in a factory. Because it is on wheels, it can easily be taken to a lot, site, or paved space in a mobile-home park. Once in place, its wheels are removed and its water and electrical systems are connected to an outside source.

Inside, a mobile home looks like a house. It is divided into rooms and often has a full range of modern appliances. But because it is built in a factory, it is usually less expensive than a traditional home. A mobile home can be a good place for a young couple to live.

Apartment Living

Like single-family houses, apartments are as varied as the needs and tastes of the people who live in them.

Apartments are more common in cities than in suburban or rural areas. People who work in cities often find that a centrally located apartment is convenient for work. They may also like being close to shops, theaters, and other facilities that cities offer.

More and more apartments are being built in suburban areas. These low buildings still use less space than single family homes.

Look closely. You'll see that this mobile home is not very mobile! Many mobile homes are part of an established community.

Because space in cities is scarce, many city apartments are in tall buildings called high rises. But sometimes older homes of two, three, or four stories are converted into apartments.

Small-town and suburban apartment buildings frequently have only two or three levels. Many people like the outdoor space that suburban apartments often include. Each unit may have a patio or a balcony. Often a playground is shared by several families.

The living space within apartments varies greatly. There are one-room studio apartments that include a small kitchen and bath. And there are two-story apartments, with a living room, dining room, kitchen, and two, three, or four bedrooms.

Apartments also differ greatly in style. There are old, historic apartment buildings, and very modern ones that feature the newest ideas in housing. Many buildings combine modern features with traditional style.

Rent or Buy?

Whether you wish to live in a single-family house or a multiple-family dwelling, you can either rent or buy.

When you buy property, you own it and are responsible for its upkeep. When you rent property, you pay a monthly sum of money to the owner or landlord. The owner is responsible for the maintenance of the grounds and building.

Many people think that owning property is a wise investment of money. Some enjoy the feeling of security that ownership gives them. They like to know that their space is actually their own.

Others prefer to rent their homes. They may be too busy to be concerned with major maintenance. Or they may want the freedom to leave an area without having to sell property.

A common belief is that single-family homes are always purchased and multiple-family dwellings are always rented. But this is not true. Single homes may be rented and apartments may be bought. Apartments that are owned by the people who live in them are called condominiums.

Only the Beginning

All this information is only the beginning of what a visitor from Lorana might find out about housing here on Earth. For you who live here, this housing information is very important. To plan for your changing needs throughout your life, you must understand the variety the housing market offers.

QUESTIONS

1. Why did human beings first develop shelters? What are the functions of today's houses?
2. Describe three types of housing. Explain possible benefits and drawbacks for each.
3. What are the benefits and drawbacks of buying a home? Of renting a home?
4. What features of our environment and society would have to change in order to do away with the necessity for housing? Explain.

5. Condominiums are becoming more and more popular. Why do you think this is so?
6. Many landlords will not rent to families with children. Why do you suppose they have this policy? What do you think of it?
7. Some housing is restricted to people in a certain group, such as single people under thirty or those who are retired and over sixty. What benefits do such restrictions offer? What drawbacks?

ACTIVITIES

1. Make a collage showing different kinds of homes people live in around the world. Explain how nature has influenced each.
2. Make a map of your neighborhood, showing the location of shopping areas, schools, recreational facilities, and so on. What changes would you make on your map?
3. Find out what housing was like in the United States 200 years ago and draw a picture of the inside of a typical home back then.

SECTION 2 · Home and Personal Space

Elementary, My Dear Watson

Look at each picture. What can you tell about the people who use these rooms? In particular, what can you tell about their:

- hobbies
- interests
- habits
- career plans
- pets
- summer vacation

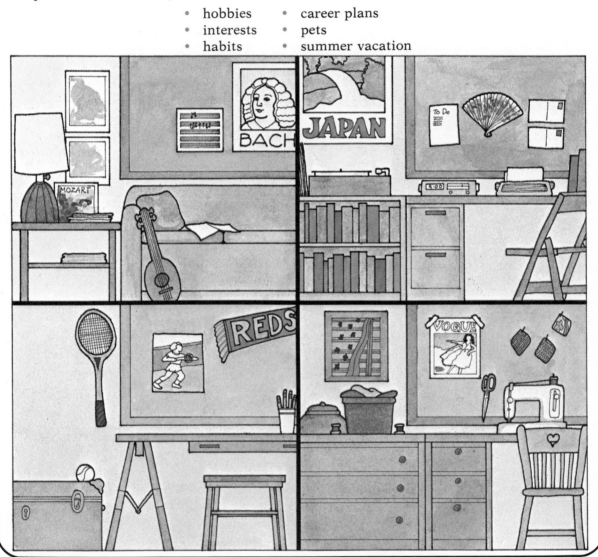

Have you ever marked your space at the beach by putting down your towel, sunglasses, and paperback book? In a library, have you ever left your books and papers on the table while you went to get a drink of water? In both cases, you were telling others, "This is my place. Please do not disturb it."

Sometimes the space you mark off is yours for just a little while. You may use your spot on the beach for a couple of hours, or perhaps a day. When you leave the beach, you will pick up your towel and other belongings. Tomorrow someone else will probably mark off the same space as her or his own.

There are other spaces that you use over a longer period of time. Because you use these spaces almost every day, they are very important to you. The room where you sleep, the drawer where you keep your sweaters, your locker at school—may all be places that have been set aside just for you. Whether you chose them yourself or whether they were assigned to you by someone else, the places that belong to you alone make up your personal space.

A Feeling of Belonging

Why do you suppose personal space is so important to people? Why do you mark off space at the beach or library? What is the purpose of having your own drawer, closet, or locker?

One reason people like having personal space is that it gives them a feeling of belonging. When you put your towel down on the beach, you know that you have a place there. By not disturbing your things, other people recognize this area as your place. When you come out of the water, you can return to your "home base."

At home and at school, personal space can give you a feeling of belonging. At home, having your own personal space is part of being a family member. This is true whether your space is small or large. What matters is that it's yours. At school, being assigned a desk means that you're part of the class. When people say, "This is Jenny's drawer," or "This is Mike's desk," it means that Jenny and Mike have a place in their home or school.

A Place for Your Possessions

One very practical reason for having personal space is that it gives you a place to store your things. Your "home base" on the beach gives you a place to put your towel and other possessions while you are in the water or at the snack bar. At home, you might have a drawer where you store your school supplies, a box where you keep your hobby equipment, a closet where you hang your clothes.

It's very important to have a place where you can store the things that belong to you. Keeping your things in the same place can help you keep track of them. Personal storage space prevents confusion by keeping your possessions separate from everyone else's.

Also, because personal space usually means "private space," others are not likely to invade it without asking you first. So personal space can also satisfy another important need: the need for privacy.

Privacy

Every human being needs a place to be alone, a place to think and dream. We all have to get away from the world and the demands it makes on us at times.

Maybe you like to lie down on your bed and listen to records by yourself. Perhaps

Absorbed in a hobby? A workspace is one place where you can have privacy.

you like to read all alone in the kitchen when no one else is there. Or maybe you "get away from it all" by going on long walks alone. Being alone gives us a chance to get to know ourselves better.

Personal space can give you the privacy you need. Your room, even if you share it, is a place where you can sometimes be by yourself. It can also be a meeting place for you and your friends.

Space that is usually shared by the whole family can be personal space at times. The kitchen, for example, may be yours on certain evenings. You might use the room to work on a project, to entertain friends, or just to be alone. Different families may make different arrangements so that all members can have the privacy they need.

Express Yourself

Everyone has a need for self-expression. One way to express yourself is by personalizing your space. This means making changes and adding objects to reflect your interests and personality. Your personal space is an extension of you. It tells the world a great deal about you.

There are many ways to personalize your space. You might paint it your favorite color. You might hang pictures, posters, and signs that you like on the walls. You might put photos, mementos, and objects that have a special meaning for you on shelves. You might also keep your hobby materials, school books, and other things that you use nearby. Because you are a unique individual, your space will also be unique.

If you move, the personal possessions you take with you will be extremely important. A rock collection, a favorite poster, or a stuffed animal may not have much dollar value. But when you unpack these belongings, you will find that they make a strange place seem familiar. They are a quick way to personalize your new home.

QUESTIONS

1. What is personal space? Give examples of personal space that is yours over a long period of time and personal space that is yours for a short period.
2. Why do people need personal space?
3. Explain the statement: "Personal space is an extension of yourself." Give two examples of how you can personalize space.
4. What areas do you consider your personal space and at what periods of time? How do you indicate that these spaces are yours?
5. How important is privacy to a teenager as compared to a young child? To an adult?
6. When do you most appreciate having personal space? Why?
7. What could be some of the effects of not having personal space?

ACTIVITIES

1. Bring from home a special object you use in your room. Tell the class why it has meaning for you and describe how you display it.

2. Describe how you would personalize your space in the classroom.

3. Write a letter to your family explaining how you feel about privacy.

SECTION 3 · Sharing Space

WHAT'S YOUR PROBLEM?

Dear Nancy,

My younger brother and I share a bedroom. There's a small table in it that we take turns using. Whenever I work on a project, I put everything away afterward. This leaves the table neat in case my brother wants to use it. But whenever he uses the table, he leaves his supplies scattered all over it. When I want to use it, I have to clear off all his stuff. This isn't fair. What should I do?

Randy

Dear Nancy,

I want to use the living room after school some days to have friends over. But my sister always uses the room at that time to do her homework. I don't know what to do. I have as much right to use the room as she does, don't I?

Paulette

Dear Nancy,

Every night at six o'clock I watch a certain show on TV. My whole family knows that this is my time to use the TV room.

But last night my sister got a phone call from one of her friends. The phone is in the same room as the TV, and she talked the whole time my show was on. That really made it hard to hear and spoiled the show for me.

I don't think my sister was being fair. Do you?

Brad

All of us live, work, eat, and play in spaces with other people. So in addition to having personal space, we also share space with others. Public buildings, streets, sidewalks, theaters, and restaurants are all shared spaces.

Your home is space that you share with your family. Each member of the family has some personal space within the home. But many spaces are shared with other family members—for example, the living room.

Shared space means any space that is used by more than one person. Limited space makes sharing necessary. Bedrooms may be shared. Bathrooms are usually shared. Smaller spaces such as closets and drawers may also be used by several people.

Shared space also means space that people use together. A family usually eats together in the kitchen or dining room. All family members may use the same room for reading, working, or watching television. This shared space gives family members a place to meet, talk, eat, play, and simply enjoy one another.

By sharing space, people share experiences. Families can watch television or work on projects together. Each family member may be doing something different in the same room and still enjoy being with the others. Sharing space is an important part of being a family.

Yours, Mine, and Ours

Families are made up of people, and no person is exactly like another. Each family member has different needs, tastes, and interests, as well as different friends. So it's easy to understand why families disagree about how space is to be used.

Sometimes, these disagreements are about personal space. Suppose someone in the family is out of tissues and takes some from your drawer. If you don't mind, then all is fine. On the other hand, if you feel that your privacy has been invaded, an argument could result.

Other disagreements are about spaces everybody uses. The living room, for example, belongs to everyone in the family. Yet, on the same evening, three people may want to use the room in different ways. You may want to play records, your sister may want to watch television, and your mother may want to talk quietly with a friend. These plans interfere with one another.

At times, sharing space can be difficult. But by respecting the rights of others and trying to see their points of view, space problems can be solved.

Your Space and My Space

When people share a home, it's important that they respect one another's personal space. This means letting other people have their privacy. If your brother is in his room with the door closed, he might not want you to walk in without knocking. In his place, you might feel the same way. Respecting the space of others also means not going into their dressers and closets without asking. It means leaving their things alone.

There may be times when entering another's space is necessary. For example, if you do the laundry in your family, you may have to go into another person's room to put clothes away. Except in special cases, however, don't go into anyone else's space without asking first. Respecting others' space prevents disagreements.

Our Space

When using shared space, be considerate. To share space fairly, you have to think

Sharing a room has its pros and cons. It can be fun to talk things over with a brother or sister—but it can also be hard to get work done.

about the wants and needs of other people. If each member is considerate, then life will be easier and more pleasant for the whole family.

One way to be considerate is to leave a place neat after you've used it. Rinsing out the bathtub after you've finished bathing is being considerate of the next person who takes a bath or shower. If you clean up after fixing a snack in the kitchen, the next person who uses the kitchen will be happy. Nobody likes having to clean up before starting to cook or bake!

Remember the letter from Randy on page 195? He was upset because his brother left supplies scattered all over the work table they both used. By leaving the table a mess, his brother was not being considerate. He was not thinking about Randy's feelings.

Helping to keep the rooms in your home clean is also considerate. If you accidentally spill something on the floor, you owe it to everyone else to clean it up. This way the shared space stays tidy—and safe.

Shared Space and Other People

Everybody needs quiet sometimes, even when using shared space. It would be thoughtless to make noise in the kitchen while your sister is doing her homework there. If your parents are chatting quietly in the living room, you should try not to disturb them. When people share space, it's important that they respect one another's need for quiet.

Sometimes being considerate means being willing to share your personal space. If your older sister comes home from college for the weekend, you might share your bedroom with her.

You may even give up your personal space when someone visits. For instance, when your grandmother stays overnight, you may sleep on the couch so that she can use your bed. At the dinner table, you may give up your usual chair. By sharing your personal space with visitors, you make their stay more pleasant.

Be thoughtful also when you plan to use shared space to visit with your own friends. For example, you may plan to invite some classmates over to watch TV. But your parents may be planning to use the TV room for a visit with their friends.

Before planning to use shared space, check with other family members. If you find that someone else wants to use the space at the same time, try to work out an agreement. That way you will avoid an argument later on.

Solving Your Disagreements

There are different solutions to disagreements about space. Some disagreements can be settled by talking things over, if the people try to understand each other's point of view. Brad, for instance, could tell his sister how he feels when she interrupts his TV program. Next time she could tell her friend that she'll call back later.

Disagreements about shared space can often be solved by taking turns using the space. Paulette's sister might agree to use the living room only on certain afternoons. Then, on other afternoons, Paulette could use it to visit with her friends.

Some families solve space disagreements by working out a compromise. Suppose you and your brother both want to use the living room on Friday night. As a compromise, you could use the room from six to eight, and he could use it from eight to ten. Neither of you would have the room for the whole evening. But both of you would have part of what you want.

Every family has its own way of handling problems about space. Does your family talk things over? Do you take turns? Do you compromise? What do *you* think is the best way of working out space problems?

QUESTIONS

1. What is shared space? Give examples of different kinds of shared space.
2. Why do we share space with others? What are the advantages of sharing space? The disadvantages?
3. Describe three techniques for enjoying shared space and avoiding conflicts with others who use the same space.
4. Why is it important to learn to share space with others? What would life be like if you never learned how to share space?
5. How can being considerate of others when using shared space benefit you as well?
6. What kind of space in the home do you think is the easiest to share? The hardest? Why?

ACTIVITIES

1. Write a skit that shows a typical disagreement over shared space in a public place.
2. Research and report on how people share space in Japan, on an Israeli kibbutz, or in collective villages in China.
3. Give a talk on how well students care for shared space in a particular area of your school. You could interview a school custodian or librarian to help you in your report.

SECTION 4 · Reorganizing Personal Space

What Changes Would You Suggest?

Jim's room badly needs reorganizing. What suggestions would you make to help him out? Have you ever reorganized your own room? What changes did you make?

How has your life changed during the past few years? Probably the activities you enjoy today are very different from the ones you liked when you were eight years old. You may have taken up a new sport or hobby. You may be thinking more about your future. As a result, you may be spending more time studying and reading.

Changes in interests and activities usually call for changes in personal space. If you take up fishing, for example, you will need a place to store your rod and tackle. More reading may mean more shelf space for books. As your interests change, you will want to reorganize your personal space.

Why Reorganize Space?

Good organization and furniture arrangement make a room more convenient to live in. Life is easier when you have enough space to store all your personal belongings. Having the things you use within easy reach helps make your day go smoother.

By reorganizing space, you often can make better use of storage facilities. Sometimes you can even create more storage space. You can also try new ways to store things so that you will be able to find them more easily.

People sometimes reorganize space to make it easier to move around in and more comfortable. Rearranging the furnishings often allows more room for walking, and more room for relaxing, too.

Space may also be organized to give the people sharing a room more privacy. A room can be divided so that each of the room's occupants has a private area. Redesigning a shared room for privacy can make life more comfortable for the people who live in it.

Box 1

Using a Floor Plan

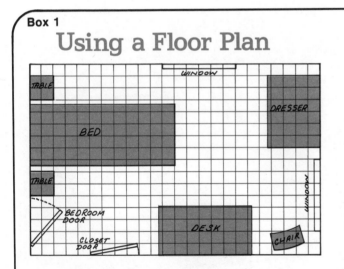

Before a designer places furnishings in a room, she or he makes a floor plan. The room is first measured, then sketched "to scale" on graph paper. In a floor plan drawn to scale, a certain number of squares is allowed for each foot or decimeter of floor space.

For example, if the scale you choose allows two squares per foot, a room measuring 8 by 12 ft would be drawn as a rectangle 16 squares wide and 24 squares long. Furnishings are also measured and drawn, allowing the same number of squares per foot. Features such as doors and windows are also shown on the plan.

By using a floor plan, you can see how furnishings will look in a particular arrangement. This can save you the trouble of moving furnishings around, deciding they don't look good, and then moving them back again. If you are buying furnishings, a floor plan can help you make sure that your choices are the right sizes and shapes. By planning first, you can avoid costly mistakes.

Getting It All Together

Getting organized means making sure that your things are where you can find them. Your clothes stay fresher when they are stored neatly. Studying is easier when your work area is in order. Besides making life more convenient, good organization can help you keep your space looking neat.

Start getting organized by taking a good look at the obvious storage space you have—for example, a closet and dresser. Making the best use of this space is a key part of solving storage problems.

The next step is to divide your belongings into two groups: items you are using right now and those that you use during a different season. Store the things you're currently using in front of your closet. The others can be put in the back of the closet, in boxes on a shelf, or in the attic. This way it will be easy to find the objects you use the most.

You can put the back of your closet door to good use by hanging a shoe holder or a laundry bag there. You can also install hooks to hang jewelry or articles of clothing. By using the door for storage, you will free more space in your closet or dresser.

Making More Storage Space

Your storage space is not limited to your dresser and closets. With a little effort and imagination, many other spaces can be used for storage.

Under your bed there is space just waiting to be used. Cut off the upper sections of cardboard boxes so they'll fit under the bed. These boxes can be used to store your sweaters, old magazines, games, or just about anything you wish.

Bookcases can be used to store other things besides books. If there are books in your bookcase you seldom look at anymore, store them elsewhere or give them to a younger relative. Then you can use the shelf space for frequently used items.

On the Wall

Wall shelves are good for storing all sorts of things besides books. Suppose you do a lot of needlework. You could put your yarn, fabrics, and trimmings in baskets on a shelf. If painting pictures is your hobby, you might keep your supplies on a shelf in colorfully painted boxes. Shelf storage space can be attractive as well as useful.

Shelves can be easily made from boards of wood or pressboard, mounted on the wall with brackets. You might want to paint them, stain them, or cover them with adhesive-backed paper.

Your walls can be used for storage in other ways. Install hooks or pegs and use them to hang jewelry, handbags, articles of clothing, or other possessions. Sporting goods such as baseball bats, fishing poles, and hockey sticks look good stored on the wall with brackets or a pegboard. Baskets of all types can be hung from the wall and used to hold anything from tennis balls to school supplies.

Organizing your storage space can make life more convenient for you. It also makes your space look neater and keeps your belongings in good condition. Thinking of ways to store things can be challenging.

Arranging Furnishings

Depending on how furnishings are placed, a room can look cramped or spacious, neat or cluttered. Think about your own personal space. How are the furnishings arranged?

Can you move freely from one area of your space to another without tripping over

In a space such as this, inexpensive shelving provides a place for your belongings and helps organize the room.

things? If you have to squeeze past a chest every time you walk into the room, try to find another place for the chest. Whenever possible, furnishings should be placed so they don't get in your way.

Does your space seem cramped? Sometimes you can make a room more spacious simply by moving the furnishings. Suppose your bed is right in the center of the room, cutting the room space in two. If you move the bed against the wall, you will have more open area. This will make the room look larger.

Grouping by Activity

Organize the areas within your space ac-

cording to what you do in them. Group together furnishings and other items you use for certain activities.

For instance, your study area might include a desk, a chair, a bookcase, and a desk lamp. Then everything you need to study will be together. Or you could store all your records near the record player and make this area a music center. The dresser where you keep your sweaters should be placed near the closet where you hang your pants or skirts.

Arrange all your belongings according to how you use them. This will save you steps and make your life easier.

Creating Privacy

When people share space, the way furnishings are arranged is especially important.

In some bedrooms, the beds make a natural division and each person takes one side of the room. In others, the space division is not so clear. There may be a studio couch or a hide-a-bed. If a bedroom is not clearly divided, the people who use it must work out a space arrangement.

Each person sharing a bedroom needs a place to keep his or her things, a place to study, and as much privacy as possible. If there is just one dresser, the drawers must be divided between the people who use the room. If there is only one desk or table, a card table might be set up so that each person can have a place to study.

Sometimes a curtain or free-standing bookcase can act as a room divider, giving a feeling of privacy. Privacy can also be increased by placing chairs and desks so that the people using them can face away from each other. When privacy is important in a shared room, furniture arrangement can help.

Creating a Look

Your space should please your senses as well as suit your needs. It's fun to express your personality by choosing and combining colors, patterns, and textures. Hanging pictures you like on the walls gives you something interesting to look at. A fake fur throw rug feels nice under your feet.

Most people find that a room is nicer to look at when everything is in order. Furniture that has been thoughtfully arranged is pleasing to the eye. By reorganizing your space, you can make it more attractive as well as more convenient.

QUESTIONS

1. Why is it necessary to rearrange personal space once in a while? What are the practical benefits of organizing storage space and arranging furniture carefully?
2. How can you arrange furniture for privacy? For spaciousness? For convenience?
3. What is a floor plan? What are the reasons for using one?
4. People sometimes put up with a badly arranged room rather than rearrange it. Why do you suppose they do this?
5. Can you think of any disadvantages to creating a great deal of storage space in your room?
6. What principles can you think of for organizing the furnishings in the living room of a home?

ACTIVITIES

1. Make two floor plans of your room. The first should show how the furnishings are arranged now, and the second should show changes you would make to gain privacy, convenience, and storage space.
2. Design a low-cost, do-it-yourself storage unit for your room. Describe what materials would be used, how much they would cost, and what labor would be necessary.
3. Describe and evaluate the space you now use for studying or working on a hobby. How could it be improved?

SECTION 5 · Getting the Look You Want

Both of these rooms are living rooms, where people sit, relax, and talk to each other. Both have comfortable chairs, tables to put things on, areas where people can talk. But the rooms are very different. They have a very different feeling, or atmosphere.

Look at the rooms for a while. Perhaps you would be more comfortable in one, perhaps in the other. What is it that makes the atmosphere of each room so different?

The use or function of a room is a major concern of the interior designer. What will the space be used for? How practical is the room's design for this purpose? Will people be able to walk through the room easily? Will the carpeting show dirt if many people walk across it?

But practicality isn't the only thing a designer thinks about. People's tastes and feelings are equally important considerations. Some people like to relax in a cool, spacious setting. Other people prefer a warm, cozy atmosphere. How does a designer create effects to suit people's feelings?

Elements of Design

Why do the living rooms shown on this page have such a different feeling to them? You may think the colors are important—one room has a warm red glow, the other is stark black and white. Perhaps it's the shapes—curved in one picture, mostly square in the other. Or maybe it's the space in the center—rectangular in one room, informal and almost circular in the other.

Spaces, shapes, colors—every room contains them. Good designers use them to create an atmosphere. Color, shape, and space are three important elements of design which you can use to produce the look you want.

Spaces

Although rooms are fixed in size, they can be made to look larger or smaller through a careful use of space. A spacious or cozy feeling can be created in a room in a number of different ways.

In many rooms, such as those shown on the previous page and on this page, furniture may outline a single space for sitting and talking. This gives a spacious look. In other rooms, the furniture may be placed so that many smaller spaces are created. This may give the room a cozy look.

Spaces can have a strong effect on people's feelings. One person may feel threatened by too much open space. She or he may like the protection and privacy that small spaces offer. Another person may feel trapped by small spaces, preferring a feeling of airiness.

Shapes

The shapes of objects in a room can have a strong effect on the atmosphere of that room. So can the shapes of the spaces. A set of furniture usually repeats particular shapes—the arms of chairs and a sofa may both be curved or straight. Repetition helps set a tone for the room. If a curved shape is repeated often, the effect will be soft. If most of the furniture is angular, the effect will be harder. And if a lot of different shapes are mixed together, the effect will be informal—or confusing. Designers need to think carefully about how different shapes look together.

Colors

Colors sometimes look good together, and sometimes they clash. Just as clothing de-signers think carefully about the effects of colors, so do interior designers plan the colors to be used in a room. Some color combinations are vivid and startling—bright red and yellow, for example. Other color combinations are more relaxing—like beige and brown. People have different tastes in colors. One person may love vivid purple, but another may find it disturbing.

Using color in a room is a simple and inexpensive way to get the look you want. Painting an old desk a new color, for example, is much cheaper than buying a new desk. Painting a special design on a wall (with permission!) won't cost as much as wallpapering. Color is one element of design that is fairly easy to change.

Lines

Lines are another important element in design. Every room has a great many lines. There is the line at the top of a door, for

The quilted fabric and curved lines of the furniture soften the effect of the many straight lines and angles in this room.

The simplest kind of balance is symmetrical (left), with similar shapes on both sides of the room. But asymmetrical balance (right) is also possible.

example, and the line around the base of a lamp. But the atmosphere of a room is most affected by the boldest lines—lines that stand out for one reason or another.

A room may have tall windows. You could use floor-to-ceiling drapes for the windows and paper the walls with vertically striped wallpaper. Add a tall bookcase and perhaps some full-length portraits or posters. Then the vertical lines would be the boldest element in the room.

Once again, taste is important. Some people will feel good in such an "upright" room. Others will prefer a horizontal effect. This effect might be achieved with low-backed chairs and sofas, long, low coffee tables, and other furnishings that repeat

this line. Still other people may like diagonals, curves, or a mixture of different lines.

Textures and Lighting

Another important element of design is texture. How do the surfaces feel? Are they silky or fuzzy? Hard or soft? Rough or smooth? A deep pile carpet will give a different effect than an indoor-outdoor carpet, even though they both have the same color and pattern. Our eyes can tell us a lot about the textures of a room. Just by looking, we can often tell how comfortable a room is.

Lighting is another major design element. It can affect all the other elements. Two shaded lamps placed on low tables can

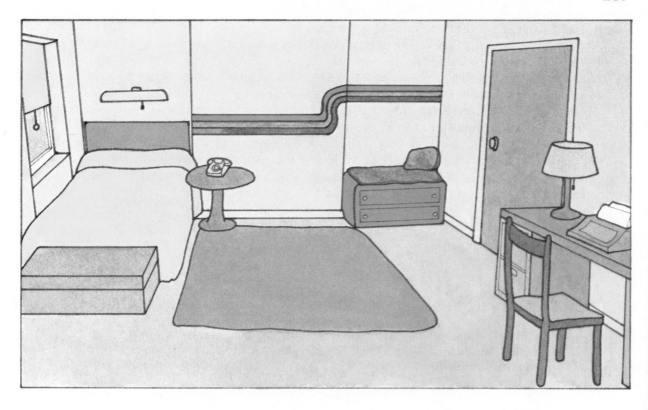

make the room appear larger than it is. Tinted bulbs can change the whole color effect. Bright ceiling fixtures can draw the eye upward in rooms with a horizontal design.

Interesting shapes can be shown off by well-planned lighting. Textures, too, can be made more interesting by the way they reflect or absorb light. Apart from its importance for activities in a room, lighting has an important design effect.

Putting It All Together

Different design elements can all work together. Or they can work against each other. Interior designers have thought about how design elements combine. They

have discovered several ways to help produce pleasing effects.

Imagine a room with square chairs, curved chairs, tall chairs, and short chairs of many styles and colors. It might be hard to relax in such a room. Designers usually decide on one color scheme, and perhaps one general style of furniture. This helps create a feeling of **unity,** or oneness.

If you use fabrics of different colors for each window drape in your room, and yet another color for your bedspread, you may have a very unusual effect. You certainly won't have unity of color.

A room may be more interesting if it has a center of interest. This can be created by the use of contrast. A brightly patterned wing chair, for example, stands out when solid colors are used elsewhere in the room. This effect—called **emphasis**—is stronger if the boldest lines in the room lead the eye toward the center of interest. In the picture on page 205, for example, the lines of the wood floor and the sofa lead the eye to the fireplace.

Another effect designers work to achieve is **balance.** Balance means an even, steady feeling. Lack of balance can be disturbing.

Suppose all the straight lines, rough textures, and cool colors are to one side of the room, and all the curved lines, warm colors, and smooth textures are to the other. Such a room would look unbalanced.

Balance, emphasis, and unity are some of the principles you can use to organize the elements in a room. These principles are not rules, however. In the end, the total look is a matter of taste, of getting the feeling you want.

QUESTIONS

1. What are two major concerns interior designers have when decorating a room?
2. List five elements of design and give an example of how each can affect the look of a room.
3. Explain three basic principles to use when combining the different elements of design. Why are they considered principles rather than rules?
4. Which element of design do you consider the most important? The least important? Why?
5. How would you feel if someone walked into your living room, looked around, and said, "Who's your decorator?" Why?
6. Why do you think some colors have an exciting effect while others are relaxing?

ACTIVITIES

1. Choose any emotion (for example, joy, anger) and design a collage using colors, lines, textures, and shapes to express the feeling.
2. Analyze a magazine picture of an attractive room, explaining how the basic elements of design create the special look of the room.
3. Using the elements and principles of design, describe the changes you would make in your classroom. You could bring in pictures, fabrics, etc., to help demonstrate the changes you would make. What would be the overall effect of your decorating plan?

SECTION 6 · Accessories Can Make the Difference

One Room—Three Different Looks

If you were asked to choose one of these three looks, which one would you prefer? Why do you think you would prefer living in the room you have chosen rather than in one of the two other rooms?

When planning rooms, designers often speak of "major furnishings" and "accessories." In a bedroom, the major furnishings might be a bed, a dresser, a chest of drawers, and a desk. The lamps, pictures, vases, throw pillows, and other small touches would be the accessories.

Accessories and Design

Accessories add something interesting to a room. Often, this is a splash of color. They can accent or highlight an area, especially if chosen with the room's color scheme in mind.

They can also give a room beauty and personality. A painting, for example, is usually pleasing to see.

Other accessories have a dual purpose. Besides improving the appearance of a room, they add convenience. A calendar that features art prints not only looks attractive, it also tells you what day it is.

Just about everything that adds to the appearance of a room can be called an accessory. Books piled up on your desk are not accessories. But if you cover them in bright colors and arrange them on a shelf, they can be an eye-catching display.

Your tennis racket can become an accessory if you hang it on the wall as a decoration. Simple, everyday objects that have interesting colors and shapes can be very exciting accessories.

Enjoying Your Accessories

Your accessories say a lot about you. By looking at them, a stranger could begin to build some picture of the kind of person you are.

A wicker sewing basket, for example, might show that you like to do needlework. Posters of snow-covered mountains might suggest that you like winter sports. Cards tacked up on your bulletin board might say that you have recently had a birthday.

People enjoy expressing their personal tastes by using certain accessories. By hanging your watercolors or displaying your sports trophies, you are saying something special about yourself.

Besides expressing your individuality, accessories please your senses. They help satisfy your sense of beauty. Your plants may give you the pleasant feeling of being in a garden. Even on the darkest day, a bright patchwork quilt may make you feel cheerful.

Accessories can also bring back memories of places you have been and people you have known. By looking at a collection of seashells, you can walk along the beach in your imagination. You can remember how much fun it was to be there and dream about going back.

Accessories give your personal space warmth and individuality. They help create a look that is yours alone. By pleasing your senses and reminding you of past experiences, accessories enrich your life.

Getting the Most from Accessories

Accessories are an inexpensive, easy, and practical way to give your personal space the look you want.

Posters, for example, don't cost very much money, and can reflect your interest in rock music or foreign countries. Attractive items can be made from household materials—an old teapot, for example, can become an attractive planter. Many of the things you use every day can be arranged as accessories.

Unlike major furnishings, accessories are easy to change. If you get bored with the way your space looks, you can rearrange or change accessories to get a brand-new look.

Give your room a personal touch with accessories that reflect your hobbies.

Ideas

Here are some ideas to help you use accessories to decorate your space. As you read through them, try to think of ideas of your own to share with the class.

Show off your collections: Do you collect shells, rocks, miniature dolls, or bottles? Storing your collection in a closet is a waste. Collections make interesting accessories, and they say a great deal about you. To get the best effect, group the things you collect in one place.

Put your memories on display: Do you like to save ticket stubs, programs, postcards, and other souvenirs? Why not take them out of the drawer and display them? You could paste them on a sturdy piece of cardboard to make a collage. Or you could

tack them to a bulletin board. The things you save are part of your life experience. They can add to the individual look of your room.

Perk up your furniture: Is your desk or dresser dull or always a mess? Does it need perking up? One way to add color and convenience is to make colorful containers for items such as paper clips, cosmetics, or loose change. Buy some colorful adhesive-backed plastic and use it to cover tin cans and small gift boxes to use as holders. Your wastepaper basket could be covered to match.

You can also add color with new accessories. A new blotter can brighten the surface of a desk. A well-chosen comb or brush, or even a colorful box of tissues, can change a dull dresser to an attractive one.

What to Do with Four Walls

Tacking posters on your walls is a quick and easy way to give your space a new look. Many different types of posters are available. Some picture famous people, others show landscapes, animals, or scenes of outer space.

Some posters are offered free by travel agencies. Most others are fairly inexpensive.

Before you tack up your poster, you may want to paste it on a piece of cardboard. This will keep it from wrinkling and give it a more solid look.

Prints of paintings can be a wonderful way to add interest to your walls. Like posters, prints are often fairly inexpensive. Bookstores, department stores, and gift shops frequently carry prints. If you visit a museum, check the gift shop for interesting prints.

Plants can be a good way to accessorize any room in the house.

Frames are often more expensive than the prints themselves. Check local discount stores for inexpensive frames. Also, look in the family storage area for old frames that are no longer being used.

Hanging your favorite photographs is another way to give your walls a personal look. To show off photos best, group them on one wall. For variety, use photos of different sizes. Frames of different shapes—round, square, rectangular—can add interest to your grouping.

Bring Nature Inside

Many people use plants to personalize their space. Plants give space a fresh, natural look. Small plants are usually not expensive. They often look good on a window sill. When they grow larger, you might want to repot them and hang them in the window or from the ceiling.

Remember that all plants are not strictly green. Some plant leaves have purple or orange tones. You may wish to select your plants to fit the color scheme of your room.

When choosing plants, consider the lighting in the room. Different plants need different amounts and kinds of light. Check your local library for books on plant selection and care before making your choice.

Learning More about Accessories

By surrounding yourself with things you really like, you can add enjoyment to your life and make a space truly yours. Besides, choosing accessories can be fun!

You probably have your own ideas about what accessories you would like for your space. But if you'd like to find out about other ideas, look through various magazines. *Family Circle, Woman's Day,* and *Apartment Life* feature articles that show you how to choose or make low-cost items. *Seventeen, Co-ed,* and *Teen* magazine also have articles on room decoration.

The world of accessories is as unlimited as your imagination. Using accessories can be one of the most exciting parts of personalizing your space.

QUESTIONS

1. What are accessories? List the different aspects of a room that can be made more attractive with accessories. Where can you find new ideas for using accessories?
2. Give examples of accessories that add to both the convenience and the look of a room.

3. How can accessories reflect your experiences and interests?
4. What kind of effect do you think a room without accessories has on a person?
5. What accessories do you see in your classroom? What others would you add?

ACTIVITIES

1. Turn an ordinary item into an accessory. Describe to the class your reasons for choosing this item, and what you did to turn it into an accessory.
2. Brainstorm a list of suggestions to be presented to the principal for using accessories to improve the look of your school. Explain why these changes would be important.
3. Using magazines, make a portfolio of good ideas on how to use accessories and display them.

SECTION 7 · Caring for Space

An Obvious Quiz

1. What do you do with your clothes when you take them off at night?
   a. hang them on a chair or lay them on a dresser or desk
   b. throw them in a pile on the floor in the corner of the room
   c. hang them in a closet or put them in the hamper if they're dirty

2. How often do you clean the room where you sleep?
   a. once a month
   b. when I finally can't stand the mess
   c. once a week

3. If you were looking for a three-month-old issue of a magazine, where would you probably find it?
   a. under the bed
   b. could be anywhere!
   c. in a stack of magazines

4. After you've listened to a record, what are you most likely to do?
   a. leave it on the record player turntable
   b. remove it from the turntable and put it down somewhere without its jacket
   c. put it in its jacket and return it to where the other records are stored

5. Suppose you got hungry during the night and decided to get a snack from the kitchen and bring it back to your room. How long would the plate and glass stay in your room?
   a. until the next morning
   b. until the end of the week or the next time the room was cleaned
   c. until I finished the snack

(*For answer key see page 219.*)

Everyone has feelings about how neat a space should be. One person may feel at home in a room where there are magazines strewn about and sporting goods in the corner. Another may want the magazines in a neat stack and the sporting goods in the closet.

People may disagree about how often space should be cleaned. Some rush for the dust cloth at the first speck of dust. Others remove dust only occasionally.

Whatever your feelings about keeping things neat, there are advantages to maintaining some sort of order in your life.

Why Keep Space Neat?

Helping to clean your own space and the spaces you share with your family is good practice for several reasons:

- Clean and well-cared-for space is usually more attractive.
- Neatness, and sloppiness, affect people's moods.
- Keeping your space in good order can save you time and energy by making your belongings easier to find.
- Your belongings stay in better condition when the space they are kept in is neat.
- You owe it to other family members to maintain your own area.
- You have a responsibility to pitch in and do your part to care for spaces that are shared.

Looks and Feelings

A clean, well-cared-for space is more pleasant to look at than one that's messy.

Imagine a room with an unmade bed, piles of dirty clothes all over, and dust everywhere. Now compare it to a room where the bed is made, the clothes are in the closet, and the furniture shines.

Even people who say they don't mind clutter would probably prefer the neat room—especially if it were cleaned by someone else!

As human beings, we are influenced by the space around us. Whether a place is neat or messy can affect the way we feel.

People's ideas of neatness differ. Many standards may be acceptable but too relaxed an attitude may damage your belongings, and also offend those around you.

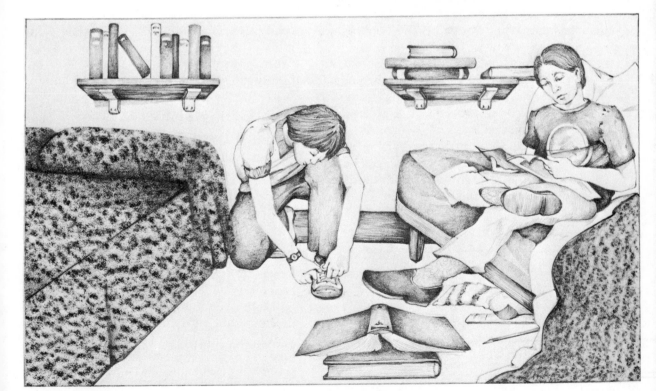

A dirty, messy room can be depressing. It can make working or studying more difficult. On the other hand, many people find that a clean, neat room is restful. Some say a neat space helps them think more clearly. Studying tends to be easier in an area that's neat and well organized.

Do you feel better about your surroundings when everything is in order? That in itself is a good reason for taking care of your space.

Save Time and Energy

Tidy areas are generally easier to live in than messy areas. Life is much more convenient when you know where everything is. Why should you have to rummage through cluttered drawers every time you want to find something?

Putting everything back where it belongs is a good habit. When you finish reading a book, for example, return it to the bookshelf. When you want the book again, you'll know where to find it.

It's almost as easy to put the book back on the shelf as it is to leave in on the floor. If you make a habit of returning things to their places, your space will stay neat almost automatically.

If you've been putting up with a messy room, your life is harder than it need be. By cleaning and straightening your personal space, you could make life much easier for yourself.

Caring for Your Belongings

Clothes, school supplies, and recreational equipment are more likely to get damaged in a messy room than in a neat one. Records, for example, can easily be scratched if they are left lying around. Damp clothes tossed on the closet floor can be spoiled by mildew.

By taking care of your belongings, you make them last longer. Instead of spending your money to replace damaged goods, you can spend it on other items.

Your Space and Your Home

Your personal space may be strictly your own area, but it is in the home where your family lives. How you keep your own space will have an important effect on the condition of this home.

If you have your own room, its neatness may seem to you strictly an individual matter. But if it is damaged through neglect or carelessness, who will pay for that damage?

Always clean up spills right away so that the floor or carpeting will not be stained. Be careful not to spill nail polish, airplane glue, or anything else that may damage furnishings. Don't mark the walls more than is necessary.

Housing and home furnishings are costly. Home repairs take a lot of time and money. By caring for your space and preventing damage, you help conserve your family's resources.

Maintaining Shared Space

At home, you share space with others. The kitchen and living room are shared spaces. Most people also share a bathroom with other family members. Except for very young children, everyone in the family is responsible for maintaining shared space.

Shared space should be cared for well enough to suit everyone who uses it. If you leave your shoes in the middle of your bedroom floor, you may be the only person who will trip over them. But, if you leave them in the middle of the living room, the rest of your family may trip over them. You should take even more care of family rooms than you do of your bedroom.

Keeping shared spaces clean is important everywhere, but especially in the kitchen, where dirt may lead to illness.

Some maintenance chores should be done on a daily basis. For example, the tub and wash basin need to be rinsed out after each use. Wiping off the kitchen counter after you've made yourself a snack helps keep the kitchen neat.

In addition to daily upkeep, many areas occasionally need major maintenance. Floors may need to be waxed. Windows have to be washed. Wash basins and bathtubs must be scrubbed. If these tasks aren't done, a shared area can become dirty in spite of everyone's day-to-day efforts.

Who Does the Work?

In some families, one person may do all these chores. Even so, when you notice that this person is very busy, it's thoughtful to offer help.

Other families may divide up major maintenance jobs. For example, one person might take responsibility for vacuuming, another for dusting.

Sometimes a cleaning job is passed around from one family member to another. You might be responsible for cleaning the bathroom one week. The next week, your brother or sister would have the job. This kind of system is called rotating chores.

Safety First

When using either personal or shared space, it's important to think about safety. Skateboards, boots, and other belongings should not be left in hallways or on the stairs where people can trip over them. Knives, needles, and other pointed objects should always be carefully put away to safeguard against injury.

Medicines and cleaning substances should be stored out of the reach of young children. Toddlers are curious and are likely to swallow any fluids and pills they happen to find. They don't realize the danger of being poisoned. But you do. So, if there are young children in your family, protect them by locking away any medicine or poisonous cleaning fluid you see lying around your home.

Care should also be taken to prevent fire. Leaving electrical appliances turned on for long periods of time can be dangerous. Unplugging an iron before you leave it unattended, for example, is a good safety precaution. Remember—unplug it by pulling the plug, not the cord. Grease spills should be wiped up to prevent kitchen fires. In general, it's important to be careful when around a stove, lighted fireplace, candles—anything that could possibly cause a fire.

A large percentage of accidents happen in the home. By watching out for safety, you can help reduce the chance of accidents in your home.

Increasing Space

As you grow older, you will be responsible for more space. For example, when you leave home to live on your own, you'll probably have more space to care for. If you decide to have a family, you may be responsible for an even larger space.

Many of the skills and ideas you use for maintaining your personal space right now will help you later on. So, with an eye to the future, make it a habit to care for your surroundings. That way, as you get older, you'll be prepared to handle the responsibilities that come with having more space.

QUESTIONS

1. What are the advantages of caring regularly for your belongings and your personal space? How can regular care save money?
2. How does each person have an effect on the condition of the home? What safety factors should be considered when caring for the space in a home?
3. Describe some of the chores that should be done daily, monthly, or seasonally in a home. Why are they necessary?
4. What are the advantages of having each person in a home always responsible for the same tasks? The disadvantages?
5. Where in the home do most accidents happen? Why?
6. Do you think that it's possible to be too neat? Explain.

ACTIVITIES

1. Interview someone of your grandparents' generation about his or her chores as a teenager. How do these chores compare with the household tasks you perform?
2. Make a list of everything you use in your home in a single day, and note what you do with it when you are finished using it. What pattern do you see in this list?
3. Make a cleaning carryall to hold the supplies used for general cleaning in your home.

Answer Key to Obvious Quiz

As with many quizzes in magazines, the "correct" answers are obvious. If you wanted to seem a very neat person, you would check all the *c* answers. To show how casual you are about maintenance, you would check all the *b* answers.

However, if you take this quiz seriously, you could learn something about yourself. If you answer each question honestly, you may see a pattern emerge. A majority of *a* answers means that you like to keep your belongings in some kind of order. A majority of *b* answers means that you don't care—many of your belongings are probably damaged. A set of *c* answers means that you really do care about neatness.

People have different ideas about neatness. It's good to examine your ideas and think how they affect your daily life. It could be the first step toward making life easier for yourself.

SECTION 8 · Home and Neighborhood

ONE PLACE, THREE VIEWS

KRISTIN OLSON

I moved to this neighborhood last summer. At first, I didn't know anybody. I didn't even know my way around. I felt like an outsider. I'm glad that feeling didn't last long. It was awful!

When school started, I met other people my age, and before long, I had lots of friends. I also found out that there's plenty to do around here! Sometimes after school we all go to Sancho's for tacos or we get ice cream at Cone Corner. There's a shopping mall right near the school. I like to go there to buy records and clothes. The neighborhood theater's called The Majestic. The admission is really low, so my friends and I go there a lot.

Now that I don't feel like a stranger anymore, I really like my neighborhood.

HELMUT OLSON

I still miss my old neighborhood. I don't know if I'll ever like this one as much.

I've made friends around here, but I still miss Joe and Manny. I miss Lake Silver, too. It was only a few streets away from where I used to live. In the summer, Joe, Manny, and I would go swimming there. In the winter, we went ice skating. The lake was big and there were pine trees all around it.

There's a pool around here. There's an indoor skating rink, too. But things just aren't the same—you know? I miss Lake Silver. And I miss my old friends.

MR. OLSON

We moved here mostly for convenience. Before we moved, I had to drive a long way to work every day. Here I get to see more of my family.

At first, I was worried about Helmut and Kris. I hoped they wouldn't have a hard time changing schools and making friends. But Kris seems to be doing fine, and I think Helmut will be okay once he's been here a bit longer.

I like it here. There are some nice foreign restaurants—inexpensive family places. It's fun to try them out.

Zoolis's Bookstore is on my way home from work. I like to drop in and browse. I love to read, so it's nice to have a bookstore right in my neighborhood.

A few months ago, I joined the neighborhood association. This community group has dances and art shows to raise money for neighborhood improvements. Right now we want to buy some playground equipment. I think that working together is part of what a neighborhood's all about.

What do you like about your neighborhood? What do you dislike? If you could make one big change in your neighborhood, what would you change?

Have you ever stopped to think about how much neighborhoods differ from one another? Think about your own neighborhood. Then think about other neighborhoods you know. Most likely, you'll find that each has its own look, its own style. Each neighborhood has a distinct personality.

In some neighborhoods, houses of many different sizes and shapes are mixed in with apartment buildings. The streets are busy, and you can always hear the sound of traffic. People can usually walk to stores to get what they need.

Other neighborhoods don't have as much variety. The houses are all similar in size and style. Each has a lawn and a front walk. You hear children playing and dogs barking. People usually have to drive to do their shopping.

There are many kinds of neighborhoods, both in the city and in the country. But there is one way in which all neighborhoods are alike—they all are places for people. In a neighborhood, people live, and sometimes work and play, together.

People Make the Difference

Think about the people in your neighborhood. What are they like? What types of things do they like to do?

Do they sit outside during the summer? Do they support a Little League team? Do they put lanterns in their windows on Halloween? Is it the custom to "drop in" for a visit, or are you expected to call first? People and customs differ from neighborhood to neighborhood.

Some neighborhoods may be tightly knit, with everyone knowing everyone else. Others may be quiet and reserved. People may know their neighbors' names but little else about them.

Neighborhoods made up of people with the same cultural background may have stores and restaurants that sell special kinds of food. Some may celebrate religious feast days with special carnivals. Others hold bazaars and church suppers. These events can be fun for everyone in the neighborhood.

Differences in neighborhoods, like differences in people, add a great deal to your experience. They make your world a more interesting place.

Close to Home

Just as the people in every neighborhood are different, so are the facilities. Every neighborhood needs facilities, places where people go for the goods and services they need.

Small businesses serve the people who live in an area. For example, your neighborhood may include a dry cleaner, a shoe repair shop, and a bakery. You may also live close to a movie theater, a restaurant, or both.

Many people like being able to shop at a nearby store or use a service that's right around the corner. The owners of these businesses depend greatly upon neighborhood support. Without it, neighborhood stores could not exist. This is one of the ways in which people in neighborhoods depend on one another.

Along with privately owned businesses, each neighborhood usually has its share of public buildings, parks, playgrounds, and schools. There may be a library or a museum. Sometimes there are health-care facilities such as a clinic or hospital.

Choosing a Place to Live

When people choose a place to live, they usually think about which facilities they

a

b

There are many different types of neighborhoods. These are just a few: (a) a garden apartment; (b) a high rise apartment; (c) a housing development; (d) a country neighborhood; (e) a row home; (f) a mobile home. Your type of residence depends on where you live, how much land space there is, the climate, your family's income, and personal preferences.

e

will use. A family with school-age children may wish to live near a school. A person who doesn't drive a car may choose to live where stores are within walking distance. Having a bus stop or train station nearby might also be important to someone who doesn't drive.

Few people use every facility their neighborhood offers. But just about everyone uses some of these facilities. When the Olson family explored their new neighborhood, each member looked for a different kind of place. Kristin found the shopping mall. Helmut used the swimming pool. Mr. Olson got into the habit of browsing at Zoolis's Bookstore.

Everyone looks for something different in a neighborhood. Most neighborhoods offer something for everyone.

Neighbors

Neighborhoods give us a chance to meet other people and get to know them. This

c

d

f

advice, and love. We need to be able to share our thoughts, feelings, and experiences with others. Warm relationships with neighbors can add a great deal of happiness to life.

Sharing a Neighborhood

Like a family living in the same house, the members of a neighborhood share a certain amount of space. The sidewalks, the streets, the parks, and similar areas are all shared spaces. Everyone in the neighborhood should take an interest in the care of these places. The beauty of a neighborhood depends greatly on the efforts of the people who live there.

Taking an interest in your neighborhood means caring about your environment. Keep your neighborhood looking nice. Don't litter. Pick up papers, bottles, and cans whenever you see them lying about.

Sometimes people who live in a neighborhood get together to improve it. They form community groups that try to find ways to make the neighborhood a better place to live. For example, the community group Mr. Olson joined was raising

helps satisfy our built-in need for human companionship. We share both joys and sorrows with our neighbors. Neighbors often become lifelong friends.

In your neighborhood, you are recognized as a unique person. The rest of the world may not care whether you win a basketball tournament. But to your neighbors, you're more than just a name and a face. They know you. So your success or failure may really mean something to them.

Human beings need one another's help,

money for playground equipment. Joining this group also gave Mr. Olson a chance to meet other people in the community. When people in a neighborhood know one another and work together, they are said to have a "sense of community."

Being a Good Neighbor

One of the best things about living in a neighborhood is being near people you can count on to help you. But if you want the help and support of other people, you, too, must be a good neighbor.

Being a good neighbor means caring about the people around you. When you know that a person in the next house is sick with the flu, try to be more quiet in your back yard. If the boy next door wins a prize in an art contest, stop to congratulate him. People who are new in a neighborhood especially need friendly neighbors who make them feel welcome.

Neighbors also offer one another safety and protection. Being a good neighbor sometimes means getting involved. If you hear a cry for help or see a person committing a crime, call the police. If you see smoke coming from someone's house or if you notice a broken window in the house of neighbors who are away, report the matter quickly. By watching out for others, people can reduce crime in their neighborhoods.

Our neighborhoods are what we make them. We can help to keep them clean and safe. We can try to be considerate of the people around us. In these ways, we can make our neighborhoods pleasant places in which to live.

QUESTIONS

1. What things make up the personality of a neighborhood? Give two examples of how different kinds of neighborhoods fill the needs of different kinds of people.
2. What kinds of shared space exist in a neighborhood? What responsibilities does each individual have toward these spaces?
3. Describe some of the responsibilities neighbors have toward each other.
4. What facilities in your neighborhood does your family use regularly? Are there facilities which you know about but don't use? Why?
5. How do you think people's ideas about neighborhoods have changed over the years? Do you think these changes are for better or for worse?
6. There's an old saying that "Good fences make good neighbors." What do you think that means? Do you agree?

ACTIVITIES

1. Draw a rough map of your neighborhood. Then compare your drawing with that of your classmates. What differences and similarities are there?
2. Interview someone who has lived in your neighborhood for a long time about the changes she or he has seen over the years. Describe the interview to your class.
3. Draw or paint a picture of your street the way it looks now. Make another picture showing how you would like it to look.

SECTION 9 · Housing and the Future

A City on a Farm

Imagine playing in your neighborhood on the twentieth floor! This could happen if an architect's dream comes true. His name is Paolo Soleri. The picture shows how compact his city would be. People live and work in one gigantic building. There are no expressways or parking lots, because cars are not needed. Travel is all by elevator and moving sidewalks.

Soleri calls his cities "arcologies"—from "architecture" and "ecology." He thinks we must change the way we live in order to survive in the future. Right now in the Arizona desert, a small "arcology" called Arcosanti is being built. A few parts are completed, but construction is very slow. It was started in 1970 and may take decades to finish. The workers are students, who contribute money

to work there. Already there are apartments, stores, artists' workshops, and a restaurant inside the complex.

In a full-size arcology, there would be tall towers with shops and schools. Thousands of people would live there. The buildings would rest on top of a large greenhouse, where food would be grown for the city. A large roof would collect solar energy to provide heat in the winter and hot water all year round. It would act as an awning in the summer.

With this design, the maximum amount of land could be used for growing food. Between the tall city structures, there would be outdoor farms and parks. The land beneath the buildings, too, could be productive. The question is, what would an arcology be like to live in?

Some important questions concerning the future of our planet must be answered. In order to plan the housing and communities of tomorrow, architects must think carefully about our natural resources. They must try to find ways to use these resources wisely.

One problem the world faces today is overpopulation. As the earth becomes more crowded, resources and space are getting more and more scarce. As a result, houses in the future may have to be smaller than those of today. Single-family homes may give way to many more tall, multiple-family dwellings that make better use of space.

Energy Problems

Architects who plan housing must figure out ways to conserve energy. There was a time when energy was cheap and plentiful. But today energy is both scarce and expensive. So new buildings will have to be more energy efficient.

Solar power may become much more common. Scientists and engineers are finding new ways to use the sun's energy. Just as people use energy from the sun to dry clothes outdoors, they can use the sun's energy to heat their homes.

To make the wisest use of natural resources, future communities will have to be more carefully planned. Housing will be linked more closely with other buildings in the community. The community's streets, buildings, and transportation system will all work together within a planned energy-saving system. Through planning, communities will make the wisest use of space.

Although future architects and city planners will all deal with the same problems, they will find many different solutions. So people in the twenty-first century

A geodesic dome can support itself, and is a good roof for large buildings, such as the library shown here.

will probably have just as many choices in housing and communities as we do today.

A Domed City

Another famous architect, Buckminster Fuller, has made plans for a community that, like Arcosanti, would be contained within one building. This building would be a large version of the geodesic dome, a dome-shaped structure that supports itself.

There are geodesic domes today that house one family, but Fuller's plan calls for a dome that would house 300,000 families. Each family within the dome would have an apartment of 2,000 square feet with a balcony leading to the outside. All the

Homes powered by solar energy are rare today. But more families may choose this form of clean energy in the future.

HOME COMPUTERS

Box 1

Home computers are already on the market. One day they may be as common as television sets.

Here are just a few of the things that they may be able to do:

- serve as an encyclopedia, dictionary, and film and book collection through connections with various videotape libraries across the country
- provide a wide range of video games for one or more people, provide instruction in almost any subject, transmit written material like letters, newspapers, and weather reports

- control and monitor all heating and lighting equipment within the house for the most efficient use of energy
- keep track of all standard food items and automatically order replacements from the store when supplies get low
- act as a combination smoke detector and burglar alarm that will automatically alert authorities when there is a problem

Right now home computers are very expensive. But as more people buy them, their price will go down. Home computers will probably be common in future households.

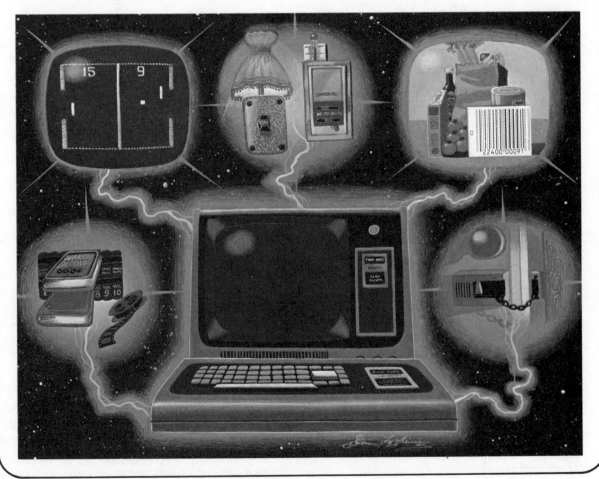

machinery needed to run the city would be inside the dome. Fuller says that his dome would be so light that it could float on water. So, someday floating cities may be possible!

New Towns

Since open space is becoming far less available, planned communities will be more important in the future. Several planned communities called new towns have already been built. Two of the most famous are in Reston, Virginia, and Columbia, Maryland.

A typical town is made up of "neighborhoods" of 2,000 to 5,000 people. Each neighborhood has a school, park, playground, pool, and community building.

Two to four "neighborhoods" make up a "village," with a population usually of 10,000 to 15,000. The village center houses businesses such as a bank, supermarket, drugstore, barber shop, beauty salon, and professional offices.

Finally, six or seven "villages" make up the town itself. In addition to the village centers, there is a downtown core. That core may include a shop-lined mall, office buildings, restaurants, a downtown park, a theater, a tennis barn, and a medical clinic.

A new town often reserves more than 20 percent of its total acreage for permanent open spaces. These spaces include golf courses, jogging and bicycling trails, and school playgrounds. The villages in the town are often separated by woods, streams, parks, or lakes.

Many experts think that new towns are a big improvement over the spread-out cities, or "urban sprawl," of the past. They believe that careful planning of cities and towns will lead to a wiser use of land and resources.

Modular Housing

An entire apartment building can be made out of housing units called modules. Each module may contain two or more rooms complete with plumbing and wiring.

Modules are built entirely in a factory. Then they are shipped to the building site and lowered by crane onto other modules. These modules combine to make an apartment building.

Because they are mass-produced, modular homes are less expensive than those built by other methods. Also, since they are designed to be fitted together, modules can be used to add new rooms whenever people want them.

Modular housing is being used in some parts of the country. A newly married couple can start off with five basic rooms: a utility core room, a living room, a kitchen, a bedroom, and a bathroom. Then, if they have children, they may add another bedroom module and perhaps a recreation room module.

Modular housing makes it possible for people to have the exact amount of space they need when they need it.

Going Underground

Underground may seem a strange place for buildings. But there are many advantages to building beneath the earth's surface. One is that the earth provides natural insulation. So underground housing uses less energy both for heating during cold weather and for cooling during hot weather. The earth also provides insulation from noise and vibration. Privacy, too, is easily available underground.

One of the disadvantages of underground housing is the lack of natural light. But this problem can be overcome by building an entryway with glass doors, perhaps looking out onto a patio or garden.

Underground buildings have been more widely used for commercial purposes than for housing. The city of Montreal has a system of attractive underground shops, offices, restaurants, and pedestrian walkways. Because this system is underground, it functions normally even during the worst snowstorms. Some people predict that in the future there will be much more underground building in cities.

Using Solar Energy

Capturing the sun's energy is one way to conserve the world's fuel supply. Recently, the National Aeronautics and Space Administration designed a home that makes efficient use of solar energy.

Nineteen rooftop solar collectors collect the energy from the sun's rays. This energy heats the house. It also heats water, which is stored in an underground tank. When the sun does not shine for a long time, the heated water is used to help warm the house. Eighty percent of the energy used in this model home comes from the sun. The remainder comes from conventional fuel.

Although solar houses are more expensive to buy than conventional ones, the energy savings are great. If solar heating systems could be halved in price, they could pay for themselves within ten years. They could also help preserve the energy resources of the world.

Playing Your Part

The solutions to the housing needs of tomorrow will be largely up to you. You will help determine whether cities are rebuilt. You may also have a part in planning new towns.

As consumers, you will shape the future housing market. Your knowledge, your ideas, and your purchasing decisions will help determine how houses are designed, built, and furnished. And your involvement with local governments and political issues will help influence where housing is built and how it is planned.

No one can say exactly what homes and neighborhoods will be like years from now. But whatever happens, you will certainly play a part.

QUESTIONS

1. What environmental problems and concerns will affect the style of housing in the future?
2. Describe three kinds of planned communities that might shape housing trends of the future.
3. How will the decisions and choices made by individual consumers affect the housing of the future?

ACTIVITIES

1. Find out more about one of the housing trends discussed in this section and report on it to the class.
2. Sketch your idea of a model community of the future. Keep in mind such problems as

4. Which of the housing possibilities described in this section would you most like to live in? Least? Why?
5. What functions other than those listed in box 1 of this section would you like to see a home computer perform?
6. How might it be possible to adapt the urban sprawl of today to the needs of the future?

limited resources and explain how you have solved them.
3. Pretend you live in a community of the future and write an entry in your diary that describes a typical day.

SECTION 10 · Careers in Housing

INTERIOR DESIGNER

Mark Thomas, a reporter for his school newspaper, is writing a series of articles on careers. Here and in box 1 of this section are interviews he recently held for the series. This one was with John Richezza, a professional interior designer.

MARK: Why did you decide to become an interior designer?

MR. RICHEZZA: Interior design appealed to me for two reasons. I like working with designs and colors. I also like working with people. Interior design gives me a chance to do both.

MARK: What courses did you take to become an interior designer?

MR. RICHEZZA: I finished a professional education program in interior design. I had to take courses in the principles of design, freehand and mechanical drawing, architecture, and art history. In order to plan homes, interior design students also learn all about fabrics, furnishings, antiques, and art pieces.

MARK: What experience have you had since you've been out of art school?

MR. RICHEZZA: For five years, I worked in the interior design studio of a large store. Then I took some exams and was admitted to the AID. That's the American Institute of Interior Designers. To qualify for the best jobs in the field, it's good to belong to either the AID or the NSID—the National Society of Interior Designers. Instead of working for someone else, though, I decided to open my own studio. I've been in business for three years now.

MARK: Could you describe your work?

MR. RICHEZZA: I help people plan their homes. First, I talk to them about what they want

and what they can afford. Then I make a few suggestions, and together we work out a plan. My clients' needs are so different that each job is a new challenge.

MARK: What kinds of plans do you work out?

MR. RICHEZZA: All kinds. I may plan one room, or an entire house. The client may want to see fabric swatches, wallpaper samples, paint chips, pictures of accessories—you name it. Sometimes I even draw a sketch of what I have in mind.

MARK: If your client approves the plan, what happens?

MR. RICHEZZA: That's the fun part. I arrange to buy all the materials and have them installed in the home. I or one of my assistants must supervise the work, of course, to make sure that everything goes right.

MARK: Is there anything you dislike about the job?

MR. RICHEZZA: Not really. But sometimes it can be frustrating when I work hard on a decorating plan and the client doesn't like it. Then I have to start all over again.

MARK: What do you enjoy most about your work?

MR. RICHEZZA: What I like best is that designing homes gives me a chance to be creative. I really enjoy thinking up a plan and then seeing it come to life in a room. And as an interior designer, I'm not limited to the rooms in my own home. I have a whole city full of rooms to work on.

The field of housing and interior design offers a wide variety of jobs. This section features interviews with two people who help others to select and arrange living space to meet their needs.

Living space extends beyond the home, however. The design of living spaces actually starts with decisions on where to build homes and community facilities. These decisions are made by urban planners. Urban planners try to solve the physical and social problems that occur when many people live in an area.

Most urban planners—sometimes called regional or community planners—work for local governments. Often their job is to help the governments prevent future problems by guiding the growth of an area.

Researching the problems of an area and trying to predict its needs are important in urban planning. Planners must know the future housing, transportation,

Interior designers use samples of different material to coordinate the elements of a room.

recreational, social, and business needs of a city, town, or neighborhood.

Once their research is complete, urban planners suggest ways to meet the needs of the area. Their plans show how underdeveloped land might best be used, and how roads and buildings could be laid out. They also may suggest what kinds of transportation systems would be practical.

As people's needs change, the use of space in cities and towns changes, too. Urban planning is likely to remain a very important field.

Construction

Building a house requires the efforts of people in many different occupations. An architect draws up the plans. A contractor supervises the actual building and hires workers such as carpenters, electricians, and plasterers. Landscapers and plant nursery workers may also be needed to plan the yard and gardens.

One part of urban planning is deciding what new facilities are needed in an area, and where they will be located.

Although there are many job opportunities in housing construction, the employment is irregular. One year, many houses may be built; the next year, only a few may be started. Changes in the number of houses being built greatly affect employment in the housing industry.

Home Furnishings Sales and Service

In order to furnish and maintain their homes, people need a variety of goods and services. The thousands of businesses that serve these needs provide a great number of jobs.

Many of these jobs are related to the inside of the house. For example, there are jobs for people who know how to make draperies and slipcovers. Some of these people own their own businesses. Others are employed by department stores or fabric shops. Usually they visit a home to take the necessary measurements. Then they make the slipcovers or draperies in the shop. Finally, they return to the home to hang the draperies or to make sure that the slipcovers fit right.

Houses need furniture, carpets, and appliances. The people who sell these products must know something about home space and interior design. There is another area of jobs concerned with the installment of these products. Many of these jobs require special skills. For example, carpet installers must be able to fit pieces of carpet into a room in such a way that the seams joining them aren't noticeable.

There are also many job opportunities in the maintenance and repair sections of the housing industry. Carpets, for example, are often professionally cleaned. Dishwashers, clothes washers and dryers, and

Box 1

SELLING HOUSES

For his next article, Mark interviewed Carol Siagh, a real estate salesperson. She specializes in selling houses.

MARK: What made you decide to go into real estate?

MS. SIAGH: After high school, I worked in a business office for a while. I wanted to change jobs, but I wasn't sure about what I wanted to do. Then a friend suggested that I might like selling real estate. I went to the library to find out about careers in real estate. Then I went out on calls with a local realtor.

As I learned about real estate, I decided I would enjoy helping people choose houses. So I took the required real estate courses and passed the state realtor's exam. Now I have a license to sell real estate.

MARK: What does your job involve?

MS. SIAGH: In a nutshell, my job is to match people and houses. But, of course, it's not as simple as it sounds.

I work for a real estate broker. People in the community who want to sell houses contact this broker. Buyers also contact us to find out what's available. I show buyers the houses and answer their questions.

Most buyers have a general idea of where they would like to live, and what they need in the way of space, and what they can afford. But sometimes their ideas are a little vague. They don't work with real estate every day, so they don't know exactly what to look for when buying a house.

That's where I can help. I know houses, and I know this area. I help people get a clearer idea of what they need and what's available.

MARK: How do you do that?

MS. SIAGH: Well, let me give you an example. Just the other day a family came in—Mr. and Mrs. Flynn and their two young boys. They said they wanted a three-bedroom house. They wanted a fireplace, a back yard, a formal dining room, and a family room off the kitchen.

I checked our listings of available houses. None of our houses within their price range had everything the Flynns wanted.

Then I remembered Mr. Flynn saying that carpentry was his hobby. One house had all the features they had mentioned except one—a family room. But it did have a big porch right off the kitchen. I suggested that Mr. Flynn enclose the porch and use it as a family room.

When they saw the house, the Flynns decided it was perfect for them. Mr. Flynn felt that enclosing the porch would be no problem. They decided to buy the house.

Because I remembered that Mr. Flynn was a good carpenter, I found the Flynns a house they liked at a price they could afford.

MARK: Is there anything you dislike about your job?

MS. SIAGH: Well, it takes a lot of patience. I may show someone more than a dozen houses and never sell them one. Or I may spend a lot of time with people trying to learn exactly what they have in mind. Then when I show them a house that fits their description, they change their minds about what they want.

MARK: What do you like best about your job?

MS. SIAGH: I enjoy the challenge of helping people find the right house. Sometimes people don't see the possibilities of a house right away. I like pointing out how they can make rooms look different by changing the color or the draperies.

Homes are very important to most people. It gives me a good feeling to help people find a house they like.

refrigerators sometimes break down. Skilled experts are needed to repair them.

Whatever your interests and abilities, the housing field offers a wide range of employment possibilities. Do you enjoy drawing? Do you like repairing mechanical things? Are you happiest when you're meeting people? A career in housing will let you use your special talents to help people meet their housing needs.

QUESTIONS

1. List five careers in housing and explain the function of each.
2. What interests, skills, and/or education are helpful in each of the careers you listed above?
3. Why will careers in housing be important in the future?
4. If you had to choose a career in the housing field, what would it be? Why?
5. Which careers in the field of housing probably did not exist 100 years ago? Why not?

ACTIVITIES

1. Arrange to spend a day on the job with someone in the housing field. Keep a diary of what the job involves. Also note what other things affect the work day.
2. Look through the classified section of your local newspaper for jobs in the housing field. How many jobs are listed for each category described in this section? Which workers seem to be most in demand? Which jobs seem to offer the best salaries and chances for advancement?

Foods & Nutrition

CHAPTER 7

Nutrition

SECTION 1 · Why We Eat What We Do When We Do

Who Ate What?

Here are pictures of three people and the meals they ate in a day. Can you match the diet time line to the person? Think about why you make the guesses that you do. What might the food a person eats tell you about him or her?

GLORIA

HARRY

SAM

TIME LINE 1

7:00 A.M.
Banana and milk
Sausages and two fried
    eggs
Sweet roll with butter
Orange juice

12:30 P.M.
Large plate of meat stew
Rice and beans
Fried banana
Pound cake
Soft drink

4:30 P.M.
Bag of potato chips
Two large cookies
Soft drink

6:30 P.M.
Large serving of meat
    and gravy
Baked potato with butter
Two ears of corn with
    butter
Small serving of spinach
Milk

10:30 P.M.
Piece of chocolate cake
Large dish of ice cream

TIME LINE 2

7:30 A.M.
Glass of tomato juice
Soft-cooked egg
Glass of low-fat milk

1:30 P.M.
Fruit salad
Medium-size hamburger
    patty
Slice of whole wheat
    bread
Green peas
Apple
Low-fat milk

4:00 P.M.
Low-fat milk

7:30 P.M.
Wonton soup
Chow mein
Oriental-style vegetables
Rice
Egg roll
Fruit
Fortune cookie
Tea

11:30 P.M.
Ice-cream sundae

TIME LINE 3

6:00 A.M.
Half a grapefruit
Large helping of
    scrambled eggs
Several pieces of bacon
Two slices of whole
    wheat toast with
    margarine
Large glass of milk

12:30 P.M.
Hamburger steak
Two slices of bread with
    margarine
Large mixed fruit salad
Large glass of milk

6:00 P.M.
Large plate of meatballs
    and spaghetti with
    sauce
Green beans
Large tossed salad
Three pieces of Italian
    bread with butter
Pastry and ice cream
Milk

10:00 P.M.
Two tacos
Beans
Rice
Milk

Does the family that just moved into your neighborhood trace its roots to Italy, Puerto Rico, or Mexico? Does a boy you see each day in the cafeteria play an active sport like football? Has the new girl in school moved to your town from the southern United States or from New England? Why does your classmate's family always eat such a late evening meal?

Food choices and meal patterns can tell a lot about a person or a family. There are nearly always reasons that people choose to eat the way they do. Sometimes the reasons are obvious. Other times they are not.

Harry

Perhaps it was easy for you to guess that Harry belongs with time line one, just by looking at Harry's size. Harry's parents like to see their family eat, as you might be able to guess by the size of his breakfast and dinner.

At lunchtime, Harry usually eats with friends in the cafeteria. They often enjoy Puerto Rican dishes, like rice and beans, and fried bananas. Through his friends, Harry has learned to like Puerto Rican cooking, although his heritage is Hungarian. While watching television with his family after school and studying at night, Harry likes to have a snack, though you might think he doesn't really need the extra food.

Gloria

Time line two might have been harder to decide. But notice that the eater avoids sweets most of the time, drinks low-fat milk, and eats very little bread at meals. This sounds like a weight-control diet. And Gloria is slim.

Gloria is a very busy girl. She has a job in the office at school, so she often eats a late lunch. She has a lead part in the school play, too. With rehearsal after school, she just managed to get home in time to join her family for a special Friday night treat.

Next, Gloria met friends to go to a movie, after which they all went out for ice cream. Gloria forgot about her weight watching then, but you can tell by looking at her that it probably didn't matter much.

Sam

By now you know that Sam belongs with time line three. Perhaps you figured this out before, however, for not many people eat like this every day. Sam is a member of his school's football team. He needs large amounts of food to build up strength and maintain energy to play his sport well.

To keep in especially good shape, Sam jogs two miles to school every day. This fact explains why he eats such a large breakfast at an early hour.

After school on the day shown here, Sam worked hard at football practice. Then he went home to celebrate his brother's birthday. For this event, Sam's parents prepared an Italian feast. Sam's grandparents on both sides of the family came from Italy. His family often celebrates special occasions with Italian dishes.

After dinner, Sam went to a dance with his girl friend. Later, they had a snack at one of Sam's favorite places—a Mexican restaurant.

Many People, Many Patterns

Observing what people eat can reveal a lot about them, but it doesn't tell you everything. Sam's ancestors, for example, might have been either Italian or Mexican, if you judged only by what he ate this one day.

Whether it's Gaspé salmon in the north, fried chicken in the south, baked beans in the east, or enchiladas in the west—throughout North America we all can enjoy the spice and variety of regional foods.

But the time lines do reveal some important facts about North America. First, they suggest that the United States and Canada have many kinds of people with many very different ways of living. Second, the time lines show what is happening more and more—people are learning to enjoy one another's traditions. One of the ways people can share their heritage with others is through serving their family's traditional foods.

The time lines also show that people have different eating patterns, for many reasons. Sometimes people eat what they do because of special activities. Sam, for example, eats hearty meals because he plays a very active sport.

The times at which people choose to eat meals vary, too, depending on each person's schedule. We saw that Gloria eats a late lunch because of her job. And Sam has an early breakfast because of his training schedule.

People often eat certain foods to celebrate special events or holidays. A large turkey dinner on Thanksgiving is common for many Americans. A big feast, like the one Sam's parents prepared, often marks birthdays and other happy occasions in families of every cultural background. The food served at such celebrations often reflects the family's heritage.

Your friends can influence your choice of foods, too. If they often gather at the pizza parlor or ice-cream shop, the specialties of those places are bound to be part of your diet. And at times you'll enjoy snacks or a meal in a friend's home. Food plays a big part in most people's social life.

Are All Patterns Good Ones?

With so many possible meal patterns and so many kinds of food to eat, you might be

---

Box 1

Oranges and Peppers

Nutritionists learn many interesting facts as they study people's eating habits.

Before 1800, many people all over the world died of a disease called scurvy. No one knew what caused this disease. Sailors and prisoners especially suffered from it. Fresh fruits and vegetables were not available on long voyages or in prisons, and this provided a clue. By 1800, it had been shown that oranges and lemons cure scurvy. But it wasn't until 1932 that the "secret ingredient" in these fruits, vitamin C, was discovered.

Mexicans, as far back as their Aztec ancestors, who lived thousands of years ago, have rarely eaten citrus fruits such as oranges or lemons. But Mexicans have always eaten peppers, and peppers of all sorts are also rich in vitamin C. So, long before anyone knew the word *vitamin*, Mexicans were getting an important vitamin they needed.

---

wondering if all eating habits are equally healthful. The answer is no!

To start with, eating regular meals is very important. If you skip breakfast and try to make up for it at lunch, your body will suffer. You won't have as much energy during the morning. Also, your body won't use the food you eat effectively if you have to digest a very large amount all at one time. It is best to eat at least three well-spaced meals each day.

Food is one of the most important factors in making a person healthy, lively, and attractive. What people eat, and when they eat it, can help them feel good all the time. Or it can keep them from doing any task as well as they might.

The Food Experts

The best judges of what makes a healthful diet are scientists called nutritionists. They study food and its effects on the body. For example, some nutritionists are studying the relationship between different kinds of fat and heart disease. Others are trying to find out how high-protein, low-fat diets affect the body.

From their studies, nutritionists can tell what makes a healthful diet. Using these findings, people of different ages, with different ways of living and different needs, can plan to get the most from their daily diets.

Be Your Own Nutritionist

Obviously you cannot have a nutritionist standing by to tell you if you are eating a healthful diet. But with a little time and effort you can become your own nutritionist. All you need to do is make yourself familiar with some of the basic facts nutritionists have learned over the years. Then keep up to date on new knowledge as researchers continue to learn more about foods and nutrients.

First of all, however, you need to do some careful thinking about your own eating habits. You can start with some personal research. For one week, keep a list of everything you eat and when you eat it. Write down *everything*—not only what you have at meals, but what you eat for snacks as well. Also write down how much of each item you eat.

Your list will help you see your own individual eating pattern. As you learn more about nutrition, you will be able to check your list to see if what you eat is helping you stay healthy.

QUESTIONS

1. List as many things as you can think of that influence a person's eating habits.
2. What one feature do special occasions all over the world usually have in common. Why?
3. What are some of the effects good eating habits can have on a person's life? Bad eating habits?
4. Why should you become aware of your personal eating habits?
5. An old saying about good eating habits is "Eat breakfast like a king, lunch like a prince, and dinner like a pauper." What does this saying mean? What are the benefits of eating this way?
6. When you are offered a new food, how do you usually react? What is it about a food that makes you decide whether or not to taste it?
7. Have you ever had a bad experience with a food that affected your attitude toward that food? What happened? Have you eaten that food since?

ACTIVITIES

1. See how many of your family's food preferences are shared by the families of your classmates. Make a list of the food items you find in your kitchen. Compare lists in class. Which foods are the most popular? What conclusions can you draw from the survey?
2. Interview someone from your grandparents' generation to find out how food habits have changed over the years. Find out what foods they ate, and how these foods were obtained and prepared. What do they think of the changes that have occurred?
3. Bring in a family recipe that is special to you, along with a story that describes why it is special.

SECTION 2 · Nutrients and What They Do for You

WHAT DO THESE PEOPLE HAVE IN COMMON?

Look at these pictures. All the people you see have something in common.

Can you think what it is?

Everyone pictured here is using energy with his or her body. That's perfectly easy to see for the mountain climber, the bicycle riders, and the runners. You can see they're exercising, and you know that takes energy.

But what about the others? They're using energy, too. It takes energy to read and think and work in an office. It even takes energy to sleep. While you sleep, you still breathe, your heart keeps beating, your blood continues to flow. Your body builds and repairs itself in many little ways. All these functions take energy.

Perhaps most important, you are growing—whether you are asleep or awake, studying or running. And growing takes a great deal of energy.

Where Does Your Energy Come From?

You know that energy for electricity can come from water power, from the sun, and from other sources. Energy for a car comes from burning gasoline. How do *you* get energy? You get it from the foods you eat.

As you know, food comes in many shapes, colors, sizes, and tastes. All food is made of a number of substances. Some of them are called nutrients. Each nutrient does something for your body.

Some nutrients provide the energy for everything you do, awake or asleep. Others build up your muscles and other body tissues. Still others keep your body working smoothly by helping to digest food, make new muscle tissue, or fight off sickness.

Nutritionists and other scientists usually talk about five kinds of nutrients. All the nutrients of one kind are alike in their makeup and do similar things for your body. The five kinds of nutrients are proteins, fats, carbohydrates, minerals, and vitamins.

Proteins: The Tissue Builders

The word protein comes from an ancient Greek word meaning "of first importance." While all the nutrients are very important, proteins are the one nutrient you can't afford to skimp on for even a short time.

Protein forms the base of all your body's cells. There is more of it in your body than of any other nutrient. Protein is necessary for building and repairing body tissues, and anyone who is growing needs a great deal of it.

Your body must have certain substances called amino acids in order to make the protein it needs. There are at least twenty-two amino acids needed for building human body cells. All of the twenty-two must be present in your body if you want to stay healthy. Your body can manufacture most of the necessary amino acids if you eat a varied, balanced diet. But there are eight that cannot be made by the body. These eight must be present in the food you eat. They are known as the essential amino acids.

Animal products, such as meat, fish, milk, and eggs, supply the essential eight. For this reason, these products are called "complete" protein foods.

The proteins in vegetables, fruits, and grains are "incomplete." They contain many amino acids, but they don't contain the essential eight in amounts great enough to support life and growth.

Still, these other protein sources help us get the amino acids we need, especially when they are combined with complete protein foods. People who don't eat meat or other animal products can get the essential amino acids from a carefully chosen diet of fruits, vegetables, and grains.

Box 1

What Is a Calorie?

When you look at a list of nutrients, you may be surprised to find one term missing. People always mention calories when talking about diets. But a calorie isn't a nutrient. What is it?

Very simply, a calorie is a measure of energy. When you ride a bicycle, you are using energy. This energy can be measured in calories. You might use up about 250 calories in a half-hour bicycle ride.

This energy may come from carbohydrates that you have eaten. It may come from fat that you are working off. If your carbohydrate and fat reserves are low, the energy may come from burning up the protein in your muscles—something you should avoid.

Carbohydrates, fats, and proteins can all be described by the amount of calories, or energy, they can produce. If the foods you eat would produce more energy than you need, many of those foods are turned into fat, which holds the calories in reserve. This is why people count calories to keep from gaining weight.

This is also why it is essential to consider nutrients as well as calories in your diet. If all the calories you eat are carbohydrate calories, you will have no proteins for body growth. With a little thought, you can keep your calories down *and* eat a healthy diet.

Fat: The Most Misunderstood Nutrient

A certain amount of fat is necessary for good health. The body stores up reserve energy in fat tissues. When a person has not eaten for a while and needs some energy, that energy can come from body fat.

Fat is also necessary so that the body can store and use certain vitamins, substances necessary to good health. Good growth, too, is aided by fat. Without fat in the diet, skin and hair problems develop. Fat also helps the body digest food and helps keep body temperature normal.

Too much fat in the diet, however, can cause serious health problems. It clearly plays a big part in being overweight. Excess weight can lead to heart disease and high blood pressure. Some experts believe that eating too much fat leads to other health problems as well. So watch for the latest scientific findings about fat in the diet. Such information is often discussed on television programs and in the newspaper.

Also, consider how much fat you eat normally. Some fats are easy to notice—the fat on meat, the oil in salad dressings, and the butter or mayonnaise on sandwiches. Some foods that you might not suspect, though, also provide large amounts of fat. Nuts, for example, contain a great deal. So do milk, cheese, baked goods like cookies and pastry, and snack foods like potato chips and chocolate candy. When considering your fat intake, don't overlook these less obvious sources.

Carbohydrates: Ready Energy

We need carbohydrates in our diet for energy. Our most healthful sources of carbohydrates are the starches and natural sugars in cereals or grains, fruits, and many vegetables. These foods not only supply energy, but also provide vitamins and minerals.

Candy and other sweets, and snack foods like potato chips and corn chips, are high in carbohydrates and do provide energy. However, they are not the best source of carbohydrates. They provide few, if any, other nutrients.

Carbohydrates are essential for good health. If you eat more than your body can use up in energy, though, the extra carbohydrates turn into body fat. In order to get energy and good nutrition without putting on extra pounds, it's important to choose your carbohydrates wisely.

Minerals: The Body Protectors

Small amounts of minerals are found in most foods. Nutritionists are still learning how each mineral works in the body. They already know that minerals form part of many tissues and are needed to keep body processes operating smoothly. Iron, calcium, and iodine are among the minerals necessary for good health. Special care must be taken to see that these minerals are included in the diet.

Iron is essential for building red blood cells. When people do not get enough iron, they develop a condition called anemia. They lack energy and have a hard time resisting infection. Anemia is the most common form of malnutrition in the United States today. Teenage girls are among those most likely to suffer from anemia. They must be especially careful to get enough iron.

Calcium is the chief mineral forming the bones and teeth. The correct amount of calcium must always be circulating in the blood so that the heart will beat regularly and the blood will clot normally. Calcium keeps nerves and muscles healthy and allows normal growth to occur.

Iodine makes the thyroid gland work

Even where food is plentiful, people don't always eat enough foods with the right nutrients. Ads such as this one are designed to help people learn about nutrition.

Some undernourished American kids have never missed a meal.

You can be overweight and your body can still be hungry for the right foods.

And America has more undernourished, overweight children than you would ever imagine.

That's why the Department of Health, Education and Welfare has published a free booklet, *Food Is More Than Just Something to Eat.* For a free copy, write: Nutrition, Pueblo Colorado 81009.

FOOD IS MORE THAN JUST SOMETHING TO EAT.

The better you eat, the better you are.

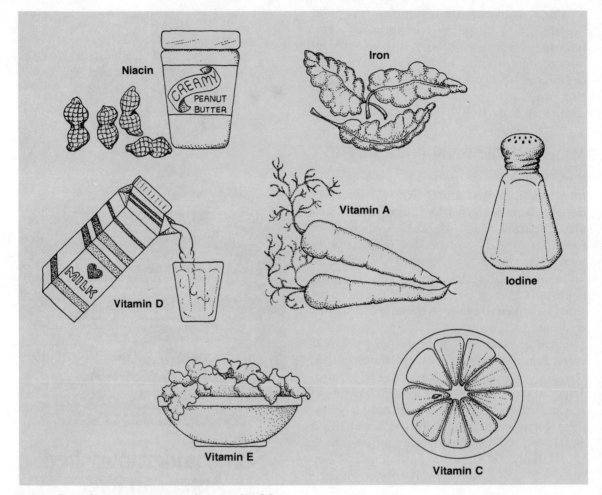

Niacin

Iron

Vitamin A

Iodine

Vitamin D

MILK

CREAMY
PEANUT
BUTTER

Vitamin E

Vitamin C

Minerals and vitamins are vital to our health, though we need only small amounts. So we should know which foods contain them. Some are so rare in nature that they need to be added—vitamin D to milk, iodine to salt.

correctly. When the diet lacks iodine, the gland does not produce enough thyroid hormone. This condition can cause such problems as excess weight gain, lack of energy, and a swelling of the neck called a goiter.

Other important minerals, such as phosphorus and potassium, are widely available in the foods we eat. There is little chance that the average diet would be lacking in these minerals.

Vitamins: "Miracle" Nutrients

Scientists did not discover the substances called vitamins until the turn of the century. Even today we have much to learn about these amazing nutrients.

Vitamins are present in the body in *very* small quantities. They provide no energy.

They form no part of the tissues. But without the necessary amount of each vitamin, serious—even fatal—illnesses develop.

Vitamin A is necessary for good vision, healthy skin, good teeth, and strong bones. **Vitamin B** is really a group of vitamins. The most important of these are thiamine, riboflavin, and niacin. Without them, your body cannot use any of the other nutrients well. The B vitamins are especially important for nerve and brain tissue to develop and function well.

Vitamin C helps your body fight off infection and heal wounds and cuts. It is also necessary in forming strong teeth and bones and in keeping gums healthy.

Your body can make **vitamin D** if you get enough sunlight. Otherwise, you must get this vitamin from food. Vitamin D is necessary for using calcium well. Sometimes doctors prescribe it in pill form for growing children and teenagers.

Vitamin E helps to make red blood cells and to keep your body strong.

Water and Bulk

Water and fiber, or bulk, are also necessary for good health. About seventy percent of your body weight is water. Water is the basic material of blood and is in all the cells.

Fiber, or bulk, comes from the parts of fruits, vegetables, and grains that your body does not digest and use. Although bulk passes through your body, it helps you digest other foods.

Teamwork

All the nutrients work together. If you get too little vitamin C, for example, your body will not be able to use calcium or iron well. If you don't get enough of the B vitamins, you will be unable to digest the other nutrients properly. There are many other examples of the way nutrients work together. Each example shows why it is necessary to get the right amount of each nutrient. If you don't, your whole body will suffer.

QUESTIONS

1. List all the ways you can think of in which your body uses energy each day. When is your body *not* using energy?
2. Name the five major nutrients and give one example of what each nutrient can do for you.
3. Name some ways in which two different kinds of nutrients work together.
4. What is a calorie? How are calories related to nutrients?
5. How is it possible to be overweight and undernourished at the same time?
6. Do you think there is one nutrient that is more important than all the others? Explain your answer.

ACTIVITIES

1. Collect pictures of snacks that provide good nutrition and snacks that provide "empty calories." Mount the pictures in related pairs (for example, orange juice and orange soft drink) and list the nutrients and calories found in each.
2. Make a poster of a human body. Label each part of the body with the nutrient(s) that help keep it in good working order.
3. Write a report on the history of a particular vitamin.

SECTION 3 · Which Foods Have Which Nutrients?

GROUP THESE FOODS

Look at the foods pictured here. Do you see any that are alike in some way? Take a few minutes and try to arrange these foods into groups, so that all the foods in each group have something in common.

Maybe you grouped the foods by color. Or maybe you put all the foods together that you usually have at one meal, like breakfast. Or maybe you made two big groups—foods you like and foods you don't!

Whichever way you grouped the foods is correct, for they all have different qualities in common. There is one way, however, of grouping that you might have overlooked. Did you put the orange and the broccoli together? The oatmeal and the spaghetti? The steak and the egg?

Perhaps not. After all, how *is* steak like an egg?

Nutritionists divide foods into a few large groups according to the nutrients most common in different foods. A piece of steak and an egg are both higher in protein than in any other nutrient. They both provide quite a bit of fat, some iron, some calcium, and varying amounts of vitamins. Neither has any vitamin C.

The balance between protein and the other nutrients isn't *exactly* the same in steak as in egg. But it is close enough for nutritionists to consider steak and egg in the same food group.

What Are the Food Groups?

Today, American nutritionists talk about four food groups. Knowing what foods are in each group and the main nutrients in each helps people plan balanced diets.

Milk and milk products—such as cheese, cream, yogurt, buttermilk, and ice cream—form one group. These foods are very rich in calcium, as well as in protein and vitamins. Nutritionists say that teenagers need 32 ounces, or 960 milliliters, of milk group products every day. That's about four glasses of milk, for example.

Meat and eggs are in another group. They are both important as sources of protein. Fish and poultry—such as chicken and turkey—are also in this group. Dried beans, lentils, and peas are rich in protein, too. So is peanut butter. But these plants aren't a *complete* protein source. People need at least 4 to 6 ounces, or about 160 grams, from this group daily—about two servings.

Fruits and vegetables are a third group. If you grouped the tomato and the strawberries together because they are both red,

you had them in the right group—even if it wasn't for the right reason!

Fruits and vegetables provide important amounts of vitamins and minerals, and they also add fiber to the diet. Nutritionists suggest eating four or more servings from this group every day.

Cereals, or grains, form a fourth group. Cereal doesn't only mean what you eat for breakfast with milk and fruit. Rice is a cereal, and so is wheat. Corn is a cereal, too, when it is dried, ground up, and made into corn bread, tortillas, or cornflakes.

Grains form the major part of the diets of most of the world's peoples. Foods in this group, which includes all kinds of bread, are important for the carbohydrates they contain. Cereal products also contain protein, B vitamins, iron, and important fats. Four servings a day from this group are recommended.

Other Foods

Some foods don't fit into any of the four groups. Like so many things for which no suitable name exists, this group is called "other." Butter is in this group. Although made from cream, butter does not fit in the milk group because it contains no calcium and almost no protein. Margarine and all kinds of oils are in this group, too.

Butter and margarine provide large amounts of vitamin A. Along with various types of oil, they add good flavor to foods, too. But these products have a high fat content and provide many calories Use them in small amounts that do not overpower the foods with which they are served.

Sweeteners, such as sugar, honey, and molasses, are also in the "other" group. They provide flavoring, but they also contain many calories and should be used sparingly.

Box 1

IN MORE DETAIL

To plan a healthful diet, people must know what their nutritional needs are, and how different foods can help to meet those needs. Understanding the four food groups is a good start. But you may want to go further. Nutritionists have carefully studied human needs. Some of their findings have been published in the form of tables.

First, nutritionists have developed tables of Recommended Daily Dietary Allowances (or RDA s for short). These tables suggest how much of certain nutrients different people should eat each day to remain healthy. Because different people have different needs, RDA s are provided for males and females of most age groups. Below is RDA information for boys and girls aged eleven through fourteen.

Nutritionists have also prepared Tables of Food Values, showing how much of the

KEY + Probably present − No data Tr—Nutrient present but in very small (trace) amounts		Calories	Carbohydrates (g)	Fat (g)	Protein (g)	Calcium (mg)	Iron (mg)	Vitamin A (IU)	Thiamine (mg)	Riboflavin (mg)	Niacin (mg)	Vitamin C (mg)
MALES RDA	11—14 years	2800			44	1200	18	5000	1.4	1.5	18	45
FEMALES RDA	11—14 years	2400			44	1200	18	4000	1.2	1.3	16	45

FOOD VALUES

		Calories	Carbohydrates (g)	Fat (g)	Protein (g)	Calcium (mg)	Iron (mg)	Vitamin A (IU)	Thiamine (mg)	Riboflavin (mg)	Niacin (mg)	Vitamin C (mg)
Milk	(1 c/240 ml)	150	12	8	8	291	.1	307	.1	.4	.2	2
Milk, skim	(1 c/240 ml)	86	12	.4	8	302	.1	500	.1	.3	.2	2
Ice Cream, plain	(½ c/120 ml)	175	16	12	2	75	.05	448	.02	.14	.57	1
Yogurt, plain, skim	(1 c/240 ml)	127	17	.4	13	452	.2	16	.1	.5	.3	2
Eggs	(1)	80	Tr	6	6	28	1	260	.05	.15	—	0
Beef, hamburger, 21% fat	(1)	235	0	17	20	9	2.7	30	.07	.17	4.4	0
Beef	(3.5 oz/100 g)	266	0	15	30	10	4	50	.1	.4	4.5	0
Tuna Fish, canned in oil	(3 oz/85 g)	170	0	7	24	7	1.6	70	—	.1	10	0
Peanut Butter	(2 T/30 ml)	190	4	17	9	10	.6	0	.02	.02	4.2	0

Note: Today scientists know of almost fifty nutrients needed for human health. RDAs have been established for only eighteen of these. The above tables list only ten.

To be sure of getting enough of the other nutrients, a varied diet is essential. In general, unrefined foods provide a wider variety of nutrients than refined foods. Even fortified foods won't give all the nutrients you need.

Among the nutrients not listed above, *Iodine* is obtained from seafood, or from iodized table salt. *Vitamin D* is made in the body with the help of sunshine—it can also be obtained from fortified milk.

nutrients are provided by portions of different foods. Tables of Food Values can be very large, because there are so many foods. The values of some common foods are shown below.

If you compare the RDA s with the Food Values, you can find out how much any one food serving will contribute to your own needs. For example, the RDA table shows that each day both boys and girls need 45 milligrams of vitamin C. A look at the Food Values will tell you which foods give you a lot of vitamin C—oranges, and potatoes. Notice how much vitamin C is lost by french frying.

Check out some other important nutrients too. As you can see, it is quite complicated to keep count of all the nutrients you eat in a day!

KEY- + Probably present − No data Tr—Nutrient present but in very small (trace) amounts		Calories	Carbohydrates (g)	Fat (g)	Protein (g)	Calcium (mg)	Iron (mg)	Vitamin A (IU)	Thiamine (mg)	Riboflavin (mg)	Niacin (mg)	Vitamin C (mg)
MALES RDA	11—14 years	2800			44	1200	18	5000	1.4	1.5	18	45
FEMALES RDA	11—14 years	2400			44	1200	18	4000	1.2	1.3	16	45

FOOD VALUES

		Calories	Carbohydrates (g)	Fat (g)	Protein (g)	Calcium (mg)	Iron (mg)	Vitamin A (IU)	Thiamine (mg)	Riboflavin (mg)	Niacin (mg)	Vitamin C (mg)
Orange	(3 in/76 mm)	75	18	Tr	1	61	.6	300	.15	.06	.7	75
Orange Juice	(¾ c/180 ml)	80	19	Tr	1	20	.4	370	.17	.06	.7	83
Spinach, cooked	(½ c/120 ml)	20	3	.5	3	84	2	7290	.06	.12	.5	25
Corn, sweet	(½ c/120 ml)	83	19	.5		3	.6	400	.11	.10	1.3	7
Potato, baked	(1 med)	140	31	Tr	4	13	1	+	.15	.06	2.5	30
Potatoes, French fried	(10 pieces)	135	18	7	2	8	.7	Tr	.07	.04	1.6	11
White Bread, enriched	(1 slice)	70	13	1	2	21	.6	0	.10	.06	.8	0
Whole Wheat Bread	(1 slice)	65	14	1	3	24	.8	0	.09	.03	.8	0
Pasta, enriched (macaroni cooked, etc.)	(1 c/240 ml)	190	39	1	7	14	1.4	0	.23	.13	1.8	0
Cornflakes, fortified (25% RDA)	(1 c/240 ml)	110	25	Tr	2	1	1.8	1250	.38	.43	5	15
Bacon	(2 slices)	85	0	8	4	2	.5	0	.08	.05	.8	0
Margarine, regular	(1 T/15 g)	100	0	12	0	0	0	470	0	0	0	0
Honey	(1 T/21 g)	65	17	0	Tr	1	.1	0	Tr	—	—	Tr
Sugar	(1 T/12 g)	45	12	0	0	0	Tr	0	0	0	0	0

Note: These tables are adapted from Food and Nutrition Board, National Academy of Sciences—*National Research Council Recommended Daily Dietary Allowances*, revised 1974, and from McGill, Marion and Pye, Orrea—*The No-Nonsense Guide to Food and Nutrition*, Butterick Publishing, 1978. More complete tables are given in back of this book, starting on p. 480.

The foods on page 248 are arranged here in the four food groups: fruits and vegetables, dairy products, cereals and grains, and meat and other protein products.

Are the Foods in Each Group Equal?

Within each group, there are great differences in the amount of the main nutrients each food provides. In the meat group, for example, a 3-ounce or 85-gram serving of steak gives 2.5 milligrams of iron. The same amount of clams gives much more iron—5.2 milligrams. But the steak has 20 grams of protein, while the clams contain only 11 grams.

Fruits and vegetables offer another example of such differences. This group is an important source of vitamins A and C. Some of these foods provide only a little vitamin A and much vitamin C—for example, oranges and grapefruit. But dark leafy vegetables such as collard greens, and deep yellow vegetables such as carrots are excellent sources of vitamin A.

Even the same food can differ, depending how it was handled and prepared. Overcooking broccoli, for example, can destroy some of the vitamins. Storing foods improperly—for too long a time or in places that are too warm—can also rob them of essential nutrients.

Getting a Balanced Diet

Clearly you must think about the differences in nutritive value among the foods in each group. The best way to make sure you get all the nutrients you need is to eat many different foods from each group. And you must take steps to preserve these nutrients by handling foods properly.

The fact that we can choose from a huge variety of foods to get the nutrients we need is part of what makes eating fun. But how are you to know whether an orange or an apple gives you more vitamin C? Does one cup of cottage cheese give as much calcium as a glass of whole milk? Which has more protein—a hamburger or a hot dog?

Also, you need to know how much of each nutrient your own body requires.

Knowing Your Nutrient Needs

Nutritionists and other scientists have studied these questions very carefully. They have developed tables that list how much of each nutrient different foods provide. They have also developed tables showing the nutrients needed by people in different age groups. You can see material from these tables in box 1 of this section.

Knowledge of nutrition is continually growing. As scientists discover new facts, these tables are revised. Keep up with the latest news on nutrition on television and in newspapers and magazines. It can help you to improve your diet.

But as a simple guide to healthful eating, the four food groups are very helpful. Follow the serving suggestions—three or four from the milk group, two from the meat group, four from the fruits and vegetables, and four from the cereal group. If you also eat a variety of foods *within* each group, you are unlikely to miss out on your nutrient needs.

QUESTIONS

1. Name the four food groups and describe the major nutrients in each one.
2. List five foods from each of the four basic food groups.
3. How many servings from each food group should a balanced diet contain each day?
4. Why should you eat more than one kind of fruit daily? Why should you vary the kinds of protein foods you eat each day?

5. How do you think referring to a table of food values might change your family's eating patterns?
6. What do you think of the old saying, "An apple a day keeps the doctor away"? How would you rewrite it?
7. Do you think your own daily calorie requirements are above or below the average amounts listed in box 1 of this section? Why?

ACTIVITIES

1. Keep a food diary of everything you eat for three days. Determine whether you had the required servings from each of the four groups. Did you have enough variety within each group? Did you get the nutrients you need daily?
2. Design a poster illustrating the four food groups and the recommended number of daily servings for each. Try to include pictures of as many foods in each group as possible.
3. Plan a nutritious three-day menu for a thirteen-year-old female athlete who needs 7,000 calories a day.

SECTION 4 · Developing Healthy Eating Habits

THE DIET BUSINESS

Diet is a word with many shades of meaning. At its simplest, diet means the foods that you regularly eat. But the word is also commonly used for special diets that are followed when for some reason people have to watch what they eat.

Sometimes special diets are called for because of sickness. A doctor knows that some foods are particularly good for the patient, while others are bad. But the most common special diets are needed because people have developed poor eating habits.

Overweight

Controlling eating habits to avoid extra weight is very important. Overweight has been called America's number one health problem. Extra pounds may look bad, but what they can do to your health is even more serious.

Being overweight can harm the kidneys and the blood circulation. It can cause, or make worse, painful diseases of the joints and bones. It can also damage the liver.

Most doctors believe that being overweight makes heart disease and high blood pressure worse. And statistics show clearly that extra pounds take years off a person's life.

Learning to eat wisely, then, will help you become not only more attractive, but healthier too.

Who Needs to Lose Weight?

How can you tell if you really should lose some weight? Your eyes can sometimes tell you. If your mirror reveals an unflattering bulge or a too-tight pair of jeans, you may need to think about your eating habits.

Mirrors can fool you, though. Occasionally, people limit their calories more than they should. They think they look good when they are actually too thin. Dieting to this extreme can be as harmful as carrying around extra weight. A diet that is too strict may not provide the nutrients needed for energy, growth, and good health.

Scales are a better guide to whether or not a person is overweight. Box 1 of this

Box 1

Average Heights and Weights of Females and Males, Ages 11–17								
	FEMALES				**MALES**			
	HEIGHT		WEIGHT		HEIGHT		WEIGHT	
Age	Inches	Centimeters	Pounds	Kilograms	Inches	Centimeters	Pounds	Kilograms
11	57.00	144.8	81.47	36.95	56.42	143.3	77.84	35.30
12	59.65	151.5	91.57	41.53	58.94	149.7	87.71	39.78
13	61.85	157.1	101.65	46.10	61.61	156.5	99.11	44.95
14	63.15	160.4	110.87	50.28	64.21	163.1	111.95	50.77
15	63.70	161.8	118.36	53.68	66.54	169.0	125.05	56.71
16	63.94	162.4	123.24	55.89	68.31	173.5	136.93	62.10
17	64.21	163.1	125.00	56.69	69.37	176.2	146.21	66.31

Adapted from National Center for Health Statistics: *NCHS Growth Curves for Children; Vital and Health Statistics*, ser. 11, no. 165 (DHEW publication; (PHS) 78-1650), November, 1977, pp. 37–38.

section gives average heights and healthy weights for people your age and older. Box 1 is only a guide. If you think it shows that you are unusually heavy, or light, check with a doctor, and consider going on a weight-control diet.

Mind Over Matter

Someone once said that taking off weight was just a matter of learning one exercise—pushing your chair away from the table! In a sense, that old joke is true. To reduce, all you need to do is eat food with fewer calories than you use.

People who are successful in shedding pounds and keeping them off, however, usually use more than will power. They exercise to work off stored calories. And they plan their meals carefully.

They make sure they get enough of all the nutrients. But they also know that by limiting their calories they can keep their weight down.

What Are Crash Diets?

Crash diets promise quick and easy weight loss. But crash diets—and all the other "wonder" plans for losing weight—fail to help people reach the one goal that really can help control a weight problem. This goal is to change bad eating habits to good ones.

Many crash diets allow only a few kinds of food and little else—grapefruit and lamb chops, for example, or bananas and buttermilk. Other diets eliminate one kind of nutrient, such as carbohydrates.

Crash diets are almost always dangerous to health. Following them prevents a person from getting a balanced diet. Though you may lose several pounds quickly on a crash diet, those pounds will not stay off when you go back to your old eating habits.

Up and Down

People may get into a bad eating pattern with crash diets. They follow one plan strictly for a short time and lose weight. Then, because the diet allowed only a limited number of foods, they become bored with their meals. Or they may be extremely hungry most of the time. In either case, they often start eating their high-calorie favorites again.

Soon the lost weight is back, and sometimes extra pounds as well. At this point, some people decide to try yet another crash diet. This pattern can go on, and it can damage the dieter's health.

Many doctors and other scientists believe that constantly gaining and losing weight puts a strain on the body and can do lasting damage. It's much healthier—and much less trouble—to learn to eat so that extra weight has no chance to build up.

If a person usually consumes the right number of calories and all the nutrients as well, a special occasion does not present a problem. Once in a while, a few treats may add a pound or two, but that weight is easily lost with a few days of sensible eating.

Watch What You Eat

Dieting for weight control need not be unpleasant if you use your knowledge of nutrition—and your imagination. A sensible weight-loss program doesn't have to be dull. Learn to enjoy the natural taste of foods—without thick sauces or a lot of butter or mayonnaise. Fix low-calorie snacks and limit yourself to small amounts of high-calorie foods. Eating one dip of ice cream instead of two, or one piece of cake instead of several, cuts many calories.

Box 2

Beyond the Four Food Groups

Most people can easily get all the nutrients their bodies need by eating a balance of foods from the four food groups. But what about those who cannot, or will not, eat food from one of these important groups? Such people must plan their diets with special care in order to get all the nutrients they need.

For example, you—or someone you know—may be unable to digest the lactose in milk. People who cannot drink milk must get the necessary nutrients provided by milk from some other source.

Many people in the world have lactose intolerance, as this condition is called. Some get by with a diet totally lacking in milk. In North America, fortunately, there are many milk group products that are almost lactose-free. Yogurt and many cheeses, for instance, lose most of their lactose as they are made. And a special lactose-free milk is also available at some supermarkets.

Vegetarians are another group who need to take special care with their diet. They eat no meat or meat products. Some also avoid all milk products and eggs.

People are vegetarians for a variety of reasons. Some believe it is wrong to kill living creatures for food. Others believe that meat and other animal products are bad for health. There may also be an economic reason. Vegetables are generally cheaper than animal products.

Making sure they get enough protein is important for vegetarians, especially for those who eat no milk products or eggs. With careful planning, though, a vegetarian diet can be as healthy as one that includes meat.

For people in your age group, a good vegetarian diet would include the following foods, in at least these amounts, every day:

   4 cups or 960 ml of milk
   4–5 servings * of fruits and vegetables, including one that is rich in vitamin C and one that is green and leafy
   2–3 servings of vegetable protein, such as cooked dried beans, nuts, and soy products
   4–5 servings of breads and cereals
   1 egg
   2–3 t or 10–15 ml of vegetable fat (oil or margarine)

Here is an example of such a diet:

Breakfast:
   Egg
   Whole grain cooked or dry cereal with milk
   Whole wheat toast with margarine
   Orange sections
   Milk

Lunch:
   Soybean patty
   Potato
   Carrot
   Tossed green salad
   Whole wheat bread with margarine
   Pear
   Milk

Dinner:
   Vegetable soup
   Peanut butter sandwich
   Cottage cheese with fruit salad
   1 or 2 oatmeal cookies
   Milk

(*Serving sizes depend on the food and the form in which it is served.)

Some high-calorie foods, such as soft drinks and potato chips, have little or no nutritive value. These foods are said to provide "empty calories." One glass of soft drink, for example, contains enough sugar to provide about 90 calories, but not one other nutrient. And ten potato chips contain 115 calories. That's a lot, considering

Exercise helps you keep in shape. Running burns about 14 calories per minute; skiing 10; basketball 8; and tennis 6.

how little they satisfy hunger and how few nutrients they offer. Eaten in large quantity, foods with empty calories may add to your weight without doing you any good at all.

Watch How You Eat

The *way* people eat can contribute to weight problems almost as much as *what* they eat. Eating slowly is especially important for dieters. Even when enough food has been eaten, it takes time to get a full feeling. When people eat too quickly—and many overweight people do—they often consume two or three extra helpings before they get that sense of fullness. Eating slowly also gives a person more time to enjoy the flavor of foods.

When people nibble or snack between meals, they are apt to put on many extra pounds. They get in the habit of eating while watching TV. They eat to relax before going to bed. If this kind of eating is a problem for you, try doing something else at these times. Practice a craft such as nee-

dlepoint while watching TV, or play a game such as backgammon. And to relax, try reading a book or magazine instead of snacking.

Are You Really Hungry?

Emotions often play a part in overeating. Some people turn to food when they are nervous, lonely, or bored. They use food to satisfy some need that would be better met in another way.

Do you find yourself eating when you are not hungry? Do you want more food than your body really needs? If so, you need to think about the cause. It may take your best efforts to turn your attention away from food and face what is causing you to overeat. Eating to make yourself feel better is a poor solution to an emotional problem. It doesn't help you deal with what is bothering you. And the weight you are sure to gain will only add to your unhappiness.

When you are tempted to overeat, try getting away from food altogether. Go for a long walk. Use the time to think about why

you are unhappy and what you might do about it. You may want to talk to a friend about your problem. Perhaps you need help from a counselor at school.

Recognizing an emotional dependence on food is the first step. If you often find yourself thinking about food and wondering what to eat next, ask yourself instead, "Am I really hungry?"

Many Different Diets

Limiting food intake for weight control is common. But people follow special diets for many other reasons, too.

Some people need to gain weight. It is not unusual for teenagers to weigh too little. If you are underweight, you should make it a point to eat foods high in calories and rich in all the nutrients.

Often a physical condition requires a certain diet. People with food allergies, for example, must avoid foods that make them feel ill or break out in a rash. People with high blood pressure need to limit their intake of table salt and salty foods. And light,

easy-to-digest meals may be called for during certain illnesses related to digestion.

Most doctors think that skin problems are partly related to diet. Avoiding chocolate, French fries, and other greasy foods may help clear up problem skin. And cutting out candy and other sweets is a good way to keep visits to the dentist short and painless, especially for those who get cavities easily.

Don't Forget Exercise

Exercise goes hand in hand with any sensible diet. When you exercise, you burn up some of the calories you take in. This helps in taking off weight. But even if you're not trying to lose weight, exercise helps you look and feel better. It firms up muscles and gets rid of the bulges that even slender people can develop. Exercise can also improve posture. This in itself makes you look better.

You're in Charge

Perhaps your parents have done most of your food thinking for you up to now. But as you become more independent, you'll make your own diet decisions.

Now that you eat away from home more and more often, you will have to select a healthy, well-balanced diet for yourself. Even at home, you may at times politely have to refuse dessert or some other high-calorie food because you have decided a few pounds need to go. Throughout your life you can make choices to control your eating pattern. These choices may be some of the most important ones you will ever make.

QUESTIONS

1. How can you tell whether or not you are overweight?
2. What are the most important aspects of a good reducing plan?
3. List some health problems besides overweight that might call for a special diet.
4. Why does extra weight have such a harmful effect on the human body?
5. Why aren't most wild animals overweight?
6. Why do you think people often overeat when they are having emotional problems?

ACTIVITIES

1. Record for one day everything you eat, the time of day you eat each item, and what you are doing at the time. What kind of pattern do you see in your eating habits? Do you think they should be changed?
2. Visit the diet food section of your local supermarket. What types of food are sold there? Compare the advantages of these foods with regular foods of the same type.
3. Obtain a copy of Weight Watchers or Lean Line diet. Analyze the diet for your age group to see if it fulfills your nutritional requirements.
4. Using the figures on page 258, work out how many extra calories you could use up in a week if you added a daily half-hour run to your routine. If you must burn up 3,500 calories to lose a pound of body weight, how much could you lose in a month? A year?

SECTION 5 · Fact, Fad, or Fallacy?

FACT OR FANCY?

Carrots make your hair curl . . . or do they?

Potatoes make you fat . . . or do they?

A medium-size potato has about the same number of calories as a glass of skim milk. And it has many nutrients, including high-quality protein, too. Many people enjoy potatoes regularly without worrying about unwanted calories. They have learned to enjoy the natural flavor of the potato without piling on lots of sour cream, butter, or thick sauces, which add many calories.

Whether your hair is naturally curly or straight depends on what you inherited from your parents. Carrots are good for you, but they won't make your hair curly.

An apple a day keeps the doctor away . . . or does it?

No one food can keep you healthy. An apple a day may be tasty and nutritious, but you need a balance of all the nutrients to help maintain health.

What you eat has a very direct effect on how you feel and look. But people have sometimes drawn wrong conclusions about certain foods. They have not realized that it is the nutrients in food, not any one food itself, that affect health.

You know that carrots won't make your hair curly. However, vitamin A, which your body makes from the carotene in carrots, does help you have healthy, shiny hair. But another source of vitamin A—acorn squash, for example, or milk or liver—would have the same effect.

When Myths Can Be Dangerous

Most food myths are quite harmless for people who eat well-balanced meals. If a person gets enough vitamin C and niacin without eating potatoes, for example, avoiding that vegetable will do no harm. And eating an apple every day is fine, as long as it's part of an overall balanced diet.

Believing everything you hear about food, though, can be risky. Certain food products or ideas about foods become popular from time to time. Their popularity may have more to do with how they are sold to the public than with sound nutrition.

A particular food or combination of foods can become as fashionable as a particular style of dress. Following fashions in clothing and food can sometimes be expensive. But in the case of food fads, it can be dangerous to your health as well.

What Can Happen?

Every year consumers in North America spend large amounts of money on food fads. Hundreds of books and magazines making special claims for "miracle" foods or "wonder" diets are published each year. Con-

As this old ad shows, miracle remedies for weight loss have been around for a long, long time.

sumers spend large amounts of money on these publications and the products they promote. In most cases, the nutrients in these "miracle" foods are available in ordinary foods for far less money. And "wonder" diets are usually less nutritious than a normal diet guided by common sense.

Food fads can be not only costly, but also bad for your health. For example, some companies claim that we cannot get enough vitamins from the foods in our diet. These companies market expensive pills that give large doses of one or more vitamins. But large doses of vitamin A or D, for example, can cause discomfort and illness. It should be possible to get all the vitamins you need from a well-planned diet.

Most dangerous of all, following food fads can keep people from seeing doctors when they should. Instead of getting medical help, people try a "miracle" food. This can seriously damage their health.

Health Foods

Just because something has become a food fad doesn't make it automatically bad. But it isn't automatically good, either. Each fad should be judged on its own merits. Usually there are arguments on both sides. If you understand something about nutrition, you will be a better judge of these arguments.

Health foods are very popular in North America today. But the term *health food* is misleading. Actually, any clean, fresh food that offers valuable nutrients can be a healthful part of the diet.

Health food stores sell grains, flours, seeds, and nuts not always found in regular grocery stores. And often they sell special vitamin products and preparations that claim to give quick energy and build body strength.

Some people believe that these special health foods aid nutrition. But many others think that such foods are unnecessary and costly.

Stores specializing in health foods also sell "organic" products. These are grown without chemical fertilizers or pesticides. Such stores sell "natural" foods, too, which contain no chemical additives or preservatives. Additives change the flavor, texture, or color of food. Preservatives slow the process of spoiling.

A Controversy

Some people worry that chemical substances on crops or added to foods may be a danger to health. They don't fully trust the

Many health food store items aren't found in supermarkets. Are they better for you than standard foods or just more costly?

tests that are conducted to keep harmful products from being used on foods. Occasionally chemical products have in fact been used, then later banned.

Other people feel protected by the testing programs, which are required by law. They argue that without chemical fertilizers, it would be impossible to grow enough food. And without preservatives, they say, it would be hard to keep food fresh enough to reach all consumers.

As a consumer, you have to make your own decisions. Are special health foods worth the extra money they usually cost? Are chemical fertilizers, pesticides, additives, and preservatives a risk? Look for the latest news on food—in newspapers and

---

Box 1

How to Spot a Food Fad

- Does the food or combination of foods seem like a "miracle" drug?
- Does the product contain huge amounts of vitamins or other nutrients over the Recommended Daily Dietary Allowances set by nutrition experts?
- Does it contain many nutrients for which no RDA has been established?
- Does it promise fast and amazing results, with no bother?

- Is the product very expensive? Can you get the nutrients in the product from other, cheaper sources?
- Are there pills, a book, or an appliance for sale in connection with the product?

"Yes" answers to these questions mean you should suspect a food fad. Beware of making a costly, unnecessary, and possibly harmful purchase.

---

magazines you feel you can trust. Reliable publications can help you answer these important questions.

Think for Yourself

A wise consumer thinks carefully before believing food myths or following food fads.

Claims made for special foods or diets can be appealing. You must be aware of the questionable nature of some claims made by food faddists and manufacturers of special foods. It's up to you to evaluate them. By using your knowledge of nutrition, you can protect your health and save money too.

QUESTIONS

1. What kind of claims should you look out for when evaluating a food product?
2. What are organic foods? Natural foods?
3. What are some of the dangers of following food fads?
4. Why do you think so many people follow food fads?

5. Do you think the use of chemical additives in food should be reduced? Should more foods be grown without chemical fertilizers? Defend your opinions.
6. Why do you think food fads tend to be very expensive?

ACTIVITIES

1. Choose a food you like that contains additives. Write a letter to the manufacturer, asking why each additive is used. Read the reply to your class.
2. Find several advertisements for food products that make special claims to improve

health. Using your knowledge of nutrition, evaluate these claims.
3. Visit a health food store and then describe to your class the foods that are sold there. How do the prices compare to the prices of similar foods in the supermarket?

SECTION 6 · Enough to Go Around

DISASTER AREA

Chris Sanford lives in a small town in West Virginia. Just as last winter's snow was beginning to melt, a fierce rainstorm hit the area. Eight inches of rain fell in less than twelve hours. The Sanfords' neighborhood was flooded and everyone had to leave their homes. Chris saw firsthand how families can get caught in emergencies without enough food.

"Most of the area surrounding our neighborhood was already underwater. When the water began to rise in our street, the police came and told us everyone would have to leave.

"No one wanted to go. We were worried about our homes. We didn't know how high the water would get or how long the flooding would last. But the storm had knocked the power out, and without electricity we only had enough to eat for a day or two."

266

Many situations can cause food emergencies. Sometimes people are unable to work because of an accident or long illness. Perhaps they cannot find jobs. These individuals and their families may not have the money to buy enough food. Sometimes natural disasters such as floods, tornadoes, and earthquakes leave whole communities homeless and without food. And when an entire country cannot produce enough food for its people, great numbers of families face serious food emergencies every day.

What Can Be Done?

North America produces plenty of food, and yet some people here still go hungry or can-

not get enough of the right nutrients. The United States government has set up several programs to help people deal with food emergencies.

One of these is the school lunch program. The government gives money and nutritious food to schools. The schools then provide nutritious lunches at little or no cost to students who need them. Schools in some parts of the country have breakfast plans, too. The government also provides milk, which schools sell at a low price to their students.

Surplus food can help feed the hungry. Farmers sometimes produce a bigger crop than they can sell. Or a company may make

When people are driven from their homes by natural disasters, they may need emergency food supplies from outside sources.

more of a food product than people buy. Programs have been developed to give this surplus to people who need food. These programs are successful only when the surplus food happens to be what people want or need.

Another plan is the food stamp program. Families or individuals with little money can get these stamps for basic food needs. Food stamps give the consumer more buying power. They help many people get through individual and family food emergencies.

All these programs help people get the food and nutrients they need. Unfortunately, these programs do not reach all who need them. The problem of feeding everyone still needs solution.

When Disaster Strikes

Fire destroys a home. A tornado rips through an area. A flood hits a community. When disaster forces people to leave their homes, obtaining food may be one of the most serious problems they face.

If an emergency hits only a few people in a community, neighbors or local religious groups can often provide food and other necessities. Many charitable organizations and social service agencies also stand ready to help.

When a disaster strikes a whole community, the Red Cross may come to the rescue. In the Sanfords' town, volunteers from the local chapter set up an emergency shelter in Chris's school. The Sanfords and most of their neighbors stayed in the shelter.

The Red Cross brought in food from a store in a nearby community. It also provided items such as juice, soup, beef stew, and milk from supplies stored in its division headquarters.

The United States government may also

Emergency food goes around the world. Here survivors of a Guatemala earthquake receive food from the United States.

help in times of emergency. The Consumer Marketing Service of the Department of Agriculture, for example, can supply food to victims of natural disasters. And when a needy area is hard to reach, the Army, National Guard or some other branch of the military uses its equipment to bring in emergency supplies.

World Food Problems

Some countries cannot produce enough food for all of their people. The climate may be dry. The soil may be poor. Old-fashioned farming methods and machines may result in poor crops and little food. In countries where farming is poor, there are often far more people than the land can feed. Shortage of food in these countries is a major problem facing world leaders.

Various national and international groups are constantly working on the world food problem in several ways. They supply and distribute food to areas that need it right away. Some of the food emergencies they handle involve whole countries and millions of people. The United Nations is especially known for this kind of work.

These agencies have long-term goals, too. Some are trying to increase crops by educating farmers about modern methods of agriculture. They also provide the seeds, fertilizers, and tools the farmers need to grow more food.

Still other organizations are trying to develop totally new food sources that could help solve the problem of world hunger.

Many organizations make a special point of sharing their knowledge with one another. They work together to ensure that more people all over the world will be well fed in the future.

QUESTIONS

1. Name some of the reasons people might not have enough to eat. Which of these situations can be taken care of by bringing in food from another part of the country?
2. List some of the programs that help people who are hungry. How do some of these programs operate?
3. What are some of the ways in which people are trying to solve the world food problem?
4. A Chinese philosopher is supposed to have said, "Give a man a fish and you will feed him for a day; teach him to fish and you will feed him all his life." How does this saying relate to the world food problem?
5. Does your school have a government-sponsored lunch program? What do you think of it? How do you think it might be improved?
6. Sometimes people who need food do not make use of new foods that are made available to them. Why do you think this happens?

ACTIVITIES

1. Give a report on *incaparina*, a protein concentrate developed for use in food emergencies, especially those that involve children.
2. Contact a local relief organization. Find out the average number of people who ask for help in obtaining food each month. How does the agency handle these requests?
3. Evaluate the nutritional content of a week's worth of lunches served in your school.
4. Obtain information on the food stamp program. Explain to your class how the program operates.

SECTION 7 · Food in the Future

THEN AND NOW

Look at the two menus on this page. The one on the left is what the Pilgrims probably ate. The one on the right is what we might eat today. Why do you think our traditional dinner is so different from the first Thanksgiving feast?

The First Thanksgiving

Venison	**Succotash**
Turkey	**Nuts of all sorts**
Duck	**Corn bread**
Goose	**Watercress and other greens**
Clams and other shellfish	**Plums**
Smoked eels	**Dried berries**

A Thanksgiving Dinner Today

Cranberry drink
Nuts
Roast turkey
Corn bread stuffing
Candied sweet potatoes
Creamed peas and onions
Tossed green salad with lettuce, tomatoes, onions, and green peppers
Hot rolls with butter
Mince pie
Pumpkin pie
Cheese and fruit—grapes, apples, bananas, and oranges

The first Thanksgiving lasted about three days. It was quite a party. The Pilgrims had nearly starved their first winter in New England. By the time harvest came, they were ready for a feast.

Today, many people in the United States celebrate Thanksgiving Day with a feast similar to that held by the Pilgrims. The idea of serving turkey, corn bread, nuts, and a large variety of food came from that early feast. But the first Thanksgiving was quite different from ours today.

Living Off the Land

There was venison (deer meat) on that first Thanksgiving table. The Indians supplied five deer for the celebration. The Pilgrims had to depend mostly on foods they could shoot or find in the forest. They had brought no cows, pigs, or chickens with them from England. And except for corn, their first crops had failed.

Turkeys and other fowl were hunted in the forest near the Pilgrim village. Because these were wild bilds, they had little fat and were not very tender. The fowl for the first Thanksgiving dinner probably had to be cooked all day over an open fire. They might have been simmered in water flavored with herbs to make them more tender and tasty.

Yesterday, Today, and Tomorrow

Many of the foods the Pilgrims ate may be unfamiliar to you. And if Pilgrims were to sit down at your Thanksgiving table, they might see many things they had never dreamed of—huge, fat turkeys, stuffing, tomatoes, bananas, oranges.

Now imagine that you are sitting down at a Thanksgiving table more than 300 years into the future. What surprises do you think that meal might have for you? Would you expect a meal such as you would have today? Or would you find great changes?

Food habits change as people's way of life changes. Few of us are like the Pilgrims, depending on what we can grow, shoot, or catch for our food. Our food comes from all over the country and from around the world. Modern methods of processing and packaging keep food fresh and nutritious for months.

Today, we have all year round fruits and vegetables that the Pilgrims could have for only a short time each year, if at all. As today's way of life continues to change, we can expect foods to change also.

Some changes may come about because the world still has so many hungry people. In finding ways to feed them, scientists may discover cheaper, more efficient and nutritious ways to use crops we already grow.

The soybean, an excellent source of protein, is a good example. New methods have been developed to make soy protein look and taste like beef, bacon, chicken, and other animal products. Since these products can cost much less than meat, they may become more and more popular.

New Ideas About Health

The soybean and other vegetable proteins may become popular for another reason. People are concerned about cholesterol and other fats in their diets. Vegetable products do not have most of these fats. We may see vegetable products take the place of much of the animal products we now eat.

As nutritionists study the problem of feeding everyone well, they may find nutrients they did not know about before. Eating habits may change to include the new-found substances.

In the future, our whole way of life may

Two-thirds of the world is covered by oceans. In the future, much of our food may come from this resource.

change. People may get less exercise than they do now, and therefore need fewer calories. Or they may have more free time, take more exercise, and need to eat more.

New Processes

New ways of processing food may also bring changes in what we eat. Dairy products with most of the fat removed are already on the market, because many people want to reduce the amount of fat in their diets.

In recent years, scientists have learned to freeze-dry some foods. These foods are very lightweight and can be stored without refrigeration. Freeze-drying was useful in the space program, and many backpackers carry freeze-dried products. But the process is costly. If it becomes less expensive, it may be more widely used in the future.

New Food from New Sources

Tables of the future will no doubt hold foods that we cannot imagine now. Some foods may be made of entirely synthetic substances, manufactured in the laboratory. Examples of such foods that exist today are artificial salt, sweeteners, and vitamins.

We already eat fish and shellfish—although not nearly as often as we might. But we may soon see new kinds of food from our oceans, lakes, and rivers.

Fish protein concentrate is an odorless, flavorless powder made from scraps of fish. It is an excellent source of protein and can be added to many foods to increase their nutritional value. Fish protein concentrate is now used in a very limited way. But in the future, it may prove to be one of the sea's greatest gifts to us.

Plankton may be another. It is made of tiny plants and animals that float in bodies of water. Plankton provides protein and fat. It is expensive to collect, but many people think it will make a good food source one day. It's a big part of the diet of whales, so it must be nutritious!

A group of plants that includes seaweed is another possible food from our water resources. These plants are called algae. They grow well in confined spaces and might easily be made into food. Algae could be especially useful during space travel. They might be grown in tanks in space ships until they are needed for food. As green plants, they would also help supply oxygen for astronauts. Some people have even suggested that such food could be grown in space stations and sent back to earth.

Food in the Future

These are just some of the new ideas about food. Many other sources are being explored, and many new ways to process and grow food are being tried.

What changes are you likely to see? How do you feel about the ones you have read about? These are important questions to keep in mind. No matter how much change the future brings, we will always have to eat. Research going on today will affect the food habits of the whole world in the future.

QUESTIONS

1. Why have eating patterns in America changed so much in the last 300 years?
2. List some of the new products that scientists have developed to increase the world's food supplies.
3. What are some of the ways to process foods that have been developed in recent years?
4. What food have you eaten recently that was processed by a new method? Why do you think this food was developed?
5. Why do you think vegetables are a more economical source of protein than animals?
6. What are some ways in which the diets of people 300 years ago might have been healthier than our modern diet?
7. What kinds of changes in eating patterns have you seen during your life? What do you think of them?

ACTIVITIES

1. Try making "soyburgers," using soybean granules that you obtain from a health food store. You can find a recipe for the burgers in a natural foods or vegetarian cookbook. You could also try making hamburger using a combination of beef and soybean granules. (The soybean package will suggest the proportions to use.)
2. Visit your local supermarket to see how many different forms of one food (oranges or turkey, for example) are available. Make a poster that illustrates all these different forms.
3. Write a report on fish farming, one possible way of increasing our food supply in the future.
4. Interview the manager of a local supermarket to find out how many new foods are added to the supermarket shelves each year. What kinds of foods do they tend to be? Do any foods seem to go out of style? Report your findings to your class.

SECTION 8 · Careers in Nutrition

MANY CHOICES

The people pictured here all chose careers in nutrition. The person in the first picture is a plant researcher. He's examining a new crop strain to see whether it is healthy and resistant to disease. Number two is a nutritionist. She's studying the soybean plant to learn about the nutrients it can provide.

In number three, you see a hospital dietitian planning meals for patients with special needs. You may be able to tell that number four is a doctor. Some doctors are very interested in nutrition. This one is taking care of a child who is suffering from malnutrition.

The field of nutrition offers a wide choice of careers. Do you like to work with people? Do you like organizing work and helping people do their jobs efficiently? Do you like research? Would you like to help people who are hungry? If you answered yes to any of these questions and have an interest in foods, a career in nutrition might suit you.

Nutritionist

You might think that *anyone* with a job in the field of nutrition would be called a nutritionist. But the word has a special meaning. Many nutritionists study foods to learn about the nutrients they can provide. Some nutritionists study exactly how nutrients are used by the body. Others look at what people need in various circumstances. Many nutritionists study what happens to nutrients in foods as they are being cooked or stored.

People often require special diets. Some volunteer jobs may let you see how dietitians meet individual needs.

Nutritionists may also work in government jobs at the local, state, or federal level to help people learn about nutrition and meal planning. Some nutritionists work with companies that produce food. They give advice on new food products and assist in development and testing.

Dietitians

Like nutritionists, dietitians know which nutrients various foods provide and how they work in the body. But dietitians usually use their knowledge to plan meals or diets for large groups or for people with special needs.

Some dietitians work in hospitals or nursing homes. These clinical dietitians plan diets for people who must eat certain foods to get or stay well. They also explain the diets to people and help them learn to follow special diets on their own.

Other dietitians manage the kitchens that prepare food for hospitals, nursing homes, schools, and colleges. These administrative dietitians may also be in charge of the restaurants that many companies have for their employees.

Doctors

Doctors have become more and more interested in nutrition over the years. Physiologists study ways in which the body uses food to produce energy. Other doctors are learning the best way to give nutrients to very sick or badly injured patients. This subject is getting a lot of attention in medicine today.

Other Scientists

Many scientists are working to solve the world food problem. Soil scientists study ways to improve land so that crops will grow better and produce more food. Plant researchers, like the one shown on the previous page, learn ways to make crops yield more produce.

Researchers may also try to develop crops that suit special areas, such as places with short summers and very severe winters, or places that get very little rain.

Some people combine an interest in animals with a knowledge of nutrition. These individuals are called animal nutritionists or animal husbandry experts. They study how animals use food and learn what diets are best for different species. Their work can be useful in helping farmers feed their livestock better. If you have a pet, their work can help you learn how to care for it.

People are always needed to work in the field of nutrition. Most of these jobs require

at least four years of college. Many nutritionists—and dietitians, doctors, and scientists—have satisfying careers teaching others the skills they have learned.

How About You?

In one sense, everyone has a job in nutrition. Whether you have a family or live alone, whether you are a man or a woman, you are in charge of seeing that you get proper nourishment every day.

If you live alone, you will plan your own diet. If you have a family someday, you may be in charge of planning and preparing meals for two or more people. Even if meals are not your chief responsibility at home, you will still play some part in planning the family's diet. So no matter how you make your living, nutrition is an important part of your life.

QUESTIONS

1. Describe some of the careers available to people who are interested in working in nutrition.
2. Why is it important for all of us to have some knowledge of nutrition, even if we do not have careers in nutrition?
3. What other jobs in the field of nutrition can you think of? Why are there so many different kinds of careers in nutrition?
4. How could the work of a plant researcher create new jobs in the field of nutrition?

ACTIVITIES

1. Choose a job that interests you in the field of nutrition and learn more about it. Report to the class on your findings.
2. Contact a local college to find out the kinds of courses you would need for a particular job (nutritionist or dietitian, for example) in the field.

CHAPTER 8

A Wise Consumer of Foods

CHAPTER CONTENTS

SECTION 1 · The Food Business

Why Is There a Difference?

One morning, Dave's mother asked him to stop after school to buy fruit for his next day's lunch. She also wanted some chocolate chips for making cookies.

After school, Dave stopped at a small store where he often bought one or two items for his mother. He liked the store because it was closer to his home. Also, it was less crowded than the supermarket, where his mother usually shopped.

He had already decided to buy dried cinnamon-flavored apple snacks. He picked up four packages, then asked the man behind the counter for chocolate chips. The store didn't carry them, the man said. A little annoyed, Dave paid for the apple snacks and set out for the supermarket.

There, as he was heading for the check-out line with his chocolate chips, he passed the same brand of apple snacks he had just bought. These, to his surprise, cost ten cents less a package.

He began looking at other items he usually bought at the small store. Here, eggs were ten cents less a dozen, cornflakes eight cents less a box, and orange juice fifteen cents less a quart!

Dave also noticed that the supermarket had a much wider selection of foods than the small store. And the supermarket carried more brands of the same item. There were four brands of orange juice, for example, while "his" store carried only one.

Why was there such a difference in prices between the two stores? And how, since the smaller store was more expensive and carried fewer items, could it compete for business with the supermarket?

Convenience food stores are open long hours, but they offer a limited variety of foods, and often at higher prices.

Supermarkets sell a wide variety of foods and other products. Their prices are lower, so to make a profit they must sell a lot.

The small store where Dave shopped is a convenience store. Much smaller than supermarkets, convenience stores sell less food per day. This means they have to buy food in smaller quantities. Since small orders of food cost more per item than large ones, convenience stores must charge higher prices to stay in business.

Different Stores for Different Needs

Convenience stores are, as their name implies, convenient. They provide services that people need—otherwise, few people would pay the higher prices they charge. They stay open longer hours than most supermarkets, and they are usually open every day—even holidays.

People often go to convenience stores for emergency purchases. Perhaps, like Dave, they need only a few items and prefer a store nearer home than the supermarket. Perhaps they need something when the supermarket is closed. Or perhaps they're in a hurry for one or two items. Convenience stores are small, and people buy only a few items at a time. So checking out usually takes less time than at supermarkets.

Convenience stores often charge competitive prices for basic items such as bread and milk. This practice attracts some customers who might otherwise go to supermarkets.

Supermarkets attract people by offering lower prices, which they can do because they sell a large volume of food. The average supermarket, for example, sells thousands of loaves of bread a week, while a convenience store may sell only several hundred. The supermarket can charge less for each loaf because it pays less. Suppliers offer discounts on large orders.

Supermarkets have enough space to offer customers many products and a variety of brands. Supermarket managers know that large numbers of customers will be attracted by a store that offers a good selection of products.

Besides supermarkets and convenience stores, many communities have **specialty stores.** Some sell only fruits and vegetables. Others carry only party foods or special imported items not available in supermarkets. Many specialty stores have delicatessens that make up sandwiches, salads, and trays of food for parties—a service that few supermarkets offer.

Specialty stores usually charge more than supermarkets because they sell much less. But, like convenience stores, they stay in business because they serve people's special needs.

Where the Dollar Goes

Supermarkets, convenience stores, and specialty stores have many expenses in common. These expenses add to the cost of each food item. All stores must pay the salaries of employees, for example. All must pay for storage equipment such as refrigerators and freezers to keep food fresh.

Some foods do lose freshness, however, because they do not sell quickly enough. Foods such as tomatoes and milk keep for only a short time. When spoiled items must be thrown away, stores lose money.

These losses are expenses that all food stores face. And they are included in the prices you pay.

The cost of food in a store also reflects the costs of growing that food. Farmers must pay for the seed, fertilizers, pesticides, and equipment they need to grow good crops. They may also have to pay for workers' salaries and animal feed. Crop failures create even more expenses.

Before every town had supermarkets, many neighborhoods relied on local markets for food supplies. Bakeries and meat markets can still be found, but such specialty stores are less frequent today.

Processing and packaging are two more steps that your food dollars pay for. These steps require factories, workers, and machinery. The materials for packaging cost money, too.

Food often travels a great distance before it gets to you, and transportation can be very expensive. Special equipment is often required to keep food fresh. The people who run the food transportation business must charge for their services, too.

All these expenses are reflected in your food bill. The next time you shop for food, consider all the processes and activities you are getting for your money. You may then feel that food is a bargain!

QUESTIONS

1. List as many kinds of food stores as you can. Why does each kind exist?
2. What are some of the advantages of doing your food shopping in a supermarket? Some of the disadvantages?
3. What are some of the expenses of a food store?
4. Imagine that there is only one food store in your community. How would that affect you and your neighbors?
5. List all the people who make their living getting a can of tomato sauce to your kitchen, starting with the person who sold the farmer the seeds for the tomato plant.

ACTIVITIES

1. Take a survey of supermarket managers in your area to find out if any of them buy seasonal fruits and vegetables directly from local farmers. Discuss the results of your survey with the class.
2. Make a poster showing the steps that go into getting one of your favorite foods from the farm to your table.
3. Choose five foods and make a survey of the stores in your area to find out how much they cost in each store. Make a chart of the foods, stores, and prices and post it on the bulletin board.

SECTION 2 · Shopping for Food

LOWEST BID

Miss Jones's eighth-grade home economics class was planning its end-of-the-year picnic. The class first formed groups for shopping, preparing the food, packing the lunch, and planning activities. Everyone, Miss Jones said, would help with cleaning up. The whole class let it be known that they would like to get out of that job—and that gave Miss Jones an idea.

The class would plan the picnic menu together. Then each group would take a week to figure out how it could buy the supplies for as little money as possible. Each group would bid for the shopping contract. The group that gave the lowest bid—that is, that found out how to buy the picnic supplies for the least amount of money—would do the shopping. And no one in that group would have to help with cleaning up.

When the class met to give the shopping bids, the estimated bills were thirty-two dollars, thirty dollars, twenty-nine dollars, and twenty dollars. The other groups were surprised at the winning group's low bid. They thought that group had made a mistake. But Miss Jones was sure the supplies could be purchased for twenty dollars. She asked the group to share its shopping methods with the rest of the class. The group then described the principles you will read about in the next few pages.

Before you even start out for the store, you can take steps to save money and effort. Careful planning of what to buy and where to buy it can pay off in savings.

Helpful Paperwork

Keep a close eye on the daily newspapers. You will find supermarket specials advertised there, items that stores are offering for a short time at lower prices than usual. Watch for advertising fliers distributed by supermarkets. These fliers, along with signs in supermarket windows, advertise current specials.

Coupons are another way to save money. They offer special prices on foods that are not otherwise on sale. You may find coupons in newspaper ads and fliers, and on food packages and labels.

Usually you simply hand the coupons to the check-out clerk as you pay for your purchases. But sometimes you must mail the coupon to the manufacturer. The manufacturer will then send you a partial refund on the price of the product.

You might think that coupons and sales will save you only a few pennies here and there. But taking regular advantage of sales and coupons can trim a food bill by several dollars each week.

What's Plentiful?

Another way to save money is to buy foods that are plentiful. Some kinds of meat, fish, and poultry are in greater supply at certain times of the year. In most areas, fall is the best time to buy turkeys, spring is the time for lamb, and summer brings a good supply of flounder.

Fruits and vegetables are cheaper when they are in season at nearby farms. Items in season travel a shorter distance from the producer to the supermarket. They are likely to be very fresh and flavorful. And they can be sold more cheaply than at other times of the year.

Newspapers often offer advice about which food items are good buys. Reading food columns, as well as store advertisements, will keep you up to date on seasonal items.

Menus and Shopping Lists

Try to plan flexible menus before going shopping. These menus can easily be changed at the store to make use of seasonal items and products on sale.

Smart menu planning also includes trying to provide the basic nutrients at the lowest price. Chicken, for example, is a less expensive source of protein than steak. You can save money by choosing lower-priced foods—so long as they provide the basic nutrients you need.

Menus for a few days or a week form the basis of the wise consumer's shopping list. Making a list of what you need before going to the market saves you from making extra trips back to the store. Following the list closely prevents you from buying tempting items you don't need.

Another way to save money on food bills is to choose the day you shop. Some specials are offered only on weekends. Shopping then can be very economical. But it may take more time and patience since the stores are crowded.

Which Store?

Once you have your list, you are ready to choose a store. Where you shop can help you save money. If one supermarket regularly offers lower prices than the others on more goods, that store may be an economical choice. If the store is also clean, well stocked with goods of high quality, and run by pleasant, helpful people, it may be a very good place to shop regularly.

Some people shop at several supermarkets to take advantage of the different bargains each offers. This practice can save money, and it may be worthwhile for particularly good bargains. Still, it uses extra time and energy. And if shoppers drive from store to store, they may spend more on gasoline than they save in grocery bills.

Unit Pricing

Once in the store, a smart shopper takes advantage of unit prices if they are posted. Unit prices appear on the shelves near the items to which they refer. These signs tell how much a standard quantity of a product costs. This helps the consumer compare prices of different-size packages of a product.

Without unit pricing, such comparisons can be difficult. Tomato juice, for example, is sold in several different-size cans. A unit-pricing label will tell you how much per quart each can costs, or how much per liter, no matter what its size. You may find out that tomato juice costs twice as much if you buy it in small cans instead of large ones. Unit pricing also helps you compare

Menu plan

Monday
  baked ham
  sweet potatoes
  cole slaw
  pineapple chunks

Tuesday
  brown rice with vegetables
  sliced tomatoes
  cottage cheese

Wednesday
  spaghetti with meatballs
  tossed salad
  french or Italian bread

Thursday
  ham and macaroni casserole
  broccoli
  biscuits
  fruit salad

Friday
  cheese soufflé
  zucchini, corn, tomatoes & onions
  grapefruit halves

Saturday
  roast chicken
  mashed potatoes
  stringbeans
  cranberry sauce

Sunday
  dinner at Grampa's

(if fish is on sale, buy,
freeze Thursday's casserole)

Shopping list
milk, eggs, margarine
buy ham large enough for two meals
  head of cabbage
(see if slices are less expensive)

whatever is on sale, tomatoes
bamboo shoots, water chestnuts
2 lbs. of cottage cheese
    (enough for lunches)

enough chopped meat for two
  batches, freeze one batch
  loaf of bread

cream of mushroom soup
broccoli (or asparagus)

block of Cheddar cheese
large can of tomatoes
6 grapefruits (breakfast, too)

6-7 lb. chicken for leftovers, soup
(another green vegetable if fresh
beans aren't available)

Making a menu plan can help in the writing of
a shopping list. Check your refrigerator supplies against the meal schedule, and you will
easily see what foods you need to buy.

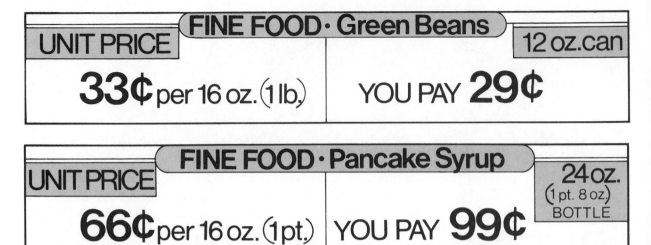

UNIT PRICE

FINE FOOD · Green Beans

12 oz. can

33¢ per 16 oz. (1 lb.)

YOU PAY **29¢**

UNIT PRICE

FINE FOOD · Pancake Syrup

24 oz. (1 pt. 8 oz.) BOTTLE

66¢ per 16 oz. (1 pt.)

YOU PAY **99¢**

Whatever a product's container size, unit prices show at a glance how much a given measure costs. By comparing you can find the bargain brand.

brands. Is the economy size of brand A cheaper than the standard size of brand B? Without unit pricing, you have to use your own math skills.

Is Bigger Always Better?

Paying attention to the size of a package can save money. As a general rule, larger packages of a product give you more for your money than smaller ones of the same brand. However, even if the economy size costs less per serving, buying it will not always save money. Sometimes you may waste a product if you know you have plenty around. If the product is one that will spoil or go stale if not used right away, you may end up throwing some out. Buying large sizes saves money only if the product will be used wisely.

Another money-saving practice is buying large quantities of goods on sale. This, too, is a good idea only if the product will stay fresh until you use it. Buying instant

coffee on sale, for example, is economical. This product keeps for a long time, even after opening. On the other hand, buying a bushel of tomatoes on sale could be a waste of money. They might spoil before you can use them all.

Looking at Labels

Paying attention to labels is an important part of wise shopping. Labels can give you valuable information. The brand name on the label is often the first thing people notice about a product. For most products, there are many brands to choose from, including the store's own brand. Store brands often cost less than other brands. This is partly because they are not advertised as much.

Some people believe that well-known brands cost more because they taste better. Others say store brands are equally good. The difference between products is often a matter of individual taste. If you like the store brand, you can usually save money.

How Much of What?

The name of a product often gives a clue to its ingredients. The United States government sets "standards of identity" for more than 250 products. These products must contain certain ingredients in certain amounts. Those ingredients need not be listed on the label. To be called mayonnaise, for example, a food must be at least sixty-five percent vegetable oil by weight. If less, it has to be called imitation mayonnaise.

For products that do not have standards of identity, the list of ingredients on the label is extremely important information. All ingredients in the product must be listed in descending order of weight.

If, for example, you were going to buy a can of chili, you might find two different brands in the store. One label might read: "Ingredients: Water, kidney beans, ground beef, salt, spices." The other might read: "Ingredients: Ground beef, kidney beans, water, salt, spices."

You would know from the label that the first can contains more water than any other single ingredient! The second can has more beef than anything else, and next to that, more kidney beans. The practice of listing ingredients in descending order by weight helps you know exactly what you're getting for your money.

Other Useful Information

Labels must also state exactly how much of a product the package contains. This information, according to the law, must be easy to see.

You can learn a lot about the foods you buy from the small print on their labels. When examining similar products, compare their contents and check the nutritive values as well.

The name and address of the company that made, packaged, or shipped the product must also appear on the label. This makes it possible for consumers to know where to write if they have questions or complaints.

In addition, many labels list nutritive values. Some labels tell what percentage of the average recommended daily allowance (U.S. RDA) of each nutrient one serving of the product provides. If a product claims to have a special nutritional purpose, this information must be included. If a product claims to be low in calories, the label must give the number of calories per serving.

INGREDIENTS—ZUCCHINI, WATER, TOMATO PASTE, SUGAR, SALT, DRIED ONIONS, FOOD STARCH MODIFIED, DRIED GREEN PEPPERS, DRIED CELERY, CITRIC ACID, DRIED GARLIC, CALCIUM CHLORIDE, SPICES.

NUTRITION INFORMATION—PER ONE CUP SERVING
SERVINGS PER CONTAINER—APPROX. 2

CALORIES 60	CARBOHYDRATE ..16g	
PROTEIN 2g	FAT 0g	

PERCENTAGE OF U.S. RECOMMENDED DAILY ALLOWANCES (U.S. RDA) PER ONE CUP SERVING

PROTEIN 2	NIACIN 4
VITAMIN A 30	CALCIUM 4
VITAMIN C 15	IRON 8
THIAMINE (VIT. B₁) .. 6	PHOSPHORUS 6
RIBOFLAVIN (VIT. B₂) 6	MAGNESIUM 8

*WT. OF ZUCCHINI (9-3/4 OZ.) BEFORE ADDITION OF LIQUID NECESSARY FOR PROCESSING
Net Wt. 16 oz. (1 lb.) 454 g
Cups ....Approx. 2
For good nutrition eat a variety of foods.

24000

Box 1

Open Dating

Showing dates on labels is called open dating. It makes information available to the public that manufacturers often keep to themselves. Open dating can help consumers to judge the freshness of a product.

Three different types of dates are used. The **pack date** tells you when the product was made or packaged. This information, which often appears on canned goods and baked products, is helpful if you know how long a product remains fresh after it is packaged.

The **pull date** is usually seen on dairy products. This date is the last day a product may be sold. If on May 1 you see a carton of milk marked April 30, you know it should not be on the shelf.

The **expiration date** is the last date on which a product can be safely used. This date lets the consumer know exactly how long it will be safe to use a product after it is purchased.

How can you tell the difference among these types of dating? It's often difficult. Some dates are put on the label by the manufacturer, others by the store. If you have a question about the date on a package, ask the store manager. Managers should have such information for all products in stock.

Open dating helps consumers save money. It helps them buy products that are fresh—and that will remain fresh for a known length of time after purchase.

Danger Signals

Finally, wise shoppers protect their health as well as their budget by watching for signs of spoilage. Bulging cans contain dangerous bacteria and should never be purchased. Point out such cans to the store manager at once.

Dented cans may have broken seams, which allow spoilage. Avoid these unless you can clearly see that all seams are intact.

Avoid rusty cans, for they may be old or may have been stored improperly.

Frozen food packages that are soft or "sweating" are probably thawing. Packages covered with stains or thin sheets of ice may have thawed and been refrozen. Such foods are not of good quality. Avoid them.

Following all these hints may seem time-consuming. But if you shop wisely, you will get value for your money.

QUESTIONS

1. Why is a knowledge of nutrition important in economical shopping?
2. Outline the steps involved in economical menu planning.
3. List some of the information you can find on the labels of modern food products.
4. Is it always a good idea to buy the cheapest food you can find? How does the term "false economy" apply to the purchase of very cheap food?
5. List some of the things that a careful shopper does to keep her or his grocery bill as small as possible.

ACTIVITIES

1. Make a list of good manners to follow when shopping for food. (Before you start, you could ask a supermarket manager about the kinds of behavior that make shopping more difficult for everyone.)

2. Draw a floor plan of the food store where your family usually shops, and label each aisle with the foods that are sold there. Then draw numbered arrows on the chart to show the best order for putting food in your shopping cart. On the bottom of the chart, explain the reasons for your system.

3. Clip out newspaper advertisements placed by three different food stores. What kinds of consumer information, besides price, do these ads offer? Is there anything in the ads that could be misleading if you didn't read them carefully? Describe any changes you would make in the ads.

SECTION 3 · Selecting and Preparing Fruits and Vegetables

DECISIONS

Imagine that you are shopping for your family. You have to choose a fruit for breakfast and a vegetable for lunch. You decide on oranges, since you love the way they taste and know they supply vitamin C. For lunch, spinach appeals to you for its good flavor and high vitamin A content.

When you get to the market, you see that more decisions await you. All the forms of oranges and spinach that appear on this page look out at you from the supermarket shelves and bins. Which ones do you choose?

Your decision depends on the answers to many questions: How do you plan to use the food? Which form seems the best buy for the money? Does one form supply more essential nutrients than the others do? Does one form come closer to your idea of "orange flavor" or "spinach flavor" than the other products do?

Today's methods of transportation, processing, and storage give us a great variety of produce—fruits and vegetables—to choose from all year round. We can buy fresh, frozen, canned, dried, or freeze-dried produce. Our decision will depend on what we like, how much we can spend, and how we plan to use the food.

As you read through this section, think about the oranges and spinach you were going to buy. Think of situations in which a particular form of each one would be your best purchase.

Getting the Most for Your Money

Really fresh fruits and vegetables supply the full value of nutrients these foods offer. Processed fruits and vegetables have been exposed to heat, air, and water. This can destroy some of their most vital nutrients, especially vitamin C and the B vitamins.

The same thing can happen to fresh produce if it is not handled properly. Some stores, for example, make their produce look fresh by misting it with water. That can dissolve vitamins. Other stores display their produce in the open air, where sunlight can take a heavy toll on nutrients.

In the home, too, fruits and vegetables can lose their nutritive value if they are not stored properly, or if they are kept too long, or if they are incorrectly cooked. A few basic principles for buying, storing, and cooking fruits and vegetables can keep their nutritive value high.

Buying Fresh—Why and When?

Have you ever tasted an orange just off the tree? If you have, you probably know the reason many people prefer fresh fruits and vegetables—flavor. Processing takes that special something away from a fresh-picked orange and turns it into an ordinary orange-flavored product.

What tastes best to you, of course, is an individual matter. You might feel that orange juice made from frozen concentrate tastes better than fresh-squeezed juice. But many people who have tried a variety of products prefer the flavor of fresh fruits and vegetables. If you're used to eating canned or frozen products, you might enjoy trying fresh produce for a change.

If you buy fresh fruit and vegetables at certain times of the year, you may also save money. Fruits and vegetables from your own area cost very little to bring to market. When these are in season, ready for eating, they can be a bargain.

At other times, fresh produce may cost much more. Winter strawberries may have been grown in a hothouse, for example, or they may have come a long distance. They will almost certainly cost more than frozen strawberries.

Wise consumers know when local fruits and vegetables are in season and use them in menu planning.

When Another Choice is Best

Sometimes processed fruits and vegetables are a better choice than fresh. Using canned, frozen, dried, or freeze-dried products can save valuable time. They usually have been washed, cut, and trimmed before packaging.

Processed fruits and vegetables can save money, too. Since processed produce keeps much longer than fresh, it is a more sensible choice in some situations. If you use a few drops of lemon juice occasionally, it's more economical to buy bottled lemon

Box 1

FRESH FROM THE GARDEN

One way of tasting really fresh vegetables is to grow your own. For some teenagers, growing plants and vegetables is a fascinating hobby. But a majority have never really thought about growing plants—and if they have, vegetables were probably low on their list.

Consider this: A vegetable garden can improve the looks of a vacant lot, your own yard, or your window. Plants that produce food can even be grown indoors instead of the more common household plants. They are just as pleasing to look at.

Many good vegetables can be grown in limited spaces. Tomato plants don't need much room, and one plant can produce several tomatoes. Sweet peppers, lettuce, endive, green onions, radishes, spinach, turnips, parsley, and chives all do well in small places. Cucumbers and pole beans can be trained to grow against a fence. What a good way to hide an ugly chain fence around a vacant lot!

Raising vegetables is like caring for any other living thing. Plants need water, food, and light. To care for them, you should learn from the experience of others. Talk to people you know who have raised plants, and check out some books on the subject from the library. Both will have excellent tips on how to get the best results. Gardening isn't a terribly difficult skill. As with most skills, it does take study, time, and practice to master.

One reason so many people enjoy the vegetables they grow is that they themselves have worked to produce a tasty and nutritious product. It's very satisfying to watch something grow when you know that your efforts helped produce it.

It is possible that there will be much less open land in the future, so home gardening may become a necessity. People may depend on their own small gardens for fresh vegetables at a cost they can afford. Knowing how to grow your own food could be an important part of eating and living well in the future.

---

juice than fresh lemons. If there is a special sale of processed produce, you can save by stocking up on fruits and vegetables you know you will use.

Occasionally, processed produce is a better buy because it is more nutritious. Sweet corn and peas, for example, lose most of their flavor and nutrients within a few hours of harvesting unless they are processed.

How to Know What You're Getting

Buying fruits and vegetables can be a tricky matter. But you can learn exactly what to look for in each kind of fruit and vegetable, whether fresh or processed. Here are some general tips that will be useful.

It's hard to go wrong when buying fresh produce if you follow one basic rule: Fresh fruits and vegetables should look *fresh*, not tired and wilted. The color should be bright, and there should be no large bruises, rotten spots, or worm holes. However, don't be put off by small blemishes. If they are on the surface, the produce is fine for most uses.

Fresh produce should also feel firm to the touch. And in most cases, they should not be oversized—very large fruits and vegetables tend to be tough and woody.

Choose your store carefully, too. A cool, clean market is not likely to sell fresh or processed fruits and vegetables that have been around too long.

The Government Helps

Government inspectors often examine fresh fruit and vegetable crops, and processed products as well. The inspectors grade each batch of fresh or processed food.

When you are buying fresh fruits and vegetables, you can judge the quality yourself. But for processed produce, see if there is a grade printed on the label. The highest grade—U.S. Grade A in most cases—is the best in quality and appearance. It's also the most expensive. When it isn't important that a fruit or vegetable look perfect, the next two grades—B and C—are fine choices. They are just as nutritious and usually just as tasty as the highest grade.

How Much Does It Really Cost?

Price is another point to think about when buying. Wise shoppers figure out how much a fruit or vegetable costs per serving. For fresh produce, this may be a matter of estimating by weight. For example, if lettuce is priced by the head, pick the heaviest head to get the best buy.

The labels on most processed foods tell how many servings the package contains. Divide the price of the whole product by the number of servings to figure out the price per serving. This lets you know whether the "giant economy size" is really a bargain.

Once You're Home . . .

Storing fruits and vegetables correctly preserves their flavor and nutritive value. Each type of produce has slightly different storage needs.

In general, fresh fruits and vegetables need refrigeration. Some, like berries and cherries, must be kept as dry as possible until they are served. Others, like lettuce and other leafy vegetables, need to be in an airtight container to retain their moisture.

A few products, such as bananas, do much better stored at room temperature. If you have a question about a specific product, the produce manager at your local supermarket would be a good person to ask.

Canned fruits and vegetables keep for long periods of time if they are stored in a cool, dry place. Storage at no more than 65°F (18°C) is recommended.

Frozen products keep well for several months *if the temperature in the freezer or freezing compartment is no higher than 0°F (−18°C)*. If the freezer or freezing compartment is not this cold, frozen fruits and vegetables should be stored for only a few days.

Dried and freeze-dried products do well on the cupboard shelf, tightly wrapped. In very humid weather, however, dried fruit should be refrigerated.

Preparing Fruits and Vegetables

Nutrition and *flavor* are key words to remember when preparing fruits and vegetables. The skin or peel and the part closest to it contain a large amount of the nutrients. Whenever possible, leave on skins and peels. Eating them helps you get the most nutrients from these products.

Vitamin A, vitamin C, and the B vitamins are easily destroyed by air, heat, and water. When cooking fruits and vegetables, whether fresh or processed, use as little water as possible. Cover the pan, too, to trap nutrients that might escape in the steam.

Using a heavy-bottomed pan lets you cook vegetables at a low, even temperature. This saves energy. So does using the right-size pan for the amount you are cooking, and the right-size burner for the pan. If you use pans and burners that are too large for the job, much of the energy heats the air instead of the food.

Vegetables should be added to water that is already boiling. The heat should be just high enough to keep the water boiling. Water cannot get any hotter than that, and using a higher temperature only wastes energy.

Another way to preserve nutrients and flavor is to avoid cutting fruits and vegetables into small pieces. Each slice of the knife exposes more surface to air and water, causing a loss of nutrients.

When the vegetables are cooked, don't throw away the cooking water. It contains a large amount of the vitamins that have escaped from the food. Save it to add to soups, sauces and stews.

We are fortunate today to have an enormous supply of fruits and vegetables. Learning a few basic principles about their use will help you make the most of them.

QUESTIONS

1. List the different forms in which fruits and vegetables can be bought in a modern supermarket. What are the advantages and disadvantages of each form?
2. What facts should you consider when deciding which form of a fruit or vegetable to use?
3. List some of the steps necessary to preserve the flavor and vitamin content of fresh produce.

4. Why do the prices of fresh fruits and vegetables go up and down so much more than the prices of canned fruits and vegetables?
5. Why do you think the larger sizes of processed fruits and vegetables cost less per unit than the smaller sizes?
6. Why do you think baby carrots and other very young vegetables are more expensive than mature ones?

ACTIVITIES

1. Find out how fruits and vegetables were preserved and stored in colonial times.
2. Make a chart listing the characteristics various fruits and vegetables must have in order to be considered grades A, B, and C. You can find the information in your library.
3. In the supermarket, some fruits and vegetables are sold by the pound, while others are sold individually. Using scales, figure out how much the ones that are sold by the pound cost individually, and how much those sold individually cost per pound. Make up a chart showing the results. What conclusions can you draw?

SECTION 4 · Selecting and Preparing Milk Group Products

GETTING HER DAILY CALCIUM

Jane's dentist told her to drink a quart (or nearly a liter) of milk per day to get enough calcium for healthy teeth. Since Jane likes many foods better than milk, she decided to find out what else would give her the amount of calcium she needs.

She learned she would have to eat 144 apples or 115 hamburgers to get the amount of calcium in one quart of milk! Jane soon decided that for calcium, milk was the best bet.

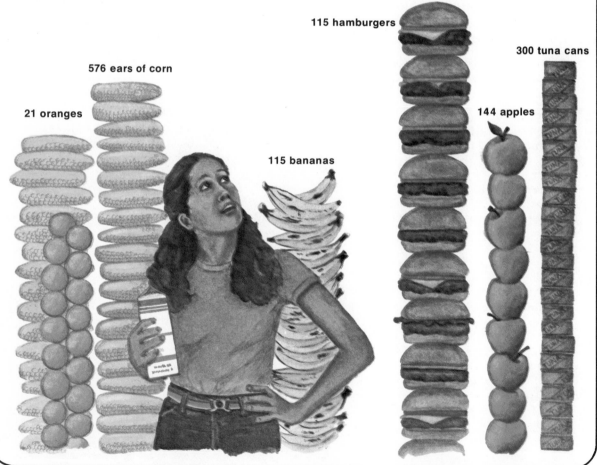

115 hamburgers

300 tuna cans

576 ears of corn

21 oranges

144 apples

115 bananas

Milk is a highly nutritious and flexible food. It has a lot of important nutrients, and can be bought in a variety of products—regular milk, yogurt, cheese, and ice cream.

Calcium and Other Nutrients

The great amount of calcium in milk and milk products makes them very valuable foods. Calcium forms a large part of our bones and teeth. A tiny amount of calcium always circulates in the blood. It regulates the heartbeat and makes the blood clot correctly. This circulating calcium is so important that if we do not get enough of the nutrient in our diets every day, our bodies will take it from our bones and teeth. These will then become weak and brittle and fail to grow properly.

Even if Jane could eat enough apples to get the calcium she needs, without milk products she would soon run out of riboflavin. This B vitamin is a must for good growth and healthy skin, hair, and eyes. Few foods contain enough riboflavin to count. But a quart (.95 l) of milk has enough riboflavin to meet the daily needs of everyone except pregnant women and nursing mothers.

Milk also supplies a great deal of high-quality protein. A quart provides about half the amount a growing person or an adult needs each day. And milk contains vitamin A, vitamin C, and thiamine.

Storing Milk Products

Keep fresh milk in the coldest part of the refrigerator. This will help retain its nutrients and freshness for as long as possible. Putting the milk container away as soon as you have used what you need is also very important. Warmth and light are both harmful to fresh milk. Warmth allows the growth of harmful bacteria, while light destroys the riboflavin content.

Other fresh milk products need the same care. Cultured milk products that have not been opened keep longer than fresh milk. The dates stamped on milk products will help you judge their freshness.

Soft cheeses, like cottage cheese, keep for a few days if tightly covered. Hard cheeses, like Cheddar and Swiss, remain fresh for weeks or even months if they are tightly wrapped.

The freezer, of course, is the place for ice cream, ice milk, and frozen yogurt. If the temperature in the freezing compartment is above 0°F (−18°C), the product should be used within a few days.

Canned and dried milk keep well on the shelf until they are opened and mixed with water. Then they must be refrigerated.

Preparing Milk Products

Like other foods rich in animal protein, milk products require special cooking tech-

Cheese is rich in protein and nutrients, but its fat content makes it rich in calories, too.

Box 1

Milk and Its Many Forms

Milk offers its rich supplies of nutrients in many delicious forms such as cheese and ice cream.

Before milk gets to you in any form, it is pasteurized. This means it is heated to a certain temperature and held there for a specific length of time. Pasteurization destroys harmful bacteria that are usually present in raw milk from even the healthiest cows.

LIQUID MILK

The dairy section of the supermarket holds many varieties of milk in liquid form. **Whole milk** contains all the nutrients milk has to offer. This includes three to four percent fat, which is often called butterfat.

Most whole milk is homogenized. This means the fat has been broken down into small particles and evenly distributed throughout the milk, so that the fat will not rise to the top as cream. Fat makes milk taste richer.

Skim milk is whole milk from which almost all the fat has been removed. It has most of the nutrients supplied by whole milk, except for fat. Vitamin A, removed during skimming, is put back in.

Two percent milk has more fat than skim milk, but less than whole milk. Although two percent milk is a little higher in calories than skim, many people prefer its flavor and texture.

Whole milk, two percent milk, and skim milk may be fortified with vitamin D. This important nutrient must be present for calcium to work well. Vitamin D occurs naturally in very few foods. Adding it to milk makes it easier for everyone to get enough.

OTHER LIQUID MILK PRODUCTS

If milk isn't homogenized, the fat, mixed with milk, rises to the top of the container. This rich substance is **cream**. An ounce of cream (29.57 ml) contains 110 calories. An ounce of whole milk has only about 20 calories.

Half-and-half is a mixture of cream and milk. It offers some of the rich taste and texture of cream with less fat and fewer calories.

Evaporated milk is whole milk that has

niques. Follow a few basic principles when preparing dishes made with milk, cream, or cheese. Then you will preserve the nutrients and get the flavor and texture you want.

Protein becomes tough and stringy at high temperatures, so *low heat* is the rule for cooking milk products. Very often the difference between success and failure is a matter of a few degrees—all the stirring in the world won't save a cream sauce that's been cooked at too high a temperature.

Heavy pots and pans are also helpful because they allow milk products to heat slowly and evenly. Slow, even heat keeps the milk from burning on the bottom of the pan. Low temperatures prevent the protein from forming a skin over the top of the food and a crust on the side of the pan. (If skins or crusts do develop, you should beat them back into the food. Otherwise, valuable protein will be lost.) Low temperatures also prevent milk products from boiling over.

Because light quickly destroys riboflavin, it is important to cover milk products whenever possible as they cook.

Milk products are a valuable part of our diet. Handling them properly will give you the full benefit of their flavor and nutrition.

been heated to remove more than half the water content. This concentrated product is canned and can be stored for long periods of time. Add the right amount of water and you once again have a product like fresh whole milk.

DRIED MILK

Milk from which all the moisture has been removed is called **dried milk.** Dried milk is an inexpensive powder that contains all the nutrients found in skim milk. It keeps for a long time. Nonfat dry milk can be used for cooking and, with water added, for drinking. One popular way to use dried milk is with flavoring such as chocolate or strawberry.

CULTURED MILK PRODUCTS

The taste and texture of milk and cream can be greatly changed by the addition of certain harmless bacteria. These bacteria are grown in colonies called cultures. They turn milk and cream into products that have a tangy taste and thick texture. That is why **buttermilk, yogurt,** and **sour cream** are called cultured milk products. Buttermilk is made from skim milk, and sour cream is made from cream. Yogurt can be made from either whole or skim milk.

SOLID MILK PRODUCTS

Cheese is one of the most important cultured milk products. It ranks as a very popular food in many parts of the world. There are more than 400 different kinds of cheeses, and over 2,000 names for them. Made from milk curd—the part of milk that contains most of the protein and fat—cheese is high in protein and other milk nutrients.

Most cheeses have much less calcium per serving than liquid milk has, and cannot be used entirely in place of it. Cheese, except for a few low-fat varieties, is also much higher in calories than milk.

Ice cream, ice milk, and **frozen yogurt** are all popular desserts made from milk products. Ice milk and frozen yogurt contain less fat and fewer calories than ice cream, but all three are sweetened with sugar and so contain many calories.

QUESTIONS

1. What are the major nutrients in milk? What do they do for your body?
2. Name some of the foods that are made from milk. How do they compare in nutritive value?
3. Describe the best way to cook milk products. What are the benefits of this method?
4. What are some of the ways that a person who does not like to drink milk can get enough of the nutrients that milk supplies?
5. What is the basic reason that milk—no matter what animal it is from—has such a rich supply of nutrients?
6. How do you think cultured milk products were discovered?

ACTIVITIES

1. Make a poster of the human body, labeling the parts and functions that the nutrients in milk keep in working order.
2. Write a skit in which you convince a child to drink milk by explaining the nutritive value of milk in simple terms.
3. Report to the class on the life and work of Louis Pasteur, who developed the pasteurization process.

SECTION 5 · Selecting and Preparing Meat Group Products

Who Is Protein Person?

One day in home economics class, Roger was half listening to a discussion of proteins and half thinking about basketball. The teacher asked him something. When Roger did not hear the question, she pointed out that if Roger listened better, he might learn something.

That night, Roger had a dream. A creature like the one on this page was dribbling the ball down the basketball court toward Roger.

"Who are you?" Roger demanded.

"Protein Person," the loud, deep voice replied. "I'm strong as an ox and smart as a wolf. I'll make meat pies out of you and the rest of your scrawny team."

"Yeah?" said Roger. "Your eyes are two fried eggs. Your nose is a sausage. Your ears look like lamb chops."

"What's wrong with that?" the creature asked coolly, as it shot two for two.

"Nothing," said Roger. "Except that's not what people are made of."

"Wrong!" shouted the creature, so loud that Roger woke up.

Protein Person was right—and Roger must have been listening more closely in class than he or his teacher thought. As the saying goes, people are what they eat. The foods that formed Protein Person's body are especially important for strong muscles, healthy blood, and healthy internal organs. These foods are very rich in protein.

Protein and Other Nutrients

Your body contains more protein than any other substance except water. Protein is part of every cell. It plays a large role in your body's constant fight against disease. It is essential for making hormones and other chemicals that control your body processes. Protein is also important in forming the genes that will transfer your characteristics to your children. Protein is one reason why meat group products are very important in the average person's diet.

Foods in the meat group also supply iron, for healthy blood, and niacin. Niacin is a B vitamin. It prevents pellagra, a serious disease that causes both physical and mental illness.

Other B vitamins, like thiamine and riboflavin, are also plentiful in meat. They help our bodies use other nutrients and are necessary for growth and good health.

Buying Fresh Meat

North Americans spend more each year for meat than they do for any other single food. So if you want to become a wise consumer of foods, meat group products are a good place to start. Find a reliable store and learn to judge the appearance and smell of the highest-quality products.

To help consumers know what they are getting, meat and poultry may carry a gov-

ernment grade. The more finely textured, tender, and juicy the meat, the higher the grade. For example, the highest grade of beef, called prime, is the most tender. The lean portion of prime is well marbled with fat.

As the grade of the beef drops, the fat content of the lean portion drops as well. Therefore, the lower grades have less fat and fewer calories per serving of lean meat. Leaner meats are less tender. The right cooking methods can increase tenderness greatly, however, making the lower grades of meat a good buy.

Cuts

The cut of meat, as well as its grade, should determine your choice. The cut tells from which part of the animal the meat was taken. The price per pound of a piece of meat depends partly on the cut. The tenderest cuts come from those parts of the animal with the least used, softest muscles.

The least expensive cut is not always the best buy. It often contains much bone or large pieces of fat and gristle that have to be thrown away. It might come from sections of the animal that are very tough.

A more expensive cut may be boneless and have less excess fat and gristle. It may come from a more tender part of the animal. The cost per serving may be less than that of a cheaper cut. A pound of round steak, for example, could provide four servings. A pound of short ribs, bones included, could provide only one.

Knowing about the different cuts of meat will help you select ground beef, a popular form of meat. Meat from the part of the animal known as the round tends to be less fatty than meat from the chuck section. So ground round is usually lower in fat than ground chuck. The color of ground

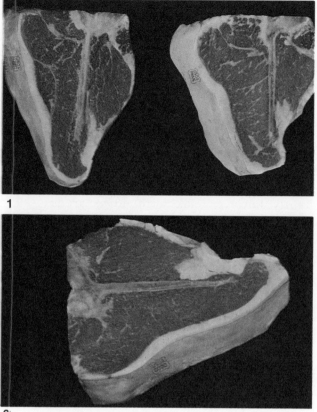

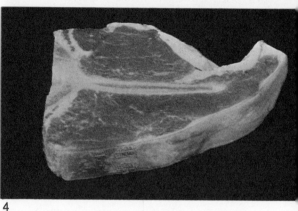

Four U.S. grades of beef: (1) Prime, (2) Choice, (3) Good, (4) Standard. It can be hard to tell the difference by sight, but streaks of fat—or marbling—within the lean meat are a clue to the better cuts.

beef is also a guide. In general, the redder, the better. As the fat content increases, the color gets lighter and pinker. Some stores include the fat content of the meat on the label.

Other Forms of Meat

Some meats go through a process called curing. Meat that is salted and then soaked in salty water, called brine, is salt-cured. Ham and bacon are cured pork. Corned beef is cured beef.

Curing can take anywhere from a few days to several months. Sugar is sometimes used in the curing process to add flavor—bacon, for example, is often cured with sugar. Cured meats have a distinct flavor. They can't be substituted in recipes for similar cuts of fresh meat.

Cured meat, meats already cooked in some way, and cooked fish (such as tuna) are often canned. Even though they tend to be more expensive than fresh meat, they're good items to have on hand for quick meals.

Meat and fish are often sold frozen. A single freezing makes no major change in flavor or nutrient content. But if meat products are thawed and frozen again, both flavor and nutrients will be lost.

DEEP FREEZE

Box 1

Food	Approximate holding period at 0°F (−18°C)
MEAT	**MONTHS**
Beef	
Hamburger or chipped (thin) steaks	4
Roasts	12
Steaks	12
Lamb	
Patties (ground meat)	4
Roasts	9
Pork, fresh	
Chops	4
Roasts	8
Sausage	2
Cooked meat	
Meat dinners	3
Meat pie	3
Swiss steak	3

U.S. Department of Agriculture, *Handbook for the Home: The Yearbook of Agriculture 1973.* Washington, D.C.: U.S. Government Printing Office, 1973.

Food	Approximate holding period at 0°F (−18°C)
POULTRY	**MONTHS**
Chicken	
Cut up	9
Liver	3
Whole	12
Turkey	
Cut up	6
Whole	12
Cooked chicken and turkey	
Chicken or turkey dinners (sliced meat and gravy)	6
Chicken or turkey pies	6
Fried chicken	4
Fried chicken dinners	4
SEAFOOD	
Fish Fillets	
Cod, flounder, haddock, halibut, pollock	6
Mullet, ocean perch, sea trout, striped bass	3
Pacific Ocean perch	2
Salmon steaks	2
Shrimp	12

Maximum home-storage periods to keep frozen foods at good quality. If your freezer temperature is not 0°F (−18°C) or below, frozen foods should be kept only for a few days.

Storing Meat Group Products

Proper storage is the first step in using meat and meat group products wisely.

All fresh meat and fish should be taken out of the store wrapper and wiped with a clean damp cloth. Then the meat or fish should be wrapped loosely in clean foil or plastic wrap and stored in the coldest part of the refrigerator.

All fresh meat products must be used within a few days of purchase. Ground meat should be cooked within twenty-four hours. Organ meats keep for only one or two days. Processed and cooked meats can be kept longer.

Eggs, too, need refrigeration to retain nutrients and flavor. Whole eggs should be stored in a covered container to keep them from absorbing food odors.

Dried peas and beans will stay fresh in the cupboard if they are kept in a tightly

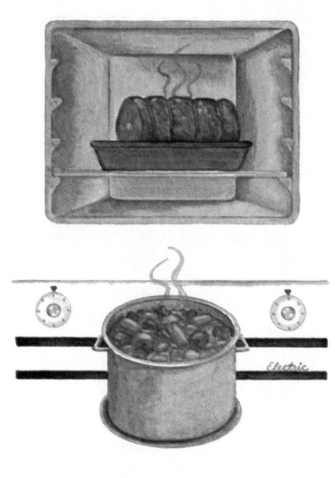

A juicy—and expensive—roast in the oven may make your mouth water. But don't ignore cheaper cuts of meat that can be cooked into very tasty stews or pot roasts.

sealed container. Canned meats and fish keep well on cool, dry shelves until they are opened.

Frozen fish and meat must be kept at 0°F (−18°C) or used within a day or two of purchase. If you plan to freeze fresh meat or fish, you should do so at once, after wrapping it in as airtight a manner as possible. Write the date of storage on the package.

Since each product has its own specific storage requirements, it's a good idea to keep a list of recommended storage times near or on your freezer. Then you'll know if that package of pork chops you put in the freezer in June is all right to use in September.

And Now—Preparing

Foods rich in animal protein become dry, tough, and stringy if they are cooked at high temperatures. Cooking at low to medium temperatures is a must, whether you are preparing fried eggs or sandwich steaks.

The cut of meat determines the method used for cooking it. **Dry heat cooking**—roasting or broiling—is good for tender, more expensive cuts. **Moist heat cooking**—which includes stewing and deep-frying—is better for less tender cuts. Moist heat makes even tough meat tender and flavorful.

A good cookbook will tell you the method of cooking, the exact temperature needed, and the length of time required for each dish.

Choosing for Variety

Vegetable proteins add variety to the diet and also save money. Delicious casseroles with dried peas or beans make excellent main course dishes. To get the most proteins these vegetables offer, mix them with each other or with animal proteins.

Don't overlook the quick, reliable standbys. Tuna salad provides plenty of protein in a tasty form. So do peanut butter sandwiches on whole wheat bread, eaten for a healthful snack. With so many foods available in the meat group, you're sure to find enough you like to get all the protein you need every day.

QUESTIONS

1. Why are foods from the meat group so important in the diet?
2. List as many different kinds of foods from the meat group as you can. Why must some of them be eaten in combination with others?
3. What are some of the things to be considered when buying meat?
4. Why is knowing how to select, store, and prepare foods from the meat group one of the most important home economics skills?
5. Why do you think meat from wild game has a tougher texture than meat from domestic animals?
6. Some experts predict that in the future more of our protein will come from vegetables than from meat. Why do you think this might happen?

ACTIVITIES

1. Make a poster illustrating the parts of the animal that various cuts of beef, pork, or lamb come from. Describe the characteristics of each cut on the chart.
2. Imagine that you are a vegetarian who drinks milk and eats milk products and eggs. Design menus for two days that give enough of all nutrients. Discuss the protein sources in detail. Then design menus for two days for a vegetarian who does not eat eggs or milk products. Show how you have provided for protein needs. Government pamphlets can assist you in this project.
3. Visit the meat department of a supermarket or go to a butcher shop. Interview one of the butchers to find out where the meat comes from and how it is bought. Find out as much as you can about different cuts of meat—for example, what makes one more expensive than another.
4. Report on the special cooking techniques, such as larding and barding, used for cooking meats with very little fat content.

Box 2

SO MANY PRODUCTS . . .

All the foods in the meat group contain a rich array of nutrients. However, some of them have more of certain nutrients than others. You can see how they vary by comparing the following products.

Beef, a meat rich in iron, comes from cattle. Because it often has a high fat content, it can be very tender.

Pork, which comes from pigs or hogs, also has a high fat content. It is especially rich in thiamine, a B vitamin. One serving of pork provides about fifteen times as much thiamine as an equal quantity of beef.

Lamb, from young sheep, is another popular meat. It is similar to beef in nutritive content.

Organ meats —including liver, kidney, heart, and sweetbread—are packed with nutrients. For example, liver contains very large quantities of vitamins D, A, and B-12, as well as iron.

Poultry —chicken, duck, turkey, and goose— provides high-quality protein with less fat than beef, lamb, or pork.

Fish is very high in protein and very low in fat. Both fish and shellfish provide iodine, a mineral the body needs to function properly. Most shellfish, such as lobsters, are also high in cholesterol, which people with certain illnesses should avoid.

Eggs supply complete protein and some degree of almost every nutrient except vitamin C. However, they too contain cholesterol.

Vegetable protein sources, such as dried beans, are often called meat substitutes. They are rich in iron and the B vitamins, but the protein they contain is not complete—they should be eaten in combination with other protein foods.

SECTION 6 · Selecting and Preparing Cereal Group Products

Sources of Life

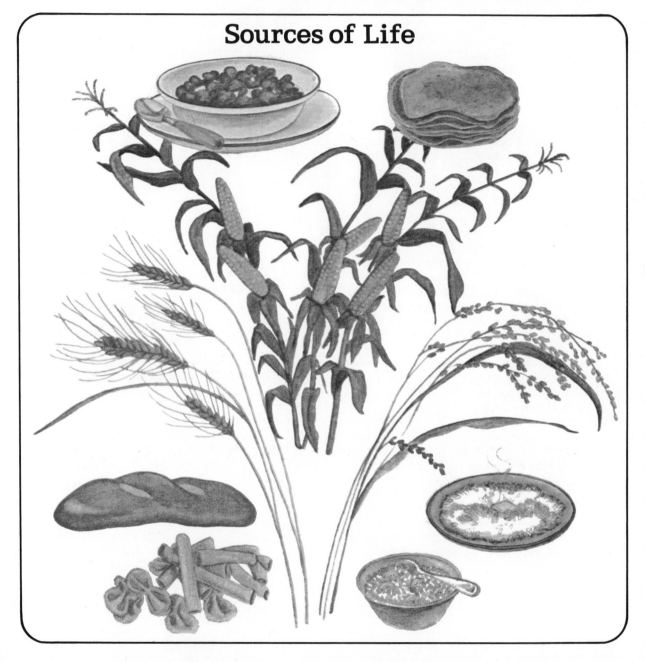

What comes to your mind when you read "cereal"? Cornflakes? Oatmeal? Perhaps white bread?

All those foods are in the cereal group, but they are just a few of the many cereal products. Cereal—or grain—products have been an extremely important part of the human diet for at least 15,000 years.

Throughout history, these foods have been the main source of nutrients in almost everyone's diet. Even today, *two-thirds* of the world's people depend on cereal products for most of their protein and calories.

The pictures on the previous page suggest the great variety of these products. The foods people eat are as much a part of their culture as their language or art.

Rice is a major food for over half the world's population. This cereal was probably first used in the Far East. But it has spread and become a standard item in meals served in lands as far from the Orient as Puerto Rico and Mexico.

Wheat is the most popular grain in Europe, the United States, and Canada. It is the major ingredient in most breads, pastries, breakfast cereals, and pasta products such as spaghetti, macaroni, and noodles.

Corn was the basic food of the American Indians. The word for corn in all Indian languages can be translated as "the source of life." When the first settlers came to North America from Europe, they had to learn to eat corn instead of the wheat, oats, and barley they were used to.

Why Cereals?

Crops that produce cereals—or cereal grains, as they are sometimes called—grow well in almost every part of the world. Uncooked cereal grains keep for long periods of time without refrigeration. They're easy to transport without special handling. They can be used in hundreds of ways for every type of meal. Most important of all, grains are rich in nutrients—vitamins, proteins, and carbohydrates.

Cereal products are our richest source of carbohydrates. This fact has given these products a bad name among people who watch their weight. Bread and breakfast cereal are often the first foods dieters cut out when they want to lose weight. This is a poor decision. Carbohydrates provide energy and help the body use up fat stores. They keep it from burning valuable protein reserves for energy.

If you have a weight problem, you should stop eating the high-sugar, high-fat foods in this group—sweet rolls, pastries, doughnuts, and other such tempting items. But cutting out nutritious, inexpensive carbohydrates completely is not the solution to your problem. You should continue to eat plain breakfast cereals, breads, and rolls.

Other Benefits

Cereal grains are an important source of protein, though unlike meats, the protein they provide is incomplete. One way to get greater value from the protein in cereal is to combine two kinds of grain. The combination, such as corn bread made from corn meal *and* wheat flour, will provide more nutrition than either grain alone.

Cereal products are also good sources of iron and the B vitamins, both of which are necessary for health and growth. Some of these nutrients are lost in the processing many cereals go through. Natural (brown) rice, for example, loses most of its thiamine when it is polished to make white rice. However, scientists have found a way to keep thiamine in white rice. The process is called conversion. Make sure the white rice you buy is converted so you get all the nutrients rice can offer.

Preparing Cereal Products

Many cereal products, including rice, hot breakfast cereals, and pastas, are cooked in water or some other liquid. Nutrients—especially the B vitamins—escape into the cooking liquid. The key to cereal preparation, therefore, is to use as little water as possible. The package will tell you exactly how much water each product needs.

Rinsing rice and pasta products before or after cooking is not a good practice. Water can wash away nutrients. Saving the cooking water is a wise thing to do since it contains the nutrients lost in cooking. The water can be used for cooking vegetables or making soup.

Cereal products should be cooked until they are "just done" and no longer. Overcooking destroys texture and nutritive value. Package directions and experience are your best guides to proper cooking times.

The Art of Baking

All cereal grains can be ground into flour. Wheat flour is a favorite for baking in this country, and white wheat flour is the most popular of all. Wheat flour loses much of its protein, vitamins, and minerals when it is milled to make white flour. Manufacturers usually replace some of the thiamine, riboflavin, niacin, and iron lost in milling. If these nutrients have been replaced, flour is labeled "enriched."

How you prepare a bread depends on many things, including the way in which you heat it, and what you use to make it rise.

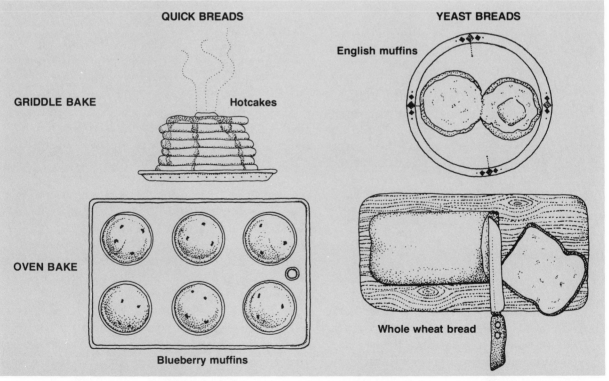

QUICK BREADS

YEAST BREADS

English muffins

GRIDDLE BAKE

Hotcakes

OVEN BAKE

Blueberry muffins

Whole wheat bread

People bake for many reasons. They like the satisfaction of doing something themselves. They enjoy taking a hot loaf of bread or a perfect pie out of the oven. Or they prefer the taste of home-baked goods. Perhaps they find pleasure in sharing what they have made with family and friends.

Like any art, baking takes skill and practice. A beginner starts with simple recipes. These may be quick breads, such as biscuits, pancakes, or banana bread, that do not require kneading and rising time. With a little experience, a baker learns how to handle dough and can move on to more difficult items such as pie crusts and yeast breads.

As you become more skillful, you can try different types of flour. You can also experiment with the many cereal dishes of other countries. For many people, baking is an enjoyable hobby.

Besides high calorie treats, bakeries provide a daily fare of bread and rolls for many.

Buying Bread and Cereal Products

Today, many people buy ready-to-eat breakfast cereals and baked goods. If they are selected carefully, these products can be as delicious, nutritious, and economical as the homemade variety.

To find out if you are getting the most nutrients for your money, check the labels on all cereal products. If the product contains white flour, make sure it is enriched flour. Experiments have shown that enriched breads are as nutritious as whole wheat breads.

Also check the labels on products that claim to have a high percentage of added nutrients. If these nutrients have been added to the usual enrichment program for cereal products, they may be unnecessary. A well-balanced diet will supply those nutrients.

When buying dry cereal products, pay attention to the weight listed on the label rather than the size of the package. At first glance, one cereal may seem much more expensive than another one the same price because it comes in a much smaller box. But the cereal in the larger box may be of the "puffed" variety, and the added air takes up much more space. The two boxes may weigh exactly the same.

Putting Them Away

Buying carefully is only the first step in becoming a wise consumer. The second is learning to store your bread and cereal products so that they stay fresh and nutritious.

Wrap bread tightly and store it in a breadbox. In hot weather, keep it in the refrigerator. Dry breakfast cereals keep well on the shelf if you close the package tightly after each use. Or you can store them in airtight containers.

Rice, pasta, and flour of all types stay

fresh for long periods in airtight containers. They need no refrigeration except in hot, humid weather, or when insects are a problem.

By choosing wisely from the great variety of cereal products, you can enjoy this oldest and most widely used food at every meal.

QUESTIONS

1. Describe the role cereals play in a well-balanced diet.
2. What happens to grains such as wheat when they are processed?
3. Describe the best process to use when cooking cereals in liquid.
4. Sometimes people use the word "bread" or "dough" as slang for money. Why do you think this is so?
5. Many traditional ethnic and regional dishes combine incomplete proteins to provide complete protein meals. Pasta and cheese, baked beans and brown bread, and black-eyed peas and rice are three such combinations. Can you think of any others? How do you suppose people developed these dishes before they knew about scientific nutrition?

ACTIVITIES

1. Make a report on triticale, a grain that has recently been developed as a new food source. You may be able to find a loaf of triticale bread in a bakery or health food store for you and your class to taste.
2. Go to the supermarket and study the dry cereals on the shelf. Which are the most expensive? What are their ingredients? Which do you think are the best buys? Why?
3. Make a map of the world, labeling each area with the cereal grain that is most popular there.

SECTION 7 · Selecting and Preparing Convenience Foods

TIME OR MONEY

Two dishes of spaghetti with sauce: the one on the left took only twenty minutes to prepare, while the one on the right took more than three hours. The difference, of course, is that the one on the left was prepared from two packages of convenience foods. That did away with the peeling, slicing, chopping, measuring, mixing, and cooking that went into making the one on the right.

The answer to the question, "Which one would you choose to make?" may seem obvious. After all, the one on the left takes much less time to prepare. But a wise consumer thinks of more than time when deciding whether to prepare a dish from scratch or from convenience foods.

What else would you base your decision on?

Although the two dishes of spaghetti shown here look identical, chances are they're not. The dish made from convenience foods may differ greatly in taste, cost and nutritive value. These differences usually affect a consumer's choices of what form of a food to buy. But not always.

More Than We Realize

Convenience foods are a much greater part of our lives than most of us realize. Some convenience foods are so commonly used we rarely think of them as convenience foods. Some foods, in fact, are not readily available in any other form.

You could call milk a convenience food because most of us buy it already pasteurized, homogenized, and packaged. Butter could also be thought of as a convenience food. So could harvested vegetables and milled flour.

Most of the ingredients we use to make almost any dish are convenience foods because some of the work in preparing them has already been done. We buy pepper that has been ground, meat that has been chopped, and peanuts that have been roasted.

From a Lot to a Little

Convenience foods differ greatly in the amount of work left to the consumer. Many reach our kitchens as prepared dishes ready to eat with little or no effort. These range from packages of baked goods that we only have to open, to whole dinners that we only have to reheat.

Some convenience foods require more work by the consumer. Cake mixes and meat extenders fall into this category. And some convenience items are simply packages of spices to give flavor to basic dishes.

All convenience foods save time—some a few minutes, some a few hours.

Other Advantages

Convenience foods can add variety to meals by expanding menu possibilities. Most supermarkets now carry ethnic foods that would be difficult for the consumer to prepare at home. Mexican tortillas, for example, are available in many stores but the special flour from which they are made may not be. The same holds true for Oriental dishes made with rice flour. Some specialty stores carry prepared dishes made with foods as exotic as whale meat and octopus.

A few food preparation tasks not only take a lot of time, but also are unpleasant. The very thought of chopping onions brings tears to some people's eyes! Frozen chopped onions that can be added to any dish do away with the necessity of chopping onions. However, there is a price to pay.

Money and Nutritive Value

Convenience foods often cost more—sometimes *much* more—than the same dish prepared from basic ingredients. For example, ready-to-eat cereal that contains a few pieces of dried fruit costs much more than plain cereal with fresh fruit. And slicing adds to the cost of foods such as meats and cheese.

Too, the process of producing convenience foods often destroys many of the nutrients the foods would otherwise provide. Dehydrated mashed potatoes, for example, contain only about half the vitamin C that fresh potatoes offer.

Convenience foods may also contain less of certain ingredients than you would expect. Frozen meat pies need be no more than twenty-five percent meat by law—not a very big contribution to your daily protein intake. Furthermore, the quality of the meat in such products may be low. If there is a lot of fat and gristle, some of the already scanty meat portion must be thrown away.

The Labels—Your Best Guide

Often, complete convenience meals are not nutritionally balanced. A frozen dinner, for example, might have to be served with a fresh salad, milk, and a fruit dessert to provide a well-balanced meal. Studying the labels on convenience foods is the only way to tell whether the nutritive content is adequate for the way you plan to use the food.

Many labels, unfortunately, do not contain enough nutritional information. Other labels are confusing and unclear. If you come across such labels, write to the manufacturer to complain. This is the best way to let the food industry know that you care about nutrition and want good information about it.

Saving Time, Saving Money?

Selecting good buys from the variety of convenience foods is a challenge. Once you are satisfied that the nutritive value of a convenience food is acceptable, you can then ask yourself, "How much time will I save compared to the money I will spend?" An extra expense may be justified when you are very rushed. When you have plenty of time—and if you enjoy cooking—it may be wiser to make a dish from basic ingredients.

Thinking about time and money will help you spot those convenience foods that save almost no time and cost a great deal. How much time does it take to add a pat of butter or margarine to a bowl of cooked carrots, for example? Almost none. But frozen carrots with butter sauce cost nearly twice as much as plain frozen carrots.

Reading the directions may also help you decide if a convenience food is a good buy. Many low-cost products require you to add ingredients that are expensive. Some cake mixes contain only flour and other dry ingredients that are relatively inexpensive. You add the costly items—eggs, butter, and milk. Another cake mix might cost somewhat more, but need only water added. It would probably be a much better buy.

Following Directions

Reading and following the directions for preparing convenience foods is necessary for good results. Ignoring directions may result in disaster.

For example, if you beat an instant pudding for more than the recommended number of minutes, the ingredients will separate and the pudding will not set. Or if you remove all the aluminum foil from a TV dinner before putting it in the oven, you will end up with dried-out peas and hard mashed potatoes by the time the meat is thoroughly heated.

Even when you follow directions carefully, the final product is sometimes disappointing. Then it doesn't matter how quick, nutritious, and economical such a product is. It is not truly convenient if you don't like it.

Write to the manufacturer, telling why you are not pleased. This will help you, and other consumers, get the most for your convenience food dollar.

QUESTIONS

1. List some basic foods that have already been processed in some way before we buy them.
2. What are the major advantages of convenience foods? The major disadvantages?
3. Why are the labels on convenience foods so important to the consumer?
4. What are some of the convenience foods (besides the ones listed in this book) that are so common that we no longer think of them as convenience foods? How many convenience foods can you recall eating during the past week?
5. Do you think your family's life style would change very much if convenience foods were not available? How?
6. How can you judge whether a convenience food is worth the extra money? Do you think someone else's judgment might be different from yours? Why?

ACTIVITIES

1. Look through your kitchen and make a list of the convenience foods you find there. Which of these foods do you think your family would eat less often if they were not available in convenience form? How would that affect your overall eating habits?
2. Pretend you lived 100 years ago and had to feed a family of five. Write an entry in your diary that describes all the food preparation you had to do during a typical day.
3. Go to the supermarket and look at all the products designed to be mixed with hamburger. Evaluate them, comparing their cost to the cost of preparing roughly the same meal from basic ingredients.

SECTION 8 · Careers in Food Processing

FEEDING NORTH AMERICA

Food goes through many steps before it comes to your table. Here, oranges are sorted for size and quality, cookies are shaped and baked, and spaghetti is machine-cut for canned soup.

For breakfast this morning, you may have had orange juice, toast, bacon, and cocoa. If so, you probably opened a can, two packages, and a box.

These foods, along with more than 9,000 others, have been processed in some way to make them more convenient for you to use. All that processing—the sorting, cleaning, cutting, cooking, freezing, drying, and packaging—requires the efforts of more than five million workers. That makes the food-processing industry one of the largest in the country.

The food-processing industry offers a large number of jobs for people with many different skills and abilities. Some jobs require skill with your hands. Others require imagination and curiosity. And there are jobs that demand a knack for organization and dealing with people.

Following the processing path of some ordinary breakfast foods will show you some of the careers open to you in the food-processing industry.

Food Freezing and Canning Workers

Orange juice is processed by some of the 250,000 production workers in food freezing and canning plants. Some of the tasks are done by hand in certain plants and by machine in others. But turning fresh oranges into frozen orange juice concentrate requires the same steps in every plant.

When fresh oranges come into the plant, hand sorters examine them for ripeness and quality. These workers must have good eyesight and quick hands.

After being sorted and washed, the inspected oranges go through huge juice extractors and other machines that turn them into concentrated juice. The juice feeds into filling machines that pour the concentrate into cans. The sealed cans are then sent through a freezing tunnel, packed into boxes, and stored in a holding room.

Workers are needed at every step of the way to operate and check the machines, to inspect cans, and to check temperatures. They make sure that sanitary procedures are being followed at all times.

For other kinds of canned and frozen foods, the steps between the first sorting and the final packing include such operations as trimming, coring, cutting, steaming, and boiling. Asparagus spears, for example, require at least half these steps.

Some foods, because they are easily damaged, require hand operations. Others, such as peas, are processed completely by machine. Workers operate these machines and keep them clean and in good working order. Because very cold and very hot temperatures are used in food processing, workers may be uncomfortable at times. Companies usually provide special clothing for those who work in extreme heat or cold.

Most production workers in food-processing plants get their training on the job after completing high school. Those who are good workers can become supervisors. But advanced schooling is needed for the more technical jobs in food processing, such as quality control.

Bakery Workers

Bread is baked by commercial bakeries. Millions of loaves are turned out each day. Some of these loaves come from small neighborhood bakeries that serve local customers. Others are produced by large industrial bakeries that sell their breads and pastries to supermarkets, restaurants, hotels, and other businesses. In all, commercial bakeries employ over 250,000 workers in jobs as varied as making dough, tending ovens, decorating pastries, and packaging final products.

In small bakeries, most of the steps involved in preparing breads and pastries are done by hand by skilled all-round bakers. Some pride themselves on their ability to create beautiful and unusual cakes and pastries.

In contrast, large bakeries are highly mechanized, and there is a much greater division of labor. All-round bakers are needed to oversee operations. But each step in the baking process is handled by a different group of workers who operate such machines as dough molders and bread slicers.

The different jobs available in bakeries require different training. Machine operators often learn their tasks on the job in a few days. All-round bakers spend several years in an apprenticeship program to master the skills that a baker needs.

Although bakeries can be uncomfortably hot, it would be hard to imagine a more fragrant place to work!

Meat-Packing Workers

Bacon comes to you from some of the more than 250,000 people who work in meat-packing and -processing plants. The hogs that are used for bacon are first killed as painlessly as possible. Then the carcasses are skinned and scalded. Assembly line workers cut the carcass into large pieces, discarding those parts that can't be eaten.

After the meat has been chilled for twenty-four to forty-eight hours, workers cut the chilled pork into smaller pieces, removing bone and fat. Those cuts that will become bacon are then sent to the curing department. Once the curing process is complete, workers feed the slabs of bacon into machines that mold, smooth, and slice them into strips. In the last step of the process, the strips are weighed and packaged by machine for the supermarket.

People who work in meat-packing and -processing plants must be mentally and physically alert at all times. Sharp tools and wet floors make safety an important concern.

Graders and inspectors work for the Department of Agriculture, rating the quality of food products and making sure they are safe to eat.

Almost all the production workers are trained on the job. Advancement comes with experience. Workers in managerial or technical positions, however, need a college education.

Food Technologists

Instant cocoa did not exist fifty years ago. We owe this and other instant foods to the imagination and skill of the men and women who work as food technologists.

Food technologists are scientists who work to improve the quality of food. "Quality" is a broad area, and food technologists work in every phase of food preparation. Besides developing new products, they may also work on new methods of processing and packaging food. They study changes that foods undergo so they can find ways to preserve or improve flavor, appearance, and nutritional content. They also study the safety of additives and decide upon the ingredients of a product. Some food technologists find ways to use the waste materials of food, such as peanut shells and corn cobs. Others work to improve the efficiency of food-processing machinery.

A career in food technology calls for scientific abilities. Food technologists must have at least a college degree. In a world whose population is increasing faster than its food supply, these men and women help ensure our future food supply.

QUESTIONS

1. Which jobs in food processing require skill with your hands? Imagination and curiosity? A knack for organization and dealing with people?
2. Describe the differences between working in a large bakery and working in a small bakery.
3. What kind of training is necessary for a job as a production worker in a food-processing plant? For a job as a food technologist?
4. Why do you think the food-processing industry will continue to grow?
5. How might the tasks of different workers in the field change in the future?
6. Which of the jobs in this section do you think you would enjoy the most? The least? Why?

ACTIVITIES

1. Write a report on George Washington Carver, who specialized in finding new uses for peanuts, sweet potatoes, and soybeans. You might also want to make a poster that illustrates some of the many new products he developed.
2. Find out how the work in a food-canning plant differs today from that done fifty years ago.
3. Check the classified ads in your local paper to see if you can find any jobs in the field of food processing. What qualifications are required? Compare the salaries and the benefits with those offered in other jobs. Is there room for advancement?

SECTION 9 · Careers in Food Distribution

Sold Out

You go to the supermarket to buy ketchup, and the shelves that usually contain ketchup are empty. How many reasons can you come up with to explain those empty shelves?

Debbie looks hungrily at the hamburger she has just made. "Ah! All I need now is ketchup, and my meal will be complete." But when she opens the refrigerator—no ketchup! Whoever finished the last bottle forgot to put ketchup on the family's weekly shopping list. Debbie ends up eating her hamburger with mustard.

In the home, that kind of oversight is more annoying than serious. But if a supermarket forgets to order more ketchup when needed, thousands of people are affected. And their attitude toward the store may be affected, too.

Supermarket Managers

Seeing that their stores do not run out of stock is the responsibility of supermarket managers. They are an important link in the chain of events that gets food from the farm to the table. They make sure that a supermarket always has the foods its customers need and want. And that's a big job,

A supermarket manager works with many people. Here she checks supplies with a seller and her meat department manager.

since a supermarket may have as many as 10,000 items on its shelves. Keeping track of so many items requires an ability to organize and a knack for detail.

Supermarket managers usually share these responsibilities with the heads of different departments in the supermarket, such as dairy and produce. Department heads keep lists of foods that are running low. The managers do the reordering. Reordering means contacting warehouses, individual companies, and local suppliers of products such as eggs and milk.

Supermarket managers must know the approximate inventory of all departments at all times. They also oversee thorough yearly inventories and keep records of the stock. Computers are helping more and more managers keep track of all the food in their stores.

Supermarket managers have many other responsibilities. They hire the store's employees and check to see that jobs are done properly. Managers are also the ones who make sure the store looks clean and attractive at all times. And if customers have complaints, managers must be able to handle them with patience and courtesy.

Bookkeeping and advertising are still other areas of responsibility for supermarket managers. If eggs are on sale one week, they let customers know by placing advertisements with local newspapers and radio and television stations.

Because supermarket managers are responsible for every area of their store's operations, they usually work longer hours than any of their employees. They must know many things—the shelf life of different foods, how to handle people, how to write reports. And managers must make sure that the store is run efficiently and makes a profit.

Supermarket managers often find a col-

Food brokers visit several stores each day. One of their main tasks is to introduce new food items to the managers.

lege degree helpful to their careers. But many start out as checkers and clerks and advance by showing good judgment and an ability to learn on the job. So, the after-school job you get in a supermarket may turn into a rewarding career.

Food Brokers

Supermarket managers depend on food brokers to supply them with ketchup and many of the other foods that appear on their shelves.

Food brokers simplify the jobs of both buyers (supermarket managers) and sellers (food companies). They do this by representing a number of companies that sell many different products. That way, supermarket managers do not have to spend time with hundreds of salespeople. The person who represents the ketchup manufacturer may also represent producers of canned goods and frozen foods. The money saved through the food broker system is passed on to the customer. Food prices would be higher if supermarket managers had to deal with each food company separately.

Food brokers also tell supermarket managers about new products and suggest attractive ways to display them. They know the likes and dislikes of customers in each area of their territory. With that knowledge, they can help supermarket managers increase sales. They may know, for example, that onion-flavored ketchup is popular in Texas, but that regular ketchup sells best in Kansas. That kind of information is vital to running a supermarket.

Truck drivers can move refrigerated, frozen, and even heated foods to their final destination.

Market Researchers

Much of the information about customer likes and dislikes comes to food brokers through the work of market researchers. They're the people who find out if onion-flavored ketchup is a good idea in the first place. They do this by making careful studies of the buying habits of customers.

You may have seen market research interviewers at work in stores and shopping centers. They talk to people to find out their reactions to new products. Some research is done even before a new product exists! In these cases, interviewers show people pictures of how the package might look, as well as a list of possible names for the new product. The results of the testing help companies decide whether their new products will sell, and if so, in which areas.

Market researchers are involved in every step of the research process. They make up questionnaires, work with computers, and analyze test results. A college education is necessary for a high-level position in market research. You can learn more about the work—and find out if you would like it—by getting a job as an interviewer for a market research firm. You may be the one who finds out what new-flavored ketchup would be most popular in your area!

Other Jobs

Many other workers are vital links in the food distribution chain. Transportation is basic to food distribution. Thousands of people are needed to drive the trucks and other vehicles that move food from the farm to the supermarket. Warehouses employ many thousands more who store and keep track of foods before they are sent to your supermarket. Food distribution is a large field that offers many different kinds of career opportunities.

QUESTIONS

1. Name some of the most important careers in the food distribution industry.
2. What do the people who have these jobs do?
3. How do workers in different areas of the food distribution field depend on one another?
4. Why are there so many more people working in the food distribution industry than there were 100 years ago? How do you think food distribution has changed in the last 100 years?
5. What kinds of questions do you think market researchers ask when they interview people about a new product?

ACTIVITIES

1. Imagine you are a food broker. Write down what you would say to convince a supermarket manager to carry a new food item (onion-flavored ketchup, for example).
2. Make a poster that illustrates how different food distribution workers depend on one another.

CHAPTER 9

Principles of Food Preparation and Service

SECTION 1· The Many Meanings of Mealtime

Eat and Enjoy!

It's often said that you can't do two things at once. But clearly the people in this picture are doing more than just eating. They are talking, laughing, sharing, enjoying one another's company—while eating a nutritious meal.

This looks like quite an event. Perhaps it is someone's birthday or a holiday. But it could be an everyday dinner. When you share a meal with family or friends, it becomes more than just a time to take in food.

Today, family members may all go to school, or work, or both. The evening meal may be a family's only chance to get together and talk. Over a nutritious meal, people can relax. They can share plans and ideas, and talk about what has happened since they last sat down together.

Meals are also times for friends to gather. At school, you can talk during lunch about all the things you can't discuss during class. After a dance, or sports event, or a movie, the fun often continues over snacks or light meals.

Some people work during mealtime. Business men and women often discuss plans and problems over lunch.

Special Times

Food plays an important part in many special events and holidays. At large family reunions, a special dinner may be the main event.

Birthdays, anniversaries, and graduations may be celebrated by a dinner party. If the party does not include a meal, snacks are usually an important part of the fun.

Special recognitions are often given at luncheons or dinners. Perhaps your school's booster or parents' club holds an awards dinner each year.

National and religious holidays are other important festive occasions that often center on a meal. What would Thanksgiving be without Thanksgiving dinner? Do you have a Fourth of July picnic? Maybe you celebrate the ancient feast of Passover. What other national or religious feast days can you think of?

You may also celebrate **special traditions** of the region in which you live—with a New England clambake, for example, or a Texas pit barbecue. You may celebrate your family's country of origin. Chinese Ameri-

Trying new foods is an adventure. Sharing the experience with others at a street fair can add to the fun.

cans often mark the Chinese New Year with traditional parties and a meal of special dishes.

Special Care

Any meal can give the person who prepares it a chance to show how he or she feels about the people who eat it. One way to show family or friends how much you care for them is to serve them nutritious and tasty meals. Taking care to select and prepare good food is an important way of expressing love. If you make a cake or some delicious snacks for a friend's birthday party, you are saying, "Happy Birthday!" with more than just words.

Everyone at the table can contribute to a pleasant time. Good manners, friendliness, and consideration for others make for a relaxed atmosphere. The finest feast in the world can be ruined by a quarrel. The simplest dinner can be a special occasion if everyone is happy and at ease.

The Price of Trouble

If people are emotionally upset at mealtime, they may not feel like eating. Then they will fail to get the nutrients they need, no matter how nutritious and tasty the food is.

People who eat when emotionally upset can harm their digestion. Tense and unhappy feelings make the stomach muscles tighten. Tight stomach muscles can cause gas pains, heartburn, and general discomfort. A tight stomach can lead to real illness, such as an ulcer, if it happens often or continues for a long time.

Feeling upset may make people eat very quickly, as a nervous reaction to their problems. This practice can make an already tense stomach even tenser. And fast eating can lead to unhealthy overeating.

Mealtimes are often used for discussing important matters. But try not to talk about topics that are unpleasant or likely to cause arguments.

Do you have something to tell your family that you know they won't like? Try to wait until after dinner, when they've had a chance to relax and digest their meal. Do you disagree strongly with your friend about a school election? Don't talk about it over lunch. If it's important to you, discuss your disagreement in the evening on the phone.

What About You?

What do mealtimes mean to you? Are they times when you can relax with the people around you? Or are you often tense or in a hurry to get somewhere else?

Mealtimes are important in everyone's life. They play a major part in celebrating holidays and traditions. They can be periods of rest in a busy day. And, every day, they are times for seeing and enjoying the people we live, study, and work with. You can help make the most of meals by trying to make them relaxed and pleasant occasions.

QUESTIONS

1. List several things people do at mealtimes besides eat.
2. How can a tense mealtime atmosphere affect your digestion?
3. How can you reduce the chances of an unpleasant atmosphere at mealtime?

ACTIVITIES

1. Which meal of the day do you enjoy the most? Write a short essay telling why.
2. Find an old book on etiquette in the library and read the section on meals. Which parts do you think still hold true today? Which

4. What are some advantages to discussing business at mealtime? Some disadvantages?
5. Can you think of any tricks to help slow down a person who eats too quickly?
6. What are some of the reasons we are eating more and more foods from different cultures and nations?

parts do you think are old-fashioned?
3. Give a talk on how your family prepares a special holiday meal. How is this different from the way your family prepares regular meals?

SECTION 2 · Handle with Care

Two Kinds of Care

There are two major reasons for taking care in the kitchen. The more important one is to protect the food, to keep it fresh and wholesome. But it's also important to protect yourself and other kitchen workers. Look at these seven pictures, and in each case decide why the people are doing what they're doing. Are they protecting the food, themselves, or both?

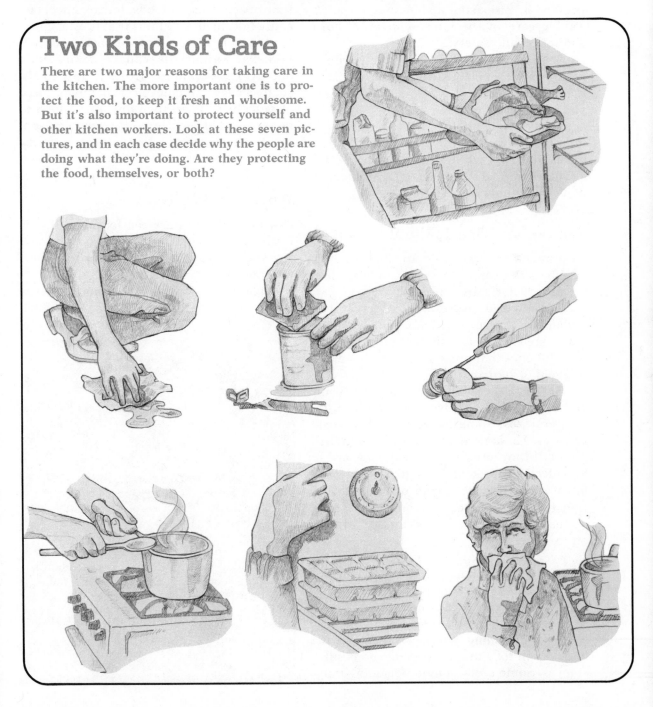

You may think the rule "Handle with care" applies only to the postal service. But careful handling is especially important in preparing and managing food. Taking care in the kitchen involves both sanitation and safety.

Sanitation keeps food free from harmful germs and dirt so that it is safe to eat. This means keeping food and equipment clean, and storing and cooking food properly.

Safety in the kitchen means using careful work habits to avoid accidents such as burns and cuts while preparing food. The kitchen can be a dangerous place if people don't know how to be careful.

Sanitation: What Is the Enemy?

Sanitation is necessary to protect the health of the eater. The main dangers are germs—bacteria and viruses.

Bacteria and viruses are tiny creatures too small to be seen without a microscope. Many are harmless. But there are enough harmful ones that great care must be taken to avoid or destroy them.

Food can carry these germs into your body. Some germs thrive on food at certain temperatures. Some thrive on soiled work surfaces. These germs can grow and multiply until they are a severe health hazard.

Infections are illnesses like colds and flu. If someone with a cold or other infection touches, sneezes, or coughs on food, germs can get into the food and be passed on to someone else.

Even when people do not feel ill, they may be carrying harmful bacteria and viruses that can make others sick. This is why it is never a good idea to use another person's drinking glass or eating utensils.

Food poisoning happens when germs multiply in food and create poisonous substances. Some types of food poisoning may cause stomach cramps, fever, and other unpleasant symptoms. Other types can cause very serious illness. Bacteria that grow in improperly canned foods, for instance, can cause botulism, an illness that is often fatal.

Another harmful type of bacteria is salmonella. Salmonella can cause infection and also poisoning. It grows in raw foods, such as eggs and chicken. Touching a piece of raw chicken and then touching a food to be served cold can cause salmonella poisoning. Such poisoning is very serious and very hard to cure.

What Can You Do?

How can you be sure the food you buy is fresh and free from bacteria and viruses? Use your eyes and nose. Don't buy food with a strange color or a bad odor.

Take a good look at canned goods. Never buy a can that is bulging at one end. Such

---

Box 1

Keeping Germs Away

- Wash hands carefully before working with food and after using the bathroom.
- Keep hair out of food. If you have long hair, tie it back.
- If you need to sneeze or cough near food, use a tissue. If a sneeze comes on too suddenly to get a tissue, turn your head away.
- Keep kitchen work areas and equipment clean. Wash them with *hot* water and soap and pay special attention to small areas, such as the cutting edges of can openers and graters.
- Wash off the tops of cans before opening them.
- Rinse all fresh fruits and vegetables to remove insecticides and dirt.

cans might contain very dangerous bacteria. If you see bulging cans in the market, tell the store manager and write the manufacturer.

Also, if you start to open a can and the liquid contents spray out rapidly, as if they were under pressure, throw the food and the can away and wash your hands.

To *keep* food safe from bacteria and viruses, a good manager of foods pays close attention to sanitation. Basic to this is **cleanliness,** which keeps germs away from food in the first place. Cleanliness requires good kitchen habits, some of which are mentioned in box 1 of this section.

Temperature and **time** are two more keys to keeping food safe. Harmful bacteria multiply quickly in food kept too long at temperatures between 40°F (4.4°C) and 140°F (60°C). Cool temperatures slow down the growth of bacteria. Freezing stops it altogether—until the food is thawed. The only way to kill many bacteria, however, is to heat the food to a high temperature.

Proper Food Storage

Most fresh foods and canned or bottled foods that have been opened must be kept in the refrigerator. There are a few exceptions to this rule. Uncut raw potatoes, for example, do not need refrigeration if air can circulate around them. Some bottled foods that are highly spiced, such as ketchup, keep well without refrigeration. And many dry foods, such as rice, flour, and sugar, keep well in the cupboard if they are tightly covered. Look at labels for specific storage directions if you are not sure. A good guideline to follow is: Refrigerate unless you learn otherwise.

Some foods spoil very quickly out of the refrigerator. Poultry, milk, and foods containing eggs are examples. If you have to

Some crops have been dusted with pesticides to keep insects away. Therefore, fruits and vegetables should be rinsed carefully before eating.

stop while preparing an egg dish, put the ingredients back into the refrigerator until you are ready to start again.

Time Tips

Cooling only *slows down* the growth of bacteria. Foods will not keep for more than a few days in normal refrigerator temperatures. Even frozen foods keep for only a limited number of days in the freezer section of the refrigerator. Box 2 of this section tells you how long some common foods will keep when refrigerated. Making sure food stays fresh is not only sanitary, it's economical as well. Spoiled food is wasted food—and wasted food is wasted money.

Heating food to the right temperature for the right length of time will destroy many dangerous bacteria and viruses. A basic cookbook will tell you how long different foods need to be cooked and at what temperatures.

Cooked food should not stand around at room temperature. As soon as possible, put leftovers into the refrigerator.

Since temperature is so important in controlling bacteria and viruses, box 3 of this section should be helpful.

Box 2

A Time to Store, a Time to Eat

How long will different foods keep in the refrigerator?

One or Two Days	Two or Three Days	Three to Four Days
Ground meat	Berries	Leftover cooked meats
Variety meats (liver, etc.)	Cherries	and meat dishes
Poultry	Asparagus	
Fish	Ham slice	
Sweet corn		

Three to Five Days	Up to One Week	Up to Two Weeks
Broccoli	Cottage Cheese	Soft cheese
Lima beans	Tomatoes	Butter
Spinach	Cauliflower	Dried beef, sliced
Green onions and peas	Celery	Oranges
Milk and cream	Eggs in shell	Grapefruit
Grapes	Bacon	Lemons
Peaches	Whole ham	Carrots (tops removed)
Apricots	Lettuce	Cabbage
Fresh meats		
Cold cuts		

Up to One Month
Apples

Based on Agricultural Research Service. U.S. Government Printing Office. Revised 1976.
Bulletin No. 78. U.S. Department of Agriculture, *Storing Perishable Foods in the Home*, Home and Garden

Kitchen Safety

Keeping food safe from bacteria and viruses is only one part of taking care in the kitchen. The other is learning to avoid accidents. There are many sources of danger in the kitchen.

The heat from a gas or electric range can give you a severe burn. It is also a fire hazard. Many foods contain grease and oil. These can coat kitchen surfaces with a thin film, which will catch fire easily.

Grease and oil can also cause slips and falls—especially dangerous if you are carrying a sharp knife or something heavy.

Knives and other kitchen tools with sharp edges need care. Keep such tools sharpened and learn to use them skillfully.

Other common kitchen hazards are electrical appliances, heavy utensils, high storage spaces, and open cupboard doors. It's important to be alert and think about what you are doing. This is especially true if many people are working side by side.

Eating Out

Sanitation and safety are as important in restaurants and other public eating places as they are in the home. Safe working conditions and habits are especially necessary in kitchens where many people work together, often under pressure to prepare food quickly. Employees must work with each other and with their employer to make sure safety standards are high.

Sanitation is a major concern of restaurant managers. Good managers want to avoid having to throw out poorly stored or poorly cooked food. And if they don't control bacteria and viruses, many people may suffer from infections or food poisoning.

How can you tell if a restaurant follows good sanitation practices? Use your eyes. Do the employees look clean and neat? Are

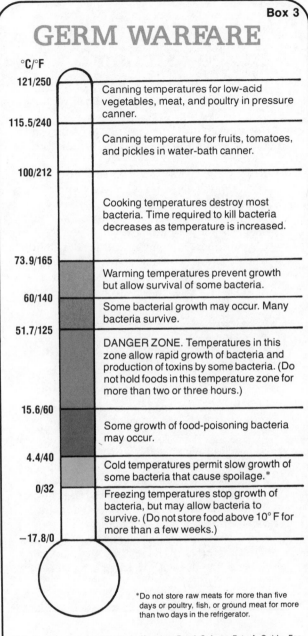

Box 3

GERM WARFARE

°C/°F

121/250	Canning temperatures for low-acid vegetables, meat, and poultry in pressure canner.
115.5/240	
	Canning temperature for fruits, tomatoes, and pickles in water-bath canner.
100/212	
	Cooking temperatures destroy most bacteria. Time required to kill bacteria decreases as temperature is increased.
73.9/165	Warming temperatures prevent growth but allow survival of some bacteria.
60/140	Some bacterial growth may occur. Many bacteria survive.
51.7/125	DANGER ZONE. Temperatures in this zone allow rapid growth of bacteria and production of toxins by some bacteria. (Do not hold foods in this temperature zone for more than two or three hours.)
15.6/60	
	Some growth of food-poisoning bacteria may occur.
4.4/40	Cold temperatures permit slow growth of some bacteria that cause spoilage.*
0/32	Freezing temperatures stop growth of bacteria, but may allow bacteria to survive. (Do not store food above 10° F for more than a few weeks.)
−17.8/0	

*Do not store raw meats for more than five days or poultry, fish, or ground meat for more than two days in the refrigerator.

U.S. Department of Agriculture, *Keeping Food Safe to Eat: A Guide For Homemakers*, Home and Garden Bulletin No. 162. Agricultural Research Service. U.S. Government Printing Office. Revised July 1975.

To control growth of bacteria, keep hot foods hot (above 140°F/60°C) and cold foods cold (below 40°F/4.4°C)

Safety Tips in the Kitchen

Box 4

- Use a dry potholder to pick up hot pots and pans. *Don't* use a corner of your apron or a dish towel—they are too thin.
- Turn pot handles inward on the range so that you don't knock the pots off and burn yourself.
- Keep apron strings, sleeves, and other parts of clothing away from flames and hot burners.
- Stir hot foods with a wooden spoon—metal ones get hot very quickly.
- If the burner on a gas range doesn't light when you turn on the gas, turn off the gas at once. Get someone familiar with the range to light it for you. Never turn on a gas range if you smell gas.
- Always cut by moving the knife away from you.
- Wash knives separately from other utensils and dishes.
- Keep cupboard doors closed.
- Wipe up all spills at once.
- Watch out for opened cans—the tops of the cans and the inside edges can be knife-sharp.
- Be careful to keep water away from electric appliances. Check the cords for fraying.
- Keep surfaces free of grease, particularly around the oven and the range top. Check the vents above burners. Grease can collect there without your realizing it.
- Never try to put out a grease fire with water. If you don't have a fire extinguisher, smother the fire with sand, baking soda, or salt.

cently received a clean bill of health? If the answer is yes to all these questions, you are probably in a clean, carefully managed restaurant.

Careful practices in the kitchen can keep you safe from illnesses caused by bacteria and viruses. They can also protect you from injury. Watching for sanitation and safety—at home and in public eating places—helps you be a good manager and consumer of foods.

QUESTIONS

1. What are the two types of care needed in the kitchen?
2. Describe two ways to keep bacteria out of food, and two ways to slow down their growth.
3. What are the main causes of danger in the kitchen?
4. Outbreaks of food poisoning occur most often in the summer. How many reasons can you give for this fact?
5. Why do you think sharp knives are actually safer to use than dull knives?
6. How could safety concerns affect the way you make a work schedule for a meal that requires many people to work together in a crowded kitchen?
7. Why shouldn't highly perishable food items be stored on the inside of the refrigerator door?

ACTIVITIES

1. Make a poster showing how to put out different kinds of kitchen fires.
2. Interview the manager of a restaurant or cafeteria to find out the kinds of sanitation practices the law requires.
3. Make a chart that lists different kinds of food poisoning, their causes, and their symptoms.

the floors, walls, tables, and linens spotless? Most important, is there a state inspection sticker telling you the restaurant has re-

SECTION 3 · Managing a Meal

OFF TO A SLOW START

(SCENE: Saturday morning. Raymond and Karen are cooking breakfast while their parents sleep.)

RAYMOND: Let's make scrambled eggs, bacon, coffee, and toast. That should be easy.

KAREN: You start the coffee. I'll get to work on the eggs.

(Karen takes butter from refrigerator, puts some in big skillet on range, flips on burner. Raymond climbs up the stepladder to look for the coffeepot, rummages wildly through cupboard.)

RAYMOND (irritated): Where's the basket for the coffeepot?

KAREN (bends down, opens bottom drawer of range): Not there. Guess you'll have to make instant . . . (stops, horrified, looking at range) Oh nuts, now look what you've done. You've made me burn the butter.

RAYMOND: Made you? Well, forget it. Just throw that out and start more butter. I'll put on water for instant coffee.

(Karen washes the skillet and puts in more butter, then opens refrigerator.)

KAREN: Hey! We're out of eggs. I'll have to go to the store fast. Be right back. (She turns off the burner and exits.)

RAYMOND (shouts after her): Okay, I'll start the bacon and the toast. (He spoons instant coffee into cups and adds boiling water. Takes second skillet, puts in several slabs of bacon, and turns on burner. Slips two slices of bread into toaster. Turns bacon with fork. Turns to make more toast, searches for butter, then gets a knife from drawer. Finally starts buttering. To himself): Toast's too cold to spread the butter.

(Karen enters with a carton of eggs and starts to work.)

RAYMOND: Bacon's done and the toast's ready—just about.

KAREN: Great—but the eggs aren't. Hey! You used another skillet for the bacon. I was going to use mine after the eggs were done. Now we have more pans to clean. And the coffee and toast are cold. You'd better throw that stuff out and start again.

RAYMOND: How could you cook the bacon in the same skillet as the eggs? How would you keep the eggs hot?

KAREN: Don't you tell me how . . . Hey—the eggs! Oh yuk!!! Now look what you . . . (She scrapes burned eggs from skillet.)

RAYMOND: Me? Us. We've been in here an hour and all we've got is cold toast, coffee, bacon, and burned eggs.

(Mother enters, looking both sleepy and surprised.)

KAREN: We were just trying to help . . .

(Mother gives a stiff smile, looks out to the audience.)

(Curtain)

W hether you're building a model airplane or making a salad, it helps to get organized before you start. Organization is especially important in preparing a meal. Any delays while you search for equipment or ingredients could spoil the dish you are preparing.

Organization starts with choosing a menu. This means deciding what dishes you will serve. Without a menu, you cannot choose specific recipes. Nor can you know if you need to shop for food. All later steps depend on your choice of menu.

You may plan only one meal ahead, or you may think about menus for the whole week. But without ideas for a menu, you can go no further.

What Makes a Successful Meal?

When planning nutritious meals, *contrast* is a word to keep in mind. Pleasing meals provide contrasts in taste, texture, and color. Spicy foods, for example, go well with mild ones, and soft foods complement crunchy ones. Appetites can be awakened by meals that please the eye with contrasting colors.

Many foods have been linked for years because they provide these contrasts—corned beef and coleslaw, french fries and ketchup, tacos and frijoles are all examples. What would you think of a meal without contrasts—creamed chicken, mashed potatoes, cauliflower, and white bread, for example?

Even the weather can be important in menu planning. Hot soup on a cold day tastes doubly good.

Selecting Recipes

Before choosing a menu, look at a cookbook. Read recipes through so you will have an idea of how long the food preparation

Planning ahead can make a dinner party more enjoyable. Be sure you have all the food and equipment you need before starting. You will be more relaxed if you follow a schedule.

will take. This is also the only way you can tell exactly what ingredients you will need and whether the recipe is costly or inexpensive to prepare. Without this information, you won't know how practical your menu ideas are.

The recipe will also help you make up a shopping list of items you need to buy. Don't forget to check your needs for equipment as well as for food. If you lack the right-size baking pan, the recipe might not succeed.

A Plan of Action

Once you've finished shopping, it's time to think about preparing the meal. A few minutes spent planning a schedule will make the work much easier and more relaxed. This schedule should tell you just what to do and in what order.

Imagine that you've chosen this menu to serve your friends:

Beans and franks **Apples**
Brown bread with **Chocolate chip**
 margarine **cookies**
Broccoli **Milk**

To make things simple so that you can spend plenty of time with your friends, you have bought bread, cookies, and frozen broccoli. That leaves only one recipe to prepare.

Beans and Franks

Servings: 4   Oven 350° F (176.5° C)

one 1-lb can pork and beans
1 lb franks, sliced
¼ t dry mustard or 1 t prepared mustard
 Preheat oven. Combine ingredients in a 1½-qt casserole. Bake uncovered for 20 minutes.

Before making your detailed plan, read the instructions on the package of frozen broccoli. Reading instructions on convenience foods is just as important as looking up recipes. If you know in advance that the broccoli will take eight minutes to cook in boiling water, then you can plan to have boiling water ready at the right time.

Making the plan is like a countdown to zero—zero being the time you will eat. Here is how you might organize the meal for your friends:

1. Set table and get out serving dishes.

Zero minus 40.

2. Start oven, set at 350°F or 176°C.
3. Mix beans, franks, and mustard and place casserole in refrigerator.
4. Put margarine on plate, and put back in refrigerator, covered.
5. Wash apples, put them in bowl, and put bowl in refrigerator.
6. Prepare salted water for frozen broccoli.

Zero minus 20.

7. When friends arrive, put casserole in oven.
8. Spend time greeting friends.
9. Start burner for broccoli.
10. Add broccoli to water when it boils.
11. Arrange cookies on serving plate and set out with apples.
12. Put bread and margarine on table.

Zero minus 1.

13. Drain broccoli and put on table.
14. Pour milk.

Zero.

15. Bring casserole to table and serve.

Be Ready to Work

Once you have made your plan, you can get down to work. Here too a little preparation can save a lot of trouble. Obviously, you should clear the kitchen counter. You can't prepare food well if your work area is piled high with things that don't belong there.

Then wipe the counter top and range to make sure they are clean before you start. A clean work surface is important in preparing food.

Be sure all the equipment you need is handy and in good working order. It's a good idea to get everything out and in place before you start preparing food.

Ingredients, too, should be on hand. Nothing is more annoying than finding you're out of dressing, for example, when a salad is half prepared. Think about the problem Karen faced on p. 329, when she found they were out of eggs. Check to see that you have all the ingredients you need *before* you start to work.

If some of the ingredients need to be prepared before you can add them to your dish, plan for this ahead of time. If you plan to serve a salad with hard-cooked eggs, for example, make sure the eggs are cooked, and cold, by the time you need them.

It's useful to have the ingredients you need laid out and ready for use. But some items need special handling. Mayonnaise and milk, for example, should be kept in the refrigerator until needed. The unused portion should be put back at once. Other ingredients should stay tightly covered until you are ready to use them.

When you're ready for items in the refrigerator, try to get everything out in one step. Use a tray if there are more items than you can safely carry with two hands. Not only will this save you steps, it will also save the refrigerator. Opening and closing the door every thirty seconds makes the refrigerator work harder than it should. It also wastes energy.

Ready at Last

Once the work space is tidy, the tools in place, and the ingredients on hand, you can get down to preparing the food. With the plan of action described earlier, this won't be too difficult.

Except for starting the oven—you want it to have reached the correct temperature when you put the casserole in, but you don't want to waste energy—you have a lot of freedom in steps 1 through 6. Even the order doesn't really matter.

But once the franks and beans go into the oven, your countdown has begun. Ten minutes greeting your friends—then the broccoli must be started. The broccoli will need some supervision, but you will have time to set out the dessert and to serve the bread and margarine. You will also have time to rejoin your friends—so long as you don't forget zero hour.

The milk goes on the table at the last minute, to protect its nutrients. Then the broccoli and the franks and beans are ready and it's time to eat.

Working as a Team

If you are working with other people—as you probably will be in the home economics laboratory—getting organized ahead of time involves still another step. Who will be doing which task?

If you and your partners decide who will do what before you start, you won't waste time later talking about who shops and who chops. List all the tasks to be done to prepare your recipe, in the order in which they must be done. Don't forget shopping, setting the table, and cleaning up. Then decide who will do each one, taking into account the equipment needed for each job. The time you save by being organized can be spent enjoying what you have made.

QUESTIONS

1. List three things you should do to get organized for preparing a meal.
2. Describe the basic steps in preparing a recipe.
3. What are some of the advantages of using a work schedule when several people are working together?
4. What are three things you must consider when choosing a menu?
5. In planning a work schedule, what are some of the things you have to keep in mind when assigning jobs to people?
6. Besides those given in this book, what food combinations are popular because their tastes complement each other?
7. Would you organize the meal plan on p. 332 differently? How?

ACTIVITIES

1. Plan a simple breakfast menu and make out a schedule to prepare it with one other person.
2. Talk to an experienced cook about the story at the beginning of this section. Ask that person if he or she ever had a similar experience. Share the story with your class.
3. Make a humorous poster to remind people to plan ahead in preparing meals.

SECTION 4 · Using Kitchen Equipment

WHAT CAN I USE?

The two pictures show a hand beater and an electric mixer. Both pieces of equipment will do a good job whipping cream.

In fact, most kitchen tasks can be done with several different kinds of equipment. As another obvious example, dishes can be washed in an automatic dishwasher—or they can be washed in a dishpan, using a dishcloth.

Here is a list of food preparation tasks. For each task, can you think of two different kinds of equipment which would help you?

Blending pastry   Roasting a turkey
Cleaning the oven   Storing leftovers in the refrigerator
Frying eggs   Cleaning spills
Making coffee   Making grilled cheese sandwiches

Read the section which follows. You will find suggested answers to these and more questions.

Every year, people spend enormous amounts of money on kitchen equipment. Some things, like ranges, are expensive but are used a great deal. Other fancy items are just like songs—popular today and forgotten in six months.

For example, this holiday season *everyone* may be giving electric meatball makers. Next year it might be automatic egg breakers. There are as many fads in kitchen equipment as there are in clothing or hair styles.

Different People, Different Needs

Good tools are a must for any worker. But a good kitchen tool for one person may be an inefficient or unnecessary one for another. It all depends on your needs.

One family may have five children and a mother and father who both work outside the home. In order to cut down on trips to the store, that family would need a good-size refrigerator, and possibly a large freezer as well. A good range would be a necessity. If the family budget allowed, time-saving electric devices would be helpful in preparing large, nutritious meals quickly.

Another family might have only two people, who care little about cooking. They would need very little kitchen equipment.

It isn't only the size of a family that counts. Someone who lives alone might enjoy cooking as a hobby. Such a person might buy special kitchen equipment usually found only in big restaurants.

Evaluating Equipment

Only the people using kitchen tools can say what they need. One question to ask when thinking about buying a piece of equipment is, "Will this help me prepare the kind of food I usually fix?" A pastry blender, for example, saves much time for someone who bakes a lot of pies and pastries. For someone who rarely bakes, two knives do the job just as well, though it takes longer.

Also, is it more important to save time or to save money? If time is the chief concern, a range with a self-cleaning oven might be worth the expense. But a family on a small budget might decide to buy a less expensive range and clean the oven themselves.

Chopping, Measuring, Mixing

The largest group of kitchen equipment includes items used to prepare foods for cooking or for serving uncooked. This group includes many simple tools, often called utensils, that are necessary even for those who cook very little. What home can do without a can opener, sharp kitchen knives, a stirring spoon, and mixing bowls?

Also in this group is some complicated and expensive equipment. Food processors, electric mixers and blenders, and other small appliances are very helpful to people who enjoy cooking. They can be used on many kinds of food, and will save time in preparing difficult recipes.

Putting on the Heat

A variety of equipment is used for heating foods. Some equipment, like kitchen ranges, provides the heat for cooking. Other items, like saucepans and skillets, hold the food as it cooks. Some appliances both heat and hold—electric skillets, for example, or electric coffee makers.

Most people need some way to heat food. But a full-size range is not a necessity for everyone. People who seldom cook may do very well with just a hot plate to heat soup or boil water for coffee or tea. An electric skillet could take care of their other cooking needs.

There are other alternatives to a full-size range. Many people are buying microwave ovens. These appliances cook food much more quickly than conventional ovens do. Although microwave ovens are expensive,

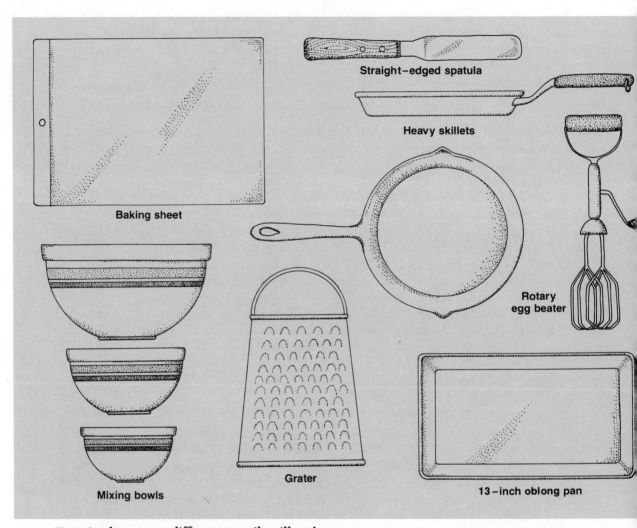

Straight-edged spatula

Heavy skillets

Rotary egg beater

Baking sheet

Grater

Mixing bowls

13-inch oblong pan

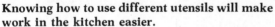

Knowing how to use different utensils will make work in the kitchen easier.

many homemakers feel the time and energy they save are worth the expense. Some people own both a microwave oven and a range.

Anyone who prepares food on a range or hot plate will also need some pots and pans. The choices among these items are enormous. For some people, one or two simple pots are enough. Others, who like to prepare different types of food, need more specialized cookware.

Storing and Cooling

Keeping food fresh before and after it has been cooked is an important part of any homemaker's job. A lot of equipment is available for this purpose.

Many foods must be kept cool to stay

Rubber scraper

Pastry blender

Saucepans

Vegetable parer

8- and 9-inch pie pans

8-inch square pan

Pancake turner

Wire strainer

fresh. Many products must remain frozen until they are ready to be used. Such items belong in the refrigerator or the home freezer, the largest appliances for storing food in the home.

Refrigerated and frozen foods often must be kept airtight—in aluminum foil or plastic wrap, in sealed plastic bags, or in containers with tight lids.

You can use regular bowls tightly covered with aluminum foil or plastic wrap. You can reuse plastic margarine containers with airtight tops. Or you can buy special airtight boxes for refrigerator and freezer storage.

Nonrefrigerated products such as flour, sugar, and cereals are also best kept airtight. Seal the open packages in plastic

Box 1

Caring for Equipment

Kitchen equipment functions best when it is kept clean and when it is used and stored properly. Keeping utensils and appliances clean not only protects your health, it also lengthens the life of the equipment. Kitchen knives, for example, stay sharper longer if they are washed immediately after use and dried thoroughly. Storing knives so that their blades do not rub against other items also helps keep the blades sharp. Dirt that builds up on can-opener blades interferes with their smooth operation. It also causes a severe health hazard.

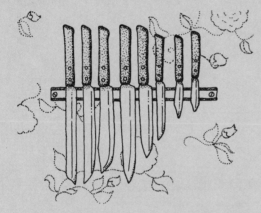

Small appliances such as blenders and toasters require special cleaning attention. Dirt and grease must be removed to keep them sanitary and working properly. However, submerging the electrical unit of such a product in water can ruin the appliance. It is dangerous as well. The manufacturer's instructions will tell exactly how to care for such equipment.

Large appliances are complicated pieces of machinery and must be treated with care. Never line the broiler of an electric range with aluminum foil. If the foil touches any part of the electrical unit while it is turned on, the entire heating element will burn out, requiring major repairs. Worse, anyone nearby could be seriously injured.

To keep a refrigerator working well and to save electricity, prevent a frost build up in the freezer. Make sure the refrigerator is not too full. Air must be able to circulate freely to maintain the correct temperature. Storing too much food in a refrigerator overworks the motor. An overworked motor may have to be replaced.

bags or transfer the contents to containers with tight-fitting lids.

When You've Finished Cooking . . .

Key items in any kitchen at cleanup time are: a dishpan, soap, a dishcloth, abrasive powder or pads, a dish drainer, and dish-

towels. A dishwasher is a convenient appliance, especially for large families. However, it is an expensive purchase and costs a lot to run. The time it saves must be weighed against the money it costs.

Paper products can be useful in cleaning up, as well as in preparing food. However, they are quite costly, and paper supplies are limited. So wise homemakers often use washable cloths or rags for mopping up spills. Old newspapers can be very useful for lining garbage cans, protecting floors from spills, and wiping out greasy pans.

Look Around You

Your school's home economics laboratory may seem very well equipped, especially if you compare it to your kitchen at home. But the home economics laboratory must meet more needs than your home kitchen.

Think for a moment about the equipment in the laboratory and at home. For each utensil, ask yourself, "Would I or my family need this to prepare the foods we eat? Would I choose one like it if I were furnishing my own kitchen on a limited budget?"

Does your kitchen at home have what it needs? Don't be too quick to say no. Some of the best meals come out of the simplest kitchens, where people make the best of what they have.

Making Do

Many families enjoy camping and have experience in making do. Maybe you know how to bake a potato without a stove. Or boil water without a pan. You can prepare excellent meals without a lot of equipment.

Do you think you need a special sandwich grill to make grilled cheese sandwiches? Try making them in an ordinary frying pan. Or grill them open-faced under the broiler.

If a recipe calls for using a double boiler and you don't have one, try floating a small pan in a larger one filled partly with water. True, you must take care that water doesn't spill into the upper pan. All the same, you have a double boiler.

While you are still learning, you should seek advice from a person with more experience before improvising equipment. Remember, you don't always have to spend a lot of money. Imagination can be the best equipment of all.

QUESTIONS

1. Describe two things that can affect the number and type of kitchen appliances a family needs.
2. What are some alternatives to buying special containers for storing food in the refrigerator or freezer?
3. Give two reasons for keeping equipment clean.
4. Most fads in kitchen equipment involve items that have just one use—bacon cookers and hot doggers, for example. How many of these single-use items can you think of? Do you think they get used or end up in the closet? Why?
5. Which pieces of equipment in your home economics laboratory would you most like to have in your home? Why?
6. How many different uses can you think of for a common table fork?

ACTIVITIES

1. As an FHA project, make up a display of unusual old kitchen utensils that you found at home or at flea markets and secondhand stores. Why aren't these utensils in use today?
2. Make a list of popular small appliances. Next to this list write the name of a utensil that could do the same job. (You could also do this as an illustrated poster.)
3. Obtain instruction books for the same appliance by two different manufacturers. Compare the kinds of information offered. Which one is better? Why?
4. Make a list of all the kitchen equipment and appliances you have at home. Number them in order from the one that gets the most use to the one that gets the least. Compare your list with the lists of other students in your class.

SECTION 5 · Following Recipes

COOKOUT

Saturday, July 16

Dear Grandfather,

We're having a cookout next Friday, the last day of camp. I thought of the great shish kebab you cook on the grill. Could you send me the recipe? I'd really love to share it with my friends here — and show off what a good cook my grandfather is! Thanks a lot!!

Love,
Alice

July 19

Dear Alice,

It's a pleasure to think you'd want to cook something I make. Here's the recipe. Good luck and have fun!

Shish Kebab

Marinate chunks of lamb or beef for a few hours in this sauce—it should be enough for several pounds of meat:

    About one cup red vinegar
    About one-third to one-half as much oil
    A good-size garlic clove—or more, if you like garlic
    A small handful of mixed herbs—I like rosemary, thyme, basil,
        tarragon, and sage
    A pinch of dry mustard
    A dash of Worcestershire sauce
    Some soy sauce (if you like)
    Salt and pepper to taste

Alternate chunks of meat with pieces of vegetables—mushrooms, cut-up green and red peppers, pearl onions are all good. Then place the skewers on a grill over a good hot fire and cook, turning once in a while, until done—usually about twenty minutes or so. And have a great feast!

All my love,
Grandpa

P.S. In case you don't know, "marinate" means soak.

Saturday, July 24

Dear Nancy,

Remember I wrote you I was going to make my grandfather's shish kebab? Well, what a mess! First, he said there was enough sauce for "several" pounds of meat. We had eight pounds, since there are 16 of us — but the sauce was only enough for about three pounds. So we had to rush to make more — after, of course, a quick run to the store for more soy sauce. And then the sauce — or marinade — didn't taste at all like Grandpa's. His recipe said: "A small handful of herbs." Well, first you couldn't taste them at all. So I kept putting in more until there were plenty, believe me. And I put in three cloves of garlic, because I like it — he said one or more, so I thought it would be OK. But was it strong! Too much garlic for some people, too many herbs for others.

Dinner was almost an hour late, because Grandfather said to cook the meat and vegetables for 20 minutes over a hot fire but it took almost 45. Probably the fire wasn't hot enough. All in all, the shish kebab was pretty awful — not like Grandfather's at all.

I'll tell you some of the good things about camp when I see you next week. I promise I won't try cooking shish kebab!

Love,
Alice

If you want a recipe to turn out well, you must follow it accurately. This means using the *exact* amounts of all the ingredients listed in the recipe. It also means understanding the language of recipes.

Alice had trouble because her grandfather's recipe used the terms "a small handful," "a pinch," "a dash." Unless you know exactly what such words mean, the dish will not taste the way you expect.

Old Measures

Many interesting recipes from years ago use exact terms that are now almost unknown. A *gill*, for example, was a measure commonly used in the last century and the early part of this one. A gill is four ounces—that is, one-half of today's customary measuring cup. Unless you already knew that, you would have to look it up if you saw it in a recipe. If you just guessed what it was, you might get a strange-tasting result.

Many delicious and economical dishes can be made from old recipes. But if you don't know what the words mean, you won't be successful at making the dish.

Going Metric

Right now, Americans need to be more aware of measurements than ever. As you probably know, the United States is changing from customary measurements to the metric system. The day's temperature is often reported in Celsius as well as in Fahrenheit degrees. Distances on road signs may be given in kilometers as well as in miles.

The kitchen may be one of the last places to go metric. Many existing cookbooks use customary measurements. And customary measuring equipment will be in many homes for a long time to come.

Many new cookbooks and individual recipes *will* use metric terms, however. And many kitchens will have metric measuring cups, spoons, and other utensils, as well as the customary equipment. So knowing which measuring system your recipe is using and which kind of equipment you have is extremely important.

If you use customary measuring utensils with a metric recipe, you will not get the results you want. The same is true if your measuring equipment is metric and your recipe is not. Always look before you cook to be sure your recipe and your utensils are based on the same measuring system.

Volume or Weight

Customary recipes make most measurements by volume—*one cup* of brown sugar rather than *six ounces* of brown sugar. European metric recipes often measure by weight, calling for grams of sugar rather than liters.

Weight measurements have a certain advantage. A *kilogram* of flour is the same amount sifted or unsifted, but a *cup* of sifted flour contains less than a cup of unsifted. However, weight measurements involve the use of scales, not a standard item in all kitchens.

Still, even under the customary system, ingredients are sometimes measured by weight. Solid shortenings—butter, margarine, lard, and similar products—are sold by the pound or fraction of a pound. Since many recipes use volume measurements for such ingredients—a cup of butter, for example—it saves time if you know that *one stick* of butter or margarine equals *one-quarter pound* and also *one-half cup*.

Some recipes may also call for a *pound* of granulated sugar or flour. Don't think these amounts have the same volume. Flour is lighter than sugar. One pound of flour fills four measuring cups. One pound of sugar fills only two.

How to Measure

Learning how to measure correctly is a big step toward becoming skillful in the kitchen. Using kitchen scales is a matter of common sense. But volume measurement needs knowledge.

It is important to use special measuring

Measure for Measure

Box 1

To be sure of success in cooking and baking, you need accurate measuring equipment and a recipe that lists exact amounts of ingredients. The amounts will be given either in metric or U.S. customary measurements. Be sure you have the correct measuring equipment for the type of measurements given in the recipe.

It will help if you know that the same amount of an ingredient can be measured in different ways. For example, 4 tablespoons is the same as ¼ cup. As you get to know what the most common measurements equal, you will gain more flexibility in using measuring equipment.

You will be able to measure the ingredients in most recipes with these basic pieces of equipment:

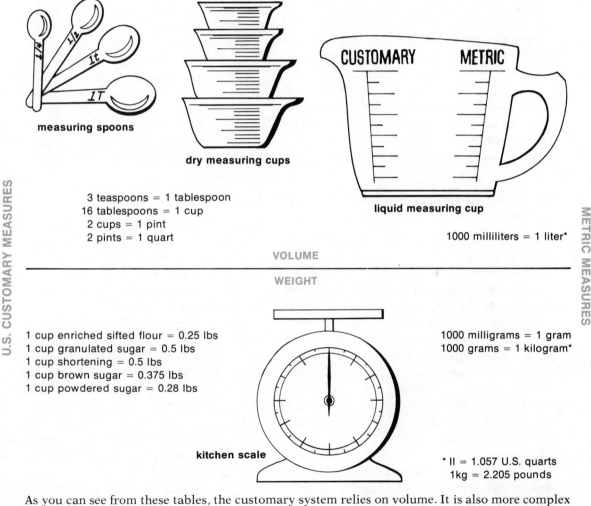

measuring spoons

dry measuring cups

liquid measuring cup

3 teaspoons = 1 tablespoon
16 tablespoons = 1 cup
2 cups = 1 pint
2 pints = 1 quart

1000 milliliters = 1 liter*

VOLUME

WEIGHT

1 cup enriched sifted flour = 0.25 lbs
1 cup granulated sugar = 0.5 lbs
1 cup shortening = 0.5 lbs
1 cup brown sugar = 0.375 lbs
1 cup powdered sugar = 0.28 lbs

1000 milligrams = 1 gram
1000 grams = 1 kilogram*

kitchen scale

* ll = 1.057 U.S. quarts
  1kg = 2.205 pounds

U.S. CUSTOMARY MEASURES

METRIC MEASURES

As you can see from these tables, the customary system relies on volume. It is also more complex than the metric system. However, people are used to using it, and it will be some time before metric measurements are fully accepted into the American kitchen.

equipment because ordinary tableware is not accurate. A measuring tablespoon, for example, usually holds much more than a serving tablespoon. The same is true for a measuring teaspoon compared to a tableware teaspoon.

To measure dry ingredients accurately in a measuring spoon, they must be leveled off. For a tablespoon of flour, for example, first fill the spoon to overflowing. Then take a straight edge—the back of an ordinary table knife or a spatula—and slide it across the top of the spoon. It will push off the extra flour. What remains in the spoon will be *level* with the edge—an exact tablespoon of flour.

For larger amounts of dry ingredients, it is more accurate to use graded cups. These cups are usually made of metal or plastic and are sold in sets that include several different sizes—see box 1 of this section.

Sifted or Unsifted, Packed or Loose?

When measuring dry ingredients by volume, you must also know whether they need to be sifted. Sifted flour has more air spaces, and is therefore lighter. If the recipe calls for sifted flour, sift *before* you measure.

A good way to do this is to put the flour through a sifter held over a piece of wax paper. Then carefully pick up the sides of the paper to make a funnel and gently slide the flour into the correct-size measuring cup. Or, after sifting, spoon the flour gently into the cup. Next, level the flour. Be careful not to press down any more than is necessary.

When flour does not need to be sifted, it should be carefully spooned into the correct-size cup and leveled off. Whether flour is sifted or not, it should never be shaken or packed to be made level.

Other ingredients, such as powdered sugar, may also need to be sifted. To measure brown sugar, pack it firmly into the correct-size metal or plastic measuring cup. There should be *no* air spaces. Measure shortening the same way. First, make sure it is warm enough to be soft.

Measuring Liquids

Liquids are measured by volume in both the metric and the standard system. Glass or clear plastic measuring cups are used. These have pouring spouts and are marked off in ounces, milliliters, or both.

Place the measuring cup on a flat surface. Then, bending over so your eyes are level with the cup, pour in the liquid until it reaches the line showing the amount you need. If you look at the cup from above, your measurement may be far off.

Other Directions

Accurate measuring of ingredients is important to success in the kitchen. At the very least, failure to measure will lead to a different taste from the one intended. At worst, it may result in a custard not setting or a cake failing to rise.

Measuring is not the only key to success. A good cookbook will give clear directions about how to prepare the food. These directions will include special cooking terms, which need to be understood (see box 2 of this section). They may also tell the heat of the oven, the size of the pan, and the length of time the food should cook. A good cookbook may explain how to know when various foods are ready.

The directions in a good recipe have been found to work. If you follow them carefully, you will prepare a successful dish.

Box 2

The Language of Cooking

Do you understand what the recipe tells you to do? Cooking has a language all its own. Most cookbooks have complete lists of cooking terms. If you don't understand a direction, you can usually look it up. Here is a short list of common terms:

TERM	MEANING
Boil	Heat a liquid until bubbles rise constantly to the surface. Also, cook something in water or another liquid that is boiling.
Bake	Cook by dry heat, usually in an oven. For baked meat, the term is "roasted."
Broil	Cook by direct heat, usually in the broiler of an oven, in an electric broiler, or over hot coals.
Blend	Mix two or more ingredients together.
Chill	Place food in refrigerator or other cold area until it is completely cold.
Chop	Cut into small pieces.
Cool	Let food stand at room temperature until it does not feel warm to the touch.

TERM	MEANING
Fry	Cook in hot fat.
Grease	Prepare a cooking surface by rubbing it with fat, such as shortening or butter.
Knead	Work dough or some other firm mixture by hand. Kneading makes a mixture even throughout. It is done by repeatedly folding and flattening the mixture until it is smooth.
Melt	Heat a solid food, like butter, until it becomes a liquid.
Preheat	Bring a heating unit, such as an oven or a broiler, to a certain temperature before using it.
Sift	Put dry ingredients through a fine sieve, mixing in air.
Simmer	Cook in liquid that is just below the boiling point.
Toss	Mix ingredients lightly.

Adding a Personal Touch

Even when you follow a recipe exactly and measure very carefully, what you prepare may not taste *exactly* as you thought it would. The difference can be caused by many things—the freshness of the food, or even the weather.

Each person who follows a recipe does things a little differently. Sometimes the changes are mistakes. But often they add a personal touch. People may use a little less salt and pepper than a recipe calls for, or a little more cream or a little less oil. With experienced cooks, this personal touch may be automatic.

If, as you grow more experienced, you decide you like your mother's apple pie better than the one in the cookbook, find out exactly what she does differently. Then follow her method, and you'll produce *her* pie. A lot of the magic of cooking is in measurement.

QUESTIONS

1. List the three things you must do to get good results from a recipe. What went wrong with Alice's shish kebab?
2. What are the two kinds of measurement systems now in use in food preparation? What are some of the basic differences between them?
3. What do you use a knife for when measuring a dry ingredient? How do you make sure you have measured a liquid accurately?
4. What do four cups of flour and two cups of sugar have in common?
5. What is the difference between *simmer* and *boil*? *Chill* and *cool*? *Bake* and *roast*? What should you do if you don't understand one of the terms in a recipe?
6. Why do you think the kitchen might be one of the last places to go metric?
7. What do you think would happen if you baked a cake in a pan that was smaller than the recipe called for? Larger?
8. How do you think recipe terms such as "a pinch" and "a handful" first came about? Why do you think people started to use standard measurements?
9. Which do you think is a better method—measurement by weight or by volume? Why?

ACTIVITIES

1. Examine the measuring equipment in your kitchen at home. Make a list of any additional pieces you need. How would they make food preparation easier and more accurate?
2. Obtain a number of different common tablespoons. Compare the number of level spoonfuls of each it takes to fill half a measuring cup with sugar. How many standard tablespoonfuls does it take? What conclusion can you draw about using common tableware when preparing recipes?
3. Interview someone who has been cooking for a while and ask her or him, "What was the worst experience you ever had using a recipe?" Report on it to the class.

SECTION 6 · Setting the Table and Serving Food

Which Is the "Right" Way to Serve Food?

Styles of serving food differ from place to place. You may have noticed this in restaurants. You may also have seen different styles in your own and your friends' homes.

Service in restaurants varies greatly. In a cafeteria, people stand in line and collect the foods they will eat. At fast-food restaurants, a person at the counter packs customers' orders. Then each customer decides where and how to eat the food.

Some restaurants offer table service. Waiters or waitresses take the orders and serve the food. Many places, like diners, have quite simple service, with one person taking care of all aspects of serving. Other restaurants are very formal, with many people waiting on each table. Most restaurant service is somewhere between the very casual and the very formal.

Service in the Home

There are also differences in the way people eat at home. How does your family usually serve the main meal of the day? Compare your serving style with that of some of your friends' families.

In some families, one person puts food on plates, then brings the plates to the table. In others, serving dishes are passed around and people help themselves.

Whether a food is served in a fast-food restaurant or at home, at an everyday meal or at a party, one point remains important.

Someone needs to know just how the meal is to be served.

Why Is It Important?

Imagine what would happen in a restaurant if no one knew how to serve the food. Waitresses and waiters might bring the dessert first and the salad last. They might forget to serve hot food until it had grown cold. Food could even end up in customers' laps as waiters and waitresses bumped into each other.

At home, too, serving must be planned. Your family probably eats its meals in much the same way every day. Having a regular custom helps make mealtimes calmer. If you had to talk about how you were going to serve before each meal, you might never get around to eating!

Styles of Serving

Perhaps your family serves each meal of the day differently. Breakfast and lunch may be quick, casual meals where people fix their own food at different times. At dinner, however, the whole family may sit down together. Your family's serving style may change for special occasions, such as holidays and parties.

No matter what serving styles are used in your family, all of you know what to expect at each meal. You have family customs, and these customs make mealtimes easier for everyone.

Setting the Table

Unless the meal is very informal, the table must be set. Tables may be set many ways. Some are very fancy, with many knives and forks and spoons for different purposes. Others are quite simple.

Box 1

A Simple Place Setting

This diagram shows the place setting that is usually found in restaurants where the service is fairly simple. This style of setting also suits most homes.

Personal touches make everyday meals special. An attractive centerpiece, tablecloth, or place setting brightens and individualizes your table.

Table settings may vary in a home when special foods are being served. Some families, for example, use separate forks for eating salads. These are placed to the left of the dinner fork. Or, when soup is to be served, a soup spoon might be placed to the right of the dinner knife. Most families make changes like these from time to time.

Buffet-Style Meals

Occasionally a meal is served buffet-style. This is a kind of cafeteria within the home. It is useful for serving food when there are too many people to sit at the table—at a party, for example.

In buffet-style service, the foods are laid out in bowls and dishes on a serving table. The plates, tableware, and napkins are stacked on the table for people to help themselves. Guests take a plate and napkin, choose tableware, then find themselves a place to sit.

No one arrangement of the serving table is correct for a buffet. Whatever allows

people to get food easily and comfortably is acceptable.

Appearance Counts

Whatever kind of meal the table is set for, an attractive setting is important to make mealtime a pleasant occasion. What does it take to set a good-looking table? For the most part, just a little care.

Neatness, with utensils lined up and napkins carefully folded, helps create a feeling of calm and order. A clean tablecloth or place mats are also important.

Colors make a difference, too. The dishes and tablecloth or place mats should look good together. They should not clash with the colors in the room. A centerpiece of fruit or flowers gives a festive touch.

For parties, you may want to take the time and care to make your table setting a work of art. But don't forget an attractive setting for everyday meals. Neatness and other careful touches make even an everyday event very special.

QUESTIONS

1. Describe three types of food service in restaurants.
2. Show where the dinner plate, knife, fork, spoon, glass, napkin, and cup and saucer should be placed in a simple place setting at home.
3. Describe two things you can do to make a table setting more attractive.
4. Compare the effects an attractive and an unattractive table might have on people who are sitting down to a meal in a restaurant or home.
5. What special problems must you think about when planning a buffet meal for a large group? What kinds of food would you choose to serve?
6. Why might formal table settings in a fast-food restaurant cause prices to rise?

ACTIVITIES

1. Ask several people what kinds of restaurants they like to go to. Find out if the type of service makes any difference to them and why. Ask them if they act differently at a restaurant depending on the service. Report on their answers to the class.
2. Find photos in magazines showing table settings that you think are attractive. For each one, tell what kind of meal or occasion you think it would be best for. Tell what it was about the setting that you particularly liked. Include the pictures in your report.
3. Make an inexpensive centerpiece for either an everyday meal or a special dinner.

SECTION 7 · A Good Host, a Good Guest

Just What Are Good Manners?

Different centuries have different ideas about good manners. But all ideas about good manners have one thing in common—consideration for others. Being considerate includes trying not to offend people—and people may be offended if you act differently than they expect. This was as true in the past as it is today.

Here are some old descriptions of table manners. Some of them may still seem sensible to you. Others you may find silly. Think about these rules. Why do you think each one seemed important then? Which would you still agree with? Why?

BAD MANNERS AT THE TABLE

- **Dip not thy thumb thy drink into. Thou art uncourteous if thou it do.**
- **Touch no manner of meat with thy right hand, but with thy left, as is proper.**
- **Rinse not your mouth in presence of others.**
- **Do not breathe too loudly at meals, for that is very inelegant.**
- **If you do lick your fingers, do not suck them noisily.**
- **Do not take both hands to raise a morsel to the mouth, but serve yourself with the right hand.**
- **Do not clean your hands on a loaf of bread.**
- **If others talk at table, be attentive, but talk not with meat in your mouth.**
- **Do not clean your teeth with the tablecloth.**
- **Do not come to the table in shirt sleeves, or put your feet beside your chair.**

What do you say to the hostess or host at a party? How do you act if you go to a friend's house for dinner? Everyone has questions about manners from time to time.

A lot of people think of manners as a list of *don'ts*—telling us what not to do. But a more useful approach is to think of manners as general guidelines for acting in ways that are acceptable to others.

A Simple Guideline

One reason manners are important is that they help people feel comfortable in many different situations. If you know what to do, you can relax and have a good time. But how can you keep all the guidelines in mind?

The job becomes easier if you realize one thing—good manners express consideration of other people. When the rule about shirtsleeves was written, it probably bothered many people to see men without coats and ties at the dinner table. Today, few people are disturbed by casual dress. Sloppiness, however—coming to the table in dirty clothes or with grimy hands and messy hair—still makes others feel uncomfortable. That's why it is good manners to be neat, no matter how casually you are dressed.

When Your Guests Arrive

When you have company for a party, what kinds of actions are considerate of others? You should make each guest feel at home and at ease with the other guests. Try to greet people right away and let them know that you are glad to see them. Help them put away their belongings. Introduce guests to one another. If it's a casual party, make sure that everyone knows where the refreshments are.

Make sure that *you* have a good time. A worried host or hostess, too busy in the kitchen to bother with guests, can't have fun. And the chances are that the guests will not enjoy themselves either. Don't invite more people than you can easily take care of.

A good hostess or host pays a fair amount of attention to every guest. You may enjoy one person's company more than another's, but both were invited to your home for a good time. If you spend too much time with one of your guests, the others may feel ignored and unhappy.

A Good Guest

Being a good guest is like being a good hostess or host. If you are pleasant and relaxed, others will feel more comfortable.

A guest should be friendly to everyone. If you don't get along well with one of the other guests, leave your disagreements at the door. Your host or hostess will thank you for it.

The parents in the home you visit deserve some special attention. Saying hello, even if they are not really part of the party, is a thoughtful thing to do. A word of thanks to the person who prepared the food is also considerate. And any effort to help clean up is always welcome.

Sitting Down at the Table

Taking a few minutes to tidy up before a meal shows good manners. A clean face and hands and neat clothes and hair make you a pleasant meal companion. Once you are at the table, be sure to help pass serving dishes around, if that is the serving style. Wait until everyone has been served to begin. Usually you should wait until your host or hostess takes a bite—unless you are told to go ahead.

Adding salt and pepper to food before you taste it suggests that you don't trust the cook. And it might be disastrous if the dish already has plenty of seasonings.

Certain ways of behaving at the table are considerate of others because they show you are concerned about health and sanitation. Never comb your hair or put on makeup at the table. Sneeze or cough away from the table and into a handkerchief, to avoid spreading germs. And, for the same reason, allow hot food to cool naturally, instead of blowing on it.

Other ideas about good manners are based on other kinds of consideration. It's hard to have a pleasant conversation when someone is slurping or munching noisily beside you. And it's hard to enjoy your food when the person opposite you is chewing open-mouthed.

The Unfamiliar

If you are not familiar with the place setting at a meal, follow this simple rule: Always use the utensil on the *outside* first. If there are two forks, for example, use the one farthest to the left for the first dish served.

If you are still puzzled about how to use a utensil correctly, watch the host or hostess. Whatever he or she does with that unfamiliar piece of tableware is what you should do, too.

At a friend's house you might be served a food you do not like or cannot eat. If you don't care for the food, try it anyway—you might be surprised. If you really dislike it, eat as little of it as possible and take a little more of other things.

Perhaps you cannot eat something because it will make you ill. Then just avoid it. If you have to say something about it, simply say you cannot eat it. That is enough—no apology is necessary. If *you* don't act as if it's a big deal, no one else will pay much attention.

An Accident?

We all spill or drop things from time to time. When you do, simply apologize. If you are home, clean it up. At a friend's house, offer to help. In a restaurant, it is the waitress's or waiter's job to mop up. Don't keep worrying about the accident. Most people will quickly forget about it if you don't look uncomfortable.

A Word About Words

Conversation at the table can make the difference between a pleasant meal and a bad experience. No one wants to listen to an argument at the supper table, or to hear unpleasant stories about food during dinner.

Dinner is not the time to talk about sad topics such as illness or death. If such subjects are on your mind, try to save them for another time.

You see, manners are really quite simple. If you think about other people's comfort, you'll be able to handle almost any situation well.

QUESTIONS

1. Why are manners important?
2. What are two things you can do to make your guests feel comfortable?
3. What are two things you could do as a guest if you realized you did not like the food that was being served?
4. Why do you think most people today are less concerned about the type of clothes worn to the dinner table than people were years ago?
5. What could you do if a guest started to talk at the table about the time she or he got sick after eating a certain type of food?
6. Which do you think is harder, being a good host or hostess, or being a good guest? Why?

ACTIVITIES

1. Ask your parents about the rules of behavior they learned as children. Are they the same or different from yours?
2. Prepare a skit of a host and guest doing all the wrong things at a party.
3. Read parts of an old book on etiquette. Find some rules that are no longer used which you think still make sense. Explain your reasons to the class.
4. Draw a cartoon strip about a funny incident involving table manners.

SECTION 8 · Careers in Food Preparation and Service

MANY, MANY JOBS

This short-order cook is preparing food in a small lunch restaurant. He cooks foods such as hamburgers, eggs, and hot dogs. These foods are prepared after the order is taken. He may also make sandwiches.

The man in the center is head chef in a large restaurant. His two assistants are learning how to prepare difficult dishes.

This waitress is one of a team of waitresses and waiters who serve customers in a large restaurant. At the peak hours of the day, she is very busy.

Perhaps someday you will be a homemaker, like the man shown here. In fact, you are a homemaker already. As part of a household, you share the responsibility for how smoothly it runs.

Do you like preparing food for other people to enjoy? Do you think you would like to be part of a business that serves good food? If you would, you're interested in one of the largest and fastest growing fields in the country.

The food preparation and service industry employs more than three times as many workers as the oil industry, the automobile manufacturing industry, and the steel industry combined! The number of workers in this business will soon top ten million.

In the late seventies, almost one dollar of every three spent for food in North America was spent for meals away from home. That figure is sure to increase—and so will the number of jobs in the food service industry.

Restaurant Owners and Managers

Owning a restaurant is a career dream for many people who enjoy food. They like the idea of serving dishes they particularly enjoy. Often they like the thought of creating a special atmosphere where people can eat in comfort and enjoy pleasant surroundings.

Running a restaurant is difficult work, however. Owners put in long hours and have to deal with many problems. They must know how a kitchen should be run and how service should be managed. They must also have good business sense. Owners often hire managers to take charge of the many details of running a restaurant. Both owners and managers find this field challenging and rewarding.

The fast-food industry is an especially promising area for people interested in food service as a career. This area is greatly expanding and needs good managers.

Chefs

Hundreds of thousands of people earn their living preparing and cooking food. Called chefs, these people work in an enormous variety of places and jobs.

Diners and coffee shops often employ short-order cooks, chefs who prepare hamburgers, sandwiches, eggs, and other fairly simple dishes. This kind of chef often learns on the job.

Other chefs work alone in small specialty restaurants that serve a few, very carefully prepared dishes. These chefs often make ethnic dishes. Some have studied in special cooking schools. Others have learned their skills from friends or relatives.

Many people work as chefs in large restaurants, in school and college cafeterias, in hospitals, and in other institutions. In such places, several chefs work together to prepare food for many people each day. Often there is a head chef who is in charge of the kitchen and directs the work of assistant chefs. Some of the assistants may be young men and women receiving on-the-job training while at vocational schools to learn the trade.

Fancy restaurants may have a specialist to prepare each kind of food. One chef may be in charge of making salads. Another may make only pastries. A third may be responsible for sauces. Chefs in such restaurants have studied for years in special schools. They spend many hours learning on the job, and may move up to become supervisors of other chefs.

From short-order cook in a diner to head chef in a fancy restaurant, people who cook for a living often regard their work as an art. So do many men and women who enjoy cooking as a hobby.

Waitresses and Waiters

People who serve food are called waitresses and waiters. A great many people wait on tables, often as part-time work. Many students earn money this way.

The job of a waitress or waiter varies greatly with the kind of restaurant. In small restaurants, like diners and coffee shops, the person who waits on tables may also make sandwiches or desserts. In larger restaurants, waiters and waitresses do not help in the kitchen. They have enough to do taking orders, serving food, and otherwise seeing to people's needs.

Waiting on tables can be very hard work. It involves being on your feet most of the time, carrying heavy trays of food, keeping orders straight, and maintaining a pleasant attitude, often under difficult circumstances. The pay for this hard job can be quite low. Good waiters and waitresses usually receive bonuses in the form of tips from satisfied customers.

In larger restaurants, dining room attendants help waiters and waitresses. They set and clear tables, pour water for customers, and bring bread and butter.

In some restaurants, a waitress or waiter may be promoted to take charge of the rest of the staff. The person who holds this job has the responsibility for seeing that everything runs smoothly.

Other Restaurant Jobs

Food counter workers serve food in fast-food restaurants, coffee shops, and cafeterias. They relay orders from customers to the kitchen, and serve food to the customer. They often take the customer's payment. In coffee shops, counter workers are usually responsible for setting places and cleaning the counter.

Restaurants, cafeterias, and dining halls hire many people who do not prepare or serve food. Some are dishwashers. Others keep the kitchen and dining area clean. Some keep track of supplies. They order items that need replacing and check deliveries when they arrive. Others work as cashiers, taking in money from customers.

Even if you don't choose a career in food service, of course, you will always have food service responsibilities. As a homemaker, whether living alone or in a family, you will sometimes prepare and serve food for yourself and others. Food service is part of everyone's life.

QUESTIONS

1. Name some jobs in the food preparation and service industry that do *not* involve preparing or serving food.
2. What makes serving tables in a restaurant very hard work?
3. What interests and qualities might make a good food service worker? Explain.
4. Compare the duties of a counter person, a dining room attendant, and a waitress.
5. Why do you think people who work in food preparation jobs often regard their work as an art?
6. What are some of the problems of owning a restaurant?

ACTIVITIES

1. With another person in the class, put on a skit portraying a careless waiter or waitress.
2. Make a chart showing all the jobs that have to be done between the time the restaurant receives the food from the supplier and the time the customer eats it.
3. Ask your guidance counselor for information about schools that train people for food preparation jobs. Describe four or five jobs that appeal to you, and list the kinds of courses you might need for each job.
4. Find a book or magazine article that describes how chefs are trained in France and write a report on it.

Clothing & Textiles

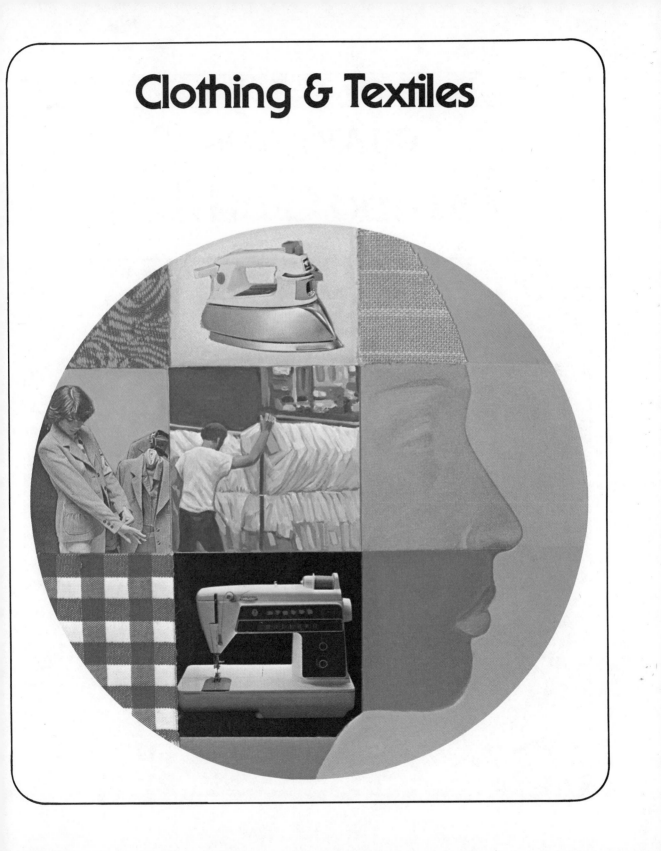

CHAPTER 10

You and Clothing

CHAPTER CONTENTS

SECTION 1 · What Clothes Do for You

Alice in Strangeland

Your shoe length doesn't tell how important *you* are. You probably don't wear a hat that shows *your* job. But your clothes do many other things for you. How you look, how you feel, what people think of you—all can be affected by what you wear.

That is why it's wise to think carefully when choosing your clothes. Clothes play an important part in everyone's life. Some of the advantages of clothing are obvious. Others are harder to see.

Clothing and Physical Comfort

Clothing has a lot to do with comfort. Depending on the climate where you live, clothes may be necessary to keep you warm, or to protect your skin from the sun, wind, rain, or snow.

It's hard to be at your best when you feel a cold draft whispering through your clothes. It's equally hard to be good-tempered when you're so overdressed that you feel like a boiled lobster. The comfort of your clothes has a great deal to do with your state of mind.

Clothes and First Impressions

Clothes serve as a kind of packaging in which you present yourself to the world. Clothing can tell other people about your life-style, your preferences, and your interests—maybe even how you're feeling on a particular day!

When you meet people for the first time, their clothes influence the way you think or feel about them. You may form an instant judgment from your "first impression" of a person.

Suppose you meet someone who is wearing a jogging outfit. You might immediately think, "There's someone who likes sports." Or perhaps you see a new student wearing a T-shirt with a famous singing group pictured on it. You naturally assume that she is interested in music.

In the same way, you might form a first impression about someone who is carelessly dressed. You may decide that that person doesn't care about himself or herself, or about what others think.

Everyone forms first impressions of others based on the clothes they wear and how they wear them.

Clothes, Personality, and Appearance

Clothes can express your personality. If you wear unusual clothes that set you off from the crowd, this may suggest that you like to think for yourself and enjoy being original. If you wear the same type of clothing that your friends wear, it may mean that you like to feel you're part of a group. Blending in with the people around you makes you feel comfortable.

A person who wears cool, quiet colors may be expressing a calm and quiet personality. On the other hand, bright colors may mean you enjoy showing your fun-loving, out-going side.

Clothes also affect your physical appearance. Certain clothing designs, for example, make your shoulders appear broader or your body seem slimmer. Other designs draw attention to your face. Colors, too, affect the way you look. The same style can have surprisingly different effects in different colors.

Try to understand how color and design can change your appearance. Knowing this will help you choose clothes that highlight your best features and help you to look your best.

Box 1

Clues from Clothes

These pictures show the same basic outfit—
a shirt and pants. Yet each gives a different
impression. What impression do you get
from each outfit?

A Time to Experiment

As a teenager, you may find that your tastes in clothing change easily. One day, you want to show that you don't care what other people think. Another day, you may want to fit in with the crowd. Experimenting with clothing is a part of finding out about yourself. It helps you to learn what kinds of clothes make you feel most comfortable with yourself and with other people.

Sometimes, even without thinking about it, you may dress the way someone you admire dresses. This is more than just copying. It's another way of experimenting to find the styles that put you at ease.

Clothes and Confidence

Looking your best can do more than create the image you'd like to present. Clothes can help you become the way you want to be.

Maybe you tend to be quiet and withdrawn. You don't really want to sit off by

Trying on different combinations of styles and colors will help you find the look you want. You can even learn from experiments that don't work out!

yourself at parties, but that's where you often seem to end up. Perhaps you just need a little more self-confidence.

Well-chosen clothes can give you that confidence. An unusual accessory—a scarf, jewelry, a belt—can be a conversation opener. Someone may ask where you bought it, what it's made of, what made you think of wearing it the way you do. When people react to you in a new way, you yourself may behave differently.

Do you usually dress in quiet colors? A brighter, livelier color might help you feel more outgoing. A style different from what you normally wear could give you a lift.

When your clothes are comfortable, fit well, and make you look the way you want to look, they can make you feel good about yourself. The right clothes can add the confidence that lets you relax at a party. They may make you feel more sure of yourself when you give a report in class. Whatever you're doing, you will do it better when you are happy with your appearance.

QUESTIONS

1. List four functions of clothing.
2. Describe two ways in which your clothing reflects your personality.
3. How might your clothing affect the way in which others see you?
4. How do you decide what to wear to school each day?
5. If you were eager to make a good first impression on someone, what would you wear? Why?
6. Name some people who *do* wear clothes which show their jobs. Do you think it's a good idea? Explain your answer.

ACTIVITIES

1. Draw a picture of your favorite outfit. Describe what it is you like about the outfit.
2. Write a story about an article of clothing that meant a lot to you when you were younger.
3. Make a list of the colors of all your clothes. Which colors do you wear the most? The least? Why do you think this is so?

SECTION 2 · Design: Color and Texture

COLOR POWER

Does the color of this man's shirt affect the color of his complexion?

Does one of these inner blocks appear to be larger than the other?

Which coat is more likely to boost morale on a rainy day?

Color can make your skin glow and your eyes sparkle. Color makes some packages seem to leap out at you from store shelves. Color reflects and influences people's moods and attitudes. That may be why people say they feel "in the pink" or "green with envy." Color can create optical illusions that make objects look larger or smaller than they really are. Color has power!

Color, Texture, and You

Color and texture are two important elements of clothing design. Both have much to do with how you look in your clothes. For example, color can bring out aspects of your skin, eyes, and hair that wouldn't be noticed otherwise. Texture—the way the surface of a fabric looks and feels—can also be used to emphasize what you like about your appearance.

You probably have favorite colors. You may like certain textures and dislike others. The best way to discover other colors and textures that suit you is to test them. Try out a whole variety of different fabrics and colors. Hold each one up to your face and think about the effect it has.

As you experiment, you may notice that your skin coloring decides, to a great extent, which colors suit you best. (However, if you use makeup, you can probably wear colors that would not look good on you otherwise.) The color of your eyes and the color of your hair also affect the way different colors look on you.

These effects are quite complex. Al-

Box 1

MANY OPTIONS

Brown eyes often have a touch of hazel. Blue eyes may seem slightly green. Look closely in a mirror at your eyes. You will notice that the iris contains flecks of several colors.

Your hair, too, has many different shades. Brown hair may have a touch of red or gold that shows up in a certain light. If you're blond, you may see some brown or red hairs.

Skin color also has variations. A blue tinge comes from the veins that lie beneath the surface. Redness comes from the capillaries that bring blood to your skin cells. The pigment melanin, a dark coloring material found in human hair and skin, makes skin color range from pale cream through yellow and tan to rich, dark ebony.

With all these colors in your skin, hair, and eyes, you can probably find many colors that will suit you.

though you may think that you have "green" eyes and "brown" hair, personal coloring isn't quite that simple. Box 1 in this section can help you see the variety in your particular coloring.

How Color Works

The color of your clothes can **highlight** similar colors in *you*. If you have blue eyes, blue clothes will make your eyes more noticeable. If you have dark-brown skin, a lustrous brown fabric—a velveteen jacket or a velour T-shirt—will give your skin a warm, glowing appearance. Gold accessories will light up bronze-colored skin.

Clothing colors can also bring out the less noticeable aspects of your coloring. By choosing colors carefully, you can emphasize that reddish streak in your brown hair or bring out the green flecks in your gray eyes.

You can also emphasize your coloring through **contrast.** By wearing opposite, or complementary, colors (see box 2 in this section), you can emphasize your skin tone, or hair or eye color. For example, shades of green make red hair more vivid. If you want to show off a suntan, very pale colors will make your tan seem darker.

Contrasting and highlighting colors can work for you, but they can also work against you. Certain colors, for example, emphasize skin blemishes. Trying on various colors will tell you which ones make the blemishes less noticeable.

Other Facts about Color

Many different colors are called by the same name. *Green*, for example, can refer to the color of pine trees or to the color of olives. The pine trees are almost blue-green: olives are closer to yellow. These two

Understanding Color

Scientists and artists have studied color for many years and have arrived at certain basic principles. Understanding some of these principles can help you use color to your advantage.

All the colors, or hues, you see on the rainbow-colored wheel here are blends of three primary colors—red, yellow, and blue. Each of the secondary colors—orange, green, and violet—is made by mixing two primary colors. Green, for example, is a mixture of yellow and blue. All other colors on the wheel are combinations of these basic six.

Every color has many values, ranging from the very light to the very dark. For example, tints and shades from the palest pink to the deepest ruby red all belong to the red family. Every color also has many intensities—from very bright to very dull.

Studies of color have produced information about combining colors in ways that please the eye. Three kinds of color schemes are most common.

A **monochromatic** color scheme uses various values and intensities of one color family. An outfit combining various yellows would be monochromatic.

An **analogous** color scheme uses colors—such as blue, blue-green, and green—near each other on the color wheel.

Complementary color schemes combine direct opposites such as red and green or blue and orange.

Box 2

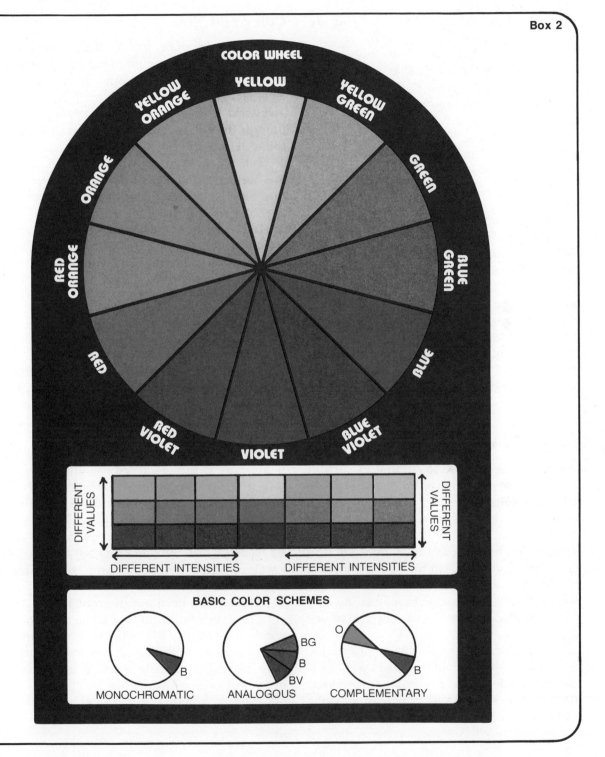

COLOR WHEEL

YELLOW

YELLOW ORANGE

YELLOW GREEN

ORANGE

GREEN

RED ORANGE

BLUE GREEN

RED

BLUE

RED VIOLET

BLUE VIOLET

VIOLET

DIFFERENT VALUES

DIFFERENT VALUES

DIFFERENT INTENSITIES

DIFFERENT INTENSITIES

BASIC COLOR SCHEMES

B

MONOCHROMATIC

BG
B
BV

ANALOGOUS

O

B

COMPLEMENTARY

types of green are very different, and are called different **hues.**

Even with the same hue, colors can vary. There are dark reds that look almost brown, and light reds that lean toward pink. Reds can be very bright, or they can be quite dull. You will understand every color better if you think of two things besides the hue. One is **intensity:** How bright or dull is the color? The other is **value:** How light or dark is the color? (See box 2 in this section.)

Intensity and value are important when selecting clothes. A garment that is *exactly* the same color as your hair or skin may do little for you. But a noticeably lighter or darker value of the same color could create an interesting effect. If you have bright-blue eyes, for example, a dark-blue shirt will emphasize their color.

Value and intensity can make a big difference in how a color looks on you. You need to experiment.

Color and Your Figure

Color can also be used to emphasize certain features of your figure and play down others. Bright colors, for example, are attention getters. If you have a small waistline, a red belt will make it far more noticeable than a navy-blue one. On the other hand, navy would be a good choice if you don't want to call attention to your waist. That's because dark colors do not draw the eye to them the way bright colors do.

Dark colors create the illusion of smaller size, while light colors make you look larger. Black pants may make you look slim, but the same pants in pale blue could make you look pounds heavier.

Color and You

There may be many colors that suit your personal coloring and do wonders for your figure. However, this doesn't mean you'll feel "right" in all of them. Some people feel awkward if they wear bright colors—even though the colors suit them. Others dislike the quiet colors they look good in.

Some people always feel better if they are wearing "cool" colors—blues, greens, and violets. Others like reds and yellows—the "warm" colors.

Decisions about what to wear can start with a study of your personal coloring, and what colors suit you. But your own personal tastes, as well as day-to-day moods, will also influence your choice of colors in clothes.

Texture

Texture is the way a fabric looks and feels. The texture of satin is smooth and slippery. Tweeds are thick and nubby. You can sink your fingers into fake furs, and you can see through voiles and chiffons.

Like color, texture can make you look heavier or slimmer. A heavy, bulky fabric will make you seem larger. A fabric with a smooth, dull surface will create a slimmer appearance. You can add to your shoulders, decrease your hips, show off your arms—all by wearing different textures.

Once again, experimenting is the best way to find the textures that are right for you. When you hold up different fabrics to your face, you will find that some bring out your good points. Others bring out features you would rather hide. A lustrous fabric may highlight shining eyes. It may also overemphasize a shiny nose.

Your personality and mood may also influence your choices. Some textures seem more conservative. Others get immediate attention.

Different textures are appropriate for different situations. A tweed fabric with its nubby surface will look sporty and casual and be great for outdoors. A sheer fabric can look soft and dressy—perfect for an evening party.

Putting It All Together

Choosing textures and colors that suit you is the first step toward finding clothes you like. Combining these elements is a very basic part of fashion design. Some colors seem to go together, others do not. A color may suit you only if the fabric has a certain texture. Two colors may look good together in one design, but terrible in another.

Once you have a general feeling for which colors and textures suit you, you can experiment with particular combinations. There are some standard color schemes that most people find pleasing (see box 2), but every outfit presents a new challenge. Learning to use color and texture will give you a real awareness of clothes. This awareness will grow as you experiment throughout your life.

QUESTIONS

1. Explain what is meant by the intensity and value of a color. What are four effects color can have on your appearance?
2. What is texture? How can the texture of a fabric affect the way you look?
3. What aspects of your appearance should you take into consideration when choosing colors and textures?
4. Why do you think blue and green are called cool colors, while red and orange are considered warm colors? What kinds of things do you associate with each group of colors?
5. Why do you think people tend to wear clothes with smoother textures in summer and rougher textures in winter?
6. Which do you think is more important when choosing a garment, color or texture? Explain your answer.

ACTIVITIES

1. Paste a variety of fabric scraps on heavy paper. Next to each piece of fabric write words that you think best describe the color and texture of the fabric (for example, bold, vibrant, gentle; stiff, silky, fluffy).
2. Interview someone who sells clothing about the popularity of different colors. Do certain colors go in and out of style? Are there any colors that are always popular?

SECTION 3 · Design: Line, Print, and Proportion

WANTING A CHANGE

Rita hates it when people say she is skinny. It doesn't matter to her that many of her friends also admire her because she is athletic and active. Her mother, who has been dieting for years, says that people tease Rita because they are jealous. Rita knows she has an attractive face and a good complexion. But she's very aware of her bony elbows and knees. She wishes she knew a way to look more "normal."

Dennis loves to play basketball. He spends every minute he can spare on the basketball court. Dennis's idol is a 6-ft-11-in professional basketball player. Dennis has a long way to go to reach that height, although he has grown a lot in the last six months. Meanwhile, he wants to look, play, and think like his hero.

Gail's grandfather always tells her that she's pleasingly plump. Gail can't see anything pleasing about it. She always skips the starches and desserts in the school lunch, but then she usually eats snacks before dinner. She can't lose any weight this way. She doesn't really *need* to be thinner, but she secretly wants to look like Suzanne, a teenage model featured in fashion magazines. One article about her lists Suzanne's height and weight as 5-ft-7-in and 110 lb. At 5-ft-2-in and 115 lb, Gail is trying to figure out how she can dress to look like Suzanne.

Do you think that you are overweight? Or that your legs and arms are too long? Or that your shoulders are not broad enough? Few people are completely satisfied with the way they look. Like Rita, Dennis, and Gail, most people believe there is something wrong with their appearance.

This is particularly true when you are young. As you grow toward your adult height, your legs and arms may suddenly seem very long. You may become thinner, or heavier, than you would like to be.

Few of these problems are permanent. Time and growth will change your build. Watching your diet and exercising will help keep your body in shape. But growth, exercise, and dieting take time to show results.

In the meantime, the right choice of clothes can help you look the way you want to look. Clothing design can change the appearance of your body. It can also affect your "style." Some designs—such as a tailored suit—make you look businesslike, while others suggest a more casual style.

What Is Clothing Design?

When you look at a garment, what do you see? In addition to **color** and **texture,** you notice certain styling **lines,** and perhaps a fabric **print.** You may also notice the **proportion,** or balance, between different parts of the garment.

What you may not see so easily is how these features of a garment can work together to change the way a person looks. When clothing designers create new styles, they create a new look for people. Through creative use of these aspects of design—color, texture, line, print, and proportion—they can make a person's shape, or silhouette, appear to change.

Shoulder pads in a jacket, for example, change the appearance of the person wearing that jacket. A flared dress makes a woman's upper body seem smaller.

The Effect of Line

Shoulder pads alter a person's shape by actually adding bulk. High heels actually add height. But a far more common way of making people appear different is by creating an illusion. The lines of a garment can fool the eye quite effectively.

Vertical lines on an outfit usually have a slimming effect. They also make the wearer seem taller. Because the eye is led up and down, the distance from side to side is less noticeable.

Horizontal lines do the exact opposite. The eye is led from side to side, and the wearer appears shorter and broader. A wide belt, for example, is a horizontal line that can make a tall person appear shorter. A rugby shirt, with its wide stripes, can make a thin person appear heavier.

Curved lines in a garment, such as curved front edges on a vest, create a softer

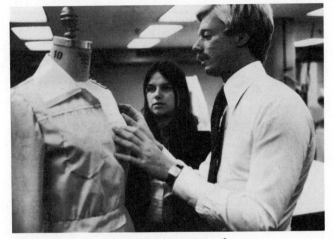

The line and proportion of a new style are adjusted on a dress form. Dress pieces can be shaped and fitted before a sample garment is made.

effect than either vertical or horizontal lines.

The effect of diagonal lines depends on the length and angle of the line. For example, a short diagonal stripe from the right shoulder to the left hip leads the eye from side to side—creating the illusion of width. A longer diagonal from the shoulder to the hem of a dress leads the eye up and down for a slimming look.

Lines on garments may be purely for decoration. They may also be structural—like the seams which hold a garment together. Both types of lines can create an illusion. A dress with a seam at the waistline can "shorten" a tall person just as effectively as a horizontal stripe on the fabric.

The Effects of Print

A striped fabric is a simple type of print. But a print can be a very much more complex arrangement of lines or figures. Whether stripes, dots, florals, or plaids,

Box 1

CREATE AN ILLUSION

If you'd rather look taller, shorter, thinner, or more filled out than you really are, these tips can help.

HOW TO LOOK TALLER

- Wear garments of matching color. Add accessories, such as neck chains, emblems, or pins, for a splash of different color that won't spoil the effect. *Don't* wear a belt with a contrasting color.
- Wear jackets or tops with long, narrow closings—such as a line of buttons or a long zipper. They give the impression of greater body length. It helps if these closings are in a contrasting color.
- Choose vertically striped fabrics. The stripes should not be too wide or too bright.
- Wear slim pants rather than flared ones. They make legs look longer.

HOW TO LOOK SHORTER

- Wear separates of contrasting colors.
- Avoid vertical lines.
- Choose wide, bright stripes in a horizontal pattern.
- Add a wide contrasting belt to an outfit.

HOW TO LOOK SLIMMER

- The most important thing to remember is that clothes should not be too tight. Nothing emphasizes bulges so much as tight garments.
- Wear tops and bottoms of the same or similar color.
- Avoid big, bold stripes in any direction.
- Choose small prints or checks rather than large ones.
- Make sure the colors you wear are not too light or too vivid.
- Avoid very bulky fabrics.

HOW TO LOOK STURDIER OR MORE FILLED OUT

- Emphasize those parts of your figure that you want to look larger by wearing bright, wide stripes, cut horizontally.
- Wear jackets and coats that are roomy at the shoulders to create the illusion of broader shoulders.
- Look for clothes with full-gathered yokes, sleeves, and skirts.
- Choose double-breasted and wrapped coats for fullness.
- Wear clothes with large collars, cuffs, and pockets.

prints can have interesting effects on your appearance.

Since prints are combinations of various colors, the guidelines for using color apply to prints. For example, a red plaid jacket attracts attention and "increases" size just as a solid red jacket does. If the main color in a print is the same blue that's flattering to your eyes in a solid color, the print will probably also be flattering. Print also allows you to wear—in small doses—colors that wouldn't suit you in a solid.

The lines of the garment and the print must work well together. For example, a curved seam loses its softening effect if the print used is a horizontal stripe. Also, some complicated lines that work well in solid colors get lost in a printed fabric.

Prints can make you appear larger or smaller than your actual size. A shirt with a large, bold print would make you look larger than one with a small, delicate pattern.

Prints can also emphasize particular features. A border print on a dress can call attention to your legs. A print collar on a solid-color shirt will make people notice your face.

Prints affect your appearance in many ways. By experimenting, you can choose the prints that work well for you.

The Effect of Proportion

Proportion is the relationship of one part to another. Your body has proportions—the length of your upper body, for example, compared to the length of your legs. Garments also have proportions—the length of your jacket in relation to the length of your pants.

In clothing design, achieving the right proportion means reaching a pleasing balance. The right proportion gives you a put-together look. For example, if you wore large hiking boots with a delicate chiffon dress, the balance of your outfit would be all wrong! A pair of evening sandals would be more in scale with your dress.

Just as the parts of an outfit must be in proportion to one another, so must an outfit suit the proportions of the person wearing it. A hip-length jacket worn with pants makes legs appear shorter. A waist-length jacket with pants "lengthens" legs. If you feel that your legs are too long, you can "shorten" them by choosing the hip-length jacket or by wearing your T-shirt outside your pants. By changing the proportions of your garments, you can change the way you look.

Different proportions are fashionable in different years. One year, low waistlines may be in. Another year, waists may be almost up to your rib cage. If you understand how clothing proportion works, you will be better able to decide which fashions you want to follow.

Design Elements and Mood

Line, print, and proportion can convey various moods. Horizontal lines seem to reflect stability and rest. Vertical lines can create a soaring, majestic feeling. Diagonal lines suggest motion and seem exciting and daring. Curved lines are playful, relaxed, and soft.

The size of a print also gives an impression. If the design is small, the effect is more delicate. Large patterns make you seem bolder. And proportion too affects the general impression given by the garment. For example, a dress with a high waistline may create a little-girl look.

The Whole Effect

The line, print, and proportion of clothing—combined with its texture and color—affect your appearance. Knowing how these elements work together can help you find the clothes that are best for you.

Design is a complicated matter, however. You learn more about it each time you study a garment. The most reliable way of deciding on a particular style is to try it on and see if it really suits you.

QUESTIONS

1. List the five basic elements of clothing design.
2. Describe three ways in which different design elements can change a person's physical appearance.
3. Explain how design elements can convey various moods.
4. In terms of the elements of design, how would you describe the "look" of today's clothing?
5. What kind of clothes do you think Gail on p. 370 should wear? Dennis? Rita?
6. Which element of design do you think most affects your appearance? Why?

ACTIVITIES

1. Make a sketch of a popular clothing style from a previous century. Analyze the way design elements are used.
2. Visit a specialty clothing shop that caters to people who are very tall, or very small, or very large. Talk to the manager about the kinds of design he or she looks for when ordering clothing for the store.
3. Sometimes two articles of clothing that look exactly alike on the hanger look very different when you put them on. Using two garments you have at home, or find in a store, describe the reasons for the differences.

SECTION 4 · Knowing What to Wear

Dressing for the Occasion

Dan's mother and father were getting ready to go to a restaurant for a dinner given by the company Dan's mother worked for. Dan was in the kitchen when his father appeared dressed in a three-piece suit Dan had never seen before.

"Why are you all dressed up, Dad?" asked Dan. "They don't make you wear fancy clothes to eat in that restaurant anymore."

"I know," said Dan's father. "But everyone else will be in a suit."

"Come on, Dad. That's their problem. You have a right to be comfortable."

"I guess that's true. But this is an important night for your mother and her co-workers. It would embarrass her if I dressed casually. I can put up with a tie for tonight—her feelings are more important."

Ann was just about ready to go shopping in the city with her mother. They were going to get something for Ann to wear at her half-brother's wedding in a couple of weeks. As Ann came downstairs in her jeans, a shirt, and heavy crepe-soled shoes, her mother exploded, "You're not wearing that into the city! And anyway, how can you try on dresses with those shoes?"

Ben's cousin Jerry, who lives halfway across the country, was visiting. Some of Ben's friends had come over to meet Jerry, and later one of them called to invite both boys to a party at his house.

When Ben passed on the invitation, Jerry thought for a moment and then said, "Should I wear a jacket and tie?"

Ben started laughing. "No way," he said. "It's not that kind of party."

Choosing what clothes to wear depends on many things. Besides your personal taste, it depends on what you are doing, the climate where you live, and the type of life you lead. It also may depend on the opinions of others.

Dressing for Activity and Climate

Different activities often demand different clothing. Sometimes this is obvious. You wouldn't wear ski pants to go swimming, or your best suit to do carpentry work. But dressing for an activity that does not require an obvious choice of clothing can take some thought.

When choosing what to wear to go shopping, for example, you might decide to dress for convenience. But if, like Ann, you are going shopping for clothes, it's smart to put on the shoes and underclothes you will wear with the garments you plan to buy.

Climate and weather affect your choice of clothes, too. You are probably so used to the climate where you live that you know automatically what clothing is most comfortable. If you are traveling, however, it may take some thought to plan your wardrobe.

Suppose you are flying from New York to Florida in November. Clothing that is comfortable when you get on the plane may be very uncomfortable when you get off. You should plan ahead.

It's always wise to travel in an outfit that includes a removable jacket or sweater, whatever the climate. Air conditioning and heating are unpredictable in trains, planes, and buses.

Respecting Others' Feelings

Today, comfort is generally the rule—so long as we don't offend other people. To avoid offending others, people usually follow the customs of those they are with. Sometimes what we are expected to wear is not what is most comfortable. But be flexible. Dan's father, for example, didn't mind getting dressed up because he knew the dinner was a special occasion for his wife and her co-workers.

Many people feel that special events call for special clothing. Getting dressed up is a way of showing that an occasion is important to them. By considering others' feelings in your own dress, you can show that you care about the occasion and their feelings too.

Feeling Comfortable in a Group

Being comfortable in a group is important to nearly everyone. This is one reason people think about what to wear. When you are dressed properly, people are more likely to accept you as a member of the group.

Knowing what to wear to school is no problem. You have been there often. You are aware of what your friends and other students wear. You know which clothes make you feel comfortable and accepted.

When you move outside your usual routine, however, deciding what to wear may take more thought. In most cases, you will not want to look out of place. You may want to wear clothes similar to those worn by your friends.

Jerry was used to putting on a jacket and tie for parties in his home town. But in Ben's neighborhood, he would have felt out of place dressed like that. And he probably would not have had a good time if he felt uncomfortable about his clothes.

The right clothes can make you feel more comfortable in a new situation.

High school proms are a time when many people get dressed up. What other occasion can you think of when people from your community wear "formal" clothing?

Special Occasions

There are times when dressing appropriately means dressing up. These are special occasions for which you are expected to wear a certain kind of clothing.

Parties—Often the person who invites you to a party will tell you what clothing is expected—"Wear jeans," for example. If someone says, "The girls are going to wear long dresses," that lets the boys know that they should come a little more dressed up than usual. Your friends will usually let you know what they plan to wear. If they don't, don't be afraid to ask.

Weddings—There aren't too many weddings in most people's lives. That is why people celebrate them by wearing more formal clothing than they usually wear. Some stores rent formal clothes. But often people borrow a formal dress or suit from someone they know.

How formally you dress for a wedding depends on the time and place of the wedding or reception. The people who invite you will give you help in deciding what to wear. Magazines also show a variety of suitable formal wear.

Funerals—At one time, black was the only color considered proper to wear to a funeral. This is no longer the rule everywhere. Still, a funeral is definitely not the occasion to wear anything flashy or daring.

Since a funeral is usually a painful emotional experience for the family involved, wearing too casual clothing might be considered an insult. If you aren't sure what dress is expected, check with others. Simple designs with dark or neutral colors are usually appropriate.

Clothing and Rules

In some cases, there are definite rules about appropriate dress. In many areas, for example, stores are forbidden by law to admit customers who are barefoot or without shirts. Restaurants usually require shirts. Some even insist on ties and jackets.

Some religious groups have strict rules about dress for their services or even within their buildings. And your school may have a dress code. In these situations, it is easy to know what to wear.

When You Have to Take a Chance

There will be times when you just don't know what to wear and can't get information from anybody else. If it is a very big gathering, you are likely to see a variety of dress. If yours is neither the most casual nor the dressiest outfit, you will probably be comfortable.

The tips in this section will help you to know how to dress for most situations.

However, you are bound to have the experience of wearing the wrong outfit. When this happens, you will probably feel embarrassed because your clothes are different. You may even think everyone is noticing you.

The best solution in such a situation is to try to forget how you are dressed. After all, your clothing is only one part of you. It's too late to do anything about it anyway, so relax and become involved in the occasion. Let people get to know you as a *person*.

QUESTIONS

1. What kinds of things affect a person's decision about what to wear for a particular occasion?
2. Describe three situations that call for specific types of clothing. What would be the results of dressing inappropriately?
3. How can your choice of clothing affect you when you are in a new situation? How can you find out what to wear for special occasions?
4. How could you find out what to wear when going on a trip to a place with a climate different from the one you live in?
5. Why do you think clothing customs for special occasions have become more liberal over the years?
6. What kinds of clothing do you think are unsuitable for school? What kind of impression would a student wearing such clothes make on you?

ACTIVITIES

1. Find an old book on etiquette and describe to your class the recommended clothing for an informal occasion, such as an afternoon walk or a visit with friends.
2. Write a skit in which a teenager wants to wear jeans to a family gathering against his or her parents' wishes.
3. Make a humorous poster showing the results of wearing clothing that doesn't fit an activity, such as jogging, gardening, or housecleaning.

SECTION 5 · Building a Wardrobe

WHAT TO WEAR?

Luis needs something to wear when he introduces a visiting speaker at a special assembly on Friday. In his school, most people get dressed up for that job, and he would like to wear a jacket and tie.

Luis has many items of clothing. When he sees something he likes, he buys it with his paper-route money. His mother buys clothes for him whenever she sees a bargain. And his grandmother gives him the brightly colored pants and shirts she loves to see him wear.

Luis's problem is that most of his pants don't go with most of his shirts. And although he has a suit, he doesn't have a casual jacket and pants—which is what he'd like to wear on Friday.

Marsha has outgrown everything from last year. After talking it over with her parents, she bought three new outfits for school. One outfit is a solid royal blue. The second has brown-and-heather tweed pants and a brown top. The third is red-and-black checked. Two of the outfits are dressy enough to wear to religious services and other special occasions. Marsha likes each of her three purchases, but she is already tired of wearing the same things over and over.

Having suitable clothes for all the different occasions and activities in your life isn't easy. This is especially true when your money is limited.

Collecting a set of clothes, or wardrobe, that can meet all your needs takes careful management.

There are many things to consider. You are growing fast, and you don't want to waste money on an outfit you won't wear more than twice. Your moods change. Sometimes you want to wear subdued shades; at other times you like brighter colors. You have to keep in mind your everyday activities. But you want to be prepared for special occasions, too.

Take the time to decide how to get the most from the clothes you already have. This will let you plan what you need to buy to round out your wardrobe. Planning will help you spend your clothing money wisely.

What Are Your Needs?

How do you decide how many outfits you really need? You can get by with just two, wearing one while the other is being cleaned. But, like Marsha, you might get pretty tired of the same things.

On the other hand, if you had twenty outfits for school, each outfit would be worn only nine times during the whole school year. Even with ten outfits, each one would get only eighteen wearings. Think about how much use you will get from each outfit that you have.

Don't forget that you are probably growing fast and this limits the wear you will get from your clothes. So avoid buying too many things that are similar. If you have several jackets, for example, you may not get enough wear from each before outgrowing them.

Most of your clothes will be worn for everyday activities. So clothing that is suitable for school, a game of tennis or bowling, and working and relaxing at home should be given first consideration.

Then there are special activities to think about. Do you need clothing for skiing or singing in a chorus? Do you play in an orchestra or take dancing lessons? How about parties, religious activities, or visits to relatives? Outfits for special events like these are part of a well-planned wardrobe.

What Do You Have?

After you have thought about the kinds of clothes you need, take stock of what you have. Go through your closet and drawers. Sort out the clothes you don't wear. You

Sorting is a key step in determining your clothing needs. Once you have organized your present clothes, you can get more use from your wardrobe, and plan better for future purchases.

Box 1

Mix and Match

Marsha did not plan ahead. She bought outfits that could not be mixed and matched. If she had chosen her three outfits in mixable colors and patterns, she might have had three times the number of outfits she bought—or nine outfits.

Though Marsha didn't start with coordinates, let's see how she can get the most mileage out of her present wardrobe, plus some new additions. What outfits might you make with these pieces if you add a camel jumper, a denim skirt, or black pants? What

may have outgrown some. Others may need repairs. Still others won't go with anything else you have. Set aside all the items that you don't wear.

Now turn your attention to the clothing that you *do* wear. Don't forget garments that are in the wash or at the cleaner's.

When you look at the clothing you actually wear, you will be able to see your clothing needs more clearly.

Filling the Gaps

Do you need a shirt or blouse for dressy occasions? What about a sweater or jacket for other pieces might be added to make several outfits?

If Luis takes a closer look at his wardrobe, he might see some unexpected combinations. Or, he might discover several shirts in his collection that would go well with one new pair of pants. Perhaps he has several pants that he could wear with one new vest.

The way to put new separates to work is to match them with old separates. Ask yourself what color and style will go with other items in your clothes collection.

school? Could you use a belt or other accessory for variety?

Do some serious thinking before adding to your wardrobe. Careful planning will help you spend your money wisely—on clothing to suit all your needs.

Think of clothes that will go with what you already have. Suppose you often wear a blue, green, and aqua plaid shirt and white pants. A matching two-piece outfit may be especially useful. Get a sweater and matching pants in either blue, green, or aqua. You can match the sweater with the pants. Or you can wear the new solid pants with the plaid shirt. This way, you will have three new outfits instead of one. This technique for expanding a wardrobe is often called mix and match (see box 1 in this section).

Plain clothes give you flexibility. They can often be used for different occasions, according to what you wear with them. Boys can wear the same pants with casual T-shirts or with a smart sports jacket. Girls can dress up a plain jumper with a sheer satin or a metallic top. The same jumper can be dressed down with a shirt or a blouse in an everyday fabric.

Getting What You Need

Once you know what you need, you can start building a better wardrobe. Begin by looking at the garments you seldom or never wear. Can you think of a way to make use of them?

Perhaps the vest you bought on sale matches something you hadn't thought of before. Is there a three-piece suit you almost never wear? Try the different pieces

with other garments. After all, they are separate, so they can be mixed and matched with other things.

Now look at the clothes that need repairs. Consider each item and ask yourself if you have anything to wear with it. Is there any activity for which you need it? In other words, is it worth repairing?

A jacket may match your gray pants and look great with your plaid or checked pants. If all the jacket needs is a new set of buttons, it's obviously worth fixing. But suppose it doesn't match anything you have. Unless you want to buy clothes to go with the jacket, fixing it may not be worth your time.

The Second Time Around

Recycling is another way to put seldom-worn clothes to use. For example, if you have grown too tall for a pair of pants, they can be recycled into shorts. A full-length dressy skirt could be recycled into a shorter, more practical style.

Your seldom-worn clothes may include some hand-me-downs that don't quite fit. Would that flannel shirt work as a jacket over a lightweight shirt until you grow a bit? Could those pants your older brother gave you be shortened to fit you? Hand-me-downs can be a great no-cost way to add to your wardrobe.

Shopping for Clothes

After you have carefully evaluated the clothes you already have, you may find that you have to buy some new pieces in order to have clothing for all your activities. Where you shop will depend in part on how much time and money you have to spend.

Department stores and specialty shops offer the largest variety, but they are also the most expensive places to shop. Discount

Box 2
Choosing Accessories

Accessories can change the look of many of your outfits. A necktie or a scarf can dress up a very simple shirt. A pendant or a belt can make many garments more interesting.

Some accessories are big financial investments and need to be planned as carefully as garments. Shoes, for example, can be expensive. Before you buy any garment, think how it will look with the shoes you already have. If you are buying shoes to go with one outfit, ask yourself if they can be worn with anything else you have.

Shoes that are the wrong style or color can spoil the effect of an outfit. So be sure to give them careful thought as you plan your wardrobe.

stores and factory outlets usually have better prices, but they are often limited in what they offer.

There are also secondhand or thrift shops to consider. These stores carry clothes that have been owned and worn by other people. The garments are in good condition, though, and you may even find an interesting style that is no longer sold elsewhere.

Secondhand clothes are much cheaper than new clothes. You are sure to get a bargain at a secondhand store—if you can find what you need, and if it fits you with little alteration.

Clothing can also be bought through mail-order catalogs. They offer a variety of styles and prices, along with the convenience of shopping at home. Shopping by mail could be a good choice if you don't need the clothing right away, and if you don't require a special fit.

Sewing is also very economical because you only have to buy a pattern and material—you supply the labor yourself. It's a good way to get additional clothing. And if you can't find a garment your size in the color and design you want, making it yourself may be the only answer.

Planning Ahead

Good management helps you get the most use and pleasure from your clothes. A good wardrobe does not just happen. It requires careful thought about what you have and what you need. And it calls for wise decision making on how to fill your clothing needs.

Give careful thought to each item you are planning to buy. Be sure it is comfortable and easy to care for. If you learn what to look for in fabric and construction, you will be even more satisfied with the clothing you select.

The more effort you put into planning, the happier you will be with your wardrobe. Planning lets you make the best use of the time and money you spend on clothes.

QUESTIONS

1. What kinds of pitfalls can careful wardrobe planning help you avoid?
2. What is the first step in planning a wardrobe? Describe the technique to use in analyzing the clothes you now have.
3. Why is mix and match important to keep in mind when planning a wardrobe? Describe three ways to add to your wardrobe.
4. What do you consider the three most important garments in your wardrobe? Why?
5. What could Luis do to help his mother and grandmother buy him clothes that he really needs?
6. What problems could arise from buying clothes a little too large that you expect to "grow into"?

ACTIVITIES

1. Make a list of your activities and one of your clothing. Can you find any new combinations? What garments could you buy or make that would go with several things you already have?
2. Find magazine pictures of other garments Marsha could use to expand her wardrobe.
3. Bring to class one or two garments that you have outgrown, along with a sketch of how you might recycle them.

SECTION 6 · Changing Fashions

FORMER YEARS

The variety of clothing fashions has been endless. Pictures of old fashions may look neat, quaint, or just plain funny to you. Chances are you would never wear such clothes without making some changes to suit your modern taste.

You are probably aware of how quickly clothing fashions change. A particular kind of garment suddenly becomes popular. A lot of people wear it. Then, as suddenly as it appeared, it is gone.

The same quick changes happen with clothing accessories. One year, bracelets are in. The next year, everyone is wearing fancy belts or a special kind of ring.

Where do these fashions come from? Why do they catch on so quickly? And why do some of them die out as fast as they came in?

What Makes Fashion Change?

Fashion has been a part of human life for a very long time. If you look at garments worn during past centuries, you will see that people often dressed differently from their parents. Even within one century, there will be a great number of different styles. If you need to be convinced, just look at the variety of clothes that have been worn in our own twentieth century!

Perhaps the simplest reason that fashion changes is that people get bored with clothes after a while. They want to dress a little differently from the way they dressed three years ago. They also like to say something special about themselves through the clothes they wear—something that tells the world that they are different from their parents and their sisters and brothers.

Most people don't like to be totally different, however. So they choose clothes that are popular with a certain group—a group that is important to them. For instance, you may like to wear clothes that your friends will admire. And your parents may choose clothes that *their* friends would like.

These two desires—to express one's own personality and to be accepted by a group—are two big reasons for fashion and its changes.

Where Do Fashion Ideas Come From?

New ideas in fashion come from many sources. Events and people in the news often lead the way. Changes in the way people live, and in what they do, may cause changes in their ideas about fashion.

Fashion designers and fashion magazines have a strong influence on what people wear. And every now and then a clothing idea that some fashion pioneer tries out catches on, becomes popular in a school, and perhaps even a city or nation.

Street fashions are started by ordinary people who like to wear familiar and comfortable clothing in a different way. For example, colorful patches on blue jeans were once a novel way of repairing holes in the pants. But now patches and emblems have become so popular that they are used for decoration rather than for hiding holes.

Other fashions may start when a few people try out a new idea, then suddenly find that everyone around them is trying the same thing. Often no one knows who invented the fashion first.

Many fashions become popular because of what people are seeing on **television** or in **the movies.** A particular TV star is very popular. Many people will want to look the same way. An event in the news is attracting a lot of attention. People may reflect this event by wearing new kinds of clothing—a French beret, for example, a Chinese-style coat, or a Moroccan caftan. You can probably think of clothes that are popular in your neighborhood because of a TV show or a news event.

The many different companies involved in producing clothing form **the garment industry.** Clothing fashions are greatly influenced by the garment industry, which is constantly coming out with fresh designs.

Fashion designers try to stay aware of

new trends. They pick up ideas from street fashion and from the media. They also create their own original designs. If a particular design becomes popular, this is good news for the designer because it means a lot of sales.

High fashion—the expensive clothes created by big-name designers—gets wide attention because of the pictures and advertisements in fashion magazines.

At one time, very expensive clothes made in Paris were the main influence on fashion. But most people could not afford the hand-sewn originals. So the American garment industry produced copies of the new styles at more modest prices.

Today, the influence of Paris fashion is not as strong as it once was. Many other fashion centers also produce original and fashionable clothes—including New York, Los Angeles, and other cities in North America. The garment industry produces versions and variations of these styles in different price ranges.

Basics and Fads

Some styles remain popular for a very long time. They become recognized as **basics.** Basics were probably worn by your parents when they were young, and may now be in your wardrobe, too. A Windbreaker, a pair of jeans, a pullover sweater—these styles have been around for quite a while, and are as popular as ever. The details may change—flared legs or straight legs on jeans, for example—but the basic design stays the same.

Other styles become fashionable for shorter periods. A few are very popular for a year or less, and then suddenly lose their appeal. These short-lived styles are often called **fads.** Some fads are very inexpensive, but others cost a lot of money. Box 1 in this section shows some clothing fads from different times and places. In their time, they were all very popular. Now they are no longer worn, and many of them seem strange to us.

The Consumer Angle

Fashion changes can make life very difficult for the consumer. Most people want to dress attractively—they want to be in fashion. But they have a limited amount of money to spend on clothes. With fashions changing so quickly, it's difficult to know what to buy.

A fad may be a very poor buy because two months after you get it, it may no longer be popular. But if you buy only basics, your wardrobe may seem dull. You'll be able to wear your clothes a long time without looking out of fashion, but you may not be too excited about them.

To have the best of both worlds, learn how to compromise. Stock your wardrobe with basics, but buy some short-term fashion and fad items to give it flair. Clothing accessories like belts, necklaces, and chains are good fad purchases because you can use them to give your basics an up-to-date look. This way you can get good value even over the short time that a fad is popular.

Following Fashions

By becoming aware of fads and fashions when you are young, you will learn to tell what kinds of clothes will stay popular and what kinds will go out of style quickly.

Check your fashion-spotting average. Would you have guessed that T-shirts with messages would become so popular? Many people thought they were a fad item, and would soon be forgotten. Would you have

Where Are They Now?

Box 1

Below are some short-lived clothing fads from the past 50 years. One of them—the Nehru suit—passed from the fashion scene so quickly that stores were left with thousands of suits they could not sell.

Can you think of any recent fads to add to this gallery of here-today-gone-tomorrow styles?

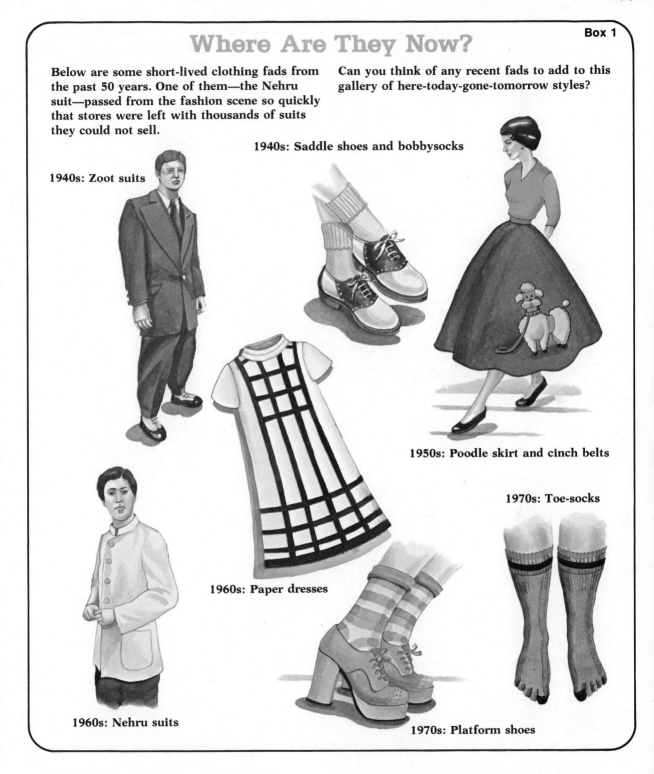

1940s: Zoot suits

1940s: Saddle shoes and bobbysocks

1950s: Poodle skirt and cinch belts

1960s: Paper dresses

1960s: Nehru suits

1970s: Platform shoes

1970s: Toe-socks

thought that jeans would become such a basic clothing item? For a long time, they were considered work pants. Are there any popular styles in your school today that you think will become basic? What do you think makes a fashion last?

QUESTIONS

1. Describe four major influences on fashion trends.
2. What is the difference between a fad and a fashion?
3. What are basics? How can an awareness of fashion help you build a good wardrobe?
4. What do you think would happen to the garment industry if styles did not change?
5. What are the current clothing fads in your school? Do you expect any of them to last? Why?
6. Name some well-known people who have affected fashion in some way, and describe the changes they have caused.

ACTIVITIES

1. Collect pictures of currently fashionable garments from newspapers and magazines. Which styles are different from anything available a year ago? Which are very much like garments on the market last year? Which do you think will be in style next year?
2. Collect pictures of high-fashion garments from newspapers or fashion magazines. Do any of them fit the life-style of the people you know? Are there features that you think might be adapted to popularly priced garments?
3. Find a garment that someone you know wore ten years ago. Could you change it to suit today's fashion? How?

SECTION 7 · Clothes of the Future

2050 A.D. – A New Machine

Rip's red-check mirafab tunic was only two days old, but he wanted to change it. The color was wrong for him. Also, he worked in a hospital, and the patients didn't seem to like the fabric pattern. One of them even told Rip that it made her *tired* to look at it. Rip also wanted to have shorter sleeves and a rougher surface.

On his way home, Rip rented the super-ultra-garment-change machine from the clothes center. He put his tunic on his special clothes form and placed the form inside the machine. He turned a few knobs, and then went to sleep to the steady hum of the machine. The next morning, his garment was ready—a plain dark-blue felt with short sleeves.

2050 A.D. – A New Attitude

Stavia came out of the recycle shop clutching the new jump suit she had chosen. She had traded the shreds of a badly worn outfit and had paid good cash as well. The shreds would be reduced to fiber again, and remade into a new fabric, then new clothes.

Getting a new piece of clothing was unusual for Stavia. She didn't really care for stiff, new clothing that was made from recycled fiber. Like most people, Stavia usually bought clothes secondhand. She much preferred comfortable reconditioned clothing.

Unfortunately, secondhand clothes were only available to those who had a wearable garment to trade in. That is why people took such good care of their clothes. If they tired of a garment, it made a good trade-in. Then they could get another piece of used clothing—and not have to break in something themselves.

No one can be sure what clothing will be like in the future. But here are some ideas to think about:

- Clothing will continue to mirror our way of life.
- As the supply of natural resources decreases, recycling will become more common.
- Improved technical know-how will change the clothing picture.
- Clothes will continue to meet individual needs and desires.
- World events will continue to influence us in ways we cannot imagine now.

Our Way of Life

As life-styles change, so does the clothing we wear. During the past thirty years, life-styles in North America have become more informal. Our clothing mirrors that fact.

Once, for example, all "proper young women" wore hats and gloves when they went shopping. Young men wore jackets and ties to all sorts of events. But today's way of life is much more casual.

The future will bring other changes in our way of life, and those changes will affect the clothing we wear. Perhaps people will have more leisure time. Then, clothing styles might become even more casual than they are today. Or perhaps people will feel a need for a more formal way of life. That desire would affect clothing choices, too.

The conditions in which we live also affect our life-styles. If the energy shortage continues, warmer clothes will be designed for indoor use during the winter. With less air conditioning, we may need more light-weight outfits for the summer months. If there are major changes in the continent's weather patterns, this, too, will affect the clothing industry.

In the more distant future, people may live on the ocean floor, and wear some ver-sion of scuba-diving equipment. They may also live on other planets and on earth's satellites, wearing streamlined versions of today's space suits.

Limited Resources

The availability of resources will also affect the future of clothing. Today, clothes are made from only a few types of fibers. Some are natural fibers, such as wool and cotton. Others are synthetic fibers made from a few basic materials, such as petroleum and wood.

The world's population is increasing. The supply of resources needed to produce these clothing fibers is not. In the future, it may be difficult to find enough land for cotton fields and sheep pastures. Less land may be available for producing wood. Petroleum resources will probably be more scarce than they are today. How we use these resources will affect the clothes of the future.

Some people think that petroleum should be saved for energy purposes, such as fuel for cars, and heat and light for homes and factories. Others say that petroleum should be saved for products such as textile fibers and chemicals. They think it may be easier to find new ways to power cars than to find new materials for fibers.

Because our supply of resources is limited, we will need to make wiser use of what we have. This may mean learning to recycle clothes in ways we haven't even thought of yet.

New Technology

The development of new fibers and fabrics might revolutionize the clothing of the future. New construction techniques may be needed. New designs may be possible.

Textile and fiber manufacturers work constantly to improve the quality of their products by developing new yarns and new production techniques.

Even today, scientists are experimenting with new sources for clothing, trying to develop new and improved fabrics. Fiberglass, for example, is a fairly new fiber made mainly from sand. Sand is in plentiful supply, so fiberglass could satisfy the world's clothing needs for a long time.

Fiberglass fabric is fireproof, which makes it perfect for outer garments for firefighters, racing car drivers, and astronauts. But the use of fiberglass in clothing is limited because it gives off tiny particles of glass that irritate the skin. In the future, scientists may develop a type of fiberglass that can be used safely in everyday clothing.

Molded foams, plastics, and vinyl may be more widely used in the near future. These materials are already used in rain-coats, boots, shoes, belts, and other items. They are useful in clothing because they are waterproof and can be molded to fit. But these materials, unlike cotton, do not "breathe," or absorb moisture. Therefore, they can be very uncomfortable. A solution for this problem will have to be found before plastics can be used in a general way.

Some fabrics developed by technology prove unacceptable. Several years ago, clothing manufacturers tried to sell disposable paper garments. But they were unsuccessful. Today, paper garments are only used for a few special purposes—hospital gowns, for example.

Clearly, new clothing ideas need more than resources and technology to succeed. New fabrics and garments have to meet individual desires and needs.

Suiting the Individual

Some clothing needs result from new jobs. Work with radiation requires special protective garments, for example. As new jobs are created, special new clothes may have to be developed.

Other garments are created for people with special needs. In the future, more clothing will probably be designed for people with physical handicaps. Wheelchair patients, for example, need garments they can put on while seated.

Children's garments of the future will probably have more self-help features, such as fasteners that can be managed by tiny hands. Clothing with self-help features gives children the satisfaction of managing their clothing themselves.

What Next?

Future world events may influence us in ways we can't imagine today. Through natural disasters or changes in weather cycles, the nature of Earth itself may change. Political change, too, may alter our lives.

No one knows for sure what the future of clothing will be. But we do know that clothes will always reflect our way of life. Clothes will always be an important way for the individual to say "I'm me" or "I'm one of you."

Even if the future brings a single garment that can be used for every activity, people will still want to express their own personalities. Fashion provides a way for people to say something about themselves to the world.

QUESTIONS

1. Explain how changes in society, technology, and available resources could affect clothing in the future.
2. Name some materials that clothing of the future might be made of. What problems need to be solved before these materials can be more widely used?
3. Name two groups of people who would benefit from specially designed clothing.
4. What kinds of changes in clothing do you think are most likely to occur in the future? Least likely? Why?
5. If a shortage of raw materials does occur, what features of our clothing do you think would be the first to change?

ACTIVITIES

1. Find out more about why paper clothing did not become popular when it was introduced in the mid-1960s. Report your findings to the class.
2. Design and sketch an article of clothing suitable for someone with a special need.
3. Pretend you live in the year 2050. Make a list of the clothing in your wardrobe.

SECTION 8 · Careers in Fashion Retailing and Merchandising

Work in the World of Fashion

A strong sense of fashion, a good head for business, and the ability to work well with others are all important in the retail clothing industry.

Do you enjoy keeping up with the latest fashions? Have you ever thought of working in one of the many stores and shops where clothing and accessories are sold?

The retail clothing industry offers many job opportunities. If you would like to combine an interest in fashion with a career in business, this may be the field for you.

First Jobs

Salespeople help customers to find what they are looking for and to make their purchases. Stores train their sales staffs so they can answer questions about fabric content, quality, and care of the clothing they sell.

Some stores require a high-school diploma for their full-time salespeople. A neat appearance and the ability to meet and work with the public are also musts. Being a salesperson is often the first step in a career in retail clothing.

Before clothes are offered for sale, incoming orders need to be checked, and tagged with the price and other information in the stockroom. All this is done by stock clerks, who keep track of the merchandise and how the stock is moving. A stock clerk does not need any special training, but being good in math and spelling helps. A talent for detailed work is also an asset.

Because there is a lot of competition for customers, a retail clothing store may use the services of a comparison shopper. Comparison shoppers check the merchandise and prices in other stores. They also study display and sales techniques. They then report their findings to the management of the store they work for.

The information gathered by comparison shoppers is used in setting prices, buying new merchandise, and developing new sales techniques.

Spreading the Word

Large clothing stores have promotion and publicity departments. The promotion department employs copywriters and illustrators to prepare advertising materials. Display workers are also part of the promotion department. They "dress" windows and set up displays throughout the store.

College writing or journalism courses will help prepare you for a copywriter's job. Illustrators and display workers need art training.

People in the publicity department work to present a good image of the store to the public. They sometimes cooperate with community groups in educational and recreational activities. They may plan or sponsor public events such as Halloween parades or spring flower shows. They may provide booklets or conduct seminars on new and useful developments in clothing and textiles. Work in a publicity department requires good writing skills and the ability to meet and work with other people.

Fashion Coordinators

Large clothing retailers often employ fashion coordinators. They have a variety of responsibilities and work with many different people.

Fashion coordinators plan fashion shows and develop advertising themes. They often involve community groups, such as school clubs, in their projects. You may have attended or modeled at a fashion show or fair put on by a store.

It is also the job of the fashion coordinator to see that clothing and accessories that go well together are available throughout the store. The fashion coordinator works closely with those who buy merchandise for the store. Together they see that various departments follow trends in colors and styles. For example, if a customer selects a suit in a new fashion color, matching accessories must be available in other departments.

A related fashion and merchandising job is that of bridal consultant. A bridal consultant not only sells appropriate costumes to the wedding party, but also advises on all aspects of the wedding.

Fashion coordinators are usually college graduates who majored in home economics or art. Experience in various positions within a retail clothing store is usually required for this job.

Garment Buyers

The position of buyer is at the center of the fashion industry. Buyers connect the designers and garment makers with the stores and shops where clothing is sold.

A buyer may work for a large department store, a chain of stores, a mail-order house, or a local specialty store. Large retail companies have a number of buyers. Each orders only the type of clothing carried in a particular department. For example, a teen buyer will order all the clothes carried in the teen department. In a local specialty store, the buyer is often the store owner.

The job of buyer has its glamorous side. Buyers are involved with the latest fashions. They travel to wholesale fashion shows in the United States. They may even go to foreign countries that manufacture clothing of interest to their customers.

In order to select and buy suitable merchandise, buyers must know the tastes and buying habits of their company's customers. For example, buyers must have a good idea of the colors their customers like. That doesn't mean they don't buy new shades. But they do make sure that they order garments in colors that are popular with their customers.

A buyer for a department store must always be aware of how well different types of clothes are selling. This requires constant contact with the salespeople and especially the managers of the various departments.

They must also know if their customers are a little larger or smaller than average. That way they can buy more of the sizes that sell best.

Buyers as Managers

Most buyers have served an apprenticeship as assistant buyer. Some even started out as stock clerks or salespeople. More and more often, though, buyers are being selected from college programs in retailing and merchandising. This training helps prepare them to assume important management responsibilities.

Models play an important role in the production of a garment. Here a sample is modeled so that it can be checked for cut and fit by the designer.

Buyers work with department managers to keep track of the goods they have bought. They have to know which items sell well and which are slow to move. This information guides them in future purchases.

There must be enough variety in the clothes they buy to suit the many different people who shop in their store. This means buyers must plan and watch their budget carefully.

Buyers must also arrange for deliveries of their purchases at the right times of the year. For instance, if they are buying summer clothes, the garments must be in the stores by spring.

As the heads of their departments, buyers must keep their sales staffs well informed. What type of merchandise is being shipped to the store? How does it represent the new fashion trends? What should cus-

tomers know about the styles and quality of the new clothes?

The buyer must be able to impart knowledge and enthusiasm to the salespeople. Then they, in turn, can pass this enthusiasm on to the customers.

The Designer

The designer is another key figure in the fashion industry. Every piece of clothing a buyer selects, every piece you wear, first took shape in the mind of a designer.

Designers choose the fabrics and plan the lines of new garments. They make sketches, and sometimes samples, from which a pattern can be made.

Designers usually get their training in college programs in fashion design, and by working with experienced designers. In order to be successful, they must keep in close touch with fashion trends and produce designs that please buyers and their customers.

Many Different Talents

Fashion retailing and merchandising involve a large network of people. Some of them are in related fields, such as publishing or advertising. Many writers, editors, artists, photographers, and models are employed by publications and agencies to bring fashion news to the public.

As you have seen, workers in the fashion industry come from a variety of backgrounds. Some are trained in retailing and merchandising. Some have studied art, journalism, or home economics. If you have an interest in any of these areas, you might consider a job in the retail fashion industry. If you like working with people and have a strong sense of fashion, this field could provide exciting opportunities for you.

QUESTIONS

1. Name the different kinds of jobs available in the retail clothing industry.
2. Describe the duties of three different kinds of workers in the field.
3. List the educational requirements for each of the above three jobs. What kinds of personal qualities would you need for each?
4. Why do you think department store managers and fashion coordinators are first required to work at different jobs in the store?
5. What other jobs in the retail clothing industry can you think of?
6. Which jobs in the retail clothing industry do you think did not exist fifty years ago? Why not?

ACTIVITIES

1. Make a chart that shows how the different workers in a department store depend on one another. You may begin your research by talking to a department store manager.
2. Interview someone in the retail clothing field about the nature of his or her job. Describe the interview to your class.
3. Look at the classified section of your local newspaper to see what kinds of jobs are available in the field. Which ones seem to offer the best chance for advancement?

CHAPTER 11

Making or Buying Clothes

CHAPTER CONTENTS

SECTION 1 · The Sewing Machine

How It All Began

In a small Massachusetts farmhouse, sometime around 1840, the evening quiet was settling in.

Elias Howe was tired after a long day's work. His wife, Elizabeth, was tired, too. But she had to keep sewing the children's new clothes. Their two little girls and small son seemed to be constantly growing out of their garments. Elizabeth sewed everything by hand. It took days to finish each garment.

Elias was concerned about his wife. Her health wasn't good. But they were too poor to hire someone to help her with all the chores she had to do.

As he watched her sew, his mind kept going back to a conversation he had overheard when he worked for Ari Davis in Boston.

Ari Davis's shop was a place where inventors came to talk about their ideas. Davis was a skilled and imaginative machinist. He, too, knew the many hours women had to spend sewing. He was sure a sewing machine could be invented. A number of people had already tried to invent one without success. But Davis boasted that he could do it. He knew it could make a fortune.

Elias was a skilled machinist, too. He believed he could become an inventor because he liked working on new ideas. Besides, his young family needed money desperately. Even more importantly, Elizabeth needed help.

Elias spent several years trying to develop his ideas about making a sewing machine,

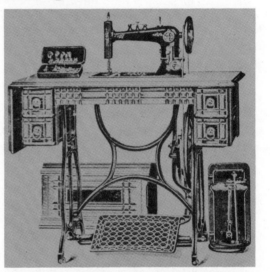

An early sewing machine—based on the inventions of Elias Howe and others.

but none of them seemed to work out. Eventually he decided to try a needle with the eye near the point instead of at the opposite end. That was the breakthrough he needed.

There were more years of trial and error before the machine was perfected and ready to patent. Fortunately for Elias, he was the first to have his invention patented. It was now 1846, six years after he had first tried to make a machine that could sew.

It was several more years before the sewing machine was accepted. Then it revolutionized the clothing industry. It also made Elias Howe a wealthy man.

The invention of the sewing machine in the last century changed the lives of many people. With sewing machines, clothing could be mass-produced in factories. Many families no longer had to sew their own clothes. And for those that did make their own clothing, the sewing machine made the work much easier and faster.

Over the years, the ease and speed of the sewing machine have turned sewing into a creative and money-saving hobby for many people. The sewing machine also saves time mending ripped seams and doing other simple repairs and alterations. Knowing how to use a sewing machine can be of value to almost everyone.

How the Sewing Machine Works

All home sewing machines use Elias Howe's idea to create an interlock stitch. This is a stitch not used in hand sewing, because it requires two threads—one thread above the fabric, and one below.

The needle carries the top thread down through the layers of fabric. There the top thread is caught by a mechanism that winds it around the bottom thread. When the needle comes back up through the fabric, the top thread pulls the bottom thread part way up with it. In a well-adjusted machine, the two threads finish up interlocked in the middle of the layers of fabric.

The fabric is moved along by a part of the machine called a feed dog. The feed dog positions the fabric for the next stitch to be made. The machine repeats this process over and over, creating a strong and even seam.

Though all sewing machines are basically the same, there are many mechanical differences from brand to brand. Before operating a particular machine, you should always read the manufacturer's directions. Keep the book nearby while sewing, in case you run into any problems.

Using the Machine

The sewing machine is a complex instrument capable of doing many different stitches. It must always be treated with care. Its many moving parts are finely adjusted to one another. Whether you are threading the machine or operating it, you need to use the correct technique.

The thread must follow a definite path on its way from the spool to the needle. It's very important to be precise, because each step of that path has a purpose. If you thread the machine incorrectly, the stitches will be poorly formed—or they may not form at all. Box 1 in this section shows how a typical machine is threaded.

The correct techniques, plus an understanding of why they work, will make it easy for you and the machine to turn out excellent work.

Adjusting the Machine

Sewing machines are made so that you can adjust the length of your stitches to suit each sewing job. The stitch regulator changes the length of the stitches by changing the distance that the feed dog moves between each stitch. Most machines have a dial or lever for this purpose.

You can also change the tightness of the stitches by adjusting the tension on the upper thread. This affects the place where the stitches interlock. Ideally, the two threads should interlock between the two fabrics. But if the upper tension is too loose, the lower thread won't be pulled into the fabric. If it's too tight, the lower thread will come right through to the top. In both cases, the stitches will not lock. One thread will just lie upon the surface of the fabric, where it can easily be pulled out. The wrong stitch tension can also make the

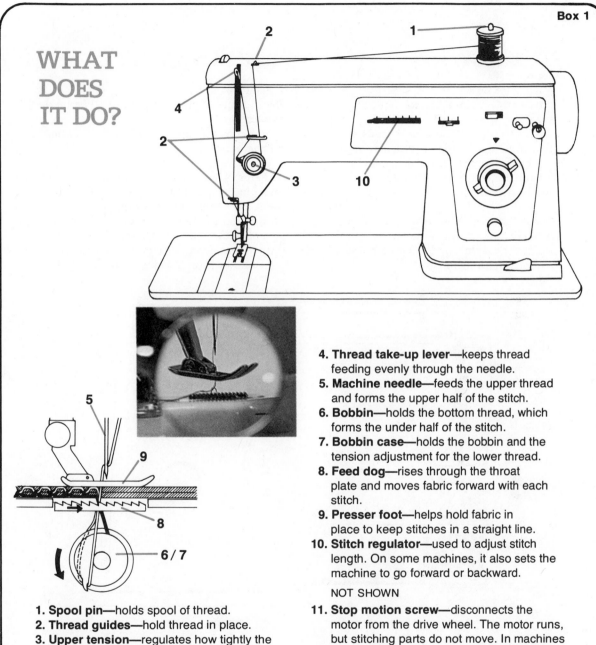

Box 1

WHAT DOES IT DO?

4. **Thread take-up lever**—keeps thread feeding evenly through the needle.
5. **Machine needle**—feeds the upper thread and forms the upper half of the stitch.
6. **Bobbin**—holds the bottom thread, which forms the under half of the stitch.
7. **Bobbin case**—holds the bobbin and the tension adjustment for the lower thread.
8. **Feed dog**—rises through the throat plate and moves fabric forward with each stitch.
9. **Presser foot**—helps hold fabric in place to keep stitches in a straight line.
10. **Stitch regulator**—used to adjust stitch length. On some machines, it also sets the machine to go forward or backward.

NOT SHOWN

1. **Spool pin**—holds spool of thread.
2. **Thread guides**—hold thread in place.
3. **Upper tension**—regulates how tightly the thread is pulled as a stitch is formed. (The tension on upper and lower thread must be just right in order to form secure, even stitches.)

11. **Stop motion screw**—disconnects the motor from the drive wheel. The motor runs, but stitching parts do not move. In machines that use bobbin winders, the sewing motion is stopped while the bobbin winder is in use.
12. **Foot or knee pedal**—controls power of the machine.

Box 2

THE HOW... AND THE WHY

- Make sure needle is in correctly. ——— This keeps stitches from skipping.
- Put stitch regulator on correct number ——— This ensures that the stitches will be made for your type of fabric. correctly.
- Pull both top and bottom threads be- ——— This keeps top thread ends from tangling tween the toes of the presser foot toward in the bobbin. the back before beginning to stitch.
- Turn balance wheel by hand when start- ——— It helps relieve strain on motor in getting ing to stitch. machine started. Controlled start allows more accurate guidance of fabric.
- Guide fabric gently. Never pull it ——— Pulling on the fabric can break the needle through the machine. or cause the seam to pucker.
- Raise thread take-up lever to highest po- ——— This releases pressure on the tension disks sition when finishing stitching. and allows thread to pull through freely.

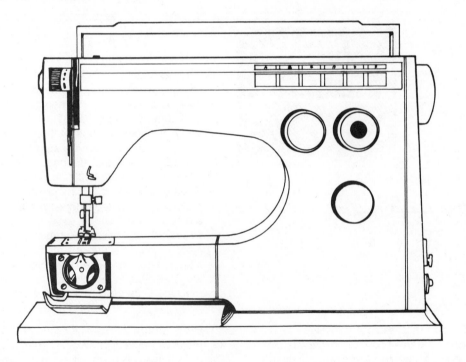

This is a freearm sewing machine. These machines are becoming more and more popular because they make sewing sleeves and trousers much more convenient. Many of today's machines can be converted from freearm, to become more like the flatbed machine shown on the previous page.

seam line pucker, or wrinkle, instead of remaining smooth.

Most tension difficulties can be solved by making an adjustment in the upper tension. It's possible to adjust the tension on the lower thread, too, but this is much more difficult. Many experts recommend leaving such work to professionals.

Special Features and Attachments

The first sewing machines could only stitch plain stitches in a forward direction. They were powered by a hand on the balance wheel. Later machines were operated by a treadle, or foot pedal. Now machines are powered by electricity. And they can do much more than the old machines could do.

Even the simplest sewing machine today can sew in reverse. This makes it very easy to backstitch, anchoring the thread firmly at the ends of a seam. Modern machines also have many special features for many kinds of sewing operations. On some machines, these features are built in. Others require the use of separate attachments.

One feature that has become standard on modern sewing machines is the zigzag stitch. With this stitch, making buttonholes is very easy. It is also used for many other stitches.

A narrow zigzag stitch, for example, can be used to sew stretchy fabric because the stitches will "give" a little with the fabric. This prevents puckered seams and broken threads. Zigzag stitches are also used to overcast, or sew over raw edges, to prevent fraying, to reinforce weak spots, and to attach patches attractively.

Some attachments are so specialized that you may never use them. These include gadgets that make hems, gather ruffles, put

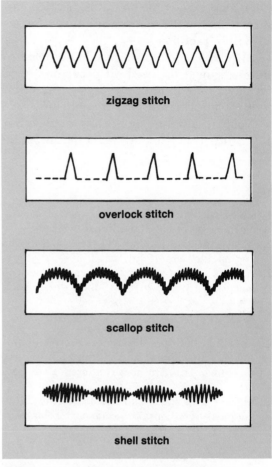

Different sewing machines offer different stitches. The zig-zag is a versatile stitch. The overlock stitch seams and overcasts at the same time. Scallop and shell stitches are used to embroider.

on binding, and make edge stitches. Though it takes some practice to learn to use these attachments, they let you do a stitch in far less time than it would take to do it by hand.

Caring for the Sewing Machine

Like all machinery, the sewing machine needs regular maintenance and careful handling. Where metal moves against metal as the machine operates, friction can put a strain on the motor and cause a harmful build-up of heat.

Although some machines do not need to be oiled, most do need oil occasionally to cut down on friction. Check your direction book for information on *your* machine.

You will also find directions for cleaning in the direction book. All machines must be cleaned regularly to keep the moving parts clear of dust and lint.

The sewing machine is a remarkable invention. It simplifies the work of mending tears, and it is invaluable for doing alterations and making new clothes. Knowing how to use and care for a sewing machine can save you a lot of time and money throughout your life.

QUESTIONS

1. How can knowing how to use a sewing machine be of value to almost everyone?
2. What is an interlock stitch? How does a sewing machine create this stitch?
3. Why is it necessary to thread a sewing machine properly? What does the tension regulator do? What problems can be prevented by regular maintenance?
4. Why wouldn't a needle with the eye near the top be able to create an interlock stitch?
5. If you were buying a sewing machine, what kinds of features would be most important to you? Least important? Why?

ACTIVITIES

1. Find out about the differences between home sewing machines and industrial sewing machines. Describe these differences to your class.
2. Make a wall chart that illustrates the different parts of either your home or the classroom sewing machine.
3. Investigate small battery-operated sewing machines. Debate the pros and cons of purchasing such an item for a single person, a family of four, and a home economics laboratory.

SECTION 2 · How Clothes Are Put Together

What Makes What?

How good are you at solving puzzles? Flat pieces of cloth or paper can often be turned into curved objects. Look at the pictures on this page. There are six different shapes and six objects they can make. Can you pick the right shape for each object?

Correct answers: **A-3:** dunce's cap, **B-6:** baseball, **C-1:** tent top, **D-4:** pouch, **E-2:** sleeve, **F-5:** collar.

Did you ever visit a fabric store and look at bolts of rolled-up cloth? When a salesperson unrolled one of them for a customer, you could see that the fabric was flat and straight.

In fact, fabric is as flat as the shapes at the start of this section. It must be cut into carefully shaped pieces to form a garment. Only by joining the edges and making planned folds in the fabric can you shape the garment to fit the roundness of a body.

Understanding how garments are made will help you to make your own clothes. It will also make you a better judge of the clothing you buy in stores. A consumer who understands how a product is made is better able to determine its quality.

The basic steps in clothing construction can be seen very clearly in the way garments are sewn at home. Once you have chosen a style, the steps are:

- selecting a suitable fabric for the style
- cutting out the right shapes
- fitting and joining the pieces correctly
- sewing them neatly and securely
- finishing and pressing the garment

Fabric

Choosing the right fabric for a style is important. A poor choice of fabric can make a garment look wrong, no matter how well made it is.

Learning which fabrics are suitable for which garments is important. Some clothes—jackets and coats, for instance—need firm fabrics that will hold their shape. Other garments—blouses and sweaters, for example—need softer fabrics that can be molded easily to the body. Studying ready-made clothes can help you learn which fabrics are right for which garments.

Fabrics have other important features. Can they be washed? Do they hold their creases? Do they resist dirt? Knowing your fabric will help you avoid disasters such as swim trunks that shrink and pleated skirts that won't stay pleated.

Patterns

The next step in garment making is cutting the fabric into pieces that will make the style you have selected. Patterns made out of tissue paper help you to do this correctly.

In the past, people had to make their own patterns. They ran the risk of ending up with garment pieces that did not fit to-

gether. Now you can buy patterns that were carefully designed to be accurate. This means that sleeves will fit into their openings properly, and the front of a garment will be the right size for the back.

Patterns come in many sizes and styles. They are sold in variety and department stores, as well as in fabric stores. They can also be ordered directly from the manufacturer.

The different styles that can be made from a basic pattern are pictured on the front of the pattern envelope. The envelope also tells you the kinds of fabric suitable for the garment, the amount of fabric required, and any notions—such as thread, zippers, and buttons—that you will need to make the garment.

The envelope contains all the tissue

Follow the cutting layout that comes with the pattern. It has been carefully planned to make the best use of your fabric without wasting any.

Box 1

GRAIN

Whether you are making clothes or buying them, it's helpful to be able to spot the grain of a fabric. Grain greatly affects the way a garment looks.

Grain is the direction of the yarns that make up the fabric. In a weave, two sets of yarns cross each other at right angles: One set of yarns runs up and down the garment, and the other runs horizontally.

Most woven fabrics will stretch very little if you pull along the yarns in these two directions. But they *will* stretch if you pull at an angle. Therefore, the pull of

gravity may stretch a garment out of shape and cause wrinkles if the yarns are not vertical.

Occasionally, a weave may be cut "on the bias." This means that the yarns run diagonally, at a 45-degree angle to the vertical. Garments cut this way are meant to stretch. It makes them more flowing.

Knits stretch in all directions, but they, too, have a grain, which can affect how they look. The yarn forms rows of tiny interlocked loops. These usually run horizontally across the garment. The vertical grain runs at right angles to these rows.

In a woven . . .

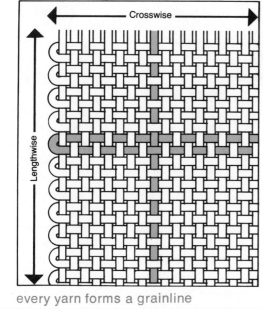

every yarn forms a grainline

In a knit . . .

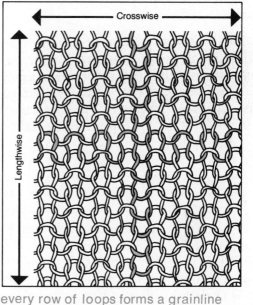

every row of loops forms a grainline

pieces you need for a garment, accurately marked. You will also find a detailed direction sheet, which explains many of the markings on the tissue pieces. This shows you how to position the pieces on the fabric before cutting the shapes. It also gives you step-by-step directions for putting the garment together.

The Layout and Pattern Markings

Pattern layouts serve several purposes. They are planned so that each piece will be placed in the correct direction for cutting (see box 1 in this section). This makes the garment hang properly. It also ensures that garments made with striped, printed, or nap fabric will look right.

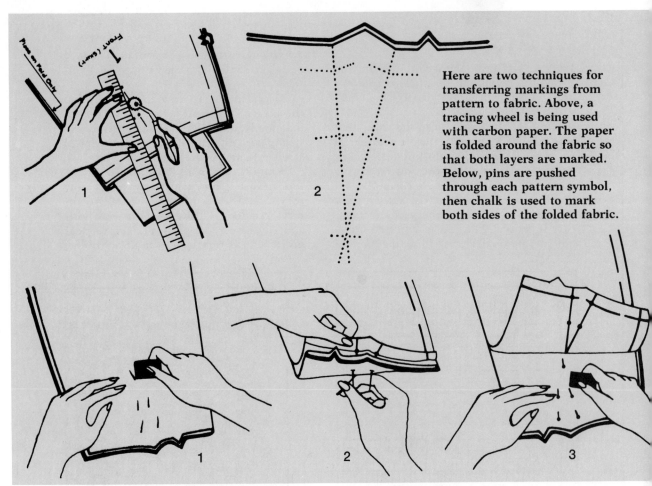

Here are two techniques for transferring markings from pattern to fabric. Above, a tracing wheel is being used with carbon paper. The paper is folded around the fabric so that both layers are marked. Below, pins are pushed through each pattern symbol, then chalk is used to mark both sides of the folded fabric.

Pattern layouts are planned so that you will waste as little cloth as possible. If you don't follow the layout that comes with each pattern, you may find yourself running out of cloth before you have finished laying out all the pattern pieces.

Most of the markings on the pattern pieces are detailed directions on what to do *after* you have cut out the material. Transferring these markings to the cloth is the first stage in fitting the pieces of the garment together accurately. This can be done in several ways.

One way is to slip a piece of special carbon paper between the pattern piece and the fabric. You can then run a tracing wheel over the pattern markings to transfer them to the fabric.

You can also transfer markings with tailor's chalk or with stitching loops called tailor's tacks. You can learn these methods easily from your teacher.

Fitting the Pieces Together

Lining up the pieces correctly is very important. If you don't do this, a collar may be attached to a sleeve, or the two edges of a seam may not match. The edge-notch or other markings on a pattern are your guides here. Baste, or loosely fasten, the garment pieces together with pins as you work.

If you are unsure about fit, it might be a good idea to baste the garment together with large, temporary hand or machine stitches. You can then try it on, check the fit, and make any needed alterations. You *can* try on a garment that has been pinned together, but that will give you a less accurate—and a far less comfortable—fit.

Basting helps in your final stitching by keeping the seams from separating as you work.

Stitching and Pressing

Once you have checked the fit of the garment, you are ready to put the pieces together with permanent machine stitches.

The usual order of stitching is to start with the small folds (called darts, tucks, and pleats) that often give shape to single pieces of the garment. Most pants, for example, have tucks or darts at the top so they go in at the waistline where *you* do.

Next, the pieces should be sewn together. Pressing as you go—that is, after each step—helps shape the garment and makes the next sewing steps easier.

Once the whole garment is sewn together, the fine details are put in. These include buttonholes and buttons or other fastenings, trimmings, and decorations. Hems are turned up and stitched as invisibly as possible. Then comes the final pressing of the completed garment.

The last step is the reward of wearing—and enjoying—what you have made.

Knowing the Answers

As you become aware of the principles of clothing construction, your judgment of ready-made clothes will probably change. Instead of thinking of two questions only—Does it fit? and Do I like it?—you will be able to look with a more expert eye at the construction of a garment. Is the stitching well done? Is the garment well shaped?

Answering such questions will make you a wiser consumer. And knowing the answers may lead you into a profitable hobby—or a rewarding career—in clothing construction.

QUESTIONS

1. How can someone who does not sew benefit from knowing how clothing is constructed?
2. List the five steps in making a garment.
3. What is the value of a pattern? What does the pattern layout help you do? What information do the pattern markings provide?
4. Which of the principles of clothing construction that you learned in this section do you think will be most helpful to you in choosing clothing? Why?
5. Some companies now make patterns with several sizes all printed on the same sheet. You cut out each piece in the size you want. What is the advantage of this type of pattern?
6. It is very difficult to make an even hem on a garment that has been cut off-grain. Why do you think this is so?

ACTIVITIES

1. Compare pattern directions from two companies for the same simple garment. Which directions do you think are easier to understand? Why?
2. Make a poster showing the basic tools needed at each step of garment construction.
3. Find a clothing pattern for a garment you really like. Look at the list of suggested fabrics. Why do you think these fabrics were chosen? Select a fabric *not* on the list, and discuss what might happen if the garment was made from this fabric.

SECTION 3 · How Clothes Are Manufactured

Different—but the Same

The equipment is different, but the steps followed by the home sewer in making a garment are much the same as those in the factory process. Before you read on, can you figure out what is happening in the factory, and why it's being done this way?

THE FACTORY PROCESS

A garment made at home has to be laid out, cut, sewn, finished, and pressed. The same operations are done in the factory—the garment is laid out (1), cut (2), sewn (3), finished (4), and pressed (5). Same operations—but the techniques are usually different.

Every year, millions of new dresses, pants, skirts, coats, suits, shirts, and underwear appear in stores. They come in every size, shape, and price range. Mass production provides us with these choices.

In home sewing, one person usually makes the complete garment. In contrast, manufactured clothes—called ready-made or ready-to-wear—are mass produced by groups of workers, each doing a specific job.

The United States was the first country to develop mass-produced clothes that could fit most people and sell at a reasonable cost. Today, the garment industry is one of the largest in North America. There are thousands of clothing factories on the continent.

Where It All Starts

The manufacture of clothing starts with design. First, sketches are made of various ideas. These ideas may come from the designer's sense of fashion trends, or they may be adaptations of high-fashion styles.

The best sketches are chosen for making samples. Sample patterns are cut from an inexpensive material called muslin. When the designer is satisfied with the pattern, a sample garment is sewn in a fabric suitable for the style.

The sample is made to fit a fashion model, who will present the style to store buyers in a showroom. If the sample garment attracts enough buyers, the style will go into production.

Industrial Patterns

As in home sewing, a pattern is needed to guide the cutting of the fabric. But industrial patterns get much greater use than home patterns, and they must last much longer. Therefore, they are made of cardboard rather than tissue.

To avoid costly errors, one test garment, called a duplicate, is sewn from this original pattern. If this were not done, thousands of garments might be produced before anyone found a mistake in the pattern. That could mean disaster for the company.

The next step is to grade the pattern. This means making separate pattern pieces for all sizes that the firm manufactures.

Finally, outlines of all the pattern pieces are transferred to a marker, a long sheet of paper that will be placed on top of the fabric to be cut. The marker must be laid out in the most economical way.

If the marker is poorly planned, a lot of fabric may be wasted. The cost of this waste would be passed on to the consumer. Incorrect planning could also result in off-grain cutting. This means the fabric yarn would run in the wrong direction and the garment would hang awkwardly.

Once the marker has been planned, the amount of fabric needed for the garments can be calculated and bought. Buttons, zippers, and threads (called notions, or findings) are also ordered at this stage. Before the fabric and findings are used, they are inspected for quality and possible damage.

Cutting the Layers

After it passes inspection, the fabric is spread on long cutting tables. It is spread many layers thick so that a lot of garments can be cut at the same time. If the fabric is a plaid or stripe that has to be matched, each layer of fabric must be positioned with great accuracy.

After the fabric is laid up on the cutting table, the marker is placed over it. It is then cut with an electric knife. Tiny holes are drilled into the pieces to mark the positions of darts, tucks, and so forth. Then the pieces are tied in bundles and sent to the sewing section of the factory.

Sewing the Garments

In most clothing factories, the sewing work on a single garment is divided among many people. This division of work resembles an assembly line in an automobile factory. And, as in an automobile factory, supervisors inspect the work as it goes from operator to operator. That way, mistakes can be corrected before the next step is taken.

Generally, the less expensive the garment, the more workers engaged in producing it. Workers who do just one sewing job all the time become very skilled and fast at it. This saves time and money.

In a factory, there are different kinds of sewing machines, all meant to speed up production. One machine, for example, can stitch, trim, and bind a seam, all in one operation. Some machines can sew on buttons and do other tasks that the home sewer must do slowly by hand. Others can perform several tasks at the same time.

In the garment industry, sewing machine operators are often classified by the kind of work they do—for example, "collar stitchers" or "sleeve finishers."

Details and Pressing

If the factory produces expensive clothes, the finishing details, such as hems, fasteners, and trimmings, are done by hand. The details on moderately priced clothing are usually machine-sewn. However, handwork is sometimes found on even low-priced garments from abroad. This is possible because the workers' wages are lower than those in North America.

Although stitched sections of a garment get a quick pressing as they move from operator to operator, the final pressing is important. It molds the garment into its proper shape and makes it look "ready-to-wear."

Garments that have durable-press finishes are heat-treated in special ovens. This sets the fabric into the desired permanent shape.

The Pressures of the Industry

To produce the clothes people need at a price they are willing to pay, the ready-to-wear industry works to avoid waste and cut costs.

Waste may occur during production, of course. But it may also occur if garments don't sell before styles change. Therefore, factories usually plan to make less rather than more than they think they can sell. And they don't buy fabrics and trimmings they may not need.

If the stores want more garments before the season ends, factories must order more fabric and make another production lot of the garments. This means that they can't plan their work too far in advance.

Because money can't be saved by long-term planning, it has to be saved in other ways. Speed is the main money saver. The more garments workers make each day, the

---

Box 1

Factory Outlets

Many clothing factories have bargain outlets that allow customers to take advantage of their mistakes. Factory outlets usually carry both first-quality garments and imperfect ones. The first-quality clothes are often there because a store canceled its order at the last minute. These garments are almost always good buys.

Imperfect garments fall into two categories—irregulars and seconds. **Irregulars** have minor flaws that you may not even notice. These flaws usually do not affect either the garment's appearance or how well it will wear. A slightly crooked seam and a tiny misprint in the fabric are typical flaws.

Seconds, on the other hand, have very noticeable defects, such as holes and tears. Sometimes these have been mended in the factory, leaving obvious stitching lines. Seconds are cheaper than irregulars, and they may suit certain purposes. But if you buy seconds without realizing it, you may be out of luck when you go back to complain about the hole under the arm. Most factory outlets sell "as is"—you can't get your money back. So look before you buy.

If you shop carefully, you can get a lot for your money in a factory outlet.

---

less each garment costs to produce. Speed also helps get out last-minute orders.

This pressure for speed sometimes leads to poor work. A machine operator may be working too fast and sew some crooked seams. One or two of these may be missed by the supervisor, who is hurrying to inspect all the work.

More frequently, some detail in finishing the garment may be missed—securing a button, for example, or finishing a buttonhole.

Before buying a garment, make sure that it is well constructed, or at least that any flaws can be easily corrected.

Consumer Beware

You should be on the lookout for such errors—particularly in less expensive garments, where the pressure to keep costs down is greatest. There may be a flaw in the fabric that was missed on the cutting table. A hem may be crooked. A seam may not be well finished.

Some of these errors you may not mind. But others could spoil your enjoyment of the garment and may be hard to fix. So check some of these points, as well as the general appearance and fit of the garment, before you buy it. There may be an identical garment on the rack that is better made. It will look, fit, and wear better.

QUESTIONS

1. What is the basic difference between the way a garment is made in a home and the way it is made in a factory?
2. Why can't mass-producers of clothing plan their work far in advance? What method do they use to save money? How does this method affect the consumer?
3. What are the advantages of mass production? List the steps in mass-producing clothing.

What role do supervisors have in this process?
4. Some clothing factories allow workers to switch tasks from time to time. Why do you think they do this?
5. Some people consider the cutter the person with the most responsibility in a garment factory. Why do you think this is so?
6. Why might a designer put false pockets on a garment instead of real ones?

ACTIVITIES

1. Find out the locations of factory outlets in your area. If possible, visit one and describe the selection and prices to your class.

2. Write a report on the rise of unions in the garment industry in the 1920s.
3. Make a chart illustrating the work flow in a garment factory.

SECTION 4 · Understanding and Judging Fabrics

Three Strikes and You're Out

1. Scott was very pleased when his older brother gave him a pair of lightweight khaki pants. He had wanted a pair for some time, but he had very little money to spend on clothes. So his brother's hand-me-down pants were very welcome. The pants were a perfect fit. They felt good, and cool.

But there was one drawback. They needed frequent washing because of the color, and then they always needed pressing. Somebody, usually Scott, had to spend time ironing them.

2. When Scott had saved some money, he made a trip to the thrift shop. There he looked for pants that didn't need ironing. He checked all the labels, and came up with a pair that felt terrific—they were really lightweight, and they were permanent press.

These pants weren't perfect either, unfortunately. Scott found that out when he wore them on a hot day. Although they were very light, the pants seemed to act like a greenhouse. Air didn't get through, and they didn't absorb moisture. He could feel prickly perspiration dripping from his legs.

3. For his birthday, Scott's parents told him to pick out some new pants. He went to a local store and tried several pairs, finally coming up with a pair that seemed perfect.

He showed them to his parents. When his father looked at the label, he pointed out that these pants had to be dry-cleaned. And for a pair of everyday pants, dry cleaning wasn't practical.

Scott was ready to give up. "Can't I even find one pair of pants without a major problem?" he said.

There are dozens of kinds of fabrics. Some are light enough to see through. Others are heavy enough to be used for trampolines. There are fabrics to keep you warm, fabrics to keep you cool, and fabrics to keep you waterproof!

The care of all these fabrics differs. Some can be cleaned with soap and water. Others mustn't get wet and need to be "dry" cleaned with special chemicals.

By learning about different fabrics, you can find out how to keep your clothes looking their best. That will help you look *your* best. You can also find out which fabrics suit your needs when you are buying or making new garments.

Fabrics Start with Fibers

Fibers are the basic ingredients of all fabrics. They are fine, hairlike strands. Some fibers are produced by nature. Others are manufactured. Fibers give fabrics many of their basic qualities.

Most fabrics are made from fibers that have been spun together into yarns. However, a few, such as felt, are made by shrinking and pressing fibers together until they are tightly tangled in a mat. Felt is thought to be the oldest fabric of all.

Natural Fibers

Until the end of the last century, all fabrics were made from natural fibers. With these

Wool (below) and cotton (above) are the natural fibers most commonly used in clothing. Here you see the fibers, yarn, and fabric.

Box 1

Natural Fibers

Natural fibers come from plants or animals. The four main fabrics from these fibers are cotton (from cotton plants), wool (from sheep and other animals), silk (from silkworms), and linen (from the flax plant).

COTTON

- is soft, strong, absorbent, comfortable to wear
- takes finishes easily because it's stronger when wet
- can be sterilized in very hot water
- dyes well
- blends with other fibers
- wrinkles easily unless specially treated or blended with synthetics

WOOL

- is warm
- dyes very well
- is naturally water-repellent
- can be damaged by moths
- usually must be dry-cleaned
- resists wrinkles

SILK

- is a luxury fiber
- can be dyed many colors
- is a very strong fiber
- should generally be dry-cleaned, but can be hand washed
- is soft, flexible, and resilient

LINEN

- is strong, cool, and absorbent
- washes well
- wrinkles easily if not treated

natural fibers, people made quite a variety of fabrics, from heavy woolens and sturdy linens to sheer silks and cottons.

Natural fibers come from plants or animals. The most commonly used plant fiber is cotton. Cotton fibers grow in the seed pod of the cotton plant. Sheep's wool is the most frequently used animal fiber. The hair of several other animals, such as alpacas and camels, is also used for wool.

Most natural fibers are fairly short—cotton fibers are rarely more than two inches, or five centimeters, long. A yarn can be made only by spinning them together. But there is one animal fiber that comes already spun—silk.

Silk is made by the silkworm. The worm spins a very long fiber to form a cocoon around itself. In nature, the cocoon is designed to protect the worm as it turns into a moth. A silk fiber can be as much as half a mile long. The long, smooth natural fiber of silk is what makes it such a soft, smooth fabric. It also makes it expensive. Unwrapping the fiber from the cocoon takes careful, skilled work. Several fibers are usually twisted together to make a heavier yarn.

Manufactured Fibers

Fibers manufactured entirely from chemicals are called synthetic. Rayon, the first manufactured fiber, is only partially synthetic since the main ingredient, cellulose, comes from plants. The fiber, however, is formed by mechanical means. Rayon fibers can be made as long as silk fibers. In fact, rayon was called artificial silk when it was developed, almost 100 years ago.

Today there are also other partially synthetic fibers. Acetate and triacetate too are made from cellulose.

The first wholly synthetic fiber, nylon, was developed shortly before World War II. Made from petroleum and other chemicals, it wasn't available for general use until after the war.

Continued textile research produced polyester, acrylic, and several other synthetic fibers. Although these fibers differ in some of their properties, they are all relatively strong and wrinkle-free.

Yarns

Fibers have been spun into yarns for thousands of years. The fibers are overlapped and twisted together to make a heavier yarn.

Long, straight fibers usually create smooth, silky strands; short, curly fibers tend to make softer and fluffier strands. The thickness of the strands also depends on how tightly the fibers are spun.

Often several strands are twisted together to make a heavier yarn. When you

---

Box 2

Cellulosic Fibers

The basic substance of cellulosic fibers is cellulose, which comes mainly from wood pulp.

RAYON
- absorbs moisture
- can be dyed many colors
- blends well with other fibers
- may not be washable
- wrinkles easily
- can be dry-cleaned
- is a low-cost fiber

ACETATE
- has attractive silklike appearance
- holds shape well
- can be dyed many colors
- usually must be dry-cleaned
- is not a strong fiber

TRIACETATE
- is washable
- can be permanently pleated
- resists wrinkles
- needs less ironing than rayon or acetate

Box 3

Synthetic Fibers

The synthetic fibers that are totally manufactured from chemical elements are based on petroleum, natural gas, coal, air, water, alcohol, and limestone.

The following synthetic fibers are used in clothing:

ACRYLIC

- is a substitute for wool and does not cause allergy
- is both lightweight and warm
- resists wrinkles
- can be washed or dry-cleaned
- is not susceptible to moths
- is sensitive to heat—wash in warm water and never use hot iron
- blends well with many fibers

MODACRYLIC

- is often used in fake furs and pile fabrics
- will not burn
- should generally be dry-cleaned (if a pile fabric or "fur")
- can be washed in warm water (if a flat fabric)
- dries quickly, therefore useful in outer garments

NYLON

- is strong and lightweight
- dries quickly, is easy to wash
- blends well with other fibers for increased strength and ease of care
- keeps its shape well
- can be dry-cleaned
- doesn't absorb moisture well, may be uncomfortable in humid weather, and may create static electricity in cold, dry

POLYESTER

- is the best wash-and-wear fiber
- resists wrinkles
- keeps its shape well
- is strong
- is the best fiber for permanent press
- blends well with other fibers
- can be dry-cleaned
- holds oily stains

SPANDEX

- is a synthetic elastic fiber
- has excellent stretch and recovery
- combines with other fibers to make stretch fabrics
- is washable—but avoid chlorine bleach

VINYL

- is a substitute for leather
- can be wiped clean with damp cloth
- can't be dry-cleaned
- is used in rainwear because of waterproof qualities

---

look at garment labels, you may see "100% cotton" or "100% polyester." More often you will see that the fabric is a blend of two or more fibers or yarns.

Blending, or combining different types of fibers, takes advantage of the best characteristics of each of the fibers in the blend. A polyester and cotton blend, for example, has the look, feel, and much of the absorbency of cotton. The polyester makes the fabric wrinkle-resistant and easy to care for.

Knit Fabrics

Knitting is one way of turning yarns into fabrics. Knit fabrics are made by looping yarn together, row after row, with special needles. Knitting can be done with just a single yarn.

Many people knit sweaters by hand, as a hobby. The knit fabrics used for suits, skirts, and other garments, however, are made by machine. These machines can produce many different types of knit, including the popular double-knits.

Knits are very popular because they have many desirable qualities. They shape to your body for an easy, comfortable fit. They stretch with movement, but return to their original size and shape. They do not wrinkle easily, even when crushed into a small space. And any wrinkles that do form will hang out quickly.

Knit fabrics are comfortable to wear even when they are made from fibers that don't absorb moisture. This is because there is usually enough space between the yarns for air to move through the fabric.

Knit fabrics are generally less costly to produce than woven fabrics. Knits are used to make everything from panty hose and T-shirts to sports jackets and evening gowns.

Woven Fabrics

Weaving is another method of fabric construction. It, too, produces many kinds of fabrics. Weaving is the interlacing of sets of yarns. One set of yarns is lined up in tight rows on a loom. Then another set of yarns is passed over and under these rows, from side to side. You may have done this yourself on a hand loom.

Industrial looms can produce many different woven patterns. Different weaves create different fabrics. The weave can determine whether the fabric will be soft or crisp, cool or warm.

Until recently, weaving was the most common method of fabric construction. Woven fabrics still have certain advantages. Their compact construction allows them to hold their shape more firmly. It often makes them more wind- and water-resistant. And weaves are often sturdier than knits, which may run, ravel, or snag with use.

Nonwoven Fabrics

Nonwoven fabrics are usually made from matted fibers. They share one special quality—their edges do not fray or ravel when cut. That means they need no special finishing. Felt, for example, is a nonwoven fabric. A felt skirt does not need to be hemmed. It can simply be cut to the right length. Felt is often used to decorate other garments.

The clean, smooth edges of nonwoven fabrics make them suitable for special uses. Many nonwoven fabrics are used where they are never seen—on the inside of garments. These "hidden" fabrics help the garment hold its form. They may give needed firmness to a collar, or shape to a shoulder.

Three of the above fabrics are identified below. Are the others knits, wovens, or nonwovens?

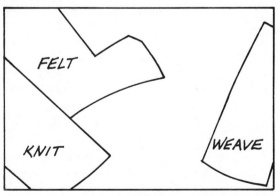

Some nonwoven fabrics are made so that they will melt when heat is applied to them. These fusible webs, as they are called, are used to attach one layer of fabric to another. Putting up a hem with fusible web is much faster than sewing. Facings and small decorations can also be attached in this manner.

Other Fabrics

Bonded fabrics go one step further. They are actually made from two different fabrics, sealed together with adhesive.

Fabrics are bonded to make them stronger and warmer. A loose knit, for example, may be bonded to a tightly woven fabric so that it will not stretch. Or fabrics may be bonded to a layer of foam to provide lightweight warmth for coats and jackets.

Some materials used for clothing are not made of fibers at all. These include natural materials such as leather and fur, and synthetic ones such as plastic and vinyl. These materials are used especially for coats, jackets, and rainwear.

Dyeing and Finishing

Fabrics come in thousands of colors and designs. A very few of these colors occur naturally in fibers such as wool. The great majority of colors, however, come from dyes. If it weren't for dyes, most of our clothes would be grayish white.

Dyes can be applied to fabrics at every stage, beginning with the fibers themselves. In synthetic fibers, dyes may even be added to the chemicals *before* they are made into fibers.

Dyeing can also be done after the fibers are spun into yarns. Yarn dyeing is one of

An entire fashion line may be planned around a certain color. Dyeing huge quantities of fabric at one time ensures that garments produced will be uniform in color.

the oldest ways of applying color to fabric. Designs can be made by weaving or knitting together different-colored yarns.

Dyeing the finished fabric is the most widely used method of dyeing. Sometimes the entire fabric is soaked in a dye bath. To make designs, though, the dye can be applied by printing it on the fabric. That allows many different colors to be used.

Besides color, other finishes are also applied to fabrics. These finishes can greatly change the qualities of the fabric. Through various finishing methods, the same piece of cloth can be turned into a number of different fabric types.

Some finishes change the look of fabrics by making them much shinier or softer than they were originally—they add texture. Other finishes improve the performance of fabrics. They may prevent shrinkage and wrinkling. Or they may make fabrics mothproof, fireproof, or waterproof.

Labels and Other Laws

Many different fibers are used to make clothing. These are manufactured into many different types of fabrics, and then treated with a variety of dyes and finishes. Each fabric requires different care.

In the past, consumers had to play a guessing game with their clothes. They had to figure out what each garment was made of. Then they had to guess how to care for it. Sometimes they guessed wrong.

Today, however, laws make guesswork unnecessary. Garment manufacturers must provide labels that name the fibers used. Instructions for washing, drying, and dry-cleaning must be sewn into clothing. You can obtain similar care instructions when you buy fabric to make a garment.

You should look for these labels when you shop so that you know what to expect from a purchase. A label may tell you that the trimming fabric must be removed before washing. This is a nuisance, but you may decide that you like the garment enough to put up with it. Or a garment may need to be washed by hand. You may decide that your schedule is so busy that you can't spare the time to wash it.

The labeling laws are meant to inform and protect you when you buy or make your clothes. If you follow label directions, your clothes should not fade, shrink, or wrinkle easily. Because of the great variety of finished fabrics used in clothing today, you need every piece of information you can get.

QUESTIONS

1. What is the relationship between fibers and fabrics? What are the basic sources of natural fibers? Synthetic fibers? How are yarns made?
2. What are the two basic methods for turning yarns into fabrics? What are the basic differences between fabrics made in these two ways? What other factors contribute to the characteristics of a fabric?
3. What information can be gained from reading the label on a garment? Give examples of what can happen to specific types of fabric if they are cared for improperly.
4. What kind of fabric do you think would be best for Scott's pants? Why?
5. What qualities would you look for in fabrics to be worn in warm weather? In cold weather?
6. Why do you think permanent-press garments can get permanent wrinkles if put into a hot dryer?

ACTIVITIES

1. Make a collage using as many different types of fabric as you can find.
2. Make a report on ways to dye yarns and fabrics using fruits, vegetables, and other natural substances.
3. Using a book on weaving, make a poster that shows in detail several basic types of weave.
4. Question your local dry cleaner on the subject of bonded fabrics. Ask if bonded fabrics present any special problems.

SECTION 5 · Judging Cut and Fit

A Question of Structure

Sarah is sorry she ever bought her new shirt. It feels uncomfortable, and it comes untucked every time she reaches across the table. It bothers her, too, that the design is printed in one direction on the front and in another direction on the back. Sarah wishes she hadn't been in such a hurry at the store.

Harvey tried on the sports jacket he'd borrowed from Frank to wear to the dance, and discovered that the sleeves felt too tight. Frank and Harvey were about the same height and weight, so why didn't the coat fit?

Carlos had struck out three batters in a row and was well on his way to the hall of fame. Then, at the top of the sixth inning, the seam in his pants split. Carlos had to retire for repairs.

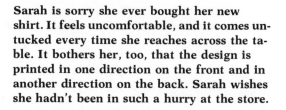

Sarah, Carlos, and Harvey are all having problems with how their garments fit. When garments don't fit right, they don't look right. They may be uncomfortable as well.

A good fit gives you plenty of room to breathe and allows you to move easily in your clothes. A good fit means that the cut of the clothes is right for your body.

Shopping Problems

If you are still growing, shopping for clothes can be a new experience every time you go to a store. You may be a different size or a different shape than you were the last time you shopped. Your ideas about styles may have changed also. But whatever your size or shape or style preferences, you want your clothes to fit right.

Clothes that fit properly and are well made can make you look good and feel comfortable. When a garment doesn't fit right or is poorly cut, it can rip at the seams—like Carlos's pants—or cause other problems—like Sarah's shirt.

A dress or shirt that seemed attractive in the store may lose its charm if it pulls on your shoulders every time you try to move. And if a garment rips, you will be even more annoyed. You can avoid problems like these by learning to judge the fit or cut of a garment.

Judging a Good Cut

Before a garment is sewn together, the pieces are cut out for the planned size and style. If the fabric isn't cut correctly, there will be something wrong with the way the garment moves on you.

Sarah's shirt, for example, wasn't cut right. The shirt pulled out at the slightest reach because it wasn't cut long enough.

Box 1

Fitting Points to Look for in Garments

When you stand straight, garments should be free of wrinkles, bulges, and gaps caused by too snug or too loose a fit.

Check that:
- center front and back of pants legs hang straight to the floor
- darts, if used, point to the fullest part of the body and do not extend beyond it
- the cut of the garment allows room to move, reach, and stretch without straining seams
- the neckline lies flat on the body without bulging
- a fitted waistline hugs your own waist

The fact that the design ran in different directions on the front and the back also shows careless work. The pattern pieces were not laid out in the same direction as the print on the cloth. If stripes or plaids are not carefully matched when a garment is cut, it won't be as attractive.

Finding Your Range

When you buy clothes, make sure that they are carefully cut—and cut to fit *your* body. The first step in buying clothes that fit is to find the size range that is right for you.

Teenagers grow at very different rates. Their body proportions change as they grow, which makes it hard for manufacturers to make one style that fits all. This is why there are different size ranges of clothes for teenage boys and girls. (A table showing these size ranges is given on p. 489 at the back of this book.)

If you are a boy, you may find that your shoulders and chest are much broader than they were last year. Check the sizes in the

Box 2

Taking Your Measurements

Depending on the garment you're buying, you will need to take different measurements to determine your size.

In a man's shirt, for example, neck and sleeve measurements are most important. For a woman's dress, the measurements needed to find the right size are bust, waist, and hips.

To find out what size you wear, take your measurements according to the following instructions. Then compare your measurements to those on a size chart. Most clothing stores have size charts available; some sample charts are given at the back of this book (on p. 489).

HOW TO MEASURE

Measuring to check your size is not difficult. Remember to stand naturally, and to hold the tape taut, but not tight.

Height: Stand against the wall (barefooted). Have another person make a mark level with the top of your head. Measure from this point to the floor.

Bust or Chest: Measure over the fullest part of the bust or chest, with the tape straight across the back.

Waist: Measure the smallest part of the natural waistline.

Hips: Measure at the fullest part of the hips in a straight line around the body.

In-seam: Place pants that are the correct length on a flat surface. Measure along inner seam from the bottom of one leg to where the two legs meet.

Neckband: Measure around the fullest part of the neck for neckband size, adding ½ in or 1 cm for wearing ease.

Sleeve: Bend arm up. Measure from base of neck across center back to elbow, across elbow crook, and up over wrist bone.

Accurate measurements can help you select garments which fit perfectly.

various other ranges besides the "boys" range. You might find a better fit. However, if you are slim, stick with the boys range for a while. A jacket that is too big can be as awkward and uncomfortable as one you have outgrown.

If you are a girl, there are even more ranges to choose from. You may wear "young teen," "junior," or "misses" clothes. If you select from the wrong range, your clothes will probably neither look good nor be comfortable.

Finding Your Own Size

Once you've located the right size range, the next step is to find your exact size.

This usually means measuring your own body. For directions on how to do this, see box 2 in this section. Measure yourself whether you are buying ready-made clothes or patterns to make your own clothes.

Knowing your exact measurements makes shopping easier. Boys' and girls' jeans, for example, are often sold by waist and in-seam measurements. The many lengths and waist sizes available in jeans usually make alterations unnecessary. (Boys' pants are often sold unhemmed. The pants must be hemmed to the correct length after they are sold.)

Some clothes—particularly sweaters, T-shirts, and other stretch garments—are marked small, medium, and large. With these sizes, the only way to know what will fit you is to try on the clothes.

Buying for Growth

Buying clothes that will fit for several seasons is not easy when you are constantly growing. But it is an important consideration when shopping for clothes—especially if you have to watch your budget.

Pants (and skirts) with elastic or drawstrings at the waistline allow for a certain amount of growth. However, not many boys' styles incorporate such features.

When choosing new clothes, check whether they allow for growth or can be altered if your size changes. For example, on some waistbands the buttons can be moved a little. Some hems can be let down without leaving a marked crease—especially if the fabric isn't a solid color. Other styles such as sweatshirts or jogging suits look all right if they are extra roomy to begin with.

So when you buy clothes, consider the fact that you will be growing. And, to get the most for your money, plan to get as much wear as possible out of garments while they fit.

Fit and How You Feel

Knowing the basic facts about fit will help you find clothes that are cut right and that fit you well. Fit is very personal. It affects how you feel and the way you move in your clothes. Well-fitting clothes can give you the satisfying feeling that you look your best.

QUESTIONS

1. What kinds of problems can occur if your clothing does not fit properly?
2. Why are there different size ranges? What two points should you remember when measuring yourself?
3. What special problem do people in your age group often have when buying clothes? How can you take this problem into account when choosing garment styles?
4. Why is it that clothes made by one manufacturer fit you just right, but the same-size clothes made by another manufacturer do not?
5. What kinds of movements should you make to check the fit of a pair of pants? A shirt?
6. Describe some situations in which the future fit of a garment would not be a consideration when shopping.

ACTIVITIES

1. Make a list of all the different sizes of clothes in your wardrobe. What does this list tell you about shopping for clothes?
2. Using a pattern book or a mail-order catalog, compare the styles offered in clothing for teen sizes with those for adult sizes. What kinds of differences are there? Draw pictures to illustrate these differences.
3. Choose a garment from your wardrobe that fits especially well and is comfortable. Compare your measurements with those of the garment. What does this tell you about the amount of extra room, or ease, you need to be comfortable in a similar garment?

SECTION 6 · Understanding Basic Construction

A JOKE IS A JOKE

You've probably seen this comedy routine many times—one person tugs on another's jacket, and it just falls apart. These garments are deliberately made with loose stitches and weak seams so that they will come apart easily and make us laugh.

That quality of work in the clothes we wear ourselves would make us cry! We want our own garments to have snug stitches and strong seams, so they won't fall apart.

Good construction may not belong in a comedy routine, but it *does* belong in our clothes.

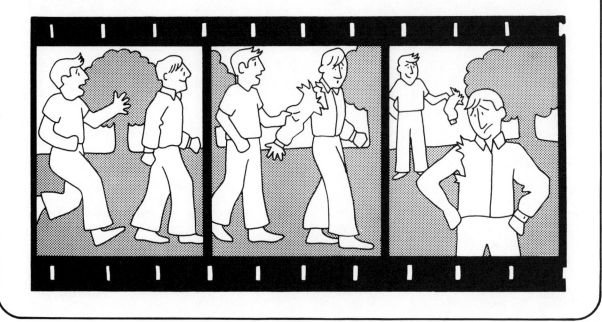

You have tried on a garment and decided that it is well cut. It hangs properly and the fit is comfortable—neither too tight nor too loose for the style. Now is the time to see how the sewing part of the construction was done.

The Seams

Seams are the basic lines of stitching that join the pieces of a garment. If the seams are badly made, a garment may tear or fall apart.

The most common seam is the open seam. The two pieces are stitched together, usually about one-half inch from the edge of the fabric (for home sewing, ⅝ in or 15 mm is the standard). Then the edges are pressed open. This seam can be used on all woven fabrics, and on many knit ones as well.

To examine the strength of a seam, pull gently on each side of a seam line, as though you were trying to pull it apart. If you see more than a pin dot of space between the stitches, you will know that the seam might split if too much strain is put on it. All seams should be smooth and even.

You can check seams in more detail by looking at:

• the type of thread used (how well does it match the fabric, and how strong is it?)
• the size of the stitching (how close together are the stitches?)
• the type of seam (see box 1 in this section)

Checking the Thread

When you examine the seams, you should note what kind of thread was used in the stitching. Fabric should be sewn with thread of similar fiber content. This way, the thread and fabric will take the same kind of use and care. If the thread and fabric are made of different types of fiber, the thread may shrink and make the fabric pucker. Or the fabric may shrink, making the thread seem loose.

The fiber content of the thread used in a ready-made garment is not usually shown on a label. However, you can see if the color and texture of the thread match the fabric. On thick and heavy fabrics, the thread should be heavy and strong. On thin, delicate fabrics, a finer thread should be used.

You may have seen garments sewn with a clear no-color nylon thread. This is often called invisible thread, and is never used in better garments. That's because it melts when touched by a moderately warm iron. Unless you intend to resew the seams right away, avoid buying a garment sewn with this thread.

Different Stitches for Different Fabrics

The number of stitches for every inch of seam depends partly on the type of fabric. Heavy, thick cloth can have only eight or ten per inch. Thin or sheer fabrics take as many as fifteen—though the thread is finer, the seam can be as strong.

All stitches should lie flat on both sides of the seam. Loops in the thread mean the sewing machine wasn't properly adjusted.

Knit fabrics with a lot of stretch to them are often sewn with a zigzag stitch. This allows the seam to have as much "give" as the fabric.

Seam Widths and Finishes

A seam that is stitched too near the edge of the fabric is likely to pull apart easily. That is why fabric is left on each edge of a seam. This is known as the seam allowance. It keeps the stitches from running off the edge. It also allows you to let out the garment as you grow.

Box 1

Special Seams for Special Needs

The double-stitched seams you often see on jeans are called flat-fell seams. They are used on garments and articles that get a lot of wear. Work clothes, active sportswear, camping gear—all use this strong seam.

Top stitching may be used for decoration on most fabrics. A blazer usually has top stitching around the edges of the collar. Top stitching also helps to keep the edges flat and in place. Look for it on polyester fabrics, where it can give a sharp edge to a cloth that does not crease easily.

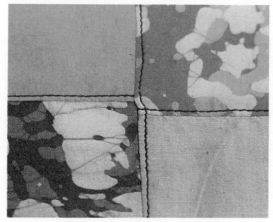

The French seam is used to enclose the edges of sheer, delicate fabrics to keep the edges from raveling. Delicate, sheer blouses and lingerie have this finish. French seams are also often used for clothes which may have to stand up to frequent washing.

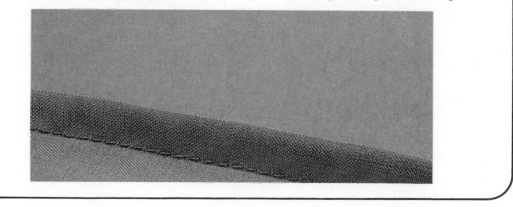

Even with a seam allowance, the seam could come apart if the edges ravel enough. To keep this from happening, seam allowances are usually "finished."

Seams on some fabrics can be "pinked," giving them a special zigzag, saw-toothed edge. The tiny points are much less likely to ravel. With many new fabrics, however, the seam allowance should be overcast with loops of thread over the edges of the fabric. Seams may also be finished with a zigzag stitch, or with a plain straight stitch near the edge.

All these finishes help hold the fabric edges together so they won't ravel. Fabrics that don't ravel, such as felt, can be left without any finish.

Shaping the Garment

Another important question in judging construction is: How is the fabric shaped to fit the curves of the body? There are several different methods of shaping, depending on the garment design. Knowing something about each method will make you a wiser clothing consumer.

One method is simply to shape the seams. If two edges are cut with carefully designed curves, when they are sewn together, they will give shape to the garment. Very few seams are the result of joining two straight edges. Shape is designed into most garments during the cutting of the fabric.

Frequently, though, more shaping is needed. The back of a shirt may need to be a little looser, or fuller, than the shoulders. The hips of a garment must be fuller than the waist. If the cut does not provide enough shaping, extra shaping can be given by folding the fabric as it is sewn together.

Darts, Tucks, and More

A **dart** looks like a seam from the outside of a garment, except that it suddenly stops in the middle of the fabric. It is a stitched down fold that provides fullness where the body rounds out, and takes the garment in where the body comes in. You will often find darts on a pair of slacks between the waist and hips. You will also find darts on

Darts help shape a garment to the body.

Tucks can both shape and decorate.

shaped jackets—from the chest to the waist, and often from the chest to the armpit.

When judging darts, look for these two aspects of their construction:

- Darts should taper gradually to a point and give a rounded appearance to the garment on the outside.
- Threads at each end of the dart should be knotted or secured in some way so that they do not pull loose.

A **tuck** is a small stitched fold that doesn't taper at the end. Instead, the fabric is allowed to make a tiny unpressed pleat.

Tucks are used instead of darts wherever a more casual appearance of fullness is desired. A tuck doesn't define the curve of the body so closely as a dart, and this gives the garment an easier look and fit.

A tuck is stitched an even distance from the fold. The thread at the ends must be firmly knotted or secured, just as in a dart.

There are other ways of shaping a garment. The fabric can be **gathered,** just as an elastic waistband gathers the top of a pair of slacks. Sometimes the gathers are so small that you cannot see them. This is called **easing.**

Well-constructed garments are made to give you enough fullness to be comfortable. If you understand how fullness is created, you will be better able to see how well this has been done in a particular garment.

Linings

Sometimes the inside story on a garment is concealed by a lining. A lining hides seams and gives a smooth, finished quality. It can add body. It can also hide an interlining that is added to a jacket or coat for warmth.

The lining must be cut and stitched with the same care as the top fabric. Above all, the lining must have a little more "give" than the outside fabric.

When you buy a garment with a lining, be sure that both fabrics require the same kind of care. When a washable fabric is used with a nonwashable lining, you have to have the garment dry-cleaned. If the outer fabric stretches in laundering, or the inner one shrinks, the garment will look too unattractive to wear. So be very careful when you buy lined garments.

Choosing Clothes to Fit Your Needs

Now you know the points of basic construction to consider when looking for a good-quality garment. If you plan to wear a garment frequently and for a long time, you will want the best you can afford. However, if you are growing very fast, or if you need a dressy garment for a special occasion, you may decide that strong construction is not so important. Then you may decide on a garment that looks nice, even if it won't wear too long. There may also be times when a current fad seems irresistible.

Knowing the basic features of good garment construction allows you to judge how long a garment will last—when that is important to you. You will know whether you are paying for quality or for style—or for both. Therefore, you will be able to decide how much of your clothes budget to invest in a garment. And you will not be disappointed with what you choose to buy.

QUESTIONS

1. List three ways to make strong seams. What is the purpose of a seam allowance? Why should the fiber content of the thread match that of the garment?
2. What should you look for in a lining?
3. In what kinds of garments is strong construction not a major concern?
4. Sometimes seams in very curved parts of a garment are sewn with smaller stitches than straight seams. Find out why.
5. Why would a manufacturer make garments with small seam allowances?

ACTIVITIES

1. Make a poster illustrating the different kinds of darts that are used on clothing. Include an explanation of when these different darts are used. You will find descriptions of the different kinds of darts in a basic sewing book.
2. Compare a pinked edge with an unfinished edge by doing the following: Cut a piece of woven fabric into two pieces. Pink the edges of one piece and leave the other piece unfinished. Wash the two pieces in a machine and dry them. Show the results to your class.

SECTION 7 · Judging Construction Details

Spotting the "Lemon"

Cars with defects are often called "lemons." Sometimes clothing deserves that name. The trained eye can spot a defect in a piece of clothing—and decide whether it's just a surface blemish that can be easily fixed, or a real problem.

Agarment's details can make the difference between enjoying it and burying it in the back of the closet and hoping you will soon outgrow it.

If a garment has good basic construction, the chances are that the details will also be well handled. Still, you should carefully examine all details, asking yourself the following questions:

- Is the garment neatly and evenly finished at the neck, hem, and sleeves or armholes?
- Are collars, pockets, waistbands, and trimmings correctly cut, sewn, and positioned?
- Do the fastenings—buttons, hooks, zippers, snaps, or grippers—suit the garment? Are they attached firmly? Are the buttonholes well sewn?

Certain faults can be corrected if you like the garment, but others should be a signal not to buy it. The trick is to distinguish one from the other.

Facings, Bindings, and Hems

Facings, bindings, and hems are used to finish the raw edges of a garment. They also

This garment was cut on the bias—the yarns reach the edge diagonally, making the hem particularly flexible.

keep the outside fabric neat and in place. Facings and bindings are often used to complete a collarless neckline or sleeveless armhole. You will also find them on coat and jacket lapels.

Facings are pieces of fabric cut in the same shape as the edges they line. Necklines and armholes that require no additional stretch for getting into the garment use facings.

In well-made clothes, facings lie flat and are sewn down invisibly from the inside, to prevent them from slipping out.

Bindings are narrow stretchable strips of fabric that are used when some extra stretch is needed to let your arm or head go easily through the opening. They are found on T-shirts and other pullovers.

Sometimes bindings are used for decoration. Then they are part of the fashion design. All bindings should be sewn to lie flat. They should not pucker or sag.

Hems are used on skirts, pants, sleeves, and any open bottom edge of a garment. A hem is simply a width of fabric folded under and secured with stitches or tape.

The way a hem is turned under and fastened greatly affects the appearance of a garment. A plain hem should lie flat and be even all around; the stitches should not be visible from the outside.

The inside edges of hems are often finished with bindings. This helps the hems to keep their shape. It also makes them less bulky.

Collars, Cuffs, and Pockets

Collars are popular style details in clothes. Though the designs vary a great deal, they all require careful construction to look attractive.

Curved edges should be smooth, for example, and the two sides should be evenly matched. If the collar stands up, it should have an inner lining to keep it firm and upright. Where the collar meets—usually center front—the ends must be the same width and evenly stitched.

It is often impossible to fix a poorly made collar. Since collars are frequently the center of attraction on a shirt or dress, it might be wise to pass up a garment with a collar that looks bad.

Cuffs present some of the same problems as collars. They must be roomy enough to slip over your hands without tearing. They must not be too loose, though, or they will keep sliding back over your hands.

Although they are sometimes decorative, **pockets** are generally applied to clothes because they are useful. A pocket meant to hold objects must be strongly stitched, from top to bottom, whether it is sewn inside—into a seam—or on the outside of a garment.

Outside pockets must be carefully cut to match in size and shape. They must also be accurately placed so the garment looks good and your hands can reach them comfortably.

You will probably want to avoid any garment with badly placed pockets because moving or straightening a pocket requires patience and experience. Also, the fabric might remain marked where the pocket was originally placed.

Waistbands and Trimmings

Many **waistbands** do little more than hold a skirt or pants firmly to the body. Others are carefully shaped and stitched to suit a garment's design.

All waistbands should match at the point where they meet. If one end of the band is higher than the other, there will be a bulge when the garment is fastened. This may be hard to fix, because it usually means that one side of the garment is longer than the other.

Many garments have elastic waistbands. The elastic should be stitched into the band to keep it from twisting and bulging.

Garments can be decorated with bands, embroidery, ribbons, and other ornaments. These **trimmings,** of course, should be securely and evenly stitched. Trimmings must also be able to take the same kind of care as the clothes they decorate. A washable garment should have washable trimmings. Otherwise, you may end up with a shirt or dress stained with dye from an emblem or ribbon that wasn't colorfast.

Fastenings

A fastening holds an opening together. It can be a button, a zipper, a hook and eye, or any of a number of other closings. Most fastenings can be decorative as well as useful. But the wrong kind can damage a garment's looks or its wearability.

Here are things to look for: Do the buttons go well with the garment? Are the fastenings sewn on securely? Are they well positioned, so that there are no bulges or gaps? Is a fastening too light or too heavy for the material? For example, a light snap will not hold a waistband together—something with more grip is required.

Gaps and bulges can occur when fasteners are not positioned correctly on the garment. If the right type of fastener is properly attached, the closing of the garment will be smooth.

What Can Be Changed?

Although details contribute to a garment's overall quality, it is sometimes worthwhile

Box 1

KEEPING THINGS TOGETHER

Taking the major fastenings one by one, here are points to check:

BUTTONS

Look for buttons that are stitched securely and placed properly. They should be located exactly opposite the buttonholes for a smooth closing. The buttonholes should be firmly stitched, without dangling ends that could unravel the buttonhole stitching. Bound buttonholes should have no raw edges that could fray and come apart with use.

HOOKS AND EYES

This type of fastener is suitable where a moderate amount of grip is needed—for example, at a neckline. Be sure the stitching is secure.

HOOKS AND BARS

These heavy stamped metal fasteners are strong enough to use for waistline closures without adding unwanted bulk. Firm stitching is needed here also.

SNAPS

Snap fasteners are most often found where a corner of fabric needs to be held in place above or below another, stronger fastener.

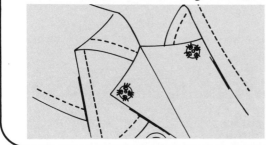

They can also be used inside any opening that has no pull or stress. Snaps should be sewn securely, but the stitches must not show on the outside of the garment. There should be no dangling threads. A luxury touch is sometimes provided on coats and suits by covering snaps with the garment fabric.

GRIPPERS

Gripper fasteners work in the same way as snaps, but they are stronger and close more securely. They are attached by forcing the metal parts together through the fabric. No stitching is involved. Grippers place a severe strain on the surrounding fabric. They should only be used on firm cloth that has added layers of fabric for reinforcement.

ZIPPERS

Zippers must lie flat on the fabric. They should be evenly positioned to avoid bulging, and the stitching should be straight. In most cases, the zipper itself should be covered by the edges of the fabric to give a good appearance.

VELCRO

A less common type of fastener is Velcro, a closure that uses two strips of bur-like

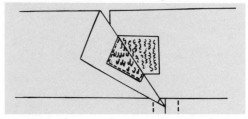

material that stick to each other when pressed together. Velcro fasteners are the easiest type to open and close, but they are not as secure as most other closures. They should usually be used where there isn't too much stress.

to choose a piece of clothing that is not perfect.

Before making such a decision, ask yourself:

• What quality do I need for the use I will make of the garment?
• How much quality am I willing to pay for?
• Can I fix the garment's flaws so I can wear it comfortably?

Some mistakes in construction, such as a crooked collar, cannot be corrected. Others are fairly simple to repair. For example, hems can be evened out, buttons changed, and stitches reinforced where necessary.

You may decide that such flaws aren't important to you if the price or style suits your needs. Can you repair the flaws? Can you live with them? Or will you look further before you spend your money? Once you have examined a garment and seen any flaws it may have, you will be better able to make your decision.

QUESTIONS

1. List the details you should check before purchasing a garment.
2. Describe the proper construction for each of these details.
3. Which mistakes in the construction of details are easy to correct? Which ones would be difficult or impossible to repair?
4. On which kinds of garments would you accept construction flaws? On which kinds wouldn't you?
5. Have you ever bought a garment with a flaw because you liked the garment very much? What happened?

ACTIVITIES

1. Make a poster illustrating the kinds of poor construction to look out for when shopping for clothes.
2. Write a humorous story about someone who bought a garment with a flaw that caused a problem.
3. Find out about the kinds of fasteners used on clothes several hundred years ago. Describe them to your class.

SECTION 8 · To Make or to Buy?

DO IT YOURSELF?

"I designed it myself."

"Wow! That's four times my allowance! I guess this is one of the times I should make my own."

"This fits perfectly. What a great buy!"

"Will you stop! Just because it's a one-hour pattern . . ."

"Just what I was looking for—I'll shorten them and wear them tonight."

Pattern companies beckon you with their ads: "Your clothes say more about you when you sew." "Make it tonight, wear it tomorrow." Other ads point out that you can make a garment for much less than it would cost to buy a similar piece of clothing.

Store windows and advertisements are equally appealing. They promise you an instant improvement in your appearance if you buy their new clothes. The stores also have frequent sales with bargain prices for many garments.

There are good reasons for learning to sew your own clothes. You may enjoy sewing and the individual look you can achieve. And there are equally good reasons for buying clothes. You may not have the patience to sew, or you may not have a sewing machine at home. To help you decide which way will suit you best, compare the advantages of making and of buying clothes.

Saving Money by Sewing

In most cases, a garment that you make yourself will cost you much less than the same kind of garment sold in a store. And the fabric can be as good as, or even better than, the fabrics you will find in similar ready-mades.

The most expensive single item in your sewing budget will be the sewing machine. Your family may already have one. In that case, all you will need is permission to use it.

If your family doesn't have a machine, you will have to decide whether you are serious enough about sewing to justify the investment. Eventually, if you keep on making your own clothes, you will make up in savings the price paid for the machine. It will pay for itself—especially if other members of the family sew, too.

Suiting Yourself

Sewing your own clothes allows you to get an exact fit. Many people have arms or legs a little longer or shorter than average, or a waistline that's a little high or low. If you sew your own clothes, you will learn to alter the pattern where necessary.

Also, you may find a pattern that is especially comfortable or flattering to you. Then you can use it several times, changing fabrics and some details. The style and the good fit will stay the same. But each garment made from the pattern will look different.

Once you are an experienced garment maker, you can use your imagination. You can adapt current styles to your own taste. You can choose the colors that suit you best, and find unusual trimmings not often seen on ready-made clothes.

A Convenient, Creative Hobby

Sewing is a convenient way to coordinate your wardrobe. You can plan the next sea-

Skill in using a sewing machine gives you flexibility in building your wardrobe. You can even become your own designer.

son's clothes in advance and shop for fabrics and patterns at your convenience. If you have a special place in your home for a sewing corner, you can pick up your work whenever you have the time or the urge to sew.

If you learn to make your own clothes now, the skills will be valuable to you for the rest of your life. Knowing how to sew clothes will also help you to recognize good construction and good fit in ready-made clothes.

For many people, sewing is a creative and satisfying hobby. It allows them to express their own ideas about how they want to look.

Why People Don't Sew

Most people buy clothes ready-made rather than sew their own. Among the many reasons they choose to buy clothes is that they don't have the skills to sew well.

Lack of skill is certainly a good reason to buy clothes that are hard to make. But if you practice, you should be able to develop the necessary skill. If you have the opportunity to learn, it's worth the effort to see what you can do.

Frequently, people buy clothes because they don't have the time, the space, or the patience to sew. And ready-made clothes sometimes offer other advantages.

Faster Results in the Store

Many people simply can't imagine what a garment will look like before it is made. When you shop for clothes, you can see at once if the style or color is becoming. Try-ing on a garment can also tell you if it is suitable for the times you plan to wear it.

Sometimes special clothing is needed very quickly, and could not be sewn in time. Or a garment may be too complicated for home sewing.

Many people have the same measurements as manufactured clothes. This gives them a wide choice when shopping in stores. As long as they can find their size, whatever style they try on fits them well. If they like the style, they can walk out of a store wearing their new clothes.

The Best Solution

Some clothes are difficult to make at home, except for the most experienced sewers. These include coats, jackets, suits, and tailored pants and shirts. Jeans and work clothes, and permanently pleated garments that require special pressing, are also quite difficult to sew. The possible savings in making these clothes at home may not be worth the bother or the risk that the garments won't come out right.

Also, home sewing machines often don't have the proper attachments for some kinds of work. Even expert sewers sometimes decide that buying a garment is the better choice.

Still, many kinds of clothing can be easily made at home. And the many advantages of sewing your own clothes should not be overlooked.

Perhaps the best solution is to learn how to sew so that you can make at least some of your own clothes. You will also be a better judge of good fit and construction in ready-made clothes.

QUESTIONS

1. In two columns, list the advantages of sewing your own clothes and the advantages of buying them.
2. How can sewing skills be of value to you when choosing ready-made clothing?
3. What kinds of clothes are usually better bought than made? Why?
4. Why are jeans so difficult to make on a home sewing machine?
5. What kind of garment would you most like to be able to sew? Why?

ACTIVITIES

1. Interview an experienced sewer about the kinds of garments he or she makes. Why did this person start to sew? What tips can she or he offer a beginning sewer?
2. Find an article of clothing that you especially like in a store. Note the price. Then find a pattern for a similar garment and compute the cost of making it in the same kind of fabric. Which would be the better choice?
3. Look in a sewing book to find the correct way to adjust a pattern. How would you fit any unusual features, such as a high waist or long legs?

SECTION 9 · Careers in the Textile and Garment Industries

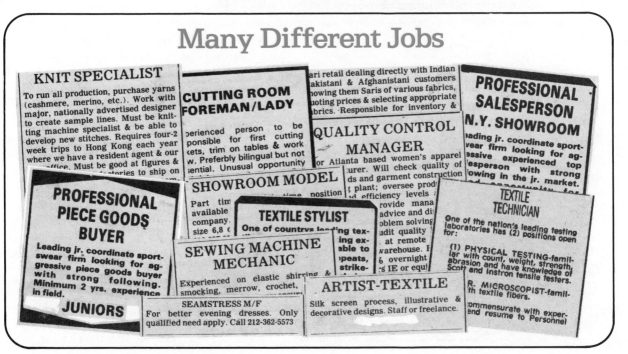

Many Different Jobs

KNIT SPECIALIST
To run all production, purchase yarns (cashmere, merino, etc.). Work with major, nationally advertised designer to create sample lines. Must be knitting machine specialist & be able to develop new stitches. Requires four-2 week trips to Hong Kong each year where we have a resident agent & our office. Must be good at figures & ...tories to ship on

CUTTING ROOM FOREMAN/LADY
...perienced person to be ...ponsible for first cutting ...kets, trim on tables & work ...w. Preferbly bilingual but not ...ential. Unusual opportunity

...ari retail dealing directly with Indian ...akistani & Afghanistani customers ...howing them Saris of various fabrics, ...uoting prices & selecting appropriate ...brics. Responsible for inventory &

QUALITY CONTROL MANAGER
...or Atlanta based women's apparel ...urer. Will check quality of ...ds and garment construction ...t plant; oversee prod... ...d efficiency levels ...rovide mana... ...advice and di... ...oblem solving ...udit quality ...at remote ...varehouse. ...6 overnight ...s IE or equi...

PROFESSIONAL SALESPERSON N.Y. SHOWROOM
...eading jr. coordinate sport... ...wear firm looking for ag... ...ssive experienced top ...esperson with strong ...owing in the jr. market.

PROFESSIONAL PIECE GOODS BUYER
Leading jr. coordinate sportswear firm looking for aggressive piece goods buyer with strong following. Minimum 2 yrs. experience in field.
JUNIORS

SHOWROOM MODEL
Part tim... available company. size 6,8 ...

TEXTILE STYLIST
One of country... ...ding tex... ...ing ex... ...able to ...peats, ...strike-

SEWING MACHINE MECHANIC
Experienced on elastic shirring & ... smocking, merrow, crochet,

SEAMSTRESS M/F
For better evening dresses. Only qualified need apply. Call 212-362-5573

ARTIST-TEXTILE
Silk screen process, illustrative & decorative designs. Staff or freelance.

TEXTILE TECHNICIAN
One of the nation's leading testing laboratories has (2) positions open for:
(1) PHYSICAL TESTING-famil... iar with count, weight, strength, abrasion and have knowledge of Scott and Instron tensile testers.
R. MICROSCOPIST-famil... th textile fibers.
...ommensurate with exper... ...end resume to Personnel

Fibers are the raw materials of clothing. Before fibers are used to make fabrics, they are usually spun into yarns.

Today, many synthetic yarns, such as nylon and polyester, are manufactured in the chemical plants where the fiber is made. But other synthetic fibers, like natural fibers, are spun into yarn in the same mills where the yarn is woven into cloth.

The Textile Industry

People have been making textiles for clothing since ancient times. Until 200 years ago, most of the tasks involved in the making of cloth were done by hand. Today, large machines do much of the routine work. Many of the workers in the textile and garment industries are involved with running these machines.

Some of these workers operate the fiber-making machines in chemical plants. Others run the spinning machines that produce yarn. Then the yarns—either natural

or synthetic—are knitted or woven into cloth in the textile mill.

Textile mills employ production workers who tend the giant looms and knitting machines. Many of these workers are trained in the mills, under the supervision of experienced workers. The more highly skilled workers are trained in technical schools or in apprentice programs in the mills. These programs take from two to four years and combine classroom and on-the-job training.

Jobs with Converters

Fabrics made in textile mills are often colorless. They are commonly called gray goods—for greige goods, which is the traditional term. These fabrics are sent to a converting plant to be dyed or printed.

Converters finish fabrics in a variety of ways. Some finishes make a fabric more attractive or easier to care for. Others make it fire- or waterproof. But because much of the work deals with color and design, firms that do converting offer job opportunities to people with artistic talents.

Those who select the formulas used to dye the textiles are called dyers. The chemicals and dyes are mixed by dye weighers. Dye range operators run the machines that dye and dry the fabrics.

Sketches of fabric designs are done by assistant designers and sketchers. Samples of colorings on fabrics are done by colorists.

Textiles can be printed in several different ways. In one important method, the dyes are applied to the fabric through a screen. Workers who print the designs are called screen printing artists, screen makers, and screen printers.

Most workers involved in dyeing or printing fabrics are supervised by a textile designer. The textile designer is also responsible for picking the particular fabric

This textile worker is called a rover. He removes the giant spools from the machines when they are fully wound with yarn.

Garment manufacturers depend on their textile buyers to select the right cloth for each new style. Here a buyer discusses fabric with a textile salesperson.

weave or knit to be used. He or she chooses the colors, designs, and finishes to be used as well.

Production work in firms that do converting can be learned in a few weeks or months. However, highly skilled workers—such as designers or colorists—need more advanced training. Some attend art or design school. Others study clothing and textiles in a home economics program.

Textiles Research

Research is an important part of making textiles that are suitable for clothing. Textile chemists and textile engineers are constantly working on techniques for making yarns and cloths, improving quality, and keeping down production costs.

They also search for new fibers and finishes. Thanks to textiles research, we have wrinkle- and soil-resistant finishes. Effec-

tive new blends of fibers may be developed in a textiles laboratory.

A college background in a related area—textile engineering, textile chemistry, or textile technology, for example—is required for jobs in textiles research.

Jobs in the Garment Industry

Garment firms take the products of the mills and converters and turn them into clothing for men, women, and children. The people who buy the fabrics for the garment makers are called fabric buyers. The fabric buyer works closely with the designer, and is responsible for getting all the fabrics needed for the firm's current styles.

Garment companies use the skills of a great many workers. Designers, pattern makers, sewing machine operators—all help to produce the clothes we wear.

Because they have special abilities, workers in the designer's studio, or sample room, are very well paid. Designers have assistants who cut and drape the fabric for the sample garment that is made from each new design. Then sample hands and tailors sew the sample garments. They are expert sewers.

The pattern maker holds the highest paid and most important production job in a garment factory. She or he makes a pattern from the original sample. Then the pattern grader makes a pattern for each of the various sizes in which the garment is to be made.

Duplicate makers are highly skilled sewers who make garments from these master patterns. These garments ensure that the patterns are correct in every detail. Then the patterns are laid out on a marker, the fabric is cut out by the cutters, and the garment pieces are sent on to the sewing department.

Stitching It All Together

The largest number of workers in the garment firm are sewing machine operators. These are the people who do the stitching.

Machine operators are trained on the job. Beginners start out stitching the easiest seams. Their wages begin with the legal minimum pay, but they can work their way up in responsibility and income. The most capable and experienced machine operators become tailors and sample makers in the designer's studio.

Factories need supervisors to direct workers. Supervisors are usually machine operators who have shown ability in working with people, as well as knowledge of plant operations.

Selling the Textiles and Clothing

Both the textile and the garment industries employ large sales staffs. Textile salespeople sell fabrics to the garment makers

When garments are finished they must be moved from the factory to a distribution center, and from there to a retail store.

Box 1

Do-It-Yourself Fashions

Pattern companies make patterns for people who sew their own clothes. These companies employ designers, pattern makers, and sample makers to prepare and test the patterns. They also hire writers who understand sewing to prepare instructions for the patterns.

Artists and photographers illustrate patterns, to make them easier to follow. They also illustrate pattern books and pamphlets. These publications show the many different styles of patterns available.

Pattern and textile companies hire people to prepare educational and advertising material. Sometimes they send consultants to schools and stores to give talks and demonstrations on how to make your own clothes. These people are usually college graduates, with a background in fashion, education, or home economics.

Retail stores that sell patterns and fabrics employ salespeople with a knowledge of sewing. Because of their experience with fabrics and patterns, they can give good advice to customers.

---

and to retail fabric stores. Garment salespeople sell their firm's products to retail clothing stores. Salespeople are usually trained by the companies they work for. Many companies hire only college graduates for their sales positions.

To be successful in sales, a person must have a lot of enthusiasm for the product and be able to impart that enthusiasm to the customer. Salespeople must be willing to travel and to work with little supervision. A career in sales can be satisfying and profitable. And it can lead to a successful career in management.

Textiles and clothing are bought and sold throughout the world. Both the garment industry and the textile industry employ salespeople and buyers to do business in other countries.

A career in international trade can be very exciting. It offers the opportunity to travel and to work with people from other parts of the world.

Finding Your Place

Are you considering a job in the textile or garment industry? If the kind of firm you want to work for is not located in your area, would you be willing to move to another part of the country?

New York City has the biggest concentration of clothing manufacturers. But there are many firms on the West Coast, as well as in other areas. Textile marketing is also centered in New York, though there are regional or district sales offices throughout North America.

Converters are generally located in the Northeast, though the industry is spreading to other areas. Most of the big textile plants are in the South. The fiber-making firms are in the mid-Atlantic and southern states.

If you are interested in textiles or garment making, find out where you can get on-the-job training. Check out technical schools and college programs in these fields. If you are artistic, like to work with your hands or with machinery, or enjoy selling—there is a place for you in the textile or garment industry.

QUESTIONS

1. List five different job areas in the textile and garment industries.
2. Name two specific jobs in each of those areas.
3. Explain the tasks involved in working at three different jobs in the field.
4. Which jobs in the textile and garment industries probably did not exist 100 years ago? Why not?
5. Why do you think so many textile plants are located in the South?
6. What kinds of things must a fabric buyer be aware of when choosing fabrics?

ACTIVITIES

1. Visit the guidance office of your school to find out more about one of the jobs in the textile or garment industry.
2. Make a map showing the location of the major centers of the textile and garment industries. (An encyclopedia can help you in this activity.)
3. Talk to someone in the field about the nature of the work she or he does.

CHAPTER 12

Getting the Most from Your Clothes

SECTION 1 · Toward a Long Life

The Clothes Care Game

The purpose of this game is to stay on the board as long as possible. The player who reaches FINISH *last* is the winner. Players throw a die in turn, and follow the directions on the square where they land. Unless routed down a detour, players should follow the main path. (If you really want to try this game, cut out small playing pieces to look like garments.)

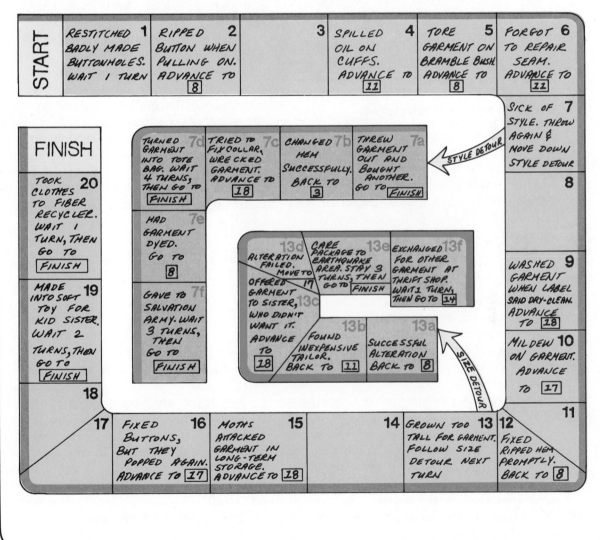

START

1 RESTITCHED BADLY MADE BUTTONHOLES. WAIT 1 TURN

2 RIPPED BUTTON WHEN PULLING ON. ADVANCE TO 8

3

4 SPILLED OIL ON CUFFS. ADVANCE TO 11

5 TORE GARMENT ON BRAMBLE BUSH. ADVANCE TO 8

6 FORGOT TO REPAIR SEAM. ADVANCE TO 11

7 SICK OF STYLE. THROW AGAIN & MOVE DOWN STYLE DETOUR

STYLE DETOUR

7a THREW GARMENT OUT AND BOUGHT ANOTHER. GO TO FINISH

7b CHANGED HEM SUCCESSFULLY. BACK TO 3

7c TRIED TO FIX COLLAR, WRECKED GARMENT. ADVANCE TO 18

7d TURNED GARMENT INTO TOTE BAG. WAIT 4 TURNS, THEN GO TO FINISH

FINISH

7e HAD GARMENT DYED. GO TO 8

7f GAVE TO SALVATION ARMY. WAIT 3 TURNS, THEN GO TO FINISH

13d ALTERATION FAILED. MOVE TO 17

13e CARE PACKAGE TO EARTHQUAKE AREA. STAY 3 TURNS, THEN GO TO FINISH

13f EXCHANGED FOR OTHER GARMENT AT THRIFT SHOP. WAIT 1 TURN, THEN GO TO 14

13c OFFERED GARMENT TO SISTER, WHO DIDN'T WANT IT. ADVANCE TO 18

13b FOUND INEXPENSIVE TAILOR. BACK TO 11

13a SUCCESSFUL ALTERATION BACK TO 8

SIZE DETOUR

20 TOOK CLOTHES TO FIBER RECYCLER. WAIT 1 TURN, THEN GO TO FINISH

19 MADE INTO SOFT TOY FOR KID SISTER. WAIT 2 TURNS, THEN GO TO FINISH

18

17

16 FIXED BUTTONS, BUT THEY POPPED AGAIN. ADVANCE TO 17

15 MOTHS ATTACKED GARMENT IN LONG-TERM STORAGE. ADVANCE TO 18

14

13 GROWN TOO TALL FOR GARMENT. FOLLOW SIZE DETOUR NEXT TURN

12 FIXED RIPPED HEM PROMPTLY. BACK TO 8

11

10 MILDEW ON GARMENT. ADVANCE TO 17

9 WASHED GARMENT WHEN LABEL SAID DRY-CLEAN. ADVANCE TO 18

8

447

The length of a garment's life depends on the fabric it is made from, the skill of the designer, and the quality of the work. It also depends on the care you give it.

How well do you take care of your clothes? Do you recycle them? You may recycle cans, bottles, and newspapers, but did you know that you can and do recycle your clothing?

Actually, people recycled clothes long before there were any bottle and can collection centers. When fabrics and garments were made at home, it made sense to reuse them. The longer fabrics and garments could be made to last, the less work there was for the people who made them.

Many Ways to Recycle

Every time you have your clothes washed or dry-cleaned, you are recycling them. Instead of throwing away the dirty clothes, you have them cleaned so that they can be worn again. And every time you repair your clothing, you are recycling it—or saving it for another wearing.

The older your clothes get, the more creative you need to be in recycling them. Perhaps you have grown taller—can you alter those pants? Perhaps a shirt has faded or gone out of fashion—can you make it fresher or more fashionable? As long as the fabric lasts, there is probably some way you can recycle it.

Even when a garment is beyond repair or alteration, think twice before throwing it away. Perhaps you could use some of the fabric for another purpose. Perhaps someone in your family could use it. Or perhaps you could give the garment away or sell it.

The longer you manage to keep recycling your clothes, the better. You are getting more for your money. And you are also saving clothing fibers, which are becoming a precious world resource.

Besides Recycling

There are other things that you can do to save your clothes. If you wear them and store them with care, they will last much longer.

Clothes can be pulled out of shape permanently by careless treatment. Hanging knits such as sweaters or T-shirts on wire hangers can ruin the shape of the neck and shoulders. Crumpling a shirt carelessly into a drawer can leave permanent creases in the fabric.

With a little regular care, your clothes will stay in good shape. They will always be ready to wear when you need them.

If you take care of your clothes, your wardrobe will seem larger. For example, if the jacket of your two-piece suit is ripped or dirty, you can't wear it. The chances are that you won't wear the pants without the jacket. You may have another pair of pants that you wear only with that jacket. So, because one garment isn't wearable, you've lost the use of two or more.

Daily and Weekly Care of Clothes

Daily care of clothes begins when you put them on and ends when you take them off and put them away. As you pull garments on, take care to prevent strain on seams and fastenings. This will save you repair time later.

While you are wearing your clothes, try to protect them from stains and tears. If you're making spaghetti sauce, wear an apron. Don't play soccer in your best slacks and sweater. And when you take your clothes off, take care to remove them without strain.

Before you put a garment away, check to see if it needs repairs. A small rip or a loose button takes only a few minutes to fix. If you ignore it now, the button may be lost or the rip may become worse. Then the repair will be a major job.

Take a few extra seconds to hang or fold your clothes. Not only will this save ironing time, it will also avoid spoiling a permanent-press finish. Carelessly throwing a garment on the bed or floor will sometimes shorten its life.

A weekly routine will keep your clothes looking their best and ready to wear whenever you need them. Set aside some time every week for recycling chores that take longer than small daily repairs. This is the time to do any sewing that isn't a quick repair. This is also the time to wash by hand any items that can't be put in the machine. If you do all your ironing at this time, you will save both effort and energy.

Box 1

Daily Clothes Care

- Put on and take off garments carefully.
- Open buttons and zippers fully when getting in and out of clothes.
- Put dresses and skirts on over your head.
- Use a deodorant or an antiperspirant.
- Eat carefully and protect your clothes with a napkin.
- Wear protective garments or old clothes when cooking, painting, gardening, or doing other messy chores.
- Take care of stains immediately.
- Check clothes for rips and loose buttons or snaps.
- Clean or press garments whenever necessary.
- Store clothes properly.

Storing Clothes

Proper storage is important in clothes care. Garments need space to hang without crowding or they will become wrinkled. Curved wooden or plastic hangers help them keep their shape.

Drawer or shelf space for folded garments should be clean. It should also be smooth so that garments don't become snagged. A good way to protect garments stored on shelves is to keep them in plastic bags or in boxes.

Some clothes need to be aired before they are stored. Sweaters, for instance, absorb body moisture and should be left out to dry before being put away. To air a sweater, spread it flat on your bed or over the back of an easy chair.

If a garment doesn't need airing, cleaning, or repair, it should be hung or folded and put away to keep it fresh.

In many climates, certain clothes are not worn for several months. When clothes

A well-arranged closet not only helps you feel organized. It also keeps clothes looking their best and lets you see at a glance what is clean and ready to wear.

are not worn for a long time, they can become damaged in several ways. Perspiration and skin oils may weaken the fabric. Insects such as silverfish may attack food stains, and damage the fibers too. If the cloth contains wool, clothes moth larvae may eat the fibers even though they are clean. And mildew—a fungus—may grow on damp fabric, causing stains.

To protect stored clothes, make sure they are clean and free of stains. Treat woolens with a moth repellent; if possible, seal them in an airtight bag. Before you put them away, make sure your clothes are completely dry, and will remain dry, to prevent mildew.

The Payoff

Regular clothes care and recycling will allow you to dress and look the way you want. Knowing that your clothes are always neat and clean will give you self-confidence.

Get in the habit of keeping your clothes ready to wear. It will make your life much easier, and you will find that your clothes last longer.

QUESTIONS

1. Name three ways in which clothing is commonly recycled.
2. What are the benefits of regular clothing care?
3. List steps you should follow in the daily and weekly care of your clothes.
4. What might happen to clothing that is allowed to remain dirty for a long period of time?
5. How could you arrange drawer or closet space to help you care for your clothes?

ACTIVITIES

1. Make a list of clothing maintenance chores that should be done on a seasonal basis.
2. Describe your current clothing care habits. How could you improve them?
3. Brainstorm techniques for recycling clothing that are not mentioned in this section.

SECTION 2 · The Washing Cycle

Many People, Many Methods

All these people are doing the same thing—cleaning their clothes. Why are they doing it differently?

How you wash your clothes may depend in part on your culture. The women washing their clothes at the riverbank don't have access to a washing machine. Perhaps they wouldn't want one, because washing is a social occasion for them.

The people in the Laundromat may be there because they have no laundry equipment in their apartments or homes. But perhaps they wouldn't want a washing machine, either. Paying for each wash at the Laundromat can be more economical than buying a machine and paying for its upkeep.

How people choose to clean their clothes, however, depends on more than culture and economics. Why do the people in the pictures use so many different ways of cleaning their clothes?

Why do people wash clothes? The answer is obvious—to remove soil and dirt so that the clothes will look clean and smell fresh. Washing is the most basic method of recycling clothes.

There are many ways to wash clothes. Some clothes must be hand-washed, others can be washed in a machine. Some should be washed in hot water, others in cool water.

Some clothes are washed in detergent only. Others come out better if bleach or some other special laundry product is added to the water. And some clothes cannot be washed at all. They must be dry-cleaned, or sometimes merely wiped clean by hand.

Fabrics and Dirt

All fabric collects dirt when it is worn. Some of this dirt comes from pollution in the air. Some of it is the result of things we do—gardening, playing ball, or working at dirty jobs. And some dirt collects on our clothes in the form of perspiration and skin oils. All these types of dirt are absorbed slightly into the fibers and yarns from which our garments are made.

Occasionally, soil becomes more ingrained. An ink spot soaks deep into the fabric, or ketchup splatters a shirt front. This concentrated soil becomes a stain—which is much more visible than general dirt, and usually harder to remove (see box 1 in this section).

General soil may be caused by several substances, and stains may be caused by many more. This is one reason for using several methods to clean clothes.

Special Materials, Special Care

Another reason for cleaning clothes in different ways is the variety of fabrics used to make clothes. No one has yet invented a cloth that is strong enough for shoes, yet soft enough for underwear; warm in the snow, yet cool in the tropics. Until such a miracle material appears, many cleaning methods will be needed for all the different fabrics.

Woolen garments, for example, usually need special care. If they are machine-washed in hot water, they may come out matted and shrunken. The manufacturer's directions for cleaning should be followed. Some manufacturers suggest washing woolens in cold water. Others may specify on the label that a garment should be dry-cleaned.

The *finish* on a fabric may also be spoiled by wrong treatment. Too much heat can damage the permanent-press finish on a cotton fabric. The fabric may set in a pattern of permanent wrinkles!

Other materials—such as leather, vinyl, and very delicate fabrics—obviously need special treatment. If you check the care labels on your clothes, you will note the variety of fabrics and cleaning methods (see box 2 in this section).

Clothes That Don't Get Along in the Wash

Another concern in washing clothes is deciding which clothes can be washed together. Clothes can be damaged not only by the wrong water temperature, but also by each other.

Dyes from darker fabrics may discolor white or light-colored clothing. Some materials, such as terry cloth and corduroy, shed lint that may stick to other items in the wash load. Heavy items such as sheets may tangle with and tear delicate clothes.

In fact, some clothing may be harmed just by the action of being washed. This is

Box 1

BEAT THAT STAIN

Few people realize that stains can actually damage clothing. Stains may weaken clothing fibers and yarns so that the fabric tears easily. Stains may even erode the fibers, causing holes. Food stains often attract damaging insects, which may eat both stain and fabric.

In removing stains, it helps to understand the principles of stain removal. Stain-removal agents work in four basic ways:

- They may soak up or **absorb** staining material from the fabric surface. For example, you can remove candle wax by placing fabric between paper towels, then ironing with a warm iron. The wax melts, and is absorbed by the paper.
- They may **dissolve** the staining material and wash it away from the fabric fibers. Water and dry-cleaning solvent are both agents of this type.
- They may **coat** particles of the staining material in such a way that these can be washed out of the fabric. Liquid detergents remove oil stains by this method.
- They may **react chemically** with the staining agent, making it colorless, or changing its form so that it can be washed out. Bleaches and vinegar both work this way.

Many stains must be removed by a combination of these techniques. You need up-to-date information on which combination is best for which stain. A technique may work well on one type of dirt in one type of fabric. The same technique may cause damage when used on another type of dirt in another type of fabric. For example, nail-polish remover is very effective against ball-point ink in most fabrics. But it will melt holes in acetates and triacetates.

Stain removal needs careful planning. Fortunately, there are many stain-removal charts available to help you. Washing-machine direction books usually include such charts. Charts can also be found in libraries. And a chart for common stains is given at the back of this book (on p. 492).

One last point: The longer a stain remains in the fabric, the deeper it penetrates—and the harder it is to remove. Always try to treat stains when they occur, or as soon as possible afterward. Otherwise, the chances of clothing damage are much greater.

---

particularly true of garments that are already torn or ripped.

Steps in Preparing to Wash

The first step in washing, therefore, is to make sure that all garments are in good shape. If a button is loose or a seam is coming apart, or if the fabric is torn, make repairs to avoid further damage.

Certain stains may be set permanently by the water or detergent. Repairs and stains need to be dealt with *before* washing.

The second step is to sort the clothing into piles that can be washed together. This means setting apart all the clothes that need a special laundry product—bleach, for example—because of the type of dirt. It means dividing clothes according to the water temperatures called for on the care labels. And it means separating those clothes that don't get along in the wash.

Box 2

What Kind of Care

Though there is a great variety of fabrics today, knowing how to clean them is not hard. This is because, by law, care labels—labels that give washing, drying, or dry-cleaning directions—must be sewn into nearly all ready-made garments. They are also provided by stores that sell fabrics for home sewing.

Garments may have hang tags as well as care labels. Occasionally, these hang tags carry washing directions that differ from those given on the care label. The reason is that some labels refer only to the fabric, while the hang tag also considers garment construction. If, for example, a garment has a braid trim that needs special care, the hang tag may say "Hand-wash only," while the care label may say "Machine-wash in warm water." In such cases, always follow the more cautious directions.

A common way to sort wash is to separate heavy items such as towels from lighter-weight clothes. Then the clothes are separated into whites (for bleaching), light colors, and dark colors that may run. And in each group, permanent-press garments are separated from others.

You may not care if your pajamas lose their permanent-press finish because they were washed in hot water. The groups you use are up to you. But remember when you are doing your wash—or your family's—that careful sorting will keep clothes looking better longer.

The Washing Process

When you squeeze soapy water through clothes by hand, or when a washing machine is agitating the garments, water is being forced between the yarns and fibers. The water either dissolves the soil or lifts the particles of dirt away from the clothing. Adding soap or detergent to the water helps remove the soil.

In most cases, the hotter the water, the cleaner the clothes will become. Hot water dissolves more soil. It also kills bacteria, which may cause skin irritation. If hot water cannot be used, a bleach or disinfect-

Sorting clothes for the wash can sometimes seem like rush hour traffic! Here a shirt is the traffic controller. In real life, of course, it's up to you to keep apart clothes which might cause damage to each other.

ant can be added to cool water to kill bacteria. (Other laundry products added to the wash perform other functions—see box 3 of this section.)

When the detergents and other products have done their work, the clothes are thoroughly rinsed in fresh water. This floats away the soil or dirt particles, and removes the soap or detergent. Finally, most of the water is squeezed out—by hand ringing or by spin drying.

Final Drying

The traditional way to dry clothes is to hang them outdoors on a clothesline and let the wind and sun dry them. On a rainy day, clothes are hung inside—perhaps in front of a fire on a clothes horse, or on a line stretched across the basement or kitchen. Garments that would stretch if hung are laid out on a towel and dried flat.

These methods are still used, of course. For one thing, they are very economical. For another, some care labels *call* for line drying or for drying flat. However, many modern fabrics look their best after tumble drying.

Most natural and synthetic clothing fibers tend to regain their original shape in an atmosphere of moist heat. This is the atmosphere of a clothes dryer. So garments that were wrinkled during the spin-dry cycle of a washing machine can usually be removed from a dryer wrinkle-free—if they are removed as soon as the dryer turns off.

If they are not removed promptly, the heat in the dryer and the weight of the clothes may cause new wrinkles to form. Also, some fabrics, such as untreated cotton, do not come out smooth when dried in a dryer. In either case, an extra step is needed before the clothes are ready to wear.

Remedies for Wrinkles

There are several ways to make clean, dried clothes that are wrinkled smooth again.

Don't run for the iron immediately. Some garments shed wrinkles if hung in the fresh air for several hours. You can also steam out wrinkles by hanging clothes in the bathroom while you take a bath or

---

Box 3

Choosing Laundry Products

Every wash needs a soap, or detergent, and water. Other products, such as bleaches and presoaks, may also be used for special purposes. Always check the care label on a garment—it may warn against the use of some product, or call for the use of another.

Soap—cleansing agent based on animal and vegetable fats; requires soft water.

Detergent—cleansing agent based on petroleum and other chemicals; works well in hard or soft water.

Enzyme presoak—helps soak out protein stains such as egg, meat juices, blood.

Prewash spray—helps remove many types of stains.

Water softener—softens hard water.

Disinfectant—destroys bacteria; needed if the water isn't very hot or if there is a contagious illness in the family.

Bleach—removes stains and soil; whitens white items, disinfects.

Fabric softener—decreases static and makes fabrics feel softer.

Starch—stiffens fabrics; used mostly on cottons.

All laundry products carry detailed directions for use. The directions must be followed carefully for best washing results, and for safety.

Tips on Using an Iron

Box 4

For the garment's sake:

- Learn how to iron *and* how to press. Ironing means sliding an iron back and forth over the garment. Pressing means lifting the iron, then lowering it onto the garment.
- To smooth most woven garments, *iron* them in the direction of the yarns. This usually means from top to bottom of the garment, or from side to side. If you move the iron diagonally, you could shift the yarns.
- To remove wrinkles from woolens and knits, *press* the garments. This avoids sideways movement, which could stretch the fabric.
- Always check the care label for any special ironing directions.
- To prevent shine, lay a press cloth on top of the garment before ironing. Special transparent cloths are available, but a lint-free cotton cloth will do the job. Another way to avoid shine is to iron (or press) the garment on the *inside*.
- To make an embroidered pattern stand out, lay it face down on a towel and press. The same method works on fabrics with raised surfaces, such as corduroy.
- To press a sleeve or a pants leg without making a crease, use a sleeve board. Or roll a magazine tightly and wrap it in a towel. Slip your sleeve roll into the sleeve and press all around without making a crease.

For your own sake:

- Always read the manufacturer's directions for your iron. Irons can be hot, and often use both electricity and water—a dangerous combination.
- Always rest the hot iron standing—*not* face down on the ironing board.
- Unplug the iron as soon as you finish using it.
- Pull on the plug, not the cord, and check to see if the cord is fraying before putting the iron away.
- Store the iron where there is no chance of its falling on anyone's head. Irons are usually quite heavy.

shower. This method is good for woolens and many knits.

The most common way to remove wrinkles from a garment is by ironing them. An iron provides heat, pressure, and often steam to relax and soften the fibers and smooth the surface of the fabric. The care label will tell you what fabric you are dealing with, and often the correct ironing setting as well. (Box 4 in this section gives you tips on how to use an iron.)

Once your garments are wrinkle-free, they are fully recycled and ready to be worn.

Economy and the Future

Today's washing and drying methods use quite a lot of water and energy. To conserve these resources, and to save money, be careful to

- run the washing machine only for a full load, or choose a setting that fits the size of the wash
- use water no warmer than necessary to get clothes clean
- dry clothes properly to keep ironing to a minimum

If you follow these suggestions, you will preserve clothing fibers and save other resources, too.

The future may bring new fabrics and new cleaning techniques. But if you develop careful habits now, you will help to ensure that the world's resources will last. And you will also look your best.

QUESTIONS

1. How does the washing process get clothes clean?
2. What are the reasons for sorting laundry into different wash loads? Describe the different groups laundry should be sorted into.
3. List several ways to keep clothes from wrinkling when drying and storing them.
4. How are the principles of stain removal similar to the principles of washing? How are they different?
5. Why do you think many modern fabrics look better when tumble dried than when line dried?

ACTIVITIES

1. Read a consumer magazine article on stain-removal agents and report the magazine's recommendations to your class.
2. Assemble a classroom display of empty laundry-product packages. Read the directions for use and discuss the reasons for using them.
3. Using two samples of each kind of fabric mentioned in the chapter, iron one the wrong way and one the right way. Demonstrate the results in class.

SECTION 3 · Dry Cleaning

THE DRY-CLEANING STORE

Clothing is sometimes cleaned at a dry-cleaning store. Some dry cleaners are small family-run businesses that serve the immediate community. Others are branches of large chains.

A dry cleaner's most important equipment consists of dry-cleaning machines and pressing forms. Sometimes this equipment is in the store itself. Often it is in a separate plant.

Dry-cleaning Machines

Dry-cleaning machines look like very large washing machines. Many stores have just one big machine, although some use several smaller ones instead.

The machine works in much the same way as a front-loading washer. Instead of water, however, it is filled with a liquid called dry-cleaning solvent. A specially prepared detergent is added. Then the clothes are put in, and the machine is tightly locked and turned on.

The special detergent works on stains and soils that would normally wash out if the fabric had been washed in water. The cleaning solvent dissolves grease and removes dirt. The solvent is carried through a filter, where the particles of dirt are trapped. Then, free of dirt, the solvent is recycled through the clothes to clean them further. This process continues for ten to twenty minutes, depending on the amount of soil.

Finally, the solvent is drained off. The garments are spun to force out any remaining solvent. Then they are tumbled dry, frequently in the same machine.

Pressing Forms

To finish the garments and restore their smooth look, the clothes are put on forms similar to dress forms. There is a difference, though. Pressing forms blow steam through the garment, removing any wrinkles.

Blowing steam through garments is usually the only process needed to give a smooth finish, because dry cleaning leaves fewer wrinkles than washing. For special purposes, however, such as putting creases in trousers, there is a steam pressing machine. And when further touching up is needed, it is done by hand with a steam iron.

Special Stains

Dry cleaners use a variety of chemicals and methods to remove spots and stains. Usually they work on special stains before the garment goes into the dry-cleaning machine. But if spots remain after the cleaning cycle, they must be removed before pressing.

Some stains cannot be removed by any method. But good dry cleaners are experienced at removing stains. They have up-to-date information about new fabrics and cleaning methods. That's why a good dry cleaner can help with all spots and stains—even those on washable garments.

To stay up to date, many dry cleaners belong to groups that do research on new clothing fabrics and methods of cleaning them. The largest research group is The International Fabricare Institute. When a dry cleaner displays the emblem of a research group, it means that the store has access to expert advice.

What Dry Cleaning Doesn't Do

Some fabrics and trimmings are harmed by dry cleaning. Vinyl, for example, can't be dry-cleaned. Bonded fabrics—those made of two layers of fabric held together with an adhesive—may separate when dry-cleaned.

And plastic buttons have been known to melt or dissolve in dry-cleaning machines.

Some dry cleaners remove buttons or trimmings from garments before cleaning. But most dry-cleaning stores post signs saying that they are not responsible for trims and buttons. So if you aren't sure whether the buttons and trimmings will hold up while the garment is being cleaned, check with the manager of the store. The manager can tell you if they should be removed.

Cleaners may miss spots and stains unless you point them out to the counter clerk. And if you know what caused the stain, say so. Otherwise, the stain may not be identified correctly. The more information *you* provide, the better you will be served.

Coin-operated Dry Cleaners

Some Laundromats offer coin-operated dry-cleaning machines for customers' use. This kind of cleaning usually costs much less than professional cleaning. However, you have to do everything yourself, although there may be an attendant to advise you. To get good results, you must follow the instructions given for the machine.

Coin-operated dry-cleaning machines remove most soil quite well, but they do not

---

Box 1

Before You Dry-Clean

- Always read the care label. If it says "Do not dry-clean," don't.
- Empty all pockets.
- If you remove buttons and trims, leave threads hanging to mark where they were.
- Point out all spots and stains to the clerk.
- If you know, tell the clerk what caused the stains.

---

provide special treatment for spots and stains. If garments don't require sharp creasing, place them on hangers as soon as they come out of the machine. Then they can be worn without pressing. If a smell of the cleaning solvent clings to the clothes, airing will remove the odor.

Do-it-yourself dry cleaning can save you money. You also get your clothes back faster. But, as with all projects you tackle yourself, it helps to learn as much as you can. Knowing about fabrics and the cleaning process can help you keep your clothes in top condition.

QUESTIONS

1. Explain briefly the steps in the dry-cleaning process.
2. What should you do before taking clothes to a dry cleaner? What information should you give the dry cleaner?
3. What are the advantages of doing dry cleaning yourself? The disadvantages?
4. Why do you think spots and stains are treated *before* garments are dry-cleaned?
5. Some dry cleaners advertise that they do all the dry cleaning themselves instead of sending it out. What advantages does this method offer?

ACTIVITIES

1. Compare the cost of having a variety of garments dry-cleaned professionally with the cost of dry cleaning them yourself in a coin-operated machine.
2. Find out about changes in the dry-cleaning industry during the past fifty years.
3. Tour a dry-cleaning plant to see how the clothes are handled. Find out what other services the dry cleaner offers.

SECTION 4 · Fitting and Fixing

Plenty of Clothes, Nothing to Wear

Aaron was going through his closet trying to find a shirt to wear to the school dance. He pulled out his favorite plaid shirt, put it on, and discovered that two buttons were missing. No problem—he'd wear his striped shirt. But that one had a ripped pocket. And his blue one had a torn sleeve. The only shirt left was plain white. No one else would be wearing a white shirt to the dance, but he put the shirt on anyway. He had no choice.

Ginny had a clothes problem, too. She'd grown a lot lately, and all her jeans were too short. She'd bought some new pants, but they were too long. Her blazer seemed okay, until she buttoned it—then it felt too tight. Everything in Ginny's closet seemed to be too short, too long, or in need of some other alteration. Ginny looked at the pile of clothes that had come from her cousin last week. They were all too big. So tomorrow Ginny would have to wear her too-short jeans and leave her blazer open. But what about the day after tomorrow?

Most people have clothing that cannot be worn—either because the garments are damaged in some way, or because they are the wrong size. Aaron and Ginny had let things slide further than most. But nearly everyone's clothes could use a little fixing and fitting.

Fitting and fixing clothing are sometimes very easy to do. A button can be sewn on in two or three minutes. A snagged knit can be repaired in ten seconds or less. Letting down a hem takes more time, but it isn't hard. If you can learn to do basic jobs like these, you will be more independent. Perhaps you can save your parents some work, or save yourself some money.

For other repairs and alterations, you may need help. If a seam has come undone on the shoulder of your shirt, you may need the advice of an experienced sewer. You could also have some of your restitching done for you. Though this costs money, it may still be cheaper than buying a new garment.

When Damage Occurs

When you find your clothes need repair, think about how the damage occurred. Knowing the cause of damage can help you decide what kind of fixing or fitting is needed.

You may decide that repair isn't your best choice. If, for example, the knees of your pants are worn through, perhaps the pants are so old that the seat is about to go, too. Check to see how thin the fabric is. Perhaps your garment has reached the end of the road.

Most kinds of damage, however, are worth repairing. A button thread may have worn through. The fabric may have been torn by accident. Such damage can be easily fixed—and if the repair is well done, it will last.

Personal habits sometimes cause damage. If the keys in your pocket keep making a hole, repair the pocket, but also find another place to keep your keys. If you rip the neck of your turtleneck sweater because you pull it off without unzipping the zipper, restitch the seam, but change your habit. Otherwise the same problem will happen again.

Damage also occurs when clothes don't fit properly. If a button pops off your coat because the coat is too tight, restitching the button won't be enough. The coat should be altered so that it can be buttoned without strain.

Alterations

Altering clothes is a skill with many payoffs. Some alterations are easy, some are hard. But whatever alterations you learn to do will help you to expand your wardrobe.

Altering can help you hold on to favorite clothes. When a skirt you love becomes too short or too snug, you can lower the hem or let out the side seams.

If you inherit oversize clothing, you can alter it to fit you instead of waiting to grow into it. You can shorten a hem or take in seams.

If you know how to alter clothes, you will have more choices when buying new clothes. Many garments need only minor corrections to fit you. You may be able to take advantage of a great bargain by buying on sale a garment that needs only simple changes to fit perfectly.

Can I Do It?

Many common alterations can be learned with a little practice. Simply moving buttons over may make a tight garment com-

Box 1

FIXING

BUTTONS

Buttons are easy to replace. Here's how. Using a double thread, sew through the button several times. You can avoid sewing the button on too tightly by placing a toothpick or a pin across the top of the button and sewing over that. When the button is secure, remove the toothpick and fasten the thread on the inside of the garment.

For heavier fabrics, form a shank by winding the thread several times around the underside of the button before fastening.

SNAPS

To sew on snaps, fix the ball part inside the top flap of the opening. Stitch closely several times through each hole. Then rub chalk on the ball and close the opening naturally. Sew the socket where the chalk leaves a mark.

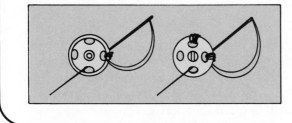

FIXING SNAGS

It takes just a few seconds to fix a snag with a crochet hook or snag fixer. (These tools are available wherever sewing notions are sold.)

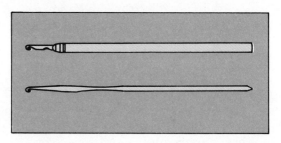

Insert the crochet hook or snag fixer through the fabric from under the snag. Grasp the snag with the hook, and pull it back through to the underside.

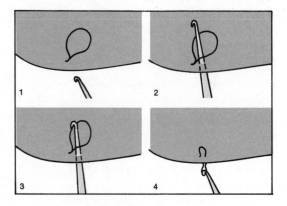

Gently stretch the fabric to smooth out any puckers caused by the snag.

fortable. Changing the length of a pair of pants or a skirt by altering a hem is not difficult. With some practice, you can learn to adjust the width of a garment by letting out or taking in seams.

There can be hidden complications, however. For example, in wrinkle-resistant garments, creases made at the seams or at hemlines may not press out. Moving buttons may leave marks on the fabric where

DARNING TEARS

You can darn, or reweave, straight tears like this:

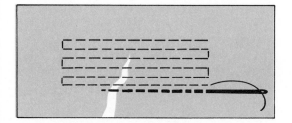

Working from the right side, place the torn edges together. Use an unknotted thread to make small stitches back and forth across the tear, beginning and ending about ¼ in (6 mm) above and below the tear. Be sure to leave a "tail" of thread at both ends to keep the stitching from pulling out.

DARNING HOLES

Even holes can be mended by reweaving:

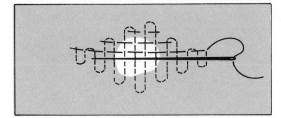

Using the technique given for mending a tear, first make lengthwise stitches up and down over the hole. Then weave rows of stitches across the first set of stitches until the hole is covered. Begin and end all lines of stitching ¼ in (6 mm) beyond the hole to strengthen the edges.

When a garment becomes faded, altering it can be a problem. The seam allowance inside these jeans kept its color. Could the seam be let out without an obvious mark at the seam line?

can rarely be made to fit evenly. If fabric was off-grain, or twisted out of shape, when the pieces were cut, no amount of sewing will correct the problem.

Creativity and Sewing

If the usual way of altering a garment does not work, a little ingenuity sometimes helps. For instance, you may think of clever ways to disguise creases, fade lines, and holes.

Creativity is a vital part of the craft of sewing. Whether you are simply fixing a tear, or altering a garment you want to save, you need to know basic techniques. But if you really understand how garments are made and how to sew, you may be able to save a garment that looks unsavable. This will stretch the life of your wardrobe, and your clothing budget as well.

the buttons used to be. Sometimes there isn't enough material to let out a seam or hem.

Some problems cannot be corrected. A neckline stretched out of shape when sewn

Box 2

FITTING

ALTERING HEMS

You can make sure all your clothes are the right length by learning how to alter hems. After removing the old hem stitching, press out the crease. Then put on the garment so the new hemline can be marked. (It's best to have someone mark the hemline for you, using chalk or pins.)

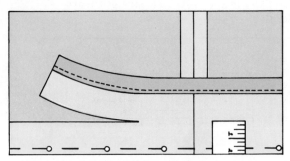

Pin the top of the finished hem to the garment, matching seams. Sew the hem to the garment with stitches that just catch the fabric. The stitches should be smooth and invisible on the outside of the garment. Press the completed hem so that it will lie flat.

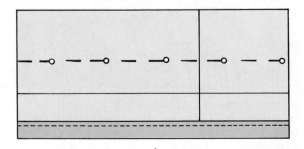

Take off the garment and turn the hem under along the chalk or pin line. Use pins to hold the hem in place. Baste the hem ¼ in (6 mm) from the folded edge. Try on the garment one more time to make sure the hem is right.

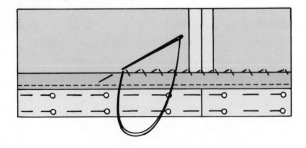

ALTERING SEAMS

Whether you have opened a seam to alter it, or are simply repairing seams, many of the same principles apply. Fix the ends of the old seam that remain, by backstitching about 1 in (24 mm) along the old seam line as you start and finish the new stitching.

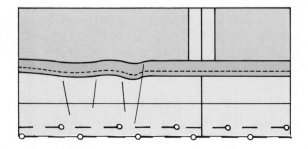

If the hem is too deep, measure and mark the desired depth. Cut off the extra fabric evenly. Finish the raw edge with a finish appropriate for the type of fabric and garment.

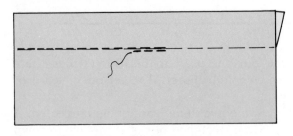

Merely restitching a seam is not hard. Pin or baste the two edges together as they were originally, and then stitch along the holes left by the old thread. But if you are altering a seam, careful planning is important.

To let out a seam, measure how much extra room you want to create, and check that there is enough fabric in the seam allowance. (If you are adjusting the body of a garment, don't forget to plan half the adjustment on one side and half on the other.) Baste the new seam in a smooth line, *then* remove the old stitching. Check fit by trying on the garment. Then stitch and press open the new seam.

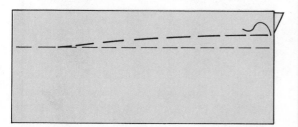

To take in a seam, the simplest method is to put on the garment inside out, and pin a new seam line so that the garment fits well. Take the garment off carefully, machine baste along the pinned line, and remove the pins. Press lightly, then check the fit of the garment before final stitching and pressing.

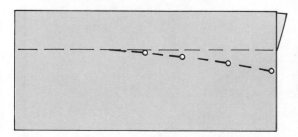

For a more accurate fit when taking in seams, put on the garment *right side* out, then transfer the markings to the inside. This is a more difficult method, but an experienced sewer will be able to help you. Ask for help too if the seam you are altering is crossed by another, as is common in the armpit of a garment. Such seams are very hard to alter.

QUESTIONS

1. List three reasons for learning how to repair and alter your own clothes.
2. What can you gain from figuring out why or how a garment was damaged?
3. What are two questions you should ask yourself before altering a garment?
4. What type of damage occurs most frequently in your clothes? What do you think causes the damage?
5. What type of alteration do your clothes most often need? Why? Who does the alterations?
6. How could you make a favorite garment larger if there is not enough of a seam allowance for letting out?

ACTIVITIES

1. Call up a local dry cleaner or tailor shop to find out the cost of various types of repairs and alterations.
2. Write a humorous story in which someone keeps letting repairs go, with disastrous results.
3. Bring to class a favorite garment that needs alteration. Have a classmate assist you in refitting the garment.

SECTION 5 · Creative Recycling

A New Look

Start with the basics, a shirt and jeans, and follow through the cycle. First the shirt was dyed to change its look. The embroidery was started to cover a stain but creativity soon took over. The star patch covered a triangular tear on the jeans. And finally, the other patch was added for balance and effect.

S ometimes—for one reason or another—a garment no longer suits you. Perhaps you have a coat that's warm and in good condition, but is a little out of style. Maybe a stain in the knee of your favorite jeans won't come out. Or perhaps the bright orange shirt you bought on sale looks a little different on you now that you're home.

When you have clothes that you no longer wear, something needs to be done. Of course, you could simply throw them away. But that would be a waste of your money—and of clothing fibers.

With a little creativity and skill, you may be able to recycle old garments. You may even end up with clothes that are better than new.

Decorating

Decorative techniques such as patches, trims, and embroidery can cover holes, hide stains, or simply liven up your clothing. Even if your jeans don't have a hole, you can decorate them with your initials, or a butterfly, or a sports team emblem.

You can make patches or appliqués yourself, or you can buy them. The simplest kind is the iron-on type sold in fabric or variety stores—no sewing ability is required!

When you use appliqués or trims such as braid, ribbon, or rickrack, make sure that the trim material suits the garment you're putting it on. It would be foolish, for example, to put a "dry-clean only" patch on a washable garment.

If you're handy with a needle, embroidery might be the answer for a garment you no longer wear. With a needle and thread, and knowledge of a few simple embroidery stitches (see box 1 in this section), you can disguise an old hemline, patch a hole, or turn a stain into a work of art.

Box 1

AN ANCIENT ART

Nobody knows when or where embroidery was developed. People all over the world use decorative stitching to brighten fabrics. Medieval tapestries and Early American samplers are only two stages in the history of embroidery.

Embroidery can decorate the yoke of a shirt, the pockets of a jacket, or the cuffs of a pair of pants. If you learn a few stitches and have patience, you can create your own personal designs. You can add a dash of color to your clothes. You can also cover small holes and stains with a unique flair. This could lengthen the life of a garment that you had given up as unwearable.

When embroidering by hand, it helps to stretch the fabric across a frame. Embroidery hoops are a convenient way to do this. They can be moved across the fabric while you work. Many sewing machines are capable of doing embroidery stitches. Whether you work by hand or by machine, embroidery is a skill that can brighten your life.

Restyling

You may want to restyle a garment that you no longer wear because it seems out of date.

The simplest way to restyle a garment is to add new accessories. A belt or a scarf, for

The material in discarded garments can sometimes be used again. A spark of imagination helped recycle these neckties into an unusual skirt.

example, can change a garment's appearance considerably. But with a little creativity and some sewing ability, you can make more dramatic changes.

When fashion magazines are featuring short dresses and all yours are long, it's not difficult to shorten the hems. Or if fashion dictates long skirts and yours are short, try lengthening them with a ruffle or a band of contrasting fabric.

Pants, too, can often be restyled to suit current fashion. Flared pants can be made straight by taking in the side seams. And straight legs can be flared by adding a triangle of new material (perhaps contrasting) to these seams.

Another way to restyle clothing is to change a garment from one type to another. For example, by removing sleeves from a sweater, you gain a vest. Pants can be cut off to make shorts. Some coats can be shortened to become jackets. Sewing books—and your own ingenuity—will give you other ideas.

A Change of Color

Sometimes the only thing wrong with a garment is its color. You don't like it, or it doesn't go with the rest of your clothes. If so, consider dyeing it.

You can dye your clothes at home, or you can have them dyed professionally. Professional dyeing costs more, of course, but some garments are worth the extra expense. For successful home dyeing, carefully follow the directions on the dye package. Dye packages give step-by-step directions for various dyeing methods.

Home dyeing works best when a light-colored fabric is darkened. However, to obtain very dark colors, you must usually simmer the fabric in the dye solution. This requires a large container and a lot of effort.

For lighter colors, you may only have to mix the dye with hot water, and then soak the garment in a sink, a container, or a washing machine.

Even light dyes can severely stain the equipment you use. It will require a great deal of cleaning and bleaching to remove all traces of the color. For this reason, you should always get permission to use the sink or container in which you plan to dye your clothes. And you should never dye clothes in a Laundromat. The dye could ruin the next customer's wash.

Creative Ways of Dyeing

Tie-dyeing and batik are two dyeing methods that create striking new designs on old garments.

In tie-dyeing, parts of the fabric are tightly wrapped, or tied, in some places so that the dye penetrates unevenly, producing a multishaded effect. One or several colors may be used in the process.

In batik dyeing, hot wax is poured onto the fabric so that it coats some areas completely. When the garment is dyed, the coated areas stay the original color. Only the unwaxed areas take the dye. During the process, the wax cracks, forming thin cracked lines in the final pattern.

When the dyeing is finished, the wax is washed out with a solvent, leaving a permanent design dyed into the fabric. The same procedure can be repeated several times for a multicolored design.

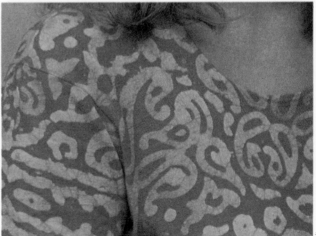

If a favorite piece of clothing is faded or stained, give it new life with a dye treatment. Special techniques, such as tie-dyeing (above) and batik (below), let you create your own designs.

Think Recycle

These are only a few ideas for giving clothes a new lease on life. Your creativity is the only limit. If you know you won't use a garment in its present form, you have nothing to lose by recycling it—and everything to gain.

If your idea works out well, you have a new garment. If you aren't happy with the change, perhaps someone else will be. And if your experiment is a disaster, you can still use the scraps of fabric in some way—the fabric needn't be wasted.

So when clothes you never wear are taking up space in your closet, think recycle. Then let your imagination be your guide.

QUESTIONS

1. Give three reasons why a garment might be creatively recycled.
2. Describe some ways in which garments can be given a new look. Which is the easiest? The hardest?
3. Could a new garment be creatively recycled? Why would one do this?
4. Are there clothes in your closet that could be given a new look? How?
5. How could you use fusible web in a creative recycling project?
6. Why are light-colored fabrics the easiest to dye?

ACTIVITIES

1. Find out how many embroidery stitches can be done by machine. Use a machine to decorate an old garment you rarely wear.
2. Make a chart showing how different-colored dyes will affect different-colored fabrics.
3. Research tie-dyeing or batiking. Give a class demonstration of the techniques.
4. Fix an iron-on patch onto one knee of some old slacks, and sew a patch onto the other. Then invent some tests to see which one lasts better.

SECTION 6 · The End of the Road?

THE FINAL CYCLE

Clothing fibers can have many lives—if you let them. Even after they seem useless for wearing, clothes can still give you, or someone else, good service. Each object shown below has lived a double life—it was once worn as clothing. What could your clothes be used for when you finally give up on them?

Even when you're certain you have no further use for an item of clothing, the life cycle of that garment needn't end. If refitting, restyling, or some other change can't make a garment suitable for you, there are other ways it can be recycled.

Saving Our Future Resources

Recycling is part of our responsibility to the future. We need to recycle clothing because the amount of fiber that can be produced in the world is limited. As more people are born, more land is needed for growing food and for housing. That means less land for growing cotton and linen, and fewer pastures for wool-producing sheep.

Machine-made fibers depend on materials that are needed for other purposes. Rayons have a cellulose base that comes mostly from wood pulp. Other machine-made fibers use coal and petroleum as basic materials. Wood, coal, and petroleum are all very important for energy production, and supplies are limited.

Today's basic materials may be completely used up sometime in the future. By then, we hope, science will have come up with new materials. In the meantime, we can help conserve our resources by getting maximum use from the fibers that make up our clothing.

Passing It On

One of the oldest forms of recycling clothing is the hand-me-down. Clothing that you no longer wear can be passed on to another member of your family, or a friend. Clothing that no longer suits you may be a real find for someone else.

During your teen years, you are likely to be growing fast. This means you may stop wearing garments *long* before they are un-

Many organizations recycle the clothes people no longer wear. Look for clothing deposit bins in shopping center parking lots.

wearable. Throwing such clothing out is wasteful. There may be several years' wear left for someone else.

If that someone else can't be found in your family, or among your friends, look further. You could earn some money by selling the clothes through a thrift shop. Or you could give the clothing to a charity organization such as the Salvation Army or CARE. (Get a receipt for the clothes so their value may be used as a deduction on your family's tax return.)

Clothes that you give away help someone else. They may help a family that has lost everything in a natural disaster. Seeing that good clothes find their way to someone who can use them is a way to help others.

Other Ways of Recycling

Garments can be recycled even when they can no longer be used as clothing. The legs of a pair of jeans, for example, can be converted into very sturdy and useful tote bags. And even if only small pieces of fabric are in good condition, these can be cut out and saved for patchwork. Such pieced fabric can be made into one-of-a-kind vests, shirts, or handbags. Or if you're feeling ambitious, you can make an old-fashioned patchwork quilt.

Worn-out garments of soft cotton make good cleaning rags. (Be sure to remove all fasteners from the rags before you use them. Otherwise, furniture could get scratched from sharp hooks or button edges.) Torn nylon stockings, panty hose, and underwear can be cut up and used to stuff toys and pillows.

Even if the fabric is totally destroyed, the fibers may still be useful. Fibers can be recycled to make fabrics suitable for padding (shoulder pads, for example). Fibers are also used for the rag content in paper. Some cities have organizations that collect old clothes for such recycling. Garments that cannot be used by thrift shops or

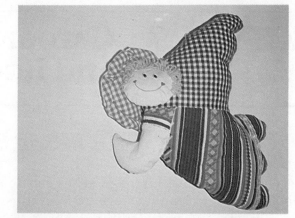

Fabrics from old clothing can be used for patchwork projects—quilts, and colorful stuffed toys.

charities may also be given away for fiber recycling.

You and Others

There are many reasons for recycling clothes. A lot of them help *you*—they stretch your clothing budget, and give you better wear for your money. But when a garment has reached the end of the road for you, don't forget other people. The garment, its fabric, or its fibers may still be useful. Don't let that usefulness be wasted.

QUESTIONS

1. Why is recycling clothing more important today than ever?
2. What kinds of groups can benefit if you recycle your clothes after you can no longer wear them? (Name some of the organizations.)
3. List all the ways you can think of to make old clothing fibers useful again.

ACTIVITIES

1. Visit a thrift shop or a charity organization. Ask about the various ways it recycles clothes.
2. Go to the library and find out as much as you can about fiber recycling. Where are the re-

4. Does your family have any hand-me-down garments that have been passed down for several generations? Why do you think families sometimes save such clothes?
5. Why is it more economical to make a worn pair of jeans into a skirt, for example, than to cut the jeans up for patchwork?

cycling plants? What is the fiber used for? Give a report to the class.
3. Collect fabric patches and turn them into a useful item. (You can find many ideas for this project in craft books.)

SECTION 7 · Careers in Clothes Care and Recycling

THE FIBER SAVERS

Everyone shown on this page is saving fibers for use in one way or another. A mender in a dry cleaning store (A), an industrial dry cleaner (B), a thrift shop (C), even workers in a paper mill (D)—all recycle materials which would be wasted otherwise. In many fields, recycling is a new idea. In the field of clothing, people have earned their living at it for years.

When you think of maintaining or recycling clothing, you probably think about your own wardrobe. Through proper care, you can keep your clothing fresh and ready to wear. But have you ever thought of maintaining and recycling clothes to earn a living? An interest in clothing care can lead to a variety of jobs.

Sewing Skills

A knowledge of tailoring and the ability to sew well are especially valuable in clothing care and recycling. Dry-cleaning plants employ menders to do repairs and alterations on customers' clothing. Secondhand clothing stores hire workers with sewing skills for repair work, too. Many large clothing stores also have alteration departments where you can get professional sewing experience.

If tailoring and sewing are your fields of interest, you should learn professional methods. Many high schools and community centers give instruction in sewing techniques.

Sewing skills are often in demand. Many clothing stores and dry-cleaning firms employ people to do mending and alterations.

Your Own Business

If you are creative and a self-starter, you may be able to develop special opportunities. Many students have earned money for college by doing mending, laundering, and even sewing new garments for others.

Starting a business of your own isn't easy. But people who started altering clothes at home for neighbors and friends have sometimes succeeded in building their own dressmaking and designing operations.

Worn-out clothes can also supply a business opportunity. Scraps of fabric, leather, and trims can be turned into "soft sculptures" and sold to stores or private customers. Patchwork quilts and pillows can also be sold. You may be able to teach these crafts in a local school or at a senior citizens' recreation center.

The Clothes Cleaners

Laundry and dry cleaning offer a number of job opportunities. Hospitals, nursing homes, and hotels often have their own plants. There are companies that supply uniforms and linen service. And, of course, there are laundries and dry-cleaning stores.

Most of these positions don't require any

special education. Employees are usually trained on the job. Of course, the better your education, the better your chances of landing a job, and of moving up to a managerial position later on.

At a laundry, a machine washer is responsible for washing the items—mostly shirts and sheets. The washer must know how to operate the controls of a huge machine that holds several hundred pounds of laundry. The machine washer must also know the right water temperature, suds level, time cycle, and amount of agitation required for different fabrics.

After the laundry is washed, the washer delivers items such as sheets to the flatwork finishers. Flatwork finishers shake the folds from the sheets and place them on belts that feed them into flatwork ironing machines. Other finishers fold and stack the sheets as they come out of the ironing machine.

Shirts, left damp after the wash, are sent to the shirt finishers. The shirt finisher presses shirts on special forms. There are round "arms" for ironing sleeves, and a form that makes it possible to iron the back and front of a shirt at the same time. After ironing the shirt, the finisher puts it on a hanger or folds it for packaging.

The jobs at dry cleaners are similar to those at laundries. There are dry-cleaning machine operators. There are finishers who see that the garments are pressed free of wrinkles. And at both laundries and dry cleaners, there are counter clerks and people who package the cleaned clothes.

Cleaners must know something about fabrics. They sort garments according to fiber, fabric construction, and the proper cleaning time. The dry cleaner may apply prespotting solution to spots before putting

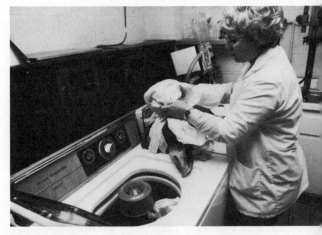

The best way to determine the effectiveness of a laundry product is to try it on dirty clothes. This researcher is testing a new detergent.

the garments into the dry-cleaning machines.

The spotters are the real fabric experts. They know how to choose the right chemicals to remove stubborn spots and stains without damaging the garment. Spotters learn the techniques to use for each type of fabric, chemical, and stain. Because the job involves so much decision making, it takes six to twelve months to learn the trade. That training can be obtained in a vocational school or on the job.

New Products

There may be fewer laundry and dry-cleaning stores in the future. While hospitals and hotels will still need someone to do their bulk work, more and more consumers will be doing their own cleaning. This is partly because of the work of new product developers in the field of clothes care and recycling.

Both the makers of laundry products and the many manufacturers of washing machines employ people to research and develop new products. These people often have a background in home economics—and their mission is to make cleaning easier.

Some research new detergent products that will safely wash more fabrics. Others seek to improve washing machines. They may make dry cleaning at home a reality in the near future—perhaps in the same machine that does your washing. Still others work to develop other equipment, such as lightweight irons, that could make a homemaker's life easier.

These new product developers need to have a good understanding of fabrics and of garment construction. Many need a background in physics and chemistry. Their inventions may decrease jobs in laundries and dry cleaners, but they will probably increase jobs in other fields.

Other Jobs

Secondhand clothing shops hire salespeople and store managers. These shops are sometimes run by charitable organizations that use volunteers as well as paid workers. Occasionally, the jobs are part time and may suit people who can work only a few hours a day.

Jobs are also available in plants that recycle fibers. Factory jobs involve running and overseeing the work of machines. The workers are usually trained on the job. Fiber-recycling plants employ managers, office workers, and maintenance people as well.

From fiber-recycling plants to the clothing alteration business, people are working to make clothes last longer. These jobs need widely different skills and qualifications. If you pursue a career in this field, you will be helping to conserve materials that may be needed in the uncertain future.

QUESTIONS

1. Name four different areas in the clothing care and recycling field.
2. Describe two jobs in each of these areas.
3. What kind of skills and education do workers in these jobs need?
4. Which of the jobs in the clothing care and recycling field do you find most interesting? Why?
5. Which areas in the field do you think will expand in the future? Why?

ACTIVITIES

1. Clip out newspaper advertisements for various jobs in the clothing care and recycling field and tack them on the bulletin board in your classroom.
2. Find out more about a particular job in the field and describe it to your class.
3. Write a story about the kind of work one of the jobs in the field might call for 200 years from now.

Appendix

FOOD AND NUTRITION BOARD, NATIONAL ACADEMY OF SCIENCES—NATIONAL RESEARCH COUNCIL
Recommended Daily Dietary Allowances, Revised 1974 †

	Age	Weight		Height		Energy	Protein	Vitamin A	Vitamin D	Vitamin E Activity
		(kg)	(lbs)	(cm)	(in)			FAT-SOLUBLE VITAMINS		
	(years)	(kg)	(lbs)	(cm)	(in)	(kcal)	(g)	(IU)	(IU)	(IU)
Infants	0.0–0.5	6	14	60	24	kg × 117	kg × 2.2	1,400	400	4
	0.5–1.0	9	20	71	28	kg × 108	kg × 2.0	2,000	400	7
Children	1–3	13	28	86	34	1,300	23	2,000	400	7
U.S. RDA (children) *							28	2,500	400	10
Males	4–6	20	44	110	44	1,800	30	2,500	400	9
	7–10	30	66	135	54	2,400	36	3,300	400	10
	11–14	44	97	158	63	2,800	44	5,000	400	12
	15–18	61	134	172	69	3,000	54	5,000	400	15
	19–22	67	147	172	69	3,000	54	5,000	400	15
	23–50	70	154	172	69	2,700	56	5,000		15
	51+	70	154	172	69	2,400	56	5,000		15
Females	11–14	44	97	155	62	2,400	44	4,000	400	12
	15–18	54	119	162	65	2,100	48	4,000	400	12
	19–22	58	128	162	65	2,100	46	4,000	400	12
	23–50	58	128	162	65	2,000	46	4,000		12
	51+	58	128	162	65	1,800	46	4,000		12
U.S. RDA (adults) **							45	5,000	400	30
Pregnant Females						+300	+30	5,000	400	15
Lactating Females						+500	+20	6,000	400	15

Note: The U.S. RDA (allowances) are based on the 7th edition of the RDA (1968).
The U.S. RDA for protein are 45 g for animal protein and 65 g for vegetable protein.
* The U.S. RDA (children) is the standard for labeling baby and junior foods (ages 1 to 4).
** The U.S. RDA (adult) is the standard for labeling all food other than baby and junior foods.
The percentage of the U.S. RDA listed on package labels are percentages of these figures.
† The Food and Nutrition board plans to revise this table early in 1979, and some RDAs may be affected.

| WATER-SOLUBLE VITAMINS | | | | | | | MINERALS | | | | | |
Vitamin C (mg)	Folacin (mcg)	Niacin (mg)	Riboflavin (mg)	Thiamin (mg)	Vitamin B_6 (mg)	Vitamin B_{12} (mcg)	Calcium (mg)	Phosphorus (mg)	Iodine (mcg)	Iron (mg)	Magnesium (mg)	Zinc (mg)
35	50	5	0.4	0.3	0.3	0.3	360	240	35	10	60	3
35	50	8	0.6	0.5	0.4	0.3	540	400	45	15	70	5
40	100	9	0.8	0.7	0.6	1.0	800	800	60	15	150	10
40	200	9	0.8	0.7	0.7	3.0	800	800	70	10	200	8
40	200	12	1.1	0.9	0.9	1.5	800	800	80	10	200	10
40	300	16	1.2	1.2	1.2	2.0	800	800	110	10	250	10
45	400	18	1.5	1.4	1.6	3.0	1,200	1,200	130	18	350	15
45	400	20	1.8	1.5	2.0	3.0	1,200	1,200	150	18	400	15
45	400	20	1.8	1.5	2.0	3.0	800	800	140	10	350	15
45	400	18	1.6	1.4	2.0	3.0	800	800	130	10	350	15
45	400	16	1.5	1.2	2.0	3.0	800	800	110	10	350	15
45	400	16	1.3	1.2	1.6	3.0	1,200	1,200	115	18	300	15
45	400	14	1.4	1.1	2.0	3.0	1,200	1,200	115	18	300	15
45	400	14	1.4	1.1	2.0	3.0	800	800	100	18	300	15
45	400	13	1.2	1.0	2.0	3.0	800	800	100	18	300	15
45	400	12	1.1	1.0	2.0	3.0	800	800	80	10	300	15
60	400	20	1.7	1.5	2.0	6.0	1,000	1,000	150	18	400	15
60	800	+2	+0.3	+0.3	2.5	4.0	1,200	1,200	125	18+	450	20
80	600	+4	+0.5	+0.3	2.5	4.0	1,200	1,200	150	18	450	25

TABLE OF FOOD VALUES

MILK GROUP	Amount	Calories	Carbohydrates (g)	Fat (g)	Protein (g)	Calcium (mg)	Iron (mg)	Vitamin A (IU)	Thiamin (mg)	Riboflavin (mg)	Niacin (mg)	Vitamin C (mg)
Buttermilk, 2% fat	1 c/240 ml	99	12	2	8	285	.1	81	.08	.4	.1	2
Cheese, American, process	1 oz/28 g	106	0	9	6	174	.1	343	–	.10	.02	0
Cheese, brick	1 oz/28 g	105	0	8	7	191	.1	307	+	.1	.03	0
Cheese, Cheddar	1 oz/28 g	114	0	9	7	204	.2	300	+	.11	.02	0
Cheese, cottage, creamed	½ c/120 ml	108	3	5	13	63	.2	171	.02	.17	.13	0
Cheese, cottage, dry	½ c/120 ml	62	1	.3	12	23	.2	22	.02	.10	.11	0
Cheese, cream	1 oz/28 g	99	0	10	2	23	.3	405	+	.05	.03	0
Cheese, Swiss	1 oz/28 g	107	0	8	8	272	.1	240	–	.10	.03	0
Chocolate milk	1 c/240 ml	208	26	8.5	8	280	.6	302	.09	.4	.3	2
Cream, heavy	1 T/15 ml	80	.4	6	+	10	+	220	+	.02	+	0
Cream, light	1 T/15 ml	45	.6	5	+	14	.01	108	+	.02	.01	0
Cream, sour	1 T/15 ml	25	.5	3	+	14	.01	95	+	.02	.01	0
Ice cream,* 16% fat	½ c/120 ml	175	16	12	2	75	.05	448	.02	.14	.57	1
Ice cream,* soft serve	½ c/120 ml	185	19	12	3	118	.2	395	.04	.27	.1	Tr.
Milk	1 c/240 ml	150	12	8	8	291	.1	307	.1	.4	.2	2
Milk, low fat 2%	1 c/240 ml	121	12	5	8	297	.1	500	.1	.4	.2	2
Milk, skim	1 c/240 ml	86	12	.4	8	302	.1	500	.1	.3	.2	2
Yogurt, fruit	1 c/240 ml	231	43	2.5	10	345	.2	104	.08	.4	.2	2
Yogurt, plain, skim milk	1 c/240 ml	127	17	.4	13	452	.2	16	.1	.5	.3	2
Yogurt, plain, whole milk	1 c/240 ml	139	11	7	8	274	.1	279	.06	.3	.2	2

* *Note:* Although ice cream is a good source of calcium, it also contains many calories, and may lead to weight problems.

MEAT GROUP *

Food	Serving											
Beef	3½ oz/100 g	266	0	15	30	10	4	50	.1	.4	4.5	0
Beef, hamburger, 21% fat	3 oz/85 g	235	0	17	20	9	2.7	30	.07	.17	4.4	0
Beef liver	3½ oz/100 g	238	6	11	28	11	9	56070	.3	4.3	.17	28
Black-eyed peas, frozen	¾ c/180 ml	169	31	–	12	32	3.7	220	.5	.1	1.8	1.2
Chicken	3½ oz/100 g	182	0	6	30	13	1.5	132	.1	.1	8.8	0
Eggs	1	80	Tr.	6	6	28	1	260	.05	.15	–	0
Fish, white	3½ oz/100 g	170	0	5	29	31	1	180	.1	.1	3	2
Garbanzos (chick peas)	¾ c/180 ml	165	27	2	9	67	3.1	23	.15	–	.9	0
Kidney beans (red beans)	¾ c/180 ml	173	32	1	11	56	3.4	8	.1	–	1.1	0
Lamb	3½ oz/100 g	260	0	16	27	8	2	–	.2	.3	7.6	0
Lentils	¾ c/180 ml	158	29	–	12	38	3.1	30	.1	.1	1	0
Lima beans, dried	¾ c/180 ml	197	37	1	12	41	4.4	–	.2	.1	1	0
Lobster	⅔ c/160 ml	95	–	2	19	65	.8	–	.1	.1	–	0
Peanut butter	2 T/30 ml	190	4	17	9	10	.6	0	.02	.02	4.2	0
Peas, dried, split	¾ c/180 ml	173	31	–	12	17	2.6	60	.23	.14	1.4	0
Pork	3½ oz/100 g	240	0	13	28	8	4	–	1	.3	4.4	0
Sardines	3 oz/85 g	175	9	9	20	372	.3	190	.02	.17	.5	0
Shrimps	3 oz/85 g	100	1	1	21	98	2.6	50	–	–	1.5	0
Soybeans, dried	¾ c/180 ml	176	15	8	15	98	3.7	37	.29	.12	.8	0
Soybean-textured patties	2½ oz/72 g	182	7	11	14	20	3	0	.23	.26	7	–
Tuna, canned in oil	3 oz/85 g	170	0	7	24	7	1.6	70	–	.1	10	0
Turkey	3½ oz/100 g	188	0	6	32	8	1.8	–	.1	.2	7.6	0
Veal	3½ oz/100 g	213	0	8	33	10	3.3	–	.2	.3	7.2	0

Key: + Probably present.   – No data.   Tr.—Nutrient present but in very small (trace) amounts.

* *Note:* Traditionally called the meat group. It includes eggs and legumes as well as meat, poultry and fish. Food values are given as for *cooked* foods in this group. Meats have visible fat removed. Chicken—no skin, half dark, half white meat.

TABLE OF FOOD VALUES (cont.)

FRUITS AND VEGETABLES GROUP *	Amount	Cal-ories	Car-bohy-drates (g)	Fat (g)	Pro-tein (g)	Cal-cium (mg)	Iron (mg)	Vita-min A (IU)	Thia-min (mg)	Ribo-flavin (mg)	Nia-cin (mg)	Vita-min C (mg)
Apple	1 (2½"/63 mm)	58	15	1		7	.3	90	.03	.02	.1	4
Apricots	3 med	51	13	Tr.	1	17	.5	2700	.03	.04	.6	10
Asparagus	6 spears	20	4	Tr.	2	21	.6	900	.16	.18	1.4	26
Avocado, raw	½	171	6	17	2	10	.6	290	.11	.20	1.6	14
Banana	1 med	127	34	Tr.	2	12	1.1	285	.07	.09	1.0	15
Beans, green	¾ c/180 ml	25	5	Tr.	2	50	.6	540	.07	.09	.5	12
Beans, lima, fresh frozen, cooked	¾ c/180 ml	126	24	—	8	26	2.1	293	.1	—	1.3	22
Bean sprouts	⅔ c/160 ml	28	5	Tr.	3	17	.9	20	.09	.10	.7	6
Beets	½ c/120 ml	27	6	Tr.	1	12	.4	17	.03	.03	.3	5
Blueberries	⅔ c/160 ml	62	15	1	1	15	1.0	100	.03	.06	.5	14
Broccoli	⅔ c/160 ml	26	5	Tr.	3	88	.8	2500	.09	.20	.8	90
Brussels sprouts	6 or 7	36	6	1	4	32	1.1	520	.08	.14	.8	87
Cabbage, shredded	⅔ c/160 ml	20	4	Tr.	1	44	.3	130	.04	.04	.3	33
Cabbage, shredded, raw	½ c/120 ml	12	3	Tr.	1	25	.2	65	.03	.03	.2	26
Cantaloupe	⅔ c/160 ml	30	8	Tr.	—	14	.4	3400	.04	.03	.6	33
Carrots	⅔ c/160 ml	31	7	1	1	33	.6	10500	.05	.05	.5	6
Carrots, grated, raw	½ c/120 ml	21	5	Tr.	—	18	.4	5500	.03	.03	.3	4
Cauliflower	¾ c/180 ml	22	4	Tr.	2	21	.7	60	.09	.08	.6	55
Celery, sliced	¾ c/180 ml	14	3	Tr.	1	31	.2	230	.02	.03	.3	6
Celery, raw	3 pieces (5" × ¾"/ 127 mm × 19 mm)	8	2	Tr.	—	20	.2	120	.01	.01	.2	5

Food	Serving											
Cherries, red sour, pitted	⅔ c/160 ml	58	14	1	1	22	.4	1000	.05	.06	.4	10
Cherries, sweet	14	70	17	1	1	22	.4	110	.05	.06	.4	10
Corn, sweet kernels	½ c/120 ml	83	19	.5	3	3	.6	400	.11	.10	1.3	7
Cranberries, chopped	¼ c/60 ml	12	3	1	−	3	.1	10	−	−	−	3
Cucumber, raw	6 slices	4	1	0	−	4	.1	+	+	.01	+	3
Dates	12	274	73	1	2	59	3.0	50	.09	.10	2.2	0
Figs, fresh	2 med	80	20	Tr.	1	35	.6	80	.06	.05	.4	2
Grapefruit, pink	½ med	40	10	Tr.		16	.4	440	.04	.02	.2	37
Grapefruit, white	½ med	40	10	Tr.		16	.4	10	.04	.02	.2	37
Grapes, seedless	20	67	17	1	3	12	.4	100	.05	.03	.3	4
Kale	½ c/120 ml	20	3	1	3	93	.8	4150	.05	.09	.8	45
Lemon juice	½ c/120 ml	25	8	Tr.	1	7	.2	20	.03	.01	.1	46
Lettuce, iceberg, raw	⅙ head	12	3	Tr.	1	18	.5	297	.05	.05	.3	5
Mushrooms, raw	½ c/120 ml	9	1	Tr.	1	2	.3	−	.03	.15	1.4	1
Mustard greens	⅔ c/160 ml	23	4	Tr.	2	138	1.8	5800	.08	.14	.6	48
Onions, boiled	½ c/120 ml	29	7	Tr.	1	24	.4	40	.03	.03	.2	7
Orange	1 (3"/76 mm)	75	18	Tr.	1	61	.6	300	.15	.06	.7	75
Orange juice	¾ c/180 ml	80	19	Tr.	1	20	.4	370	.17	.06	.7	83
Parsnips	⅔ c/160 ml	66	15	1	1	45	.6	30	.07	.08	.1	10
Peach, peeled	1 (2½"/63 mm)	38	10	Tr.	1	9	.5	1330	.02	.05	1.0	7
Pear, Bartlett	1 (3"/76 mm)	109	28	1	1	14	.5	36	.03	.07	.2	7
Peas, green	⅔ c/160 ml	71	12	1	5	23	1.8	540	.28	.11	2.3	20
Pepper, green sweet	1 med	18	4	Tr.	1	9	.5	420	.06	.07	.5	96
Pepper, green sweet, raw	¼ c/60 ml	6	1	Tr.	+	2	−	105	.02	.02	.1	32

Key: + Probably present.   − No data.   Tr.—Nutrient present but in very small (trace) amounts.

* *Note:* All fruits and vegetables fresh unless noted. Vegetables fresh *cooked* unless noted "raw."

TABLE OF FOOD VALUES (cont.)

FRUITS AND VEGETABLES GROUP *	Amount	Cal- ories	Car- bohy- drates (g)	Fat (g)	Pro- tein (g)	Cal- cium (mg)	Iron (mg)	Vita- min A (IU)	Thia- min (mg)	Ribo- flavin (mg)	Nia- cin (mg)	Vita- min C (mg)
Pineapple, cubed	⅔ c/160 ml	52	14	Tr.		17	.5	70	.09	.03	.2	17
Plums, prune, fresh	3 med	75	20	Tr.	Tr.	12	.5	1340	.03	.03	.5	4
Potato, baked	1 med	140	31	Tr.	4	13	1	+	.15	.06	2.5	30
Potatoes, French fried	10 pieces	135	20	7	2	8	.7	Tr.	.07	.04	1.6	11
Prunes, dried	4 med	80	22	1	Tr.	16	1.2	510	.03	.05	.5	1
Pumpkin, canned	1 c/240 ml	80	19	1	2	61	1	15680	.07	.12	1.5	12
Raisins (snack package)	½ oz/14 g	45	12	Tr.		9	.5	2	.01	.01	.1	+
Spinach	½ c/120 ml	20	3	.5	3	84	2	7290	.06	.12	.5	25
Spinach, raw	1 c/240 ml	13	2	.1	1	47	1.6	4050	.05	.10	.3	25
Squash, summer, cubed	½ c/120 ml	14	3	Tr.	1	25	.4	390	.05	.08	.8	10
Squash, winter, mashed	½ c/120 ml	38	9	.1	1	20	.5	3500	.04	.10	.4	8
Strawberries	⅔ c/160 ml	37	8	1		21	1.0	60	.03	.07	.6	59
Sweet potato, baked	1 med	211	48	1	3	60	1.3	12150	.13	.11	1	33
Tomatoes	½ c/120 ml	32	7	Tr.	2	18	.8	1200	.08	.06	1	29
Tomato, raw	1 med	32	7	Tr.	2	19	.7	1350	.09	.06	1	35
Tomato juice	¾ c/180 ml	35	8	Tr.	2	13	1.6	1460	.09	.05	1.5	29
Watermelon	⅔ c/160 ml	26	6	1		7	.5	590	.03	.03	.2	7

* *Note:* All fruits and vegetables fresh unless noted. Vegetables fresh *cooked* unless noted "raw."

CEREALS GROUP

Bread, white enriched	1 slice	70	13	1	2	21	.6	0	.10	.06	.8	0
Bread, whole wheat	1 slice	65	14	1	3	24	.8	0	.09	.03	.8	0
Bread, rye (⅔% rye)	1 slice	80	17	Tr.	3	27	.8	0	.09	.07	.6	0
Corn flakes, fortified (25% RDA)	1 c/240 ml	110	25	Tr.	2	1	1.8	1250	.38	.43	5	15
Corn, grits, enriched, cooked	⅔ c/160 ml	83	18	Tr.	2	3	.5	125	.1	.05	.6	0
Oats, rolled, whole grain, cooked	⅔ c/160 ml	107	18	1	4	14	1	–	.13	.03	.2	0
Oats, rolled, instant	1 pkg	107	19	1	4	24	1	0	.15	.04	.3	0
Pasta, enriched (macaroni cooked, etc.)	1 c/240 ml	190	39	1	7	14	1.4	0	.23	.13	1.8	0
Rice, instant, enriched, cooked	¾ c/180 ml	135	30	Tr.	3	4	1	0	.16	–	1.2	0
Rice, parboiled, enriched	¾ c/180 ml	139	31	Tr.	3	25	1.1	0	.14	.02	1.6	0
Rice, puffed, whole grain, restored	1 c/240 ml	60	13	Tr.	1	3	.3	0	.07	.01	.7	0
Wheat, farina, enriched	1 c/240 ml	100	22	Tr.	3	147	.8	0	.12	.07	1	0
Wheat, farina, mix & eat	1 c/240 ml	100	21	Tr.	3	10	8	0	.15	.08	1	0
Wheat, farina, quick	1 c/240 ml	100	21	Tr.	3	147	8	0	.15	.08	1	0
Wheat flakes, fortified, 25% U.S. RDA	¾ c/180 ml	100	24	Tr.	2	10	4.5	1250	.38	.43	5	15
Wheat, puffed, whole grain, restored	1 c/240 ml	55	12	Tr.	2	4	.6	0	.08	.03	1.2	0
Wheat, shredded, whole grain	1 large biscuit	90	20	1	2	11	.9	0	.06	.03	1.1	0
Wheat, whole grain cereal	1 c/240 ml	110	23	1	4	17	1.2	–	.15	.05	1.5	0

Key: + Probably present.   – No data.   Tr.—Nutrient present but in very small (trace) amounts.

TABLE OF FOOD VALUES (cont.)

OTHER	Amount	Calories	Carbohydrates (g)	Fat (g)	Protein (g)	Calcium (mg)	Iron (mg)	Vitamin A (IU)	Thiamin (mg)	Riboflavin (mg)	Niacin (mg)	Vitamin C (mg)
Bacon, fried crisp	2 slices	85	0	8	4	2	.5	0	.08	.05	.8	0
Butter	1 T/14 g	108	0	12	–	3	.03	459	+	+	+	0
Honey	1 T/21 g	65	17	0	Tr.	1	.1	0	Tr.	–	–	Tr.
Margarine, corn oil	1 T/14 g	100	0	11	0	0	0	500	0	0	0	0
Margarine, regular	1 T/15 g	100	0	12	0	0	0	470	0	0	0	0
Mayonnaise	1 T/15 ml	100	.2	11	–	3	.1	40	0	0	0	0
Nuts, almonds, salted	15	90	30	8	3	35	.7	0	.04	.14	.5	Tr.
Nuts, pecans	10	69	1.5	7	1	7	.2	13	.08	.01	.1	Tr.
Nuts, walnuts	5 halves	65	1.6	6	1.5	10	.3	3	.03	.01	.1	0
Oil, corn	1 T/15 ml	120	0	14	0	0	0	0	0	0	0	0
Oil, corn, peanut and other vegetable	1 T/15 ml	120		14	0	0	0	0	0	0	0	0
Salad dressing	1 T/15 ml	65	2	6	–	2	Tr.	40	Tr.	.01	Tr.	0
Salad dressing, oil and vinegar type	1 T/15 ml	85	2	9	–	0	0	0	0	0	0	0
Seeds, sesame	⅓ c/50 g	290	9	27	9	55	1.2	25	.09	.07	2.9	0
Seeds, sunflower	⅓ c/45 g	271	9.6	23	12	58	3.4	23	.33	.11	.6	–
Sugar	1 T/12 g	45	12	0	0	0	Tr.	0	0	0	0	0

Key: + Probably present.   – No data.   Tr.—Nutrient present but in very small (trace) amounts.

CLOTHING SIZE CHART

Note: This chart is based on size ranges offered by a major clothing retailer. * Different manufacturers have different names for their ranges. Sizes given here are considered regular. Some manufacturers also have special sizes such as "slim" or "husky." All sizes may vary from one clothing maker to another. To be sure of a good fit, always try on clothing before buying it. (Pattern sizes are more standardized. Body measurements are always given on the pattern envelope.)

FEMALE SIZES

Girls	7	8	10	12	14
Height	49–51½ in 124.5–130.8 cm	52–53½ in 132–135.8 cm	54–55½ in 137–141 cm	56–58 in 142–147.5 cm	58½–60½ in 148.8–153.8 cm
Chest	26–26½ in 66–67.3 cm	27–27½ in 68.5–69.8 cm	28–29 in 71–73.5 cm	29½–30½ in 74.8–77.3 cm	31–32 in 79–81.5 cm
Waist	22–22½ in 56–57.3 cm	23–23½ in 58.5–59.8 cm	24–24½ in 61–62.3 cm	25–25½ in 63.5–64.8 cm	26–26½ in 66–67.3 cm
Hips	27½–28 in 69.8–71 cm	28½–29 in 72.3–73.5 cm	29½–30½ in 74.8–77.3 cm	31–32½ in 79–82.8 cm	33–34½ in 84–87.8 cm

Young Teen	6T	8T	10T	12T	14T	16T
Height	59–60 in 150–152.5 cm	60½–61 in 153.8–155 cm	61½–62 in 156.3–157.5 cm	62½–63 in 158.8–160 cm	63½–64 in 161.3–162.5 cm	64½–65 in 163.8–165 cm
Bust	28½–29 in 72.3–73.5 cm	29½–30 in 74.8–76 cm	30½–31 in 77.3–79 cm	31½–32½ in 80.3–82.8 cm	33–34 in 84–86.5 cm	34½–35 in 87.8–89 cm
Waist	22–22½ in 56–57.3 cm	23–23½ in 58.5–59.8 cm	24–24½ in 61–62.3 cm	25–25½ in 63.5–64.8 cm	26–26½ in 66–67.3 cm	27–27½ in 68.5–69.8 cm
Hips	31–31½ in 79–80.3 cm	32–32½ in 81.5–82.8 cm	33–33½ in 84–85.3 cm	34–35 in 86.5–89 cm	35½–36½ in 90.3–92.8 cm	37–38½ in 94–97.8 cm

* Courtesy of Sears, Roebuck and Co.

CLOTHING SIZE CHART (cont.)

FEMALE SIZES

Junior	3	5	7	9	11	13	15	17
Height	62 in–66 in/157.5 cm–167.5 cm							
Bust	30–30½ in 76–77.3 cm	31–31½ in 79–80.3 cm	32–32½ in 81.5–82.8 cm	33–33½ in 84–85.3 cm	34–35 in 86.5–89 cm	35½–36½ in 90.3–92.8 cm	37–38 in 94–96.5 cm	38½–39½ in 97.8–100.3 cm
Waist	22–22½ in 56–57.3 cm	23–23½ in 58.5–59.8 cm	24–24½ in 61–62.3 cm	25–25½ in 63.5–64.8 cm	26–27 in 66–68.5 cm	27½–28½ in 69.8–72.3 cm	29–30 in 73.5–76 cm	30½–31½ in 77.3–80.3 cm
Hips	32½–33 in 82.8–84 cm	33½–34 in 85.3–86.5 cm	34½–35 in 87.8–89 cm	35½–36 in 90.3–91.5 cm	36½–37½ in 92.8–95.3 cm	38–39 in 96.5–99 cm	39½–40½ in 100.3–102.8 cm	41–42 in 104–106.5 cm
Misses	6	8	10	12	14	16	18	20
Height	63 in–66½ in/160 cm–168.8 cm							
Bust	31½–32 in 80.3–81.5 cm	32½–33 in 82.8–84 cm	33½–34 in 85.3–86.5 cm	34½–35½ in 87.8–90.3 cm	36–37 in 91.5–94 cm	37½–38½ in 95.3–97.8 cm	39–40½ in 99–102.8 cm	41–42½ in 104–107.8 cm
Waist	22½–23 in 57.3–58.5 cm	23½–24 in 59.8–61 cm	24½–25 in 62.3–63.5 cm	25½–26½ in 64.8–67.3 cm	27–28 in 68.5–71 cm	28½–29½ in 72.3–74.8 cm	30–31½ in 76–80.3 cm	32–33½ in 81.5–85.3 cm
Hips	33½–34 in 85.3–86.5 cm	34½–35 in 87.8–89 cm	35½–36 in 90.3–91.5 cm	36½–37½ in 92.8–95.3 cm	38–39 in 96.5–99 cm	39½–40½ in 100.3–102.8 cm	41–42½ in 104–107.8 cm	43–44½ in 109–113.3 cm

MALE SIZES

Boys	6	8	10	12	14	16	18	20
Height	44½–47 in 113.3–119.5 cm	47½–50½ in 120.8–128.3 cm	51–54½ in 129.5–138.5 cm	55–58½ in 139.5–148.8 cm	59–61½ in 150–156 cm	62–64 in 157.5–162.5 cm	64½–66 in 163.8–167.5 cm	66½–68 in 168.8–173 cm
Weight	47–51 lbs 21.3–23.1 kg	52–61 lbs 23.6–27.7 kg	62–75 lbs 28–34.02 kg	76–89 lbs 34.5–40.4 kg	90–103 lbs 40.8–46.7 kg	104–118 lbs 47.1–53.5 kg	119–129 lbs 53.9–58.5 kg	130–141 lbs 58.9–63.9 kg
Chest	24½–25½ in 62.3–64.8 cm	26–27 in 66–68.5 cm	27½–28½ in 69.8–72.3 cm	29–30 in 73.5–76 cm	30½–32 in 77.3–81.5 cm	32½–33½ in 82.8–85.3 cm	34–35 in 86.5–89 cm	35½–36½ in 90.3–92.8 cm
Waist	21½–23 in 57.3–61 cm	22½–24 in 59.8–63.5 cm	23½–25 in 62.3–66 cm	24½–26 in 64.8–68.5 cm	25½–27 in 67.3–71 cm	26½–28 in		

Waist 54.8-58.5 cm

	33	34	36	38	40	42
Teen males—suits and jackets						
Height	64–66 in 162.5–167.5 cm	66–68 in 167.5–173 cm	67–69 in 170–175.5 cm	68–70 in 172.7–178 cm	69–71 in 175.5–180.5 cm	69–71 in 175.5–180.5 cm
Chest	32–33 in 81.5–84 cm	33½–34 in 85.3–86.5 cm	34½–36 in 87.8–91.5 cm	36½–38 in 92.8–96.5 cm	38½–40 in 97.8–101.5 cm	40½–42 in 102.8–106.5 cm
—shirts and sweaters	XS	S	M	L		
Height	65–68 in 165–173 cm	67–70 in 170–178 cm	69–72 in 175.5–183 cm	70–73 in 178–185.5 cm		
Chest	32–33½ in 81.5–85.3 cm	34–36½ in 86.5–92.8 cm	37–40 in 94–101.5 cm	40½–42 in 102.8–106.5 cm		
Neck	13–13½ in 33–34.3 cm	14–14½ in 35.5–36.8 cm	15–15½ in 38–39.3 cm	16 in 40.5 cm		
Men—coats, jackets, suits	36	38	40	42	44	46
Height	over 67 in—through 71 in/over 170 cm—through 180.5 cm					
Chest	34½–36½ in 87.8–92.8 cm	37–38½ in 94–97.8 cm	39–40½ in 99–102.8 cm	41–42½ in 104–107.8 cm	43–44½ in 109–113.3 cm	45–46½ in 114.8–118.3 cm
Waist	29–31 in 73.5–79 cm	31–33 in 79–84 cm	33–35 in 84–89 cm	35–37½ in 89–95.3 cm	38–40 in 96.5–101.5 cm	40–42½ in 101.5–107.8 cm
—dress shirts (neck size)	14½	15	15½	16	16½	17
Waist—no larger than	33 in 84 cm	35 in 89 cm	37 in 94 cm	39 in 99 cm	42 in 106.5 cm	45 in 114.5 cm
—sport shirts	S	M	L	XL		
Waist—no larger than	32 in 81.5 cm	36 in 91.5 cm	40 in 101.5 cm	44 in 112 cm		

STAIN REMOVAL CHART

Warning: Chemicals used for stain removal are often dangerous. They may be poisonous or flammable. Several of these substances give off harmful vapors and should never be used in an enclosed area. Always read the label before using any stain removal agent and use with extreme care.

STAIN	WASHABLE	DRY CLEANABLE
Ballpoint pen ink	Ballpoint pen ink comes out quite easily when sponged with rubbing alcohol. Any stain which remains should be rubbed with soap or a detergent and then the fabric should be washed.	Use method for washable fabrics, followed by sponging with a mild detergent solution of 1 teaspoon detergent to 1 cup of water.
Blood	Soak in lukewarm water and detergent. If yellow stain remains, apply laundry bleach. Rinse well. For stubborn stains, apply a few drops of ammonia. (Never use ammonia and chlorine bleach together. They combine to form a poison gas.)	Treat with cold water to which table salt has been added (1 ounce per quart of water). Salt helps prevent color bleeding. Rinse and blot with towel. Try warm water and hydrogen peroxide to remove final traces.
Candle wax, chewing gum	Candle wax and chewing gum can be removed from most fabrics if they are first hardened by rubbing with an ice cube and then scraped off with a blunt knife or your fingernail. This takes time and patience but it does work. In desperate cases, you can try sponging the gum or wax with a nonflammable cleaning fluid, but this can spread the stain.	Same as washable fabics.
Chocolate	Rinse in lukewarm water. If brown stain remains, apply laundry bleach. For sturdy fabrics, pour boiling water through fabric over a bowl.	If colorfast, sponge with lukewarm water.
Coffee, tea	Simple washing will usually remove coffee and tea stains.	Sponge with cold water first, then try mild detergent.
Cosmetics	Pretreat by rubbing detergent into spot. Launder.	Use a grease solvent. Dry clean.
Fruit and berry	Launder. If stain remains, apply white vinegar. Rinse. If necessary, bleach with hydrogen peroxide.	If safe, apply small amount of detergent locally. Rinse. Or, apply white vinegar; rinse.
Grass, flowers, foliage	Work detergent into stain, then rinse. Or, if safe for fabric, sponge stain with alcohol. Dilute alcohol with 2 parts water for use on acetate. If stain remains, use chlorine or peroxygen bleach.	Same as washable, but try alcohol first, to see if it is safe for the dye.

STAIN REMOVAL CHART

Warning: Chemicals used for stain removal are often dangerous. They may be poisonous or flammable. Several of these substances give off harmful vapors and should never be used in an enclosed area. Always read the label before using any stain removal agent and use with extreme care.

STAIN	WASHABLE	DRY CLEANABLE
Greasy stains, including lipstick, tar	Start by following the ice-cube method given for chewing gum, then use lighter fluid to remove remaining stain.	Same as washable fabrics.
Mildew	Pretreat fabric as soon as possible with detergent and launder. Expose to sunlight; if any stain remains, sponge with rubbing alcohol.	Have dry cleaned.
Milk and cream	Immediately soak in cool water and detergent. Rinse and launder.	Sponge with cleaning fluid. If colorsafe and stain still remains, sponge with water.
Nail polish	Do not use polish remover. Sponge with amyl acetate. Launder. If necessary sponge with alcohol mixed with a few drops of ammonia.	Do not use polish remover. Sponge with amyl acetate or mixture of alcohol plus a few drops of ammonia.
Paint, varnish	Rub detergent into stain and wash. If stain is only partially removed, sponge with turpentine.	Sponge with turpentine. If necessary, loosen more of the paint by covering the stain for 30 minutes with a pad of cotton dampened with a solvent. If stain remains, apply one drop liquid detergent and work in with bowl of a spoon.
Pencil	Erase with soft eraser. If mark remains, work detergent into stain. Rinse. If necessary, put ammonia on stain, then repeat detergent treatment.	Erase or, if colorsafe, follow directions for washable fabrics.
Perspiration	If garment color has been affected, sponge a fresh stain with ammonia, an old stain with white vinegar. Rinse and launder.	Same as washable fabrics.
Scorch	Alternate applications of detergent, water, and ammonia. Rinse well.	Dampen with hydrogen peroxide until stain is removed. If necessary mix a few drops of ammonia with 1 tbsp. peroxide and moisten stain. Sandpaper scorch from heavy wools.

This table is adapted from Kleeberg, Irene Cumming—*The Butterick Fabric Handbook*, Butterick Publishing, 1975, and from *The Vogue Sewing Book*, Butterick Publishing, 1975.

Glossary

A

Accessory In interior design, item—such as a lamp, picture, or vase—that is not part of the basic furnishings of a room. Also, article of dress—such as a scarf, belt, or piece of jewelry—that is not part of a basic outfit.

Acetate Low-cost fiber manufactured from cellulose, resembling silk.

Acrylic Synthetic fiber often used as a substitute for wool.

Additive Substance added to food to improve its quality, flavor, or appearance.

Adolescence Period of growth during which a child matures into an adult.

Agitate In washing, to move clothes around with a back and forth or up and down motion, forcing water through the fabric.

Algae Group of water plants, including the seaweeds, which could be a food source in the future.

Allergy Adverse physical reaction to a substance—such as a food, dust, or pollen—that does not affect most people.

Alteration Change in a piece of clothing that affects the style or fit.

Amino acids Organic compounds that combine in various ways to form different proteins.

Analogous In a color scheme, describes colors that are similar and appear near to each other on the color wheel.

Anemia Disease, often caused by lack of iron in the diet, which affects the quality or quantity of red blood cells in the body.

Applique Individual fabric decoration applied to a larger fabric background.

B

Backstitch Reverse stitch to secure the beginning and end of any permanent stitching. Also, hand stitch used in needlework.

Bacteria Tiny one-celled plants that can be seen only through a microscope. Some are useful, others cause disease and spoil food.

Bake To cook food by dry heat in an oven.

Balance In interior design, effect achieved when different design elements have equal force—or attract equal attention—in a room.

Baste To hold pieces of a garment together temporarily with long stitches or pins.

Batik Method of creating a design on fabric by applying wax which is removed after the fabric is dyed.

Bias Line that is diagonal to the grain on a woven fabric. The bias has more stretch than the straight grain line.

Bindings Narrow strips of fabric used to cover raw edges, mainly necklines and armholes.

Bleach Chemical that removes color from an item. Household bleach may be used to disinfect or to remove stains.

Blend To mix two or more ingredients together.

Boil To heat a liquid until bubbles rise constantly to the surface. Also, to cook something in water or another liquid that is boiling.

Bonded fabric Fabric made from two layers of different material that have been sealed together with adhesive.

Botulism Illness caused by bacteria in improperly canned food.

Boycott Act of joining others in refusing to buy or use a product.

Broil To cook by direct heat.

Budget Detailed account of how a resource will be used.

C

Calcium Mineral essential to strong bones and teeth. Milk products are a major source of calcium.

Calorie   Unit for measuring the energy value of food.

Carbohydrates   Nutrients that provide the body with ready energy, spare the use of protein, and help use fat.

Carotene   A substance from which the body makes vitamin A, found in many yellow or orange colored fruits and vegetables.

Cellulose   Substance that forms the solid framework of plants, used to make several types of clothing fibers.

Chill   To place food in a refrigerator until cold.

Chop   To cut food into small pieces.

Communication   Act of passing along or exchanging information or ideas.

Community   Group of people sharing the same locality and government. Also, group whose members share common interests and concerns.

Complementary   In a color scheme, describes direct opposites on the color wheel.

Compromise   Method of settling differences in which each side gives in to some of the demands of the other.

Condominium   Building in which apartments are owned by the people who live in them.

Consumer   Someone who buys and uses goods or services of any kind.

Contingency   Unexpected event.

Contrast   In design, method of using widely different colors, sizes, textures, or shapes for an exciting or stimulating design.

Convenience food   Food item or combination of foods that are easy to use because much of the preparation has been done by a food company.

Convenience store   Small grocery store, open long hours, that sells a wide range of foods.

Converter   Industrial plant where fabrics are finished in a variety of ways.

Cool   To let food stand at room temperature until it does not feel warm to the touch.

Cotton   Most commonly used plant fiber. Also, fabric made from this fiber.

Credit   Privilege of buying goods or services without immediate payment.

Curd   Thick part of milk which separates from the watery part when milk sours. It is high in protein and fat.

Curing   Method of preserving foods with salt or sugar. Cured foods may also be dried or smoked.

D/E

Dart   Tapered, stitched fold which shapes fabric to the body.

Delicatessen   Store that sells prepared foods, such as cooked meats and salads.

Emphasis   Design technique in which an object, shape, or line is made to attract attention. This often gives a feeling of order.

Energy   Strength to be active.

Environment   All of the surrounding conditions that affect the development of a living thing.

F

Fabric   Cloth or material.

Fabric buyer   Someone who buys fabrics for a garment maker.

Facing   Shaped piece of fabric used to line and finish an edge—such as the neck or armhole of a garment.

Fad   Fashion or craze that is followed for a short time.

Fastenings   Items such as zippers, snaps, and hooks used to close garments.

Fats   High energy nutrients. The body stores up reserve energy in fat tissues.

Feed dog   Part of a sewing machine, located under the presser foot, which moves the material along between stitches.

Felt   Fabric made by wetting and pressing fibers until they are tightly matted together.

Fiber   Cellulose—the part of fruits, vegetables, and grains not digested by the body. Also, natural or synthetic hairlike strands, the raw material from which most fabrics are made.

Fiberglass   Very fine, threadlike pieces of glass that can be spun into yarn for making fireproof fabrics.

Freeze-drying   Process in which food is preserved by being frozen, then dried in a vacuum.

Fry   To cook in hot fat.

Fusible web   Fiber mesh which bonds two layers of fabric by application of heat and pressure.

G

Goal   Result or aim to be achieved. Some goals are short-term, to be achieved in the present. Others are long-term, to be achieved at some future time.

Genes   Tiny units in a living cell which pass on traits, such as hair and eye color, from parents to their offspring.

Geodesic dome   Structure, shaped like an upside-down bowl, with a framework of interlocking triangles or other angled shapes.

Grain   Direction of the yarns which make up a fabric.

Grease   To prepare a cooking surface by rubbing it with fat.

Greige goods   Fabric as it comes from a textile mill—before it has been dyed, bleached, or finished in any way. Also called gray goods.

H

Half-and-half   Mixture of cream and milk.

Hand wheel   Wheel at the right of the sewing machine, used to move the needle up and down by hand.

Hem   Edge of a garment that is folded under and secured with stitches or tape, for neatness and to prevent ravelling.

Home economist   Someone whose career is directed towards improving services, products, and practices that affect the home and family.

Homemaker   Someone who takes or shares responsibility for the care of a home.

Homogenized   Describes milk which has been processed so that the butterfat remains mixed with the milk and does not rise to the top as cream.

Hormones   Substances, produced in the glands, which influence body functions.

Hue   Name used to identify a color on the color wheel.

I

Infant   Baby who is not yet able to walk or talk.

Ingredient   Item that is part of a mixture or recipe.

Intensity   In colors, degree of brightness or dullness.

Iodine   Mineral that helps the thyroid gland to work properly and the body cells to use their food at the correct rate.

Iron   Mineral essential for building red blood cells.

K/L

Knead   To work dough by hand—pushing, folding, and turning it with your hands.

Knitting   Method of making fabric by looping yarn together, row after row.

Lactose   Form of sugar present in milk.

Leather   Material made by tanning the skin of animals.

Linen   Fabric made from fibers of the flax plant.

Low-fat milk   Milk from which the butterfat has been removed to 2%.

M

Management   Process of setting goals, then planning and taking the steps necessary to reach them.

Marketplace economy   Free economic system in which most decisions on what will be sold or bought are left to producers and consumers, rather than controlled by the government.

Mass production   Method of making large quantities of goods at the lowest possible price.

Media   Means of communication—such as television, radio, or the press—that reach large numbers of people.

Melanin   Pigment or coloring material found in human hair and skin.

Melt   To heat a solid food such as butter until it becomes a liquid.

Mender   Someone employed by a drycleaning firm to repair clothes.

Minerals   Nutrients belonging to a class of substances, usually inorganic, essential in small amounts to the normal functioning of the body.

Modacrylic   Modified acrylic fiber often used to make pile, or fake fur fabrics.

Module   Single ready-made housing unit that is part of a whole building.

Monochromatic   In a color scheme, describes variations of a single color.

N/O

Niacin B-group vitamin, found mainly in protein foods, that prevents pellagra.

Notch Diamond shaped marking through the cutting line of a garment pattern, used for matching one section of the garment to another.

Notions Items such as buttons, zippers, hooks and elastic, used in making clothing.

Nutrients Substances in food which the body needs in order to work properly. Nutrients are classed as proteins, fats, carbohydrates, minerals and vitamins.

Nylon Synthetic fiber, produced from petroleum, that is strong, lightweight, holds body heat, and resists wrinkles.

Organic Coming from living things. Describes foods produced without chemical fertilizers or pesticides.

Overcast To stitch over the raw edges of a seam to prevent the fabric from ravelling.

P

Paraprofessional Someone trained to assist a professional.

Pasteurization Process by which milk is heated to kill bacteria.

Pattern layout Plan for the arrangement of pattern pieces on fabric so that garment pieces are cut correctly and as little cloth as possible is wasted.

Pellagra Disease caused by lack of niacin in the diet.

Personal space Area or place—such as a room, closet, drawer, or locker—that belongs to an individual.

Pesticide Chemical that destroys insects, used to prevent insect damage to crops.

Plankton Floating plant and animal life in a body of water.

Pollution Act of making something foul or dirty, especially the environment.

Polyester Most widely used synthetic fiber. It is strong and resists wrinkles.

Preheat To bring an oven to a certain temperature before using it.

Prejudice Opinion or feeling that is not based on facts.

Preservative Substance that will slow the process of spoiling.

Priority In a list of goals, one that is of primary importance.

Produce Fruits and vegetables.

Proportion Balance between different parts of a whole or the relationship of one thing to another.

Proteins Nutrients that build and repair body tissue.

R

Raw edge Unfinished edge of fabric.

Rayon Fiber made from cellulose.

Recycle To bring something back into use which might otherwise have been discarded.

Resource Anything that can be used to meet a need.

Riboflavin B-group vitamin that helps cell tissue in the body use food.

S

Salmonella Bacteria that grow in foods.

Sanitation Activities and methods that make clean, healthful conditions.

Scurvy Disease caused by lack of vitamin C.

Seam Line created when two pieces of fabric are stitched together.

Seam allowance Amount of fabric between the stitching and the cut edge of a garment.

Shared space Area or place—such as a kitchen, living room, workbench, or yard—used by more than one person or by people together.

Sibling Sister or brother.

Sift To put dry ingredients through a sieve to make them light and airy.

Silk Fine, strong, shiny fiber that is produced by silkworms and the thread or fabric made from this fiber.

Simmer To cook in liquid that is just below the boiling point.

Solar energy Energy that comes from the sun.

Solvent Substance that dissolves another substance.

Spandex Synthetic elastic fiber.

Standard Judgment about the manner in which a goal should be accomplished, affecting the way resources are used.

Stereotype Oversimplified idea of what something or someone is like.

Stitch regulator Device on a sewing machine that adjusts the length of the stitch to suit different sewing jobs.

Surplus Amount that is over and above what is needed.

Synthetic Describes something created entirely from chemicals.

T

Tension dial Device on a sewing machine which regulates the tightness of stitches by controlling the pull on the upper thread.

Textiles Fiber-based materials often used to make clothing.

Texture The way a fabric looks and feels.

Thiamine B-group vitamin found especially in cereals, nuts, and yeast—used in the treatment of beriberi.

Toddler Baby who is just learning to walk and moves in an unsteady manner.

Tolerance Ability to accept people as they are.

Toss To mix ingredients lightly.

Traits Special qualities or distinguishing features.

Triacetate Modified acetate. Triacetate fabrics resist fading, shrinking, and wrinkling, and can be ironed at higher temperatures than acetate.

Trimmings Decorative items—such as rickrack, braid, lace, fringe—sewn onto garments to add color and design.

Tuck Stitched fold of fabric that is usually decorative, but may also be used to shape fabric to the body.

U/V

Unit price Cost of a standard amount of a product, posted to help customers compare different-size packages and different brands.

Unity In interior design, a sense of oneness which occurs when parts are related by a single idea.

Value In colors, degree of lightness or darkness.

Vegetarian Someone who does not eat meat, poultry, or fish.

Vinyl Tough form of plastic often used for outer garments.

Vitamins Nutrients belonging to a group of organic substances, essential in small amounts to the normal functioning of the body.

W/Z

Warranty Guarantee or promise concerning the quality, content, or performance of a product.

Weaving Method of making fabric by interlacing yarns.

Wool Soft, curly hair of sheep and certain other animals and the yarn or fabric produced from these natural animal fibers.

Zigzag stitch Machine stitch in which the needle moves from side to side.

Index